Living
on the
Precipice

Other Books by Greg Caton
(See: gregcaton.com)

Lumen: Food for a New Age
(1985)

MLM Fraud
(1991)

The Gospel of 2012
According to Ayahuasca:
The End of Faith and
the Beginning of Knowingness
(2012)

The Joys of Psychopathocracy:
Why Criminality is Essential
to Effective Modern Government
Our Rebirth in the Wake of
Their Destruction of Our World
(2017)

Living
on the
Precipice

Global Corruption, The Supremacy of "Fake" &
Reflections on Near-Term Human Extinction.
The Essential Internet Postings
(1996-2018)

Greg Caton

with updated commentaries

Herbologics
8345 NW 66th St., #7093
Miami, FL 33166
(305) 851-2305
Email: greg@gregcaton.com

Cover Concept and Design / Illustrations: Khushal Khatri, Sri Ganganagar, India / coroflot.com/khushal
Interior Design and Layout: Andrea Vera Tandazo

Printed in the U.S.A. by CreateSpace, an Amazon.com company

Library of Congress Cataloguing-in-Publication Data

Greg Caton, 1956 –
Living on the Precipice: Global Corruption, The Supremacy of "Fake" & Reflections on Near-Term Human Extinction. The Essential Internet Postings (1996-2018)

1. Political Science 2. Anthropology 3. Medicine

Library of Congress Catalog Card Number: 2017912442
ISBN: 978-0-939955-05-3

Published by: Herbologics -- Miami, FL

Table of Contents

"A global culture that cultivates all things fake -- fake
news, fake education, fake medicine, fake science -- as long as it
serves a financial or political agenda, is the hallmark of a system that
can ban anything useful to man . . . or even things vital to the
sustenance of life on this planet." – (June 2017)

Introduction

It's hard to believe it's 23 years ago now, but I can remember the seed out of which came my first efforts at communicating on the Internet. It was in early 1995 that I was browsing through a bookstore in Corpus Christi, Texas. I happened to come upon a book that taught the code for composing web pages in HTML. For those too young to remember, the Internet was a fledgling medium then, so primitive that there were still no "alignment tags" for placing text next to pictures. Although the first incarnation of the Netscape Navigator browser had just come out the previous December, few people were actually online yet, and so the Internet was still largely in the hands of the government and those of us who regard ourselves as technology's "early adapters."

In short order, the language did evolve, with the introduction of "Netscape extensions," CSS (cascading style sheets), CGI scripts, Java, and countless other languages and programs for making the worldwide web an increasingly more functional medium for communications and commerce.

Something else evolved, too, for those of us who were products of those early years: our own styles of expression and the maturation of the subject matter that would define so many of our careers. My first websites were natural extensions of the brick-and-mortar businesses I ran at the time: soybean.com, the online store for Lumen Foods, a vegetarian food company I founded in 1986 and sold in 2007; and altcancer.com, the online presence of Alpha Omega Labs, an herbal company I founded several years prior, among others. (Both sites exist to this day.) What followed were online newsletters, blogs, articles, essays, audio and video clips, and unending multimedia presentations in ever-changing formats. Some of us have contributed more than others – in my case, something in excess of 3,500 web pages – and yet I doubt that anyone whose career streams came out of the web's headwaters can say they were not forever changed by it.

We were shaped not only by the evolution of the technology and our own thoughts of the world around us, but by the current affairs that influenced both. The book you are about to read deals with the weighty subjects I tackled in various online activities over a 22 year period, from 1996 to 2018.

I begin with the subject of NTE (near term extinction), which I believe is now well underway and is largely an unrecognized and underappreciated fait accompli in absence of some kind of "outside intervention." Then I pan out to the factors that have contributed to our apparent demise. Included in this effort are my extractions of the very best material from my online blog, *The Ashwin* (2002-2018), in addition to my online book, *Meditopia* (meditopia.org), which I would have completed and made into a separate monograph, if only I had the time. If any of us still had the time.

I regard this work as the capstone of a career based on truth seeking, based on the desire to see the world with all preconceived social, political, religious, and philosophical filters removed. Given the gravity of the subjects covered, I can't think of a better way that this material could possibly be approached.

Greg Caton
gregcaton.com
March 27, 2018
Cuenca, Ecuador

Part I:

Ecological Intimations of NTE

(near-term extinction)

A Brief Commentary on Part I and Chapter 1

I have chosen to dedicate Part I of this monograph to the subject of NTE (near-term human extinction), which I have written about or alluded to on the web for the better part of 20 years now. I did this for a reason: it shows where mass global corruption and the elevation of all things "fake" will take us when left unchecked. In other words, it puts the other elements of the book, covering what appears on the surface to be social components of less gravitas, into perspective. It also shines light on the preciousness and fragility of life itself, something we take for granted.

We have substituted the wisdom of adherence to Natural Law for artificial constructs that are woven into all aspects of modernity, and therein lies our undoing. (I cover this quite extensively in my previous book, The Joys of Psychopathocracy.) The rest of this book can be better appreciated by the reader by beginning with a "pan out" to see the causal end result of our folly.

Naysayers will attack the seemingly hyperbolic time frames. Human extinction in 10 or 15 years – maybe less? Is this a joke? With a near record 8 billion humans currently occupying the planet, this hardly seems possible. However, as I point out in Joys,[1] a species most often achieves its largest population just prior to overshoot and "die-off," which can occur with surprising violence and rapidity. Moreover, I couldn't care less whether we are looking at 10, 20, 50, or even 100 years. Enough of the petty bickering. The trend line is clear: we're seeing habitat collapse all over the planet, and I believe we have passed a "point of no return." When you fully understand this, the precise timing becomes less important, if not irrelevant.

We are ALL living on the precipice.

And we are diminished in any refusal to fully recognize where we are all headed, how we got here, and how we spend the remaining time we have left – collectively and individually.

---

[1] Caton, The Joys of Psychopathocracy, 2017.

Chapter 1:

"Depletion of Ozone so Bad / Mass Extinction could be within 7 years."

"First we had Guy McPherson's[1] estimates of human extinction by around 2025. Now an aeronautical engineer who dubs himself, 'IRay' is indicating that crops won't grow outdoors within 7 years because of ozone layer collapse. Does it make any difference that remote viewers in the 90s provided exact details that match what's happening in the atmosphere now? Or can we simply sweep all this evidence under the rug and agree to relegate it to 'doom porn'?"

C uenca, Ecuador - December 9, 2017 -- Two days ago, an associate sent me a link to an interview put out by the YouTube channel, Leak Project,[2] run by a certain "Rex Bear," who also maintains a web site[3] by the same name. In this particular YouTube installment, which was posted on December 6, Rex interviewed an aerospace engineer, who goes by the internet moniker, iRay, who, in turn, maintains a data-rich website of his own called, *Sacred Seeds*.[4]

---

[1] See: guymcpherson.com/
[2] The interview can be found at: youtu.be/1chxX1Dzy2Q. The Leak Project channel itself is at: goo.gl/XiVucN
[3] See: leakproject.com/
[4] See: iray2017.wixsite.com/sacredseeds

Since you might not have one hour and fourteen minutes to sit through this interview,[5] allow me to give you the short version: Our sunlight has been moving from UV-A and UV-B ultraviolet light towards UV-C and even microwave rays for years now, light which is not friendly to life on this planet. Dane Wigington attributes this shift to chemtrails (geoengineering) and went so far as to put out an article in August, entitled, "Geo-engineering is Causing Lethal UV Radiation Exposure."[6]

Now, mind you, there is nothing particularly original about the suggestion that ozone depletion could wipe out most life on Earth. Why not? Well, for one, there are scientists who believe that this is precisely what caused the horrific Permian-Triassic extinction event,[7] 250-252 million years ago. (Note that Permian and Triassic refer to geological periods. The authors of this article use a different geological marking system, wherein this event marked the end of the Ediacaran era and the beginning of the Cambrian period. But regardless of the names used, we are still talking about the same event.) So as not to understate the severity of the event itself, it may be illustrative to point out that this event caused such colossal damage to ecosystems worldwide that it took 10 million years for life to recover.[8]

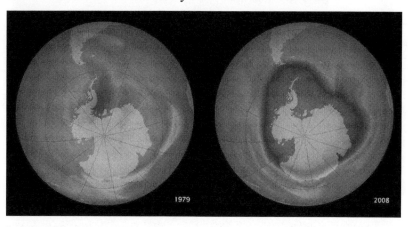

[5] Again see: youtu.be/1ehxX1Dzy2Q

[6] See: www.geoengineeringwatch.org/geoengineering-is-causing-lethal-uv-radiation-exposure/
The page was removed not long after Dane posted the article.

[7] See: www.dailymail.co.uk/sciencetech/article-3449945/Mass-extinction-550-million-years-ago-caused-Earth-s-magnetic-field-FLIPPING-new-study-claims.html

[8] See: en.wikipedia.org/wiki/Permian%E2%80%93Triassic_extinction_event

What struck me as jaw-dropping about this interview weren't simply the implications of the data that iRay had accumulated, which by themselves were quite impressive and convincing. What struck me as amazing was the correlation to one of the early chapters of *Meditopia* which I penned in September 2004, just before going to prison, which provided information that precisely matched iRay's conclusions. Though written in 2004, the information seems even more relevant now.

Entitled, "Meditopia: The Inevitable Collapse,"[9] I pointed out there are several concurrent global events that point to a near-term, great cataclysm. Prominent among these is mass die-off of life on the planet's surface, much like the Permian-Triassic event, that will be initiated by the outright collapse of the ozone layer. I illustrated that we've known for a long time that we are losing the ozone layer and that the causes are anthropogenic.

Central to my presentation were two quotes -- one by Dr. Hans C. Moolenburgh in the Netherlands,[10] with whom I had communicated personally, and the other was a passage written by the late, great investigative reporter, Jim Marrs.[11]

Of the two, Marrs relevation was more revealing and disturbing. I realize before I proceed that there is a great deal of disinformation in the media and even the alternative media about remote viewing, its accuracy, and validity of its methodologies. Nonetheless, the information provided sounded legitimate to me then, and it sounds even more legitimate now. It deals with formerly classified military reports from remote viewers on future Earth changes that he was able to uncover.

My comments are in brackets:

[Taken from 'The Enigma Files' -- gleaned from CIA remote viewers in the 1990s]: The report contains this sobering assessment: "Atmospheric ozone depletion / replenishment was

---

[9] See: www.meditopia.org/old/chap16_2004.htm

[10] Hans C. Moolenburgh, As Chance would have it: A Study in Coincidences (Essex, UK: Saffron Walden, The C.W. Daniel Company Limited, 1998), 161. Throughout this section, Moolenburgh is summarizing parts of his unpublished work, *Lilianne* (see p. 159).

[11] Jim Marrs, PSI Spies (Phoenix, Arizona: AlienZoo Publishing, 2000), 176.

perceived to be driven by a natural ebb and flow process -- a geophysical cycle. But this process has become overwhelmed by man-made activity -- The complex natural ozone cycles / patterns, in combination with the man-made alterations, make it extremely difficult for present scientists to figure out just what is happening. A long series of tests, research, and small-scale experiments, using several types of chemicals, will be undertaken -- but these efforts to stop the ozone decay will have little or no impact -- they are only 'Band-Aid' approaches. A critical point is reached, circa 2005-2012 -- [as is often the case with psychic viewing in the future, these dates were made invalid by temporal extension, a common phenomenon]. The destruction will begin a runaway course, in a fashion analogous to metastasis (the transfer of malignant cells from one location to another). During this period, the problem -- and its potential consequences -- will no longer be subject to question . . .

"The ozone decay will not necessarily be slowed down, but its effects temporarily ameliorated by coincidental volcanic activity. One such related event will be the explosion of an 'extinct' volcano in the North American Cascade chain . . . The volcanic activity will literally and figuratively eclipse the ozone problem, but decreased sunlight will wreak havoc with crop production in many places. Chaotic weather patterns in combination with decreased sunlight will necessitate the construction of huge environmentally-controlled greenhouses, so that food production can carry on without being subject to vicissitudes of climate / weather. Unwittingly, these structures form the templates for technologies that will become increasingly critical to sustaining human life. They will begin to be seen as sanctuaries -- then habitats, as society begins to 'migrate' into them . . .

"A point is reached where very little life is seen outside of the artificial structures. The atmosphere outside these 'biospheres' is almost antiseptic. The sky is striated and multi-hued. Earth's remaining (surviving) inhabitants have either been driven underground or into these very large, climate-controlled domes, which now house complete medium-sized cities. Our children's children are residents there. There is no perceivable violence.

Most creative energy is directed to questions of survival . . ."

The second quote came from Hans C. Moolenburgh, M.D., who was influential enough to get the Dutch government to suspend the practice of poisoning its citizens, as is done in most of the rest of the Western World, through the flouridation of its drinking water.[12] At that time, Moolenburgh was working on a fictional work, called *Lillianna*. Many people who find out how governmental institutions work choose to wrap their presentations inside a cloak of factionals, or "non-fiction novels." When I read the following passage about the mass culling of life on Earth through the deliberate destruction of the ozone layer, I understand why:

"'A special committee of our inner circle has discovered the real difficulty on Earth. It has carefully studied history in all its aspects, especially that of the last 250 years, and come to the conclusion that the enormous proliferation of human life, the population explosion, is the cause of all evils.'

"'We have,' he said proudly, 'at last found an ideal method to curb this teeming fertility and bring the world population back to acceptable proportions.'

"The professor then proceeded to talk about the ozone layer that protects humanity against the devastating effects of solar radiation. The layer is, as we all know, already deteriorating under the influence of several man-made factors, one of them being space missiles.

"'But now,' Dirk Slager said, 'we will destroy the ozone layer on purpose in order to cull humanity and other proliferating life to 1% of its present numbers.' . . .

"'As long as the elimination process lasts . . . the elite and their passive and totally obedient slaves will be living under enormous protective domes.'"

We know from the work of Dane Wigington[13] that **the de-**

---

[12] See: ffwireland.blogspot.com/2013/01/evidence-based-medical-science-used-to.html

[13] See: www.geoengineeringwatch.org/

struction of the ozone layer IS deliberate. We can reason that this is the true reason for the construction of over 200 deep, protective, classified, underground cities.[14] In fact, I believe that the "Planet X narrative" is just a cover.[15] If the ozone layer were "recovering," which is the position of officialdom,[16] then investigators like "iRay" would not be able to document such sharp, dramatic increases in dangerous solar radiation penetrating through to the Earth's surface. But even if the demise of humanity were not due to mass starvation and all the societal chaos that comes with habitat collapse caused by a diminished ozone layer, it would be due to something else.

Something else that gives people in power the psychopathic pleasure that they crave -- a matter I cover in exhaustive detail in my most recent book, The Joys of Psychopathocracy.[17]

I have felt for the entirety of my adult life that I would experience some kind of end of "life as we know it" as time progressed. The "what" that leads to this change is not nearly as important as how we use the unfolding events to better ourselves spiritually. This, too, I cover in detail in my previous book.

It is time to put away the things of this world that are material -- the things that are dying all around us. It is time to seek out the treasures of what is permanent, enduring, and favorable to "the good."

I can see no greater purpose for living at this time in history.

---

[14] See: www.heartcom.org/200under.htm

[15] Among those who take the position that the DUMBs (Deep, Underground Military Bases) were built to protect the Elite from the ever-elusive "Planet X" is investigative reporter, Bob Fletcher, See: socioecohistory.wordpress.com/2016/03/23/bob-fletcher-planet-x-nibiru-incoming-underground-cities-declassified-docs-reveal-world-government/ I've met and spoken to Bob personally and I do not believe that he's being disingenuous. But my opinion is that the decimation of the ozone layer is a more likely cause.

[16] This is what is communicated in the following PowerPoint presentation, which presents the orthodox ("fake news") position: slideplayer.com/slide/4617266/

[17] See: www.amazon.com/Greg-J.-Caton/e/B00J1SGU6U

Chapter 1

A Brief Commentary on Chapter 2

In an interview I had with Professor Guy McPherson on May 7, 2017, we discussed the confounding developments that are contributing to habitat collapse and the mass extinction of species worldwide.[1]

I talk at length about this discussion and our Holocene Extinction Event in my last book.[2]

Fukushima – just one nuclear power plant complex -- is noteworthy not only because of the incredible destruction it has brought to ecosystems all throughout the Pacific Ocean, but because it gives us a preview as to what we can expect from the other 500 nuclear plants worldwide. (The number is 447 active and operating, with another 61 under construction.)[3] You'll never get the truth about the extent of the damage from any major government or the mainstream media. This is a primary point that I make here.

The implications of what has been suppressed are laid bare here in Chapter 2. It was originally posted as the July 2015 edition of the Ashwin.[4]

---

[1] See: www.gregcaton.com/video/CatonMcPherson3.mp4
[2] Greg Caton, The Joys of Psychopathocracy, 2018.
[3] See: www.world-nuclear.org/nuclear-basics/global-number-of-nuclear-reactors.aspx
[4] See: www.altcancer.net/ashwin/ashw0715.htm

Chapter 2:

Fukushima:
A Verifiable ELE

Coming to Grips With the Ultimate
Conspiracy ~~***Theory***~~ ***Fact*** *And Realizing
That If the Major Governments
of the World Can Suppress An Extinction
Level Event of This Magnitude,
They Can Suppress Anything*

C uenca, Ecuador (July 2015) -- The Fukushima Daiichi nuclear disaster occured on March 11, 2011, an unfortunate accident following a magnitude 9.0 earthquake and its subsequent tsumani. At the time, I didn't think too much of it . . . partly because I learned in the fourth grade that Japan and the American hemisphere are separated by a somewhat substantial body of water, but more importantly, I was still serving time in U.S. federal prison on a trifling probation matter. (I document that nonsense in Chapter 3 of *Meditopia*,[1] and since it made me a "cause célèbre," I won't rehash particulars here.) The prison in Texas where I was detained[2] is macabrely referred to as "Bloody Beaumont" by the inmates, because of the high number of men incarcerated there who don't make it out alive. So I had better things to worry about than a malfunctioning power plant halfway around the world.

Or so I thought.

Immediately after my release from custody, five and a half months later, I jumped on the first flight I could get out of

---

[1] See: www.meditopia.org/chap3-3.htm

[2] The Federal Correctional Complex, Beaumont (FCC Beaumont) is a U.S. federal prison complex for male inmates in Texas. It is operated by the Federal Bureau of Prisons, a division of the United States Department of Justice.

the U.S., so I could return home to my wife, Cathryn, and our peaceful life here in Ecuador that the U.S. crime syndicate had so rudely interrupted. That put me even further away from the problem and on the other side of the equator, where the trade winds blow from east to west.

Some time in 2013 I began to get news from friends in the alternative media and scientific community that Fukushima was far more serious than was being reported by the mainstream media. It has been disturbing my peaceful life in Ecuador ever since.

It was an innocent enough beginning. In the fall of 2013 I had just concluded an interview with a prominent person in the alternative media. Instead of hanging up, I asked my host if we could cover some "odds and ends" off the record. At some point early on, I asked what he felt was the most pressing issue on his radar screen: NDAA, the struggling economy, eroding civil rights and increasing police brutality in the States, collapse of border enforcement, etc.?

"None of those things," my host said, interrupting me mid-sentence. **"Nothing else that is being reported by any-one, on any topic, in any media venue -- anywhere -- even begins to compare to Fukishima. I have interviewed people who work in oceanography and biology who tell me private-ly that Fukishima is an ELE -- an extinction level event."**

"That sounds like a pretty healthy piece of doom porn," I said, hyperreflexively and almost dismissively. Throughout my entire adult life, I had lived through one overstated disaster after another. Between the threat of peak oil, Three Mile Island and other "China Syndrome" wannabes, Y2K, 2012, Edgar Cayce, Mass Dreams of the Future, a lifetime of financial Armaged-don predictions, a lifetime of tension concerning the imminent sliding of my home state of California into the Pacific (begin-ning with the hype around "The Late, Great, State of Califor-nia" [1968]), etc., etc., etc., etc. this just seemed like yet another piece of eschatological hyperbole. Scratch that. Eschatological nonsense.

"No, it's extremely serious," my host interjected. "Since Hiroshima and Nagasaki, we've been making the world increasingly more radioactive and hostile to life. There were more than 2,000 nuclear bomb tests conducted from 1945 to the early 1990s alone, and those are only the ones officially acknowledged. I have friends 'in the know' who tell me with a straight face that *Homo sapiens* have perhaps 30 more years, probably less."

Less than a month following this interview, I happened to meet up with some friends at a local German pub who are, in turn, friends of Lauren Moret. A geophysicist who used to work at Lawrence Livermore National Laboratory, Moret has done more to articulate the extreme danger that Fukushima poses to all life on Earth than any other person of whom this author is aware. Her online assembly of presentations is impressive, though they are hardly restricted to the isolated accident at Fukushima.

Through studying Moret's material, I became acquainted with the work of Dane Wigington and his website on geoengineering. (The relevance is that by comparing the two phenomena, it becomes crystal clear that irradiating and poisoning the general public are interrelated and exceedingly deliberate.) This, in turn, brought me to the very same conclusion concerning our near-term destiny as that of Professor Guy McPherson, whose website contains an unusually impassioned plea to please not commit suicide, after thoroughly examining all the facts.[3]

When I stopped to reflect on the overlapping themes of these researchers' works, I couldn't help but see that their collective message had been speaking to me my entire life; I just hadn't been listening.

When I was sixteen, I read Richard Maurice Bucke's seminal work, <u>Cosmic Consciousness</u>.[4] It made such a deep impression on me that years later I delved into the work of Walter Russell, a Renaissance Man of the highest order, who entered into cosmic awareness himself in 1921. Russell then went on to dis-

---

[3] See: guymcpherson.com

[4] Richard Maurice Bucke (M.D.), <u>Cosmic Consciousness: A Study in the Evolution of the Human Mind</u> (New York: E.P. Dutton & Co., 1969). The books was originally published in 1901

cover plutonium and complete the Mendeleev chart of elements years before it would be officially recognized, crediting other, lesser minds. The current Periodic Table of Elements is vastly inferior to the one Russell created; a problem that could be readily fixed, if only modern science were not so wholly devoted to keeping people stupid; a matter I address more completely in a previous Ashwin entry.[5]

In 1957, while I was still an infant, Russell wrote and published Atomic Suicide with his wife, Lao.[6] One of the points that Russell stresses is that the damage to the environment that is created by even one power plant exceeds that of many nuclear bomb explosions. This is because the environmental damage created by tons of radioactive waste from these is incalculable -- (then and now, apparently). Part of the problem in Russell's delivery -- as Bucke made abundantly clear is his book -- is that he was speaking from a cosmically consciousness mind. The most knowledgeable and brilliant among us is still a kindergartener compared to someone who has ascended to Russell's level. In fact, there are students of Russell's work (this one included) who have spent years trying to understand his principles and still fall short. So far into the stratosphere of man's intellectual capabilities did Russell ascend that few people's work are so challenging.

This is unfortunate, because in hindsight, no message of the past century has been so vital: that if you gather together and concentrate these heavier weight metals -- these "destroyers" in the Divine Plan -- then you will destroy life itself. And destroy it, we will, for we are only in the beginning stages of the sixth great extinction and when we are finished, and I mean that in every sense of the word, our handiwork will continue on long

---

[5] "Ashwin" defined in Glossary. The previous Ashwin entry refers here to: www.altcancer.net/ashwin/ashw0914.htm. This Ashwin has been updated and is Chapter 24 in the present volume.

[6] Walter Russell, Atomic Suicide: What Radioactivity Is, Why and How It Kills, What To Do About It (Swannanoa, VA: University of Science & Philosophy, 1981). Originally published in 1957.

after we're gone.

Even most bacteria here on Earth may not make it.

I did not see the truth of this, for myself, until recently.

For the past couple of years, I've had the time to contemplate the effects of being here on South America, on the "other side" of the equator. A number of authorities have stepped forward to proclaim, or at least intimate, that the southern hemisphere is safe from Fukushima[7] (though our friend, Dr. Mark Sircus knows otherwise).[8] It has been suggested that governments should begin mass evacuation of billions to the southern hemisphere.[9] This doesn't make sense to me, though, when you consider that as early as 2012, even rains in Southern Brazil were coming up highly radioactive.[10]

In 2009, well before the disastrous events at Fukushima, I bought a Gamma Scout,[11] a Geiger counter made in Germany, so that I could stay on top of the alpha, beta, gamma, and x-ray radiation, all threatening to good health with sufficient exposure. It wasn't all that expensive. I believe I paid a few hundred dollars.

Since my return to Ecuador, my wife and I check the Gamma Scott frequently. In fact, we keep it in the office. Nonetheless, over all this time, we have never once had an "alert." Day after day, we have checked the measurements, and sure enough, we have been well within the safe zone, according to our Geiger counter.

We began to think that since the readings are "off the chart" in the U.S., and much lower in Ecuador according to our Geiger counter, that perhaps it really is safer living here. Perhaps South America is somehow protected. Perhaps the reported threats to

---

[7] GEOS-5 Nature Run Collection, see: svs.gsfc.nasa.gov/cgi-bin/details.cgi?aid=30017

[8] News You Don't Want to Read About Fukushima, see: drsircus.com/general/news-you-dont-want-to-read-about-fukushima/

[9] Fukushima Disaster Could Force Evacuation of Billions to Southern Hemisphere, see: chemtrailsplanet.net/2013/08/19/fukushima-disaster-could-force-evacuation-of-billions-to-southern-hemisphere/

[10] See: www.enviroreporter.com/2012/08/no-place-to-hide-fukushima-fallout-findings-widespread/all/1/

[11] See: www.gammascout.com/

our side of the globe are overstated.

But then, that theory got shot right out of the sky.

We were visited by a friend who owns an identiFINDER R400[12] (formerly IdentiFINDER 2), which, when you add neutron burst detection capability and all the necessary add-ons, runs somewhere around $34,000, clearly outside the reach of the average person.

Apparently, unbeknown to me, my friend had done readings in Central America and at various places in our general area (3 degrees south equator). Far more disturbing than the usual radioactive isotopes: actinium-228, antimony-124, barium-140, cerium-143, cesium-135, chromium-51, cobalt-60, iodine-131, iridium-192, molybdenum-54, neptunium-237, samarium-153, strontium-91, thorium-232, etc., were the sheer number, amplitude, and persistence of "neutron storms." Neutrons are ten times more destructive to life than gamma radiation; and in case you doubt that, contemplate the fact that neutron radiation is the basis for one of the most destructive weapons to life ever invented: the neutron bomb.[13]

What the Elite of the world have done is create a situation where all life on planet Earth is being "neutron bombed," admittedly at lower levels, but consistently nonetheless, every second of every day, regardless of where you live on this planet.

No wonder cancer rates are exploding worldwide,[14] as if they were not high enough already. There is no place safe on Earth, certainly no place to which one could safely evacuate.[15] As Leuren Moret cogently articulates, none of the governments with access to the relevant information needed to protect the public are disclosing it; only those of us who are investigating this privately and have the temerity to speak the truth openly are putting the information out there.

---

[12] See: www.flir.com/threatdetection/display/?id=63333

[13] The tactical neutron bomb is a nuclear weapon that maximizes damage to people but minimizes damage to buildings and equipment. It is also called an enhanced radiation warhead. See: www.nuclearfiles.org/menu/key-issues/nuclear-weapons/basics/neutron-bomb.htm

[14] See: youtu.be/NX6qXxxFW2E

[15] See: youtu.be/3-GCyOAiUXE

Chapter 2

A Brief Commentary on Chapter 3

From 2007 to up until the time of my illegal kidnapping in 2009, I was travelling extensively through Ecuador, particularly in the Amazonian region. I met and talked to many shamans and indigenous leaders as to what they thought was "coming" in their vision quests. I picked up a tapestry of revelations that was remarkably homogenous in its message: we are about to reap what we have sown.

This chapter is taken from a post I made in May 2009.[1]

---

[1] See: www.altcancer.net/ashwin/ashw0509.htm

Chapter 3:

Dark Messages From the Amazon: Preparing for the Ecological Apocalypse & The Revenge of Gaia

"The Earth does not belong to the white man; the white man belongs to the Earth. This we know. All things are connected like the blood that unites our family . . . If we kill the snakes, the field mice will multiply and destroy our corn . . .(And so) whatever befalls the earth befalls the sons and daughters of the Earth. Man did not weave the web of life; he is merely a strand in it. Whatever he does to the web, he does to himself."

Chief Seattle[1]
Ted Perry version of famous Seattle speech (1854)

Above: *This picture appears to show what might be three distinct lakes or large pools of water. In actuality, what it shows is the Río Pastaza, the border between Ecuador's two largest provinces, Pastaza and Morona Santiago, home to about a dozen indigenous groups, including Shuar, Achuar, Huaorani, Sarayaku, Jivaro and Chechua. There are no adults living in these expansive provinces who have not witnessed the earth changes underway. The area you see above, for instance, was one large solid river just 30 years ago. Climate changes have had dramatic effects on fresh water levels, not to mention the impact of a hydroelectric dam upstream, and even here, where population density is a tiny fraction of what it is in the urban areas, the ill-ef-*

[1] The haunting, prophetic words of Seattle are discussed in the closing (right column) section of *Meditopia* - Chapter 5.

fects of mankind's overarching footprint can be seen in untold ways, subtle and not-so-subtle. This is made all the more disturbing when considering the area's remoteness. Most of the places I now visit inside the Amazon require the employment of a small plane to reach them. They are, for all intents and purposes, inaccessible any other way.

It is the mark of these ill-effects to which this edition of the Ashwin is devoted.

Guayaquil, Ecuador -- June 8, 2009 . . . Tonight, after returning from Baños,[2] where I was visiting a fellow herbalist, I happened to get a phone call from the States.

In the course of that conversation, the subject of ***Earth 2100*** came up, a two-hour ABC program,[3] espousing an apocalyptic view of the future if humanity doesn't reform its ways soon, that aired in 2009 (see complete program).[4] For those of you who tuned in to this media event, and are still hungering for more because the ***History Channel's*** lurid renderings of 2012 doomsday predictions just didn't produce enough adrenaline, and for those of you who didn't, I have news.

It's too late to reverse what's coming, and only an uninformed observer or unabashed propagandist would think that we'll need 90 years to get there.

Given the frantic pace that underground military bases and huge city dwellings have and are being built by the Power Elite over the past 65 years, I suspect they know it, too.[5]

This chapter details how I spent five years of my life coming to that conclusion (actually, "revelation" would be more apt), how it dovetails with the work of Alpha Omega Labs, and how one amazing "vision quest" contributed to the process.

[2] Baños de Agua Santa, commonly referred to as Baños, is a city in eastern Tungurahua Province, in central Ecuador. Baños is the second most populous city in Tungurahua, after Ambato, the capital, and is a major tourist center. It is known as the "Gateway to the Amazon", as it's the last big city still located in the mountains before reaching the jungle and other towns that are located in the Amazon River basin.

[3] See: topdocumentaryfilms.com/earth-2100-final-century-of-civilization/

[4] See: youtu.be/8pcZuSDq2SE

[5] Read Richard Sauder's book, Underwater and Underground Bases, the followup to Underground Bases and Tunnels: What is the Government Trying to Hide?. Hear also Phil Schneider's comments on the subject, made in 1995, shortly before he was assassinated for talking too much.

While imprisoned in the U.S. on bogus FDA charges, an issue I summarized in my blog, Ashwin,[6] with greater expansion in Chapter 3 of *Meditopia*,[7] I devoted my time to reading over 350 books on history, medicine, politics, philosophy, agriculture, entheogens and eschatology.

The real mind-bender in the group was Terence McKenna's first book, <u>The Invisible Landscape: Mind, Hallucinogens, and the I Ching</u>,[8] which developed the concept of Timewave Zero, a numerological sequence which uses the rise and fall of "novelty" to explain critical junctures in human development, including the beginning and end of civilizations. (Reduced to a mathematical formula, Timewave Zero is available as a software program, called **Fractal Time**).[9] Therein McKenna established what appears to be the winter solstice of 2012 as an indefineable "end" to the current cycle.

I had already been exposed to people's propensity to become attracted to specific future dates as significant points of chaos in the time continuum, having witnessed the hubbub surrounding the Y2K affair.[10] Even in absorbing the material in McKenna's first book, I found the concept itself unoriginal, having first been exposed to "2012" as a significant date when reading Ken Kalb's <u>The Grand Catharsis</u> (originally published in 1969).[11]

So, for me, it wasn't about the date. It was about processes. It was about trying to figure out if my own civilization was on the verge of collapse, forget trying to nail down an exact date, with the same rapidity as the three grand examples provided in Joseph Tainter's <u>The Collapse of Complex Societies</u>.[12]

After I got out of prison in March of 2006, I read the majority of the extant literature on "2012." The following year, in May 2007, I flew to Sedona, Arizona to participate in a "Wis-

---

[6] Ashwin: see Glossary

[7] See: www.meditopia.org/chap3-1.htm

[8] See: www.meditopia.org/biblio.htm#mckenna6

[9] See: www.fractal-timewave.com/

[10] See: www.britannica.com/technology/Y2K-bug

[11] The book is still available at: www.amazon.com/gp/product/0964292769

[12] See: www.meditopia.org/biblio.htm#tainter1

dom Gathering" at the conference center of the well-known futurist and visionary, Dr. Chet Snow,[13] where five prominent leaders of different indigenous groups shared their surprisingly common visions of an imminent collapse. The two I found most compelling and impressive in their presentations were Grandfather Martin Gashweseoma,[14] who summarized the Hopi prophecies (see Frank Waters)[15] and "preparation" activities, primarily dealing with storable food and water in underground dwellings, which members of the Hopi nation are currently engaged in, and Lakota activist, Russell Means.[16] Fortunately, I was able to spend private time with both men to get more details on their views. Grandfather Martin was able to point to photos of ancient petroglyphs and divine the coming of "what you would call a police state -- right here on Turtle Island [the United States] ... and here -- do you see this? The dotted line that leads away? That represents people like yourself who are leaving because you sense what's coming!" Not long after the Elite turn the United States into a fascist hell-hole, in Grandfather Martin's view of the ancient Hopi prophecies, Earth changes would begin in earnest. In the Christian Bible, read the Book of Revelation, Chapter 18, substituting "United States of America" for "Babylon," and you'll get the general idea.

As for Russel Means, the man was almost giddy over the very idea of a complete collapse of civilization, "I'm rootin' for our Mother. I'm cheering for Mother Earth. And you know what? I can't wait! Boy, I just can't wait!!"

Three and a half months later, I left the U.S. to live in Ecuador. (My wife and son had already moved there.) And among the things I set out to do was to speak with indigenous leaders and shamans to see if there was any correlation with what I was hearing in North America. I also sought to have my own entheogenic experiences, so that I, too, could travel the path that Terence McKenna and his brother had traveled over 35 years

---

[13] See: www.chetsnow.com/

[14] See: earthenergyreader.wordpress.com/tag/hopi-elder-grandfather-martin/

[15] See: www.meditopia.org/biblio.htm#waters1

[16] See: www.biography.com/people/russell-means-21016231

earlier in the same corner of South America.

"You Have 40 Years - No More."

On May 17, 2009 I drove with friends to Coca, Ecuador to visit with Master Shaman, Francisco Siguenza ("Don Bartolo"), who runs a school for shamans in Orellana Province. He doesn't call himself a "Master Shaman," but it the only way I know to describe someone who is so well-respected among indigenous visionaries, that he is sought out by hundreds of other shamans from tribes throughout the Amazon region.

My interest was not so much centered on his extensive herbal knowledge as it was the reports I was receiving concerning his prophetic visions.

According to Don Bartolo, he first began to receive apocalyptic visions in 1984, and it was at that time that he received startling, clear images of massive, worldwide flooding, something akin to the story in Genesis of Noah and the flood. He says he has repeatedly seen the Amazon basin being covered in water and the western coastline of South America up to the Andes destroyed by massive tsunamis. Initially he was told, "You have 40 years . . no more" (which would equate to the year 2024). However, he reports that in more recent visions he has been told that the Purification would have to begin sooner.

Interestingly, his visions mimic comments I hear all over the Amazon. Don Agustin Grefa of Tena, Ecuador told me a year and a half ago that impending Earth changes were widely seen by Amazonian visionaries; that he saw early signs of these changes manifesting in 2011; so that most Earth people would be aware of their imminence by that time; and that children were already being taught how to survive in the extensive cave systems that exist throughout Napo Province.

T he day after my journey to see Don Bartolo, I visited the director of the local museum in Puyo,[17] anthropologist, Carlos Hidalgo, to discuss the recently discovered end time writings on the ancient ruins of Copataza.[18] Located in

---

[17] See: en.wikipedia.org/wiki/Puyo,_Pastaza

[18] Astonishingly, there is little information on Copataza available on the internet. Because of my busy schedule, I have been able to visit places around the Copataza ruins, but never the ruin site itself.

Pastaza Province, the stone carvings, now deciphered, talk about the changes in the Earth at the end of the current age.

Although an exact date has not been assigned to the ruins, they are so old that neither the Shuar nor other indigenous people who live in the area around the ruins, found where Río Copataza and Río Pastaza meet, have an explanation in their oral traditions as to who or what produced the monuments.

Hidalgo, himself an intense academic with extensive knowledge of the cultural anthropology of the area, speaks voluminously about the beliefs of the local people as they pertain to massive, impending changes, all linked to humanity's abuse of Earth Mother (Pachamama).

Traces of evolving "end of times" ethos in the Amazon come from the most unexpected places. In Pastaza, women of the Sarayaku community are known for their ceramic work. While visiting one ceramist, I happened to ask about a tableful of various strange looking creatures, "Oh, those," the woman from Sarayaku replied, "Those are demonic entities. They live in the trees, streams, mountains, but they are not permitted to come out until the end of the age. When this time comes, which is soon, they will be let loose."

There was a cool breeze in those early morning hours of November 11, 2006. I had gone to the beach to spend time with Ed Tuttle and his wife, Tonya, who run a retreat not far from the shore, called Samai. Appropriately, their website is called *Sacred Journey*.[19]

Back in those days I was scurrying back and forth between the United States and Ecuador, focusing on trying to solidify a budding business venture, Ecuador Passion Fruit,[20] and preparing for my exit. I had already received premonitions that corrupt FDA officials were manufacturing perjured testimony against me, standard operating procedure these days, making it impossible for me to finish my probation, no matter what I did. My choice was to leave the U.S. or go back to prison on yet more trumped up charges.[21]

The previous August (2006) I had my first Ayahuasca experience in a one-on-one vision quest which I took with Ed at the retreat. Several more journeys were taken that fall and now I had come back for a weekend of meditation and repose.[22] About 11 p.m., I drank my third glass of the concentrated concoction, then went off with Cathryn, back to our room, to finish our visionary journeys alone.

Over the next four hours, I was caught in alternating fits of profusely vomiting the bitter brew, and reclining to experience the visions, ever intent on unlocking their inner meaning.

About 2 a.m., after hours of viewing what appeared to be bands of gold ribbons passing from right to left, all with engravings, in letters consistent in form, size, and style, something I can only describe as a cross between Sanskrit and Hebrew, time momentarily froze. My heart stopped, breathing ceased, I felt

---

[19] See: www.sacred-journey.com/

[20] See: www.ecuadorpassionfruit.com/

[21] This is covered in extensive detail in the second section of *Meditopia's* third chapter.

[22] If you've never been on a vision quest, the ayahuasca variety is best theatrically represented in the movie, *Blueberry (Renegade)*, which despite its Southwest U.S. setting makes sense: its Director Jan Kounen is no stranger to South American shamanism..

as if I had fallen into some altered, super-conductive state of awareness . . . and then it happened.

"Change The World."

Not only were the letters not foreign or unrecognizeable, but the message was clearly written in English. It was the first time in several hours that I had seen anything that had any decipherable meaning.

"Change the world?" I asked within the confines of my own mind. "How can I change the world? I couldn't even save myself or my family!" I protested.[23]

"You can and you must. It is written," came the reply, clearly, unmistakably, as if God himself were speaking into my ear; except this was a level of divinity or spirit beyond anything I knew, pure, full of love and compassion, and as distinctly real as if someone I knew were standing next to me and speaking into my ear.[24]

---

[23] What came to mind in that moment was the memory of my pleading in U.S. Court, the helplessness of having to agree to charges that everyone in the Court knew were a farce, including the judge and the prosecutor, driven by threats the prosecutor made towards my wife and my 7-year old son if I didn't do whatever they wanted. This forever leaves a sense that one can do little correct or reform an endemically corrupt culture or society.

[24] Shakespeare wrote, "Many a truth has been spoken in jest," and so I find it ironic that the late stand-up comedian, Bill Hicks, crude though most of his material was, at least by my sensibilities, should have so eloquently described, in one of his routines, Five Dried Grams, the experience of using an entheogen to experience the Divine. Referring to his personal experience when taking magic mushroom (Psilocybe mexicana L.) he comments: "Ya know what happened when I took 'em? I laid in a field of green grass for four hours, going, 'My God, I love everything!' [Big laughs.] The heavens parted. God looked down and rained gifts of forgiveness upon my being, healing me on every level, psychically, physically, emotionally. And I realized that our true nature is Spirit, not body, that we are eternal beings, and God's love is unconditional, and there's nothing we can ever do to change that. It is only our illusion that we are separate from God, or that we are alone. In fact, the reality is, we are one with God, and He loves us. Now, if that isn't a hazard to this country. [Big laughs.] You see my point. How are we going to keep building nuclear weapons? You know what I mean? What's going to happen to the arms industry when we realize that we're all one? It's going to fuck up the economy! [Big laughs.] The economy that's fake anyways! [Bigger laughs.] You can see why the Government's cracking down on the idea of experiencing unconditional Love! Isn't it interesting that the two drugs that are legal, alcohol and tobacco, two drugs that do absolutely nothing for you whatsoever, and drugs that grow naturally upon this planet, drugs that open your eyes up to make you realize how you're being fucked every day of your life . . [Big laughs.] those drugs are against the Law. Wow! Coincidence? I don't know. [Big laughs.] I'm sure their motives are pure." Hysterical, but true.

Interestingly, in my psychonaut journeys, I have found that marijuana is very deleterious to the process of self-discovery, to say nothing of its damaging effects on cognitive function and memory, both short and long term. The "ayahuasca spirit" went so far as to warn against people who took entheogens for recreational purposes and not serious self-discovery

I saw many things those early morning hours -- most of which I will leave absent here because so much of the instruction was quite personal. In time, after many months of reflection, I have come to believe the admonition to change was global, as if applicable to the entirety of humanity. I also came to believe that "Change the World" embodies our embracing, rather than rejecting, the "beauty in the breakdown." That as eternal spiritual beings, a wider vision of our world will allow us to see that the Earth can and will take it upon herself to do away with this horrific, Luciferian class of Elitists who are intent on destroying the Earth, because we either cannot or will not stop them.

At Alpha Omega Labs, we deal with cancer patients all the time who begin to experience a type of Herxheimer Effect after Cansema initiates a die-off of their cancer. Fever, fatigue, sometimes nausea, these are all "Herx symptoms" through which we have to counsel people. And there are two ways to view Herx symptoms: that it's a horrible thing, having to deal with unpleasant healing symptoms, OR, more positively, that something good is happening, the inconveniences are of short duration, and the end result will be a state of health.

Mother Earth is about to unleash a die-off of her own, a pruning of what is corrupt and unreformable. I don't know the date. I wasn't told. I have only been shown the processes and how they will unfold. For its part, Alpha Omega Labs is involved, as are others in Ecuador, with growing, storing, and sharing the information on hundreds of medicinal plants in the coastal, mountain, and Amazonian regions. It is akin to the "monastic option" proposed by Morris Berman.[25]

---

and was particularly emphatic on this point concerning the use of marijuana.

[25] Taken from Morris Berman, The Twilight of American Culture. The gist of Berman's "monastic option" draws from a historical phenomenon that occurred at the close of the Roman Empire. Briefly stated, as the Dioclesian Dynasty came to a close and it became obvious to all Roman citizens with eyes to see, that the Empire was on the verge of collapse, various monasteries took it upon themselves to create hidden libraries in the attempt to save what they regarded as the most important writings (knowledge) of their civilization. Uncovered many years later, Berman claims that much recovered information from these libraries would later help in the creation of the Renaissance. He claims that sensitive individuals in today's collapsing civilization would be wise to follow suit. A fictionalized version of such a library, created for future generations, is found in Umberto Eco's The Name of the Rose, made popular by the movie of the same name.

What world we create after the Petri dish has been cleaned out should be our focus now. For our sake and for the sake of all living creatures on this planet, that world should take into account our conscious recognition that this act of house cleaning was necessary, that our unspoken Declaration of War against Mother Nature was a Declaration of War against ourselves.

And it is in that return to our roots, to our Mother, to what is pure and unspoiled, that we will find ourselves, that we will end this 6,000 year Luciferian nightmare.[26]

Viewed in that context, there is nothing to mourn or regret. In fact, it would appear that everything is running just as it should; for, in all actuality, it was probably planned this way from the very beginning.

---

[26] The themes incorporated into the closing paragraphs of this Ashwin (see Glossary) are expanded upon in Chapter 5 of *Meditopia*. See: www.meditopia.org/chap5.htm. The updated version of this Ashwin post appears in the current volume as Chapter 7 ("Seed Corrupted").

Chapter 3

A Brief Introduction to Part II

I wrote a paper in the spring of 1974 for a physics class in college about advances in the study of holography.[1] The most interesting thing I learned from that paper was that "the whole is contained within every part." You observe the same phenomenon in iridology and reflexology.

Similarly, although the machinations of the Medical Industrial Complex are, at least on the surface, representative of only a slice of modern global life, through it we can see how the entire machinery of human life has evolved and currently operates. Moreover, if we are going to isolate "just a slice," I think this just may be *the* best slice. When examining a global culture built on the supremacy of "fake," few areas provide so many rich, poignant examples of the perversity of modernity as this. You'll see.

A significant portion of Part II is taken from *Meditopia*,[2] a work I started in the summer of 2004, before I was sent off to prison. I had intended until recently to produce *Meditopia* as a separate book. However, after 13 years of intermittent work, frequently interrupted by incarceration and other roadblocks that were thrown my way, thanks to the criminally-oriented and egregiously-misbranded U.S. criminal justice system (2003-2011), followed by the time-consuming rigors of adjusting to business life in South America, I have decided to extract the very best of that work and incorporate it into the current volume. Nothing in the flow or consistency of this book has been sacrificed as a result. Perhaps this book was the intended result of *Meditopia* all along and I just didn't know it. Until now.

---

[1] I was a student at Los Angeles Valley College in that semester, a veritable institution for the mass "deplorables" who would either move on to lesser occupations or advance themselves and transfer to more respectable institutions. In my case, I graduated in 1975 and then enlisted in the U.S. Navy for three years. Nonetheless, the run of pre-med classes I took during my two years there would set the stage for my work in the "alternative medical field" years later and my subsequent epiphany for how the world really worked – the foundation for most of my writings.

[2] What has been posted to *Meditopia* to date can be found at: www.meditopia.org

Part II:

"Meditopia":
Through Modern Medicine
We Can Examine
The Seeds That
Bring Us To Planetary
Destruction and the Principles
That Would Bring
About Resolution

A Brief Commentary on Chapter 4

Meditopia[1] was my first composition following my arrest by FDA officials in 2003. It was initially my attempt to "tell my story," confronting, as I was, the innumerable, outrageous and provable false statements made by U.S. government officials in connection with their criminal case against me. I "wrote" most of the material in my head between my arrest on September 17, 2003 and my temporary release in late May 2004. The bulk of this online book was then set to text online, which I formatted in HMTL, in the summer of 2004 prior to my reimprisonment in September. So we're talking a span of slightly more than three months. Part II is exclusively drawn from *Meditopia*, which has seen changes, updates, and amendments over the intervening years. What came out of *Meditopia* was something far grander, enriching, meaningful, and relevant to the world at large than I had originally envisioned. Ultimately, "my story" took up a small, almost insignificant part of the online book (most of which is excluded here), and the largest portion of it formed a comprehensive "worldview" that would lay the foundation for all my subsequent work. (For those who are interested, I cover my case in exhaustive detail in Chapter 3 of *Meditopia* online.)[2] In the following chapters I have pieced together the most important parts of *Meditopia*, technically and until now an incomplete work, so as to provide "a complete thought," if not a comprehensive philosophy.

I have been asked by many people over the years, how I came to be the pioneer of escharotic Black Salve, which is now an international online phenomenon. Escharotic products are now sold online all over the world, but before Cathryn and I began talking about them on the web in 1995, very few people had ever heard of them.[3] This opening chapter explains how I discovered escharotics and the "deep-down-the-rabbit-hole" intellectual epiphanies I had as a result of their discovery.

[1] See: www.meditopia.org

[2] Chapter 3, told in three parts, begins at: meditopia.org/chap3-1.htm

[3] See: www.altcancer.net/ashwin/ashw0712.htm

Chapter 4:

A Tear in the Matrix
Meditopia / Chapter 1

*"For the medical profession this era may well be one of
the most shameful and ethically questionable in its history."*

Stanley Wohl, M.D.[1]
American Physician,
Author, Consumer Advocate

*"Everyone should know that most cancer research is
largely a fraud, and that the major cancer research organizations are derelict in their duties to the people who support
them."*

Linus Pauling[2]
Two-time Nobel Laureate
1901-1994

*" . . . there is no disease whose prime cause is better
known. That the prevention of cancer will come there is no
doubt. But how long prevention will be avoided depends on how
long the prophets of agnosticism will succeed in inhibiting the
application of scientific knowledge in cancer."*

Otto Warburg[3]
Also a Two-time Nobel Laureate
1883-1970

---

[1] Stanley Wohl, The Medical Industrial Complex (1984). I offer this as the first quote of *Med-itopia*, not because it represents the thesis of the book, but because it summarizes the thrust of the first chapter. As I show in later chapters of *Meditopia*, not only is orthodox medicine irreparably corrupt, but the seeds of its perversity are woven into a 6,000 year old age-defining, cultural operating system that is, in reality, its unseen foundation and influence, its apparenta-tion, to use the language, but not the argument, of Arnold Toynbee.

[2] See: www.brainyquote.com/quotes/quotes/l/linuspauli159885.html; Linus Pauling is an important figure in *Meditopia*. Pauling discusses the value of vitamin C / Lysine as an effective combination in the treatment of cardiovascular disease which we discuss further in Chapter 6.

[3] Otto Warburg, The Prime Cause and Prevention of Cancer (Wurzburg, Germany: Konrad Triltsch, 1967). A brief biograpy can be viewed at: www.nobel.se/medicine/laureates/1931/warburg-bio.html. An ironic side note is that the first of Dr. Warburg's two Nobel prizes came in 1931 for discovering that "the cause of cancer is due to a lack of cellular oxygen."

"The American public has no idea how politics secretly control the practice of medicine. If a doctor dares to introduce a natural, less costly method, no matter how safe or effective, Organized American Medicine can target this doctor for license revocation using fear tactics and legal maneuverings. Why do holistic therapies threaten medicine? (Firstly) They involve a major change in scientific thought. (Secondly) They imply that current methods are inadequate, and, (Thirdly) they threaten huge profits . . ."

James P. Carter, M.D., Ph.D.[4]
American Physician
Baton Rouge, Louisiana
Author: Racketeering in Medicine

"It is very difficult to believe that the very centers entrusted with research in cancer at such enormous expense are 'inhibiting the application of scientific knowledge in cancer' but it is not so difficult to understand once the economics of cancer is grasped.

"The treatment of cancer is, after all, a business which is very lucrative and very expensive for the customer. The goal of most exclusively profit-minded business men is to sell their commodity at the highest price possible in a market where they can eliminate all competition and customers have no choice but their commodity. Such entrepreneurs secure a monopoly by convincing their customers that theirs is the only valid product available and that competitors are frauds whose product is worthless.

"A monopoly of any market is a sure source of profit; a captive clientele has no other choice. The sellers can charge any price the market will bear and can evade any responsibility for bad results because they do not and cannot give any guarantees. They eliminate all critics of their products and challenges to their authority. Their business prospers; thousands of new customers constantly replace those that disappear.

"The original John D. Rockefeller was no mean hand at spotting the commercial possibilities in any enterprise. As his millions came in, he kept reinvesting in the most profitable businesses. One day when appendectomies were the rage in the medical profession, a surgeon told John D. that everyone should have an appendectomy before the age of sixteen as a preventative. The oil wizard saw the point at once . . . 'Why, you've got a better thing than Standard Oil' . . ."

Nat Morris[5]
The Cancer Blackout (1959)

---

[4] James P. Carter, M.D., Dr. P.H., Racketeering in Medicine (Norfolk, Vitginia: Hampton Roads Publishing Company, 1992), i.
[5] Nat Morris, The Cancer Blackout, 5th ed. (Los Angeles, California: Regent House, 1977), 199.

Great ideas and earth-shifting revelations quite often find their messengers in some state of personal tragedy at their point of discovery. Why that is, I don't know. But I can attest to its frequency in my own life; and, in fact, pathos has accompanied my life at almost every turn of substance. The greater the pain, the more sublime and consequential the noetic and spiritual epiphany that followed.

And so it was at the close of 1989, the end of a tumultuous decade, during which I'd uprooted from my home in Los Angeles to move to the provincial southern town of Lake Charles, Louisiana. That year I found myself filing for corporate bankruptcy, followed by my first run-in with U.S. federal authorities, and concluding with the end of my first marriage. At the age of 33, I began the 90's by packing a few personal items into a small car and moving into a crowded, two-bedroom apartment with a friend and her three small children. It was a winter of discontent, nor would it be my last.

Concurrent with this development and in keeping with my never-ending attraction to unusual, out-of-the-box entrepreneurial possibilities, I had just recently been put in contact with a two-man business in Texas called Medical Sciences, Inc. Armed with an herbal black goo and an encapsulated herbal formula for internal use, the merry twosome could be found scampering around the South Texas Hill Country in lab coats and carrying stethoscopes. No satirist could possibly paint a picture of two country bumpkins who better fit the archetype of snake oil doctors selling a quack cancer cure than this duo. Despite my natural openness to investigate all things unconventional if a thread of truth could be found, I had real reservations about this one. There was just one small thing that kept me from walking away without hesitation.

Their products actually worked.

They even worked on advanced stage-4 cancer with extensive metastasis[6] for which primary care physicians had completely given up hope. (A patient knows when his oncologist has reached that point when the subject of discussion centers on the

---

[6] See: www.cancer.gov/publications/dictionaries/cancer-terms/def/metastasis

status of his will and the settling of any unattended legal affairs.)

I watched a clumsily composed VCR tape showing case after case of grateful customers providing their own personal testimony. I could tell that, on the whole, their stories were genuine.[7] I also spoke directly to a number of end users who related stories that were nothing short of miraculous. In most of these cases, orthodox medicine had failed miserably, and many had no problem sharing their disdain for conventional cancer treatment, not because they were predisposed to any particular philosophical position, but because they were eyewitnesses to their own victimhood. And so, when able to obtain some of the topical salve myself, I applied the product on a rapidly enlarging mole that had been growing on my face. Apparently, the vanity that had encouraged my first wife and me to purchase a sun tanning bed for one of our bedrooms had come back to haunt me. About two centimeters below my left eye, the mole wasn't just getting larger, it was getting much darker. As a student of herbology for many years, I knew the symptoms well, and yet I had delayed in seeking out the (second) opinion of a dermatologist.

The salve created a slight sting for about two days and within two weeks the resulting scab came out. Six months later, by mid-1990, I couldn't even tell I had ever had that mole. It is now 15 years later, and the growth has never returned. Now whether or not the growth was a basal or squamous cell carcinoma, I'll never know. It didn't matter to me. What mattered was that I had accidentally stumbled upon one of the cracks in modern medicine's well-crafted mythology concerning the source of "cures." I was getting sucked into a vortex of discovery that would, in time, lead me to fully view the unseen underbelly of what some call the "medical-industrial complex,"[8] a system in which a combination of pride, profits, and prejudice has created a fabric of corruption so vast, so evil, and so breathtaking in its

---

[7] In October, 2006, I found a copy of the old Medical Sciences, Inc. Promotional Video (1989), and had it converted into WMV files. It can be viewed in its entirety on the *Meditopia* video page, broken down into four ten minute segments. To understand the more personal elements of *Meditopia*, a viewing of the video is highly recommended but is not essential. See: meditopia.org/video.htm

[8] Stanley Wohl, The Medical Industrial Complex (New York: Harmony Books, 1984).

breadth, longevity, and audacity, that it would reshape my entire worldview, but not before entering a world of intrigue that, viewed from the perspective of most "normal" people, borders on the surreal.

Impressed with what I had observed so far, I attempted to enter into a business relationship with Medical Sciences, Inc. about this same time. Zane Blanton and Calvin Taylor proved to be very difficult people to negotiate with. Basic contractual points were altered after oral understandings were reached. Then changed again. As a friend of mine who works as an investment broker, Steve Roberts, M.D., tells me, this is the classic "mad scientist negotiation game." He says, "They are so worried that the entire world is out to screw them that you basically end up wasting weeks of time on a deal that never had a chance of reaching fruition in the first place." (Years later I would relate the entire incident to Steve, and thereafter it became an ongoing joke. I couldn't conclude a phone conversation with him without hearing a reversion to his very best imitation of a frantic, 95 year old mad scientist: "You're trying to screeeeeeewww me!")

But Blanton and Taylor were not scientists, mad or otherwise. Intellectuals they were not. Knowledgeable they were not. Delusional they were. I didn't learn this until I was contacted by the man who was actually making their product.

Enter Hal Matheny.

Hal came to my office in Lake Charles, my primary work space from 1986 to 2007. He revealed that his formulations were variants of the work of one Howard McCreary, a self-styled cowboy herbalist, who went around the country passing out a black herbal paste that many thousands of people had used to remove both skin cancers and a wide variety of internal cancer tumors. He told me that the formulas were so old that it would be difficult for anyone to claim authorship. However, that would not stop them from trying.

Not long after I met with Hal, he died in a mysterious, some would say highly suspicious, plane crash. An experienced pilot with over 5,000 hours of flight time, Hal was flying a "tail dragger" near his home in Bastrop, Texas, when suddenly this "very forgiving aircraft" made a nosedive and headed straight into the ground. A couple of months later, in the spring of 1990, I was indicted, along with three other individuals, by a grand jury in Giddings, Texas for "Theft of Trade Secrets," an action obviously engineered by Blanton and Taylor with help from friends in the local city attorney's office.

Broke and "on my last nickel," I worked with my court appointed attorney to try to make the best of being arrested for, as Taylor would put it, "stealing my cancer cure."

In the course of the ensuing investigation, another defendant and I showed the prosecution a document that would end any notion that their case had merit: U.S. Patent No. 209,331, filed in 1878 (hereafter, the "Daniel patent"). Apparently, no one connected with Taylor or Blanton had thought to see if the formulary work they were so gleefully having made was proprietary. The fact is (or was), it is, indeed, very old and very much in the public domain. Made from just three ingredients: zinc chloride, bloodroot (*Papaveraceae sanguinaria canadensis*),[9] and kerosene oil,[10] it appears that with the substitution of water for the kerosene oil, plus the addition of galanga (*Alpina officinalis*, a cousin of ginger, and extraneous to the effectiveness of the formula), the "trade secret" turned out to be rarely in trade, but not very secret. Although the case, for all intents and purposes, was closed, my curiosity as to how such a miraculous "technology" (if such formulary simplicity merits the use of the term) could be in such disuse, was hardly satisfied. How was it possible for something this simple, this inexpensive, this non-toxic (when properly used), and this highly effective, to "fall through the cracks"? Further investigations only served to

---

[9] Concerning the use of taxonomy: most references use genus and species/subspecies in identifying a plant. Since the work of Dr. Jonathan Hartwell and others use "family," as their first major category, I've decided to stick to their system of nomenclature. So whenever the Latin (botanical) name of a plant is given in this monogram, note that the listing is in the family / genus / species / subspecies (if any) order. For more commonly known herbs, I have elected to eliminate "family."

[10] U.S. Patent No. 209,331. Without the addition of the kerosene oil, even in this 1878 patent there would be nothing proprietary. Twenty years earlier, Fell and Pattison published escharotics of their own, wherein the only difference is their use of water instead of a petroleum distillate.

call more issues into question. Apparently "Medical Sciences," with the help of Howard McCreary, had fallen upon a simple tradition of curing cancer, so old and effective, and so empowering to ordinary people without any intervention on the part of the medical community, that its very benefits had condemned it to be professionally reviled, thus causing it to be a permanent regulatory target.

It had a name: escharotic, a pejorative term given to it by early medical practitioners who saw their practices suffer whenever their patients were able to obtain the product. Since "eschar" comes from the Greek word for "burn," they were able to sum up their campaign to destroy the everyday use of these products in their very word to describe it.[11] The name became so prevalent that even proponents of escharotic preparations used the term. The fictitious claim that "escharotics" do nothing more than "burn the skin" is still used to this day, with every bit the sense of gravity and feigned genuineness as in the 1880s. (Small problem: it isn't true. I cover that later in this book.)

And yet, escharotics turned out to be an unkillable foe, like a stubborn crabgrass that refuses to forever depart from the dichondra lover's lawn. The patent office tells the story: beginning with U.S. Patent No. 92209,[12] filed in 1869, escharotics proceed through the Daniels patent to Patent No. 1411577[13] ("Mullins," filed in 1922), which is so close to Daniels' patent, I'm surprised it was issued. And then you have U.S. Patent No. 4,229,437[14] and 4,315,916,[15] which supposedly uses bittersweet (*Celastraceae celastrus scandens*), instead of bloodroot, with zinc chloride, although, frankly, I was confused as an herbalist, because "*Solanum dulcamara*" was the botanical name given for this new botanical variation, and everybody knows that's "climbing

[11] The use of the word "eschar" even pre-dates Paracelsus, who is covered in the next chapter. The OED traces the use of the word back to 1430, where "eschar" is defined as "a brown or black dry slough, resulting from the destruction of a living part, either by gangrene, by burn, or by caustics." See The Compact Oxford English Dictionary, 2nd ed. (1991), 387.

[12] See: meditopia.org/images/pat_92209.jpg

[13] See: meditopia.org/images/pat_1411577.jpg

[14] See: meditopia.org/images/pat_4229437.jpg

[15] See: meditopia.org/images/pat_4315916.jpg

nightshade." The claims on the wide range of skin growths this simple formula will remove is accurate, by the way.

Less creative still is U.S. Patent No. 4,515,779,[16] filed in 1981 by John Q. Elliott -- this variant based on zinc chloride, bloodroot, and ginger root in equal amounts -- again, another very close version.

And then there are "complicated versions," which, as you'll learn from reading this book, are the essence of medical advancement: complicated is good, more likely to earn a profit; simple is bad; people figuring things out for themselves, bad. BAD! Two such monstrosities include U.S. Patent No. 2,344,830[17] (1944) and 6,558,694[18] (2000). Their filings may be separated by a half century; their objective and the transparency of their *raison d'être* are not. These forays into legalistic one-upmanship weave the formulary essence into a surgical process, which, if you understand escharotic preparations, is completely unnecessary. Sure, it makes a lot more money for the medical community -- but it is, nonetheless, unnecessary. (This monstrous attempt to make surgery essential to a process for which the knife is totally unnecessary forms the basis for Mohs surgery, a dermatological procedure that is standard and approved in most Western countries. But I'll get to that later also.)[19]

Some patents use obfuscating language to try and hide what really amounts to a re-filing of something quite old. Patents 4,053,630 and 4,224,339 use the same escharotic knowledge, expand the base of metal salts claimed to be effective, add commonly used organic acids (or their metal chelates) and get

---

[16] See: meditopia.org/images/pat_4515779.jpg

[17] See: meditopia.org/images/pat_2344830.jpg

[18] See: meditopia.org/images/pat_6558694.jpg

[19] Even in the 1800s, long before Mohs surgery, "conventional wisdom" held that "escharotics" were best used in conjunction with surgery. (Based on my many years of working with escharotic materials, I have found that it was as unnecessary th en as it is now, in the vast majority of cases.) See: John Cummings Munro, "Escharotics in the Treatment of Malignant Disease," *Boston Surgical and Medical Journal*, eds. George B. Shattuck and Charles F. Withington (Boston: Damrell and Upham, 1889): 272-75. However, a deeper study of the literature of the time indicates that although caustics were begrudgingly acknowledged as being useful in the treatment of "epithelial ulcers," "when it comes to malignant disease . . . surgical intervention is the only proper resource." Cha-ching! See: *Journal of the American Medical Association* 37 (1901): 1015.

through on the basis that they are a treatment for disturbed keratinization.U.S. Patent No. 4,847,083[20] is a variant for decubitus ulcers, though a complex one.

None of this covers the variations yet to be used as an oral preparation. But don't worry, the story of Vipont Pharmaceutical is upcoming. My point in even touching upon all this patent work is simply to make clear just how widespread the discoveries involving escharotics have been. This does nothing but make the effort to suppress them all that more horrific and shameful.

Business people are often accused by those of a more singular technical or scientific frame of mind of being cerebrally challenged bean counters. They see the business, the money to be made, sure -- but they are, more times than not, incapable of grasping the "whole picture." By focusing only on the immediacy of creating profit-producing commerce, they don't allow the full blossoming of whatever science might bring. It is a recurrent theme among the technocrats of the world, and among some specialists: ecological sociologists come to mind; it is a vital tenet of their work.

One thing that business people do better, however, and I aspired to embody this trait, is identify trends. You don't have to be able to fully navigate the subtleties of linear regression, but you need to be able to spot synchronicities and ask yourself, "Why?" Is the phenomena I'm observing an isolated incident? Or does it have parallels elsewhere that I can learn from? Are there tendencies I can identify? Are others aware of these trends -- and if not, can I turn them into opportunity?

Having taken a year of my life to study the history, use and effects of escharotic preparations, it was obvious to me that they were, quite clearly, a cure for cancer, when properly manufactured and properly applied. Not a preventive. Not a palliative. A cure. Let's spell it together: C-U-R-E.

The next question, therefore, was obvious.

Just how many other similar phenomena were out there to be "re-discovered"? Were there also highly effective cures for

[20] See: meditopia.org/images/pat_4847083.jpg

strokes, heart disease, arthritis, diabetes, multiple sclerosis, Alzheimer's and God only knew how many other human ailments that were being suppressed because of their simplicity and threat to the established order?

I didn't have to look far to see evidence of this "suppression pattern." The number of exposés on the criminality of the medical establishment in this area turned out to be quite overwhelming. It wasn't that a body of work documenting this kind of malfeasance wasn't out there. It just wasn't being read. Fine.

What I wanted, however, were specifics. It wasn't good enough for me to see, with crystal clarity, that the medical industrial establishment, including the pharmaceutical companies, the HMOs, hospitals, medical specialists, all their respective lobbyists, and their enforcement hacks at the Food & Drug Administration, had a vested interest in squelching competition. I went well beyond seeing that science and its applications in the world of commerce were largely guided along lines of profit, exclusivity, monopoly, and destroying competition. I understood that. I'm a businessman. What others might call a conspiracy, I can identify as "business as usual."

My inquiry had to go farther.

I wanted to know WHAT was being suppressed. Moreover, I wanted to know precisely what the inventors knew, the first victims in the chain of suppression. I wanted to find ways of marketing what they could not. As a technically-oriented business person, as well as a scientist and inventor in my own right, I wanted to learn both the technologies, and the methods to negotiate the legal and political landmines that prevented these superior methods of treatment from getting into the marketplace.

Early in the fall of 1990, I contacted a man who had achieved considerable success in the pharmaceutical industry. Dr. Russell T. Jordan was a man with a most interesting history. A fighter pilot in World War II, Jordan initially took the academic path before becoming a co-founder of Vipont Pharmaceutical. Jordan was already semi-retired by the time I made his acquaintance. Consulting as "MedConEx," Jordan helped me fill in some of the pieces regarding the history of escharotics.

Jordan was well familiar with escharotics when I met him. He had managed to turn his own acquaintance with Howard McCreary into a business opportunity of his own: the creation of Vipont Pharmaceutical in Fort Collins, Colorado. Vipont's core business ended up being a dentifrice and mouthwash, although 15 out of their 23 U.S. patents revolved around bloodroot,[21] with most of the remaining work having at least some tangential relationship.[22] (A variety of autobiographical histories on Vipont surfaced, I even posted one,[23][24] but Jordan appeared to stay above the fray on 'credit-taking.')[25]

---

[21] U.S. Patent No. 4,145,412; "Composition for application to oral cavity and method for preparation thereof," filed February 14, 1977 by Peter A. Ladanyi for Vipont Chemical Company. U.S. Patent No. 4,406,881; "Antimicrobial agent," same stated inventor, but the company name has been changed to Vipont Laboratories; filed September 18, 1981. U.S. Patent No. 4,517,172; "Plaque disclosing agent," inventor: George L. Southard, and now it's Vipont Laboratories, Inc., the assignee for this and most of the patents that follow below through Note #25. Somebody's moving up in the world. Filed December 29, 1983. U.S. Patent No. 4,590,061; "Antimicrobial plaque disclosing agent," Southard. Filed May 10, 1985. U.S. Patent No. 4,599,228; "Antimicrobial agent," back to Ladanyi. Filed January 25, 1984. U.S. Patent No. 4,683,133; "Method for treating periodontal disease," Southard. Filed August 20, 1985. U.S. Patent No. 4,689,216; "Sanguinarine dental compositions with hydrated silica," Greene. Filed August 25, 1987. U.S. Patent No. 4,735,945; "Method for inhibiting bone resorption and collagenase release," Sakamoto, et al. Filed April 5, 1988. U.S. Patent No. 4,737,503; "Method for inhibiting the release of histamine," Sakamoto, et al. Filed April 12, 1988. U.S. Patent No. 4,767,861; "Recovery of benzo-c-phenanthridine alkaloids," Boulware. Filed August 30, 1988. U.S. Patent No. 4,769,452; "Production of purity benzo-c-phenanthridine alkaloid salts," Boulware. Filed September 6, 1988. U.S. Patent No. 4,818,533; "Production of high purity alkaloids," Boulware, et al. Filed April 4, 1989. U.S. Patent No. 5,013,553; "Drug delivery devices," Southard, et al. Filed May 7, 1991. U.S. Patent No. 5,066,483; "Oral rinse compositions," Harkrader, et al. Filed November 19, 1991. U.S. Patent No. 5,175,000; "Free amine benzophenanthridine alkaloid compositions," Godowski, et al. December 29, 1992.

[22] U.S. Patent No. 4,975,271; "Mucosal delivery systems for treatment of periodontal disease," Dunn, et al. Filed Demcember 4, 1990. U.S. Patent No. 5,060,825; "Irrigation system and method for delivering a selected one of multiple liquid solutions to a treatment site," Palmer, et al. Filed October 29, 1991. U.S. Patent No. 5,077,049; "Biodegradable system for regenerating the periodontium," Dunn, et. al. Filed December 31, 1991. U.S. Patent No. 5,199,604; "Irrigation system and method for delivering a selected one of multiple liquid solutions to a treatment site," Palmer, et al. Filed September 23, 1991. U.S. Patent No. 5,200,194; "Oral osmotic device," Edgren, et al. Filed April 6, 1993. U.S. Patent No. 5,324,520; "Intragingival delivery systems for treatment of periodontal disease," Dunn, et. al. Filed April 13, 1993. U.S. Patent No. 5,395,615; "Free amine benzophenanthridine alkaloid compositions," Godowski, et. al. Filed September 30, 1992. U.S. Patent No. 6,465,521; "Composition for desorbing bacteria," Rosenberg. Filed October 15, 2002.

[23] See: meditopia.org/images/pat_4847083.jpg

[24] "Vipont Chemical Pharmaceutical Company." www.altcancer.net/mccrear2.htm. Narrated by Clark Bigham.

[25] Jordan suspected that a product that worked this well for so many sufferers of gingivitis, one that didn't require input from doctors or dentists, would eventually be the target of the orthodox community. He was right. See: www.sciencedaily.com/releases/2001/12/011227075007.

At the time that I met him, Jordan was heavily involved in researching the properties of another medicinal chemical, nor-dihydroguaiaretic acid. "NDGA," as it is commonly called, is a catecholic butane, and the primary, active compound of another beloved specimen of Native American ethnobotany, chaparral (of which I worked with three out of the six species on the North American continent: *Zygophyllaceae larrea divaricata, L. mexicata, and L. tridentata*). Jordan began researching other medicinal herbs which could be combined with zinc chloride to get the same cancer curing effect, and sometime during the early to mid-1980s, he came upon chaparral leaves as an even better additive to the traditional zinc chloride escharotic than the bloodroot rhizome of old. Jordan's work lead to both a patent[26] and a working relationship with a struggling pharmaceutical company, Chemex Pharmaceutical, that had been trying to find its place among respectable American drug companies since its founding in 1975. Refinement of this latest embodiment of the escharotic concept lead Jordan to expand claimed proprietorship over all other catecholic butanes, besides the NDGA in chaparral.[27] It also lead to a flurry of related patent filings which did little to truly enhance the effectiveness of the original embodiment.[28] The search after Jordan's contribution, as is the case

htm "American Cancer Society funds study to show relationship between Viadent, or sanguinarine, use and leukoplakia." I suspected they would eventually target a bloodroot-based dentifrice for other reasons, so I took Jordan's advice and formulated an "escharotic toothpaste" that replied primarily on zinc chloride and chaparral instead. See www.altcancer.net/tpaste.htm

[26] U.S. Patent No. 4,774,229; "Modification of plant extracts from zygophyllaceae and pharmaceutical use therefor," Russell T. Jordan; assigned to Chemex Pharmaceutical, Inc. Filed May 7, 1986.

[27] U.S. Patent No. 4,880,637; "Compositions of catecholic butanes with zinc." Russell T. Jordan; assigned to Chemex Pharmaceutical, Inc. October 28, 1986.

[28] U.S. Patent No. 4,895,727; "Pharmaceutical vehicles for exhancing penetration and retention in the skin." Larry M. Allen; assigned to Chemex Pharmaceutical, Inc. Filed May 3, 1985. U.S. Patent No. 5,008,294; "Methods of treating tumors with compositions of catecholic butanes." Neiss, et. al.; assigned to Chemex Pharmaceutical, Inc. Filed June 3, 1987. U.S. Patent No. 5,116,149; "Methotrexate compositions and methods of treatment using same." Loev; assigned to Chemex Pharmaceutical, Inc. Filed June 10, 1991. U.S. Patent No. 5,292,731; "Methods of treatment using methotrexate compositions." Loev; assigned to Chemex Pharmaceutical, Inc. Filed July 21, 1992. U.S. Patent No. 5,409,690; "Treatment of multidrug resistant diseases in cancer cell by potentiating with masoprocol." Howell, et al.; assigned to Chemex Pharmaceutical, Inc. Note: masoprocol is the new, fancy name for NDGA. Filed June 23, 1993. U.S. Patent No. 5,541,232; "Treatment of multidrug resistant diseases." Howell, et al.; assigned to Chemex Pharmaceutical, Inc. Filed June 23, 1994.

with all modern drug companies, was the search for respectability, proprietorship, and government approval.

What resulted from this was the creation of Actinex (Masoprocol) as a registered tradename for NDGA; subsequent FDA approval[29] and now common usage for keratosis.[30] Chemex itself eventually merged with Access Pharmaceutical in Dallas, Texas.[31] At least one attempt was made commercially and quite publically to make use of the zinc chloride / NDGA combination, but it was quickly taken off the market.[32]

Most of these events happened while Jordan was still alive, but well after the period from 1990 to 1991 that I worked with him.[33] The important point to note here is that Jordan considered the reality of his discovery to be largely a case of misuse. He knew what anyone who has ever worked with the various zinc chloride embodiments in escharotics knew: they cure cancer. Relegating his findings to a treatment for keratosis marginalized the potential of the product.

Before working in the pharmaceutical industry, Jordan had been a professor of medicine at the University of Michigan. He was a good teacher who exposed me to the political realities of modern medicine. "Health care is a misnomer," he would say, "What we have today is 'disease care.' And if a product doesn't make people in high places a lot of money, it won't have

[29] Actinex (masoprocol) remains an approved drug. See: www.drugs.com/mmx/masoprocol.html; It was approved in 1992 for "skin lesions caused by overexposure to sunlight.
Block Drug (Jersey City, NJ) was listed as the manufacturer, since this was the company to which Chemex Pharmaceutical sold the rights to Actinex. See: www.fundinguniverse.com/company-histories/block-drug-company-inc-history/ (in reference to Block Drug's dealings with Chemex).
[30] Masoprocol (Actinex) is now an approved dermatological agent used primarily in the treatment of actinic keratosis. See: www.healthdigest.org/topics/category/1390-masoprocol-dosage-interactions-side-effects-how-to-use
[31] Chemex Pharmaceutical, Inc. was reverse merged into Access Pharmaceutical, Inc. This was an inevitable occurrence, following Chemex's delisting from NASDAQ in 1995.
[32] Herbalgram.com used to carry an HerbClip catalog sheet as it relates to this product. It is no longer available on the Internet. The product's primary ingredients were NDGA and chaparral. It was taken off the market in 1997 for unspecified reasons by the manufacturer, Stiefel Laboratories, Inc. (Coral Gables, FL). It has not returned to market. This catalog sheet itself was put out by ABC (American Botanicla Council), (512) 331-8868. Bin #108.
[33] Russell T. Jordan was born on January 28, 1919 and died on August 17, 2003 -- exactly one month to the day before my arrest. I was released on May 27, 2004 and spoke with Grace, Russell's wife of 57 years, on June 9, 2004. She indicated to me that Russell had become stricken with hepatitis after a botched surgery at a VA hospital. He was also diabetic and had a touch of Parkinson's towards the end. His passing was peaceful.

a chance of surviving in the marketplace. They'll just kill it, and sometimes the person who introduces it."

The "Ten Conditions":
Identifying a Recurring Suppression Pattern

Escharotics are especially offensive to the medical community for ten very obvious and powerful reasons. Because these reasons recur with such frequency and poignancy, I will enumerate them here:

1. **The Products (Escharotics) Cure Cancer.**
   (And as we'll see in further chapters, so do quite a number of other suppressed treatment approaches). The escharotic versions I went on to create worked better than 99% of the time topically, and better than 50% of the time on a wide range of internal cancers, excluding blood cancers (i.e. leukemia, lymphomas, and Hodgkin's). From 1995 to 2003, I ran and operated Alpha Omega Labs (altcancer.com), after already having five years experience in working with escharotics. I created a line of escharotic products that I named "Cansema® " (merging "cancer" with the popular trademark, Noxzema® and pronounced can-see'-muh.).[34] In only two cases did customers "claim" that the topical product did not work, and in only one case did a customer sue (Sue Gilliatt vs. Gregory James Caton, et. al.), and in even THAT case, the plaintiff admitted in sworn deposition that her cancer had been cured.[35] As to the internal ver-

---

[34] Cansema® was registered with the U.S. Trademark & Patent Office in 2004 by Herbologics, Ltd., a Louisiana corporation I created in 1993. The manner in which corrupt FDA officials have helped various entities, including Rising Sun (www.bloodrootproducts.com) , violate the trademark, and worse, turning the other way in the face of variations which are provably adulterated and misbranded, is the subject of a later chapter in the original *Meditopia* text. See Chapter 12 in the current volume: "Gresham's Law: Its Treacherous Application."

[35] Sue Gilliatt's entire deposition: www.meditopia.org/sue_depos.doc. It is in DOC file format -- nearly 1.2 megs in size, so please allow time for the download. [Case No. 1:03-CV-1183 LJM-WTL, Southern District of Indiana, Indianapolis Division; Sue Gilliatt (Plaintiff) vs. Gregory J. Caton, Lumen Foods Corporation d/b/a Alpha Omega Labs, Dan Raber, Appalachian Herbal Remedies, Pangea Remedies, The Deodorant Stone Co., and DSMC (Defen-

sions of Cansema® that were escharotic (Capsules and Tonic I), few customers failed to report some progress -- if not dramatic results. We were able to produce testimonial pages displaying an array of astonishing success stories.

2. **They're cheap.**

They are easy and inexpensive to make, not to mention inexpensive to sell (relative to orthodox treatment). Cansema® Salve, the primary salve I created and sold for $49.95 USD, could be used to cure a dozen or more average sized skin carcinomas. No monopoly, big profits, or advantages of extortionary regulation to be had here. Not good for the home team.

3. **No Doctor Is Required.**

They do not require the intervention of a doctor. They place most cancer treatments on the same level as going to the local drugstore to get a topical ointment to eliminate athlete's foot.

4. **They're Non-Toxic.**

They are not at all toxic topically. The internal variations are potentially toxic (especially with the use of bloodroot, which contain potent alkaloids, notably sanguarene), but not if properly formulated, with adherence to a clearly stated, properly tested protocol.

5. **They Expose Long-Standing Industry and Government-Based Fraud of Unimaginable Proportion.**

Their very existence makes clear what an enormous fraud that orthodox chemotherapy, radiation, and most surgery are. Moreover, their efficacy exposes what a joke the multibillion dollar "cancer research" industry is and has been for the better part of a century.

dents). Ms. Gilliatt sued even though she admitted under oath that her cancer was cured by Caton's and/or Raber's products. Read end of p. 38 through middle of p. 39 in the deposition.

6. **They're Non-Patentable.**
They cannot be meaningfully patented. Those escharotics that have been patented could not be reasonably defended. Without a basis to secure a monopoly, no faction with the drug industry could possibly condone the public becoming knowledgeable in the use of escharotics.

7. **They Do Not Lend Themselves to Proprietary Ownership and the Monopolistic Privileges It Brings.**
They've been around for so long that no one can claim credit or ownership to the essential principles behind them, the principles supporting their efficacy.

8. **Indigenous Ethnobotanical Origins Are Shown to Be Superior.**
Escharotics' origins, that is, if anyone at all is to get credit for their discovery, go back to indigenous and aboriginal sources. Nothing is more embarrassing to modern science than the admission that we have spent many hundreds of billions of dollars on a project, and still we cannot improve upon the advice of medicine men ("those brute savages!") who fail to bow to the gods of our superior, industrial, mechanistic universe. This is cognitive dissonance we shall not put up with! It is a "tear in the matrix" that threatens to create an uncontrolled stampede among the disgruntled hoi polloi who just might decide to become "unplugged."

9. **True Democracy Is Exposed as a Sham**
Escharotics' existence undermines the legitimacy of representative democracy. It allows even the more obtuse among the civically ignorant citizenry to view the mythology of "government by the people" in all its disinformation. If escharotics are not proof that most Western democracies are, in actuality, plutocracies that put the interest of the rich and influential over those

of the common man, nothing is. If the average citizen in the U.S., U.K., Australia, New Zealand, etc., knew what I knew, they would know that they possess absolute proof, in their hands, that modern medicine is the story of oppressive financial servitude. They would know that their so-called "elected representatives" are not only complicit, but are owned, lock, stock, and barrel, by the power elite. They would internalize, with unmistakeable clarity, the evidence that their houses of political representation were, in fact, little more than multinational corporate brothels. Not that many are not already aware of the fact; but it would most decidedly raise, as Alan Watts used to say, the "intensity of the concept" to a higher level of outrage. Most people, to this point, have not had the capacity to understand the cruel machinations that sit behind this kind of brutality.

10. Knowledge of their Existence and Proper Use Would Lead to the Wholesale Bankruptcy of the Medical Industry in the West

If the preparation and use of escharotics were widely known to ordinary citizens, this knowledge among the "People" would only lead to the embracing of other, equally effective natural remedies that are far superior to anything that modern medicine, generally, and more specifically, modern pharmacology, has to offer. Any significant movement in this direction would have an accelerating character and would, as I will expand upon in upcoming chapters, bring about the financial decimation of the pharmaceutical industry in the West and much of the medical industry that is allied to it.

Remember these conditions, integral to what I call the "Suppression Pattern," as they form a recurrent theme in this book. The concept is further refined as the book progresses, and, in fact, I will refer back to these points as the "Ten Conditions" in subsequent chapters.

For now, before I can complete the chronology of events that leads to the present, it is important to examine a brief history of escharotics, specifically, and trends in medical suppression, generally.

Unless you believe, with the clarity and intensity that I believe, that these Conditions are true and beyond the pale of exaggeration or embellishment, you will not be able to appreciate the latter sections of this book and what they mean for you, your family, and society.

That is why I devote enough time and attention in what follows so you can see the Suppression Pattern for what it is and what it has done to Western Civilization.

Once you internalize these concepts with clarity, you will never be the same person again.

Chapter 4

A Brief Commentary on Chapter 5

This chapter was originally composed as Chapter 2 of *Meditopia*. The first half of the chapter was written entirely in the summer of 2004, but the addendum on Dr. Perry Nichols wasn't added until 2017. Minor changes were made in the years in between.

Its primary function is to show that escharotics have a very long history of effectiveness, and an equally long history of medical authorities working very assiduously to ensure that people don't know about them; and if they do, to lead them to believe they are lacking in therapeutic efficacy, if not outright dangerous. More material and pictures related to this chapter can still be found online at the *Meditopia* site.[1]

Comparing the stark contrast between the official narrative and the provable, empirical facts forms the transition between my personal experiences in the previous chapter and the rest of Part II. In turn, Part II segues and expands into other disciplines in Part III.

---

[1] See: www.meditopia.org/chap2.htm

Chapter 5:

Escharotics:
500 Years of Suppression
Meditopia / Chapter 2

"The touchstone of true science is power of performance, for it is a truism that what can, also will, and thus attains to real existence."

Dr. Rudolf Virchow
(1821-1902)

"The universities do not teach all things . . . so a doctor must seek out old wives, gypsies, sorcerers, wandering tribes, old robbers, and such outlaws and take lessons from them. A doctor must be a traveller . . . Knowledge is experience."

Paracelsus[1]
(1493-1541)

"Any treatment of disease that claims to be in advance of what is known to the profession however clearly on scientific principles or uniformly commended by its power to heal, is sure to meet with opposition. In the treatment of cancer that is the more to be expected inasmuch as cancer has been the opprobrium of the profession. By physicians, the world over, it has for the most part been regarded as incurable. If this is not so, why the conviction universally pervading the public mind that all ordinary means to arrest it are impotent?"

T.T. Blake, M.D.[2]
Cancers Cured Without
the Use of the Knife (1858)

---

[1] The New Encyclopaedia Britannica, 15th ed, 1986, Vol. 9 (Micropaedia), "Paracelsus," 134.

[2] T.T. Blake published Cancers Cured Without the Use of the Knife in 1858. The passage cited from the book is taken from: Nat Morris, The Cancer Blackout, 5th ed. (Los Angeles, California: Regent House, 1977), 28.

"A physician once told me that nothing arouses so much bitter enmity and heated arguments among his colleagues, as the subject of cancer. This may be due to the guilty recollections of cancer victims expiring who might have been saved; or of the memories of patients pronounced hopelessly ill who recovered under the treatment of a 'quack,' or who miraculously lived without further treatment. Possibly these guilt reactions and the remorse over exhausting the money of patients and their relatives in futile cancer treatments, account for some of these psychological manifestations which are expressed in hostility and attack."

Nat Morris[3]
(written in 1958)

"I die by the help of too many physicians."

Alexander the Great[4]
On his deathbed, 323 B.C.

"Civilization originates in conquest abroad and repression at home."

Stanley Diamond[5]
*In Search of the Primitive:
A Critique of Civilization*

I t is my position that for the entirety of recorded history in Western culture, but most particularly on account of Greek and Roman influences from about the fifth century, B.C., to the present, the suppression of simple, effective medical remedies in favor of more complex systems, methods, products, and protocols, has been embedded into the very fabric of the prevailing medical establishment. We'll examine the various political, economic, and religious constructs, my version of "cultural infrastructure," necessary to sustain this system of suppression in

---

[3] Nat Morris, The Cancer Blackout, 5th ed. (Los Angeles, California: Regent House, 1977), 156.

[4] Alexander the Great quote taken from: George Crile, Jr., M.D., Cancer and Common Sense (New York: Viking Press, 1955), 51.

[5] Stanley Diamond, In Search of the Primitive: A Critique of Civilization, as quoted by Jensen, p. 189.

an upcoming section. For now, it is only important to establish and define the "suppression pattern" and apply it to escharotics, as we discussed in the first chapter, so as to first finish my initial chronology.

Paracelsus, the famous, 16th century, medical pioneer used escharotics. His success in treating cancer is well documented. He was also well-known to have been a victim of jealousy among his less competent colleagues (which included nearly everyone save himself), and was finally disposed of as a means of terminating their frightful embarrassment.

Most physicians of antiquity acquired their reputation not because they were great theoreticians, but because they were able to cure patients who found little relief elsewhere. The proof was in the pudding. Good doctors cure their patients, and grateful acknowledgement through payment is the natural consequence. (Today it's the reverse. Getting paid is primary. The cure is an afterthought. This is poignant reality that hits anyone who has ever visited the ER section of a modern American hospital.)

A master of empirical eclecticism in the medical arts, Paracelsus gave credence to neither academic credentials nor social standing. He understood the dangers inherent in ideological rigidity and was the very antithesis of monoculturalism in medical approach, in all its diverse theoretical and applied facets that are as much an infection in medicine today as back in the days of Galen.

Paracelsus is reviled for his association with mysticism, astrology, and alchemy by contemporary historians, indeed he found ways to harness them all in his practice, and yet his critics must begrudgingly note his unusual successes. Centuries before Mesmer, Paracelsus understood and employed the principles of suggestion; centuries before Freud, he understood mind/body connection; centuries before Antonio Meucci[6] or R. Raymond Rife,[7] he utilized electromagnetic therapy; he discovered hy-

---

[6] Gerry Vassilatos, Lost Science (Kempton, Illinois: Adventures Unlimited Press, 1999), 56-75.

[7] Ibid., "Ultra Microscopes and Cure Rays: R. Raymond Rife," p. 137-168; Barry Lynes, The

drogen, nitrogen; coined the term "alcohol" (from the Arabic),[8] and identified zinc. He composed his own pharmacoepia and achieved clinical success that few physicians today can match, all at a time when medical specialization, as we know it, was non-existent.

Gotthold Ephraim Lessing (1729-1781), one of the most influential figures of the Enlightenment, said of him, "Those who imagine that the medicine of Paracelsus is a system of superstitions which we have fortunately outgrown, will, if they once learn to know its principles, be surprised to find that it is based on a superior kind of knowledge which we have not yet attained, but into which we may hope to grow."[9] His knowledge of subtle energies that act upon the living organism mimic principles that only now are beginning to migrate from our recent discoveries in quantum physics into the stodgy crevices of our biological sciences. Paracelsus is widely credited with not only being the "father of modern medicine," in part because of his expansive and radical departure from the apothecary practices of his time, but the father of lesser known or respected practices and disciplines, including iatrochemistry and balneology.[10] Viewing the breadth of his work and the endurance of so many of his ideas, not to mention a universe of thought that did not endure, perhaps because we have not the sufficient collective consciousness to comprehend it, it does not seem hyperbolic to say that he was "the precursor of chemical pharmacology and therapeutics, and the most original medical thinker of the 16th century."[11]

In a facet of personality that appears common among those who rise too far above the mean intelligence of their medical

Cancer Cure That Worked! (Ontario, Canada: Marcus Books, 1987).

[8] See: www.chm.bris.ac.uk/webprojects2002/crabb/famous.html

[9] reference.allrefer.com/encyclopedia/L/LessingG.html, on background on Lessing, and Note 7, p.6 for his quotation.

[10] Nicholas Goodrick-Clarke, Paracelsus: Essential Readings (Berkeley, California: North Atlantic Books, 1999), 21, 30.

[11] Manly P. Hall, Paracelsus: His Mystical & Medical Philosophy, Philosophical Research Society, (1997), p. 5; extracted from: Fielding H. Garrison, A.B., M.D., An Introduction to the History of Medicine - with medical chronology, suggestions for study and bibliographic data (Philadelphia and London: W.B. Saunders Company, 1929), 204.

peers, Paracelsus appeared to have little by way of humility. While lecturing at the University of Basel, he is reported to have said that the soft down on the back of his neck knew more about the practice of medicine than all the professors of Basel put together.[12] A celebratory book burning of works by Galen and Avicenna, pillars of 16th century medical thought, which Paracelsus orchestrated in the spirit of religious leader and fellow German reformer, Martin Luther (1483-1546), was the last straw for many. It wasn't enough that he could cure illnesses that no one else could, he made a point to rub his colleagues' collective face in it. On one occasion Paracelsus offered to cure any patient deemed incurable. Fully prepared to disgrace this wild braggart, his colleagues presented him with fifteen advanced cases of leprosy. (One can only imagine that since his enemies got to do the choosing, these were no mean challenges. No doubt with advanced cachexia and one foot already in the grave).

He cured nine out of the fifteen.[13]

The escharotic formula that Paracelsus used was as simple and direct as the rest of this practice. Instead of zinc chloride as a caustic halide, Paracelsus used "sal ammoniac" (ammonium chloride), along with fuligo (wood soot), and orpiment (arsenic sulfide).[14] According to records of the time, it worked. (Interestingly, Paracelsus employed his own "arsenic paste" nearly 400 years before Nobel Prize-winner, Paul Ehrlich, created his own celebrated version to treat syphilis in the early 1900s.[15] Varia-

[12] Ibid.

[13] Nicholas Goodrick-Clarke, Paracelsus: Essential Readings (Berkeley, California: North Atlantic Books, 1999), 19.

[14] I found no evidence that Paracelsus used a zinc chloride base in his escharotics. It appears that ammonium chloride was his halide caustic of choice in his own formulary work. One prominent formula consisted of just three ingredients, including Orpiment (arsenic sulfide). Paracelsus used it in one cancer preparation: Arthur Edward Waite, trans. and ed., The hermetic and alchemical writings of Paracelsus the Great (Edmonds, Washington: The Alchemical Press, 1992), 18. He combined the orpiment with fuligo (wood soot), and with sal ammoniac (ammonium chloride) acting as the caustic halide in this formula. One aside: Chloride and iodine appear to be reoccurring halogens in this area, as I have never seen any compounds of bromide, fluoride, let alone astatine, used in topical escharotic preparations.

[15] Paul Ehrlich (not to be confused with the celebrated ecologist and author from Stanford) won the 1908 Nobel Prize in Medicine for his work in immunity. He is widely known for his rediscovery of an arsenic paste; his versions called Salvorsan and Neosalvorsan were used in treating syphilis in the early 20th century, and are still in use in the veterinary community. Ironically, he also coined the term "chemotherapy," a concept that was synonymous with quackery

tions in the 1800s had already been used by allopaths to treat skin cancer).[16]

Paracelsus had a separate formula that was less "intense," which he used to treat skin cancers, jaundice, and some wounds. We don't know the exact method of preparation, but it used "litharge" (lead monoxide) as the caustic agent.[17]

As one might expect, Paracelsus' reviling of tradition would eventually cost him his life, as he was unceremoniously pushed off a cliff by hired assassins "in the employ of the medical fraternity," according to supporters.[18] Though even a most orthodox review of Paracelsus' contribution to modern medicine cannot diminish his stature, the allopathic version of his end, as with most dissenters, has him in a most unflattering exit off stage, namely, a bar room brawl.[19] Or victim of a midlife stroke.[20] The reputation of more recent dissenters who produced miraculous results has fared no better, even to the point of altering a death certificate.[21]

Paracelsus is such an illustrative example, not only because he was a medical luminary nonpareil, but because the elements of suppression are so pronounced in his life and work.

Central to Paracelsus' work was the use of natural plants and mineral compounds, and what we might regard as the rudi-

---

at a time when x-ray and radiation treatment were the prominent moneymakers in conventional cancer treatment. See: Kenny Ausubel, <u>When Healing Becomes a Crime</u> (Rochester, Vermont: Healing Arts Press, 2000), 233; quoting: Ralph W. Moss, <u>Questioning Chemotherapy</u> (Brooklyn, New York: Equinox Press, 1995), 15-16; A. Gilman, "The initial clinical trial of nitrogen mustard," *American Journal of Surgery* 105 (1963): 574-78.

[16] As early as 1895, orthodox physicians were using arsenic paste to treat skin cancer.

[17] Paracelsus used litharge (lead monoxide) in a topical paste for cancer, which also contained salt water, alum (probably aluminum sulfate), and white vinegar. Litharge is a strong enough irritant, though not ideal by any means, given that the lead content can be sufficiently transdermal to cause other toxicological complications. See: Arthur Edward Waite, <u>The hermetic and alchemical writings of Paracelsus the Great</u> (Edmonds, Washington: The Alchemical Press, 1984), 7.

[18] Manly P. Hall, <u>Paracelsus: His Mystical & Medical Philosophy,</u> (Los Angeles, California:Philosophical Research Society, 1997), p. 7.

[19] Fielding H. Garrison, A.B., M.D., <u>An Introduction to the History of Medicine</u> (W.B. Saunders Company, 1929), 205.

[20] Nicholas Goodrick-Clarke, <u>Paracelsus: Essential Readings</u> (Berkeley, California: North Atlantic Books, 1999), 19.

[21] A point made in the movie, *When Healing Becomes a Crime*, by Kenny Ausubel. See www.altcancer.net/vidgal.htm#hoxsey

ments of modern chemistry. He didn't abandon Galenian concepts of herbal medicine, but his understanding was deeper, richer, and more holistic, turning empirical, "evidence-based" medical herbalism into a kind of subset of a much larger universe of thought and practice.

There are hundreds of botanical extracts, the knowledge of which come to us from indigenous sources worldwide, which have shown to have anti-cancer properties. Dr. Jonathan Hartwell, one of the founders of the National Cancer Institute, spent most of his adult life categorizing them, leaving behind a reference that would become a classic in the field of phytopharmacology and ethnobotany.[22] (Later I would write an article, in tribute to Hartwell's influence on my own work.)[23]

But escharotics are not just botanicals. They employ, by definition, a lightly caustic compound, with one or more botanical ingredients. Caustics usually involve the use of a metal salt, often a halogen combined with a metal (halide), such as zinc chloride or potassium iodide.[24] (Though in the case of one famous physician, the contribution of the dissociated potassium was considered paramount.)[25]

Another anhydrous chloride, "butter of antimony" (antimony trichloride) fits into this category. Many dermatologists are aware that along with zinc chloride, butter of antimony was

[22] Jonathan L. Hartwell, Plants Used Against Cancer (Lawrence, Massachusetts: Quarterman Publications, Inc., 1982). This book is no longer in print, and when I attempted in 1998 to contact the publisher at their address at 5 South Union Street in Lawrence, Massachusetts (USA), the current occupants said they had never even heard of the publisher.

[23] See: www.altcancer.net/hartwell.htm

[24] If you're a little weak in remembering your high school chemistry, go to www.chemicalelements.com and follow along. The halogens are the second to the last column on the right, next to the noble gases. They include (starting from lowest molecular weight to highest) flourine, chlorine, bromine, iodine, and astatine.

[25] Nat Morris, The Cancer Blackout, 5th ed. (Los Angeles, California: Regent House, 1977), 43. Dr. F.W. Forbes Ross (M.D.) treated cancer as a mineral deficiency. He employed both potassium iodide and potassium citrate (the latter not a halide) along with phosphorus supplementation in London at the turn of the nineteenth century. Says Nat Morris: "In the treatment of cancer, Doctor Ross prescribed potassium citrate and phosphate to correct the mineral deficiency, with a weekly dose of five grains of potassium iodide. His cancer patients were either the hopeless and inoperable or those who had refused surgery or irradiation. In a number of cases adjudged as hopeless, he was remarkably successful. He prescribed potassium routinely in all his other patients and claimed that over a period of fifteen years no patient under his care had contracted cancer."

one of the ingredients in a number of early escharotics of the 1900s.[26] But its use goes back even to Paracelsus in the 1500s, though it appears he used it for other maladies.[27]

I always stuck with zinc chloride in my escharotic work, and if you spend a couple hundred hours (as I have) going through patent records to uncover what caustic previous researchers have used, zinc chloride is, by far, the caustic of choice. Familiarity with its useful properties is not new. Anthropologists found traces of man-made zinc chloride in the Great Pyramid at Giza, produced at least 2,500 years ago (though one researcher attributes its use to the generation of power and not medicine).[28]

Zinc chloride, though now reviled by allopaths in an attempt to smear alternative practitioners, was one of just three ingredients in the initial Mohs surgical paste that is now central to a standard dermatological procedure approved throughout the West. The three ingredients that Mohs used in his formula and taught were: zinc chloride, bloodroot, and stibnite (antimony sulfide, another Paracelsus favorite),[29] and can be found in Mohs' own original work.[30] Ironically, the AMA, FDA and other pillars of orthodox medicine exerted enormous effort to put Harry S. Hoxsey out of business (and they succeeded),[31] and yet Hoxsey's formula was almost identical to Mohs'. The difference? Mohs called the topical a "fixative," and he artificially and unnecessarily inserted the act of surgery as a necessary part of the process.[32]

---

[26] "Secret predates Mohs method: Perry Nichols and the escharotic cancer cure." See: www. dermatologytimes.com/dermatologytimes/article/articleDetail.jsp?id=95680&pageID=1 (Access requires membership) Although this is an allopathic web site and the article's author cannot faithfully report the facts without lacing it with disparaging spin, the essential points still come through.

[27] See: www.zompist.com/versci.htm

[28] John DeSalvo, Phd., The Complete Pyramid Sourcebook (Bloomington, Indiana: Author-House, 2003).

[29] Ingrid Naiman, Cancer Salves and Suppositories (Cundiyo, New Mexico: Seventh Ray Press, 1994), 41.

[30] Frederic E. Mohs, B.Sc., M.D., Chemosurgery: Microscopically Controlled Surgery for Skin Cancer (Springfield, Illinois: Charles C. Thomas Publisher, 1978).

[31] Kenny Ausubel, When Healing Becomes a Crime (Rochester, Vermont: Healing Arts Press, 2000); 153-161. Hoxsey's Salve contained zinc chloride, antimony trisulfide, and bloodroot. Note 29, 151.

[32] J.T. Phelan, H. Milgrom, H. Stoll, H. Traenkle, "The Use of Mohs Chemosurgery Technique

Hypocrisy and suppression have appeared together time and again throughout the history of organized medicine, as we see repeatedly.

(By the way, American physicians are now taught that zinc chloride was eliminated from the Mohs paste as an ingredient because it is caustic to healthy skin tissue. There is no nice way to say this: it's a patent lie. I myself have worked with "butter of zinc" bases that were over 60% pure zinc chloride and had the thick, syrupy mess dripping from my fingers down to my elbow for the better part of an hour. Upon removal with running tap water there was only slight irritation to the skin on my forearm. I have done this not less than fifty times in a twelve year period -- 1991 to 2003.)

The suppression of effective, inexpensive, natural methods of healing has a history in the U.S. that is more extensive and egregious than any place on Earth, in any time period on Earth. I didn't realize just how true this was until I compared various escharotic patent filings in the U.S., with court filings on Hoxsey, Rife, and others, and then compared this with published work on the subject.

In late 1857 and 1858, three separate medical doctors surfaced in the U.S. and England with reports of a cancer cure that worked with amazing success.[33]

The first was Dr. J. Weldon Fell.

A man of no plebeian upbringing, Fell was born to an old and distinguished American family with a long lineage of famous physicians and professional men. Fell was one of the original founders of the New York Academy of Medicine and a faculty member of the University of New York; and as cancer writer Nat Morris noted, his was "one of the most interesting (stories) in the history of cancer."[34]

in the Management of Superficial Cancers," *Surgery, Gynecology and Obstetrics* 114 (1962): 25-30. See: Harwell, 439, who notes "of 70 patients, 42 completely healed (of which 2 recurred)."

[33] An important side note: all three doctors originally practiced in New York City, though both Fell and Pattison ended up moving to London. This should appear to the astute observer as more than coincidence.

[34] Nat Morris, The Cancer Blackout (Los Angeles, California: Regent House, 1977), 30. Most

According to Morris, ". . . a sinister cloud enveloped his career because of his cancer practice and in the prime of his life, he emigrated to London to start anew. There he engaged again in the practice of cancer treatment under very auspicious circumstances for he was singularly prosperous and lived very lavishly."

His departure from New York was shrouded in mystery, but it fits a recurring pattern for physicians whose cancer practices rise too far in success above their peers. Prior to leaving, Fell attempted to resign from the New York Academy of Medicine, but his resignation was refused. It appears his association with a "cancer quack," a certain Gilbert of New York City, had caused colleagues great animosity. His resignation was postponed in the hope of "pinning a charge of quackery upon him so he could be ignominiously ejected from the academy."

Fell's subsequent success in London provides evidence as to the cause of his mistreatment in New York, as does the sizeable fortune, earned while servicing a grateful, sizeable base of patients in the U.S., which he took with him to England. He wrote a friend of renting a castle for $100 per week, a kingly sum at that time.

In the fine tradition of Paracelsus, Fell was also a man lacking in humility. A mere guest in his new host country, he derided English surgeons for "operating and amputating without any justification whatsoever and said that limbs were cut off merely to satisfy the vanity or sadism of surgeons. He charged that practices were tolerated in England that would never be permitted in the United States and of all the physicians he had met in London, there were only two whom he would trust to treat himself or his family."[35]

Remarkably, excepting these sharp comments on the surgical practices of his contemporaries, Fell remained on good

of the material on Blake, Fell, and Pattison in this section is taken from Morris' work. Many of the following footnotes are also Morris', and I provide them only on account of the increasing unavailability of his fine work. The Cancer Blackout was produced in five editions, the last of them having been printed in 1977; Montague, M.F.A. and Musick, W.J., "A Yankee doctor in England in 1859," Bulletin of the History of Medicine 13 (February 1943): 217-288; Farrow, Ruth T., "Odyssey of an American cancer specialist," Ibid., 23 (May 1949): 236-252.

[35] Nat Morris, 31.

terms with his fellow English practitioners, and although little is known of the final years of his life, the record shows that he never again fell into professional or public disrepute.

Dr. Fell published a text on cancer, the content of which is the basis for his inclusion in the present work.[36]

To the best knowledge of this author (and I would be delighted to hear from anyone who would refute my assertion) Fell was the first one to publish an escharotic as it has come to be most popularly used in the West, namely, the use of zinc chloride as the caustic of choice, along with a cancerolytic (cancer-fighting) medicinal herb. The use of zinc chloride as a superior, though mild caustic (it has a pH of 5.0), is reflective of the experimentation that took place over the preceding centuries. Caustics known to have been used, then and prior, in orthodox practice included "nitrate of silver, quicklime, sulphate of copper (sometimes used with borax), sulphuric acid (oil of vitriol) mixed with saffron, and permanganate of pottasa. Alkaline caustics such as sulphate of zinc were also in vogue."[37] Dr. Fell dismissed them all, so he must have known of their shortcomings, as did his contemporary and fellow user of escharotic preparations, Dr. John Pattison (see below).

Fell's publication itself places him 20 years prior to the filing of U.S. Patent No. 209,311, and just four years after A. Hunton's 1855 treatise, "On some of the medical virtues of indigenous vegetables grown in the United States." We are also told by Hunton that the manner in which the medical secrets concerning bloodroot were obtained from an Indian doctor were less than honorable.[38] (None of which compares, of course, with the wanton theft of indigenous Americans' land and the taking of most of their lives.)[39]

---

[36] J. W. Fell: A Treatise on Cancer (London: John Churchill, 1857).

[37] Morris, 37.

[38] A. Hunton, "One some of the medical virtues of indigenous vegetables grown in the United States." N.J. Med. Rep. found in Hartwell, p. 433, wherein he notes, "(the ointment was) used successfully for over 30 years and obtained surreptitiously from an Indian doctor." (p. 432).

[39] Derrick Jensen, The Culture of Make Believe (White River Junction, Vermont: Chelsea Green Publishing Company, 2004). There are too many passages demanding thoughtful reflection in this book, just on the treatment of the native American Indians, to do it justice here. (And this is only one of the themes of this, Jensen's last tome). Among the more noteworthy: p.

Even apart from Fell's open admission that the central role of bloodroot in his medical product came from "native savages,"[40] there is the issue of its use in American folk medicine long before that, specifically, its widespread use in Pennsylvania, documented as early as 1811.[41] Moreover, since bloodroot is native to the North American continent, its appearance in Russia infers that it may have been exported there.[42] Internal studies by the National Cancer Institute, which have themselves been suppressed, show even wider use in recent times.[43]

But again, it is Fell that publicly announces the advancement of an escharotic by adding bloodroot to zinc chloride. Of greater importance is the final report which the board of directors of Middlesex Hospital allowed him to publish concerning the results on 25 cancer patients, substantiating his claims that his treatment was far more successful than anything then available "and justified abandoning surgery for relief of cancer."[44]

In their official communication, the board made the following cautious endorsements of the Fell cancer treatment:

122 (destruction of heritage); p. 162, 170 (General Sherman's treatment of them); p. 172, 177, 308 (open Indian slaughter); p. 175 (Montezuma slaughter); p. 193 (General Smith's "Burn and kill the natives!" campaign -- "I want no prisoners. I wish you to kill and burn; the more you kill and burn the better you will please me" . . . including children down to the age of ten); p. 246 (the holocaust of the Cherokee indians); p. 311 (wipeout of Lakota and Cheyenne people), etc., etc. I had to read this 608 page book twice while in prison. I was too busy silently weeping to catch it all on the first go-around. I underlined the parts that really struck a nerve on the second pass -- which ended up being about 30% of the book. Most people don't read footnotes -- and that's too bad -- I would have included this material in the main text (more amplified, of course) if it were more germane to the topic at hand. Actually, in a way, it is. You understand in studying Jensen's work why a sustained medical holocaust would not only be possible in the culture of the United States -- it is inevitable, a mere reflection of its very sick, inner nature.

[40] Fell, p. 95, noted in Hartwell, p. 435. Fell himself was aware that bloodroot ointment was made and used by Indians of the Lake Superior region to treat cancer, even uterine.

[41] Treatment of cancer by bloodroot. 1859. Boston Med. and Surg. J. noted by Hartwell, p. 437, wherein he notes the use of powdered bloodroot to treat cancers in Pennsylvania as early as 1811.

[42] J. Wolff, "Die Lehre von der Krebskrankheit." G. Fischer Jena, Part IIIb., 1914, p. 618. Noted in Hartwell, p. 437, who comments: "Folk remedy of the Indians of the Lake Superior region." (Breast cancer). "Folk remedy in Russia (1896-1897)" for non-specific cancers.

[43] National Cancer Institute, central files. Same citation for members of the Larrea genus by Hartwell, p. 437, footnote #691. His comments: "Cancer -- Louisiana; Pennsylvania; California; Tennessee; (Cherokee Indians); Oklahoma. All 1956-7." Apparently, Hartwell uses the same citation to communicate that the NCI was well aware of its value as a salve and its common use in Texas, with "1955-8" probably representing the dates during which an internal investigation of its usage at NCI was made.

[44] Morris, 32.

1. It was safe and conformed to surgical principles.
2. It could be employed on both operable and inoperable cancers.
3. It obviated removals of the entire breast and could be confined to enucleation of tumors only.
4. It spared patients the hazards of surgery, including hemorrhage and constitutional affections.
5. Enucleation was followed by healthy granulation and cicatrizing surface (scarring over).[45]

Despite its apparent growing acceptance by the orthodox medical community in London, a sea change that should have brought about the elimination of radically invasive cancer procedures, the remedy somehow fell into disuse. Only sporadic, historical references can be found to its use, which demonstrate that conscientious physicians would discover and bring the practice back, only to see it furloughed by medical authorities. One such instance is the use of a zinc chloride compound at St. Bartholomew Hospital in London, to treat breast cancers, no less. Our knowledge of it survives because two such cases can be found in the hospital's "Pathological Museum."[46]

For now it's important to know that Fell was not alone in his discovery, even in his own time.

At about the same time that Fell was making headway at Middlesex Hospital, Dr. John Pattison, also an expat from New York City living in London, was preaching the same message with what appears to be the same formula. Pattison, like Fell, abhorred the surgical treatment of cancer as a fraud upon the public. In 1858, Pattison, too, published his own work, a pamphlet, which provided not only the exact formula, but a precise description of its use. His ingredients? Zinc chloride, goldenseal (*hydrastis canadenisa*), flour and water. (Having experimented with variations of both formulas over many years, I can attest that the end result of either Fell's or Pattison's formula would

---

[45] Ibid., 33.
[46] George Crile, Jr., M.D., Cancer And Common Sense (New York: Viking Press, 1955), 31.

be almost indistinguishable topically.) To further punctuate his point, Pattison expanded his pamphlet to a book in 1866, entitled "Cancer: Its nature and successful and comparatively painless treatment without the usual operation with the knife."[47]

Neither Fell nor Pattison were obsessed with the elimination of more invasive methods of cancer treatment without sound reasoning. As early as 1844, a survey was compiled by Dr. Leroy d'Etoilles and published by the French Academy of Science. To this day this report on cancer survival is probably the most extensive ever released. It was based on results supplied by 174 physicians on 2,781 cases, followed "in some instances for over thirty years."[48] The short version: patients are better off, in most cases, doing nothing at all than going with surgery. Today, despite modern improvements in techniques and equipment, "the dominance of surgery in the treatment of cancer despite these ominous observations has been maintained by studiously ignoring and suppressing adverse information by the powers that be."[49] The continued practice of unnecessary surgery for financial gain is a contributing factor in "death by doctoring" as the third leading cause of death in the U.S., so says a study that miraculously managed to find its way into the pages of the Journal of the American Medical Association as recently as 2000, though it was largely ignored by the mass media.[50]

Pattison was not singular in his approach. (No physician worth his salt is.) He indicated the role of diet, reflecting the etiological role of nutrition that was a century ahead of its time. Despite the later dating of his publication, Pattison's involvement with the very same Middlesex Hospital that brought fame to Dr. Fell is quite insightful. As it turns out, Pattison's work in London came before that of Fell. In 1852 Pattison offered to

---

[47] Pattison, John: Cancer: Its nature and successful and comparatively painless treatment without the usual operation with the knife (London: H. Turner & Co., 1866).

[48] Morris, 35.

[49] Ibid., 35.

[50] Barbara Starfield, MD, MPH, "Is US Health Really the Best in the World?" *The Journal of the American Medical Association* vol. 284 no.4 (July 26, 2000): 483-485. See: jamanetwork. com/journals/jama/article-abstract/192908

demonstrate his method to the directors of Middlesex Hospital and even to work without pay. An initial agreement was worked out where Pattison would work with twenty cases and would disclose his methods, permitting disclosure of his methods and criticism of results.

The directors reneged.[51]

A subsequent request in 1854 was also sent begging. Pattison continued to work in London, where he built a successful practice that was wide and extensive. Nonetheless, Pattison was labelled a "cancer curer" and "quack" by his medical colleagues. His name was deliberately omitted year after year in the semiofficial directory of physicians, an act of mean-spiritedness that was only changed by an act of Parliament.

In comparing the life work of Fell and Pattison, one point becomes most instructive. Their formulas and protocols were, from a functional point of view, nearly identical. So why did the medical community accept one with open arms and slander the other as a quack? This is one of many anomalies in the cancer establishment that defies logical explanation. Why did U.S. Federal authorities come after me because of my Cansema, whose active principles were zinc chloride and chaparral, both of which appear or have appeared in approved cancer related products (in Mohs' surgical paste and Actinex (NDGA))? Why was I made to plead to selling "an unapproved drug"? Is it because NDGA is okay if it's made in a laboratory, but not okay if it comes from chaparral, the very plant from which the discovery was made, a plant with an extensive ethnobotanical history of use for medical purposes?[52]

---

[51] Morris, 38.

[52] Jonathan L. Hartwell, Plants Used Against Cancer (Lawrence, Massachusetts: Quarterman Publications, Inc., 1982). Section XI: Lloydia 34(4), p. 682. It remains a mystery, even to me, why despite the depth of Hartwell's work, he only cites one reference to any member of the Larrea genus (Zygophyllaceae Larrea tridentata).By the end of the 19th century, the successful use of escharotics for the better part of a half century had become so widespread that various clinics and institutions began to specialize in it, and yet he quotes a "Coville" source, noting "identified from sample of leaves and twigs by Dr. B.G. Schubert, U.S.D.A." Here is the reference Hartwell provides: "National Cancer Institute, central files." For someone like myself who has worked with indigenous sources for chaparral and knows how ubiquitous its use was and is in the Southwest, this, in and of itself, at least carries the appearance of a cover-up, and

You find these and so many other "non sequitors" and "prof-it over logic" contradictions throughout the medical industry.

The third and last practitioner / specimen from 1858 is also instructive. T.T. Blake, M.D., published Cancers Cured without the Use of the Knife. Unlike Fell and Pattison, Blake would not reveal what his formula was. Nonetheless, the description he gives of the process follows so closely those of all other es-charotics, and taking into account the uncanny origin of Pattison and Fell in New York during the very same time period, I would agree with Nat Morris' interpretation that it was most probably an escharotic formulation that was close to theirs.[53]

The Extraordinary Case of Perry Nichols, M.D.: A 20th Century Story of a Cancer Clinic That Cured Cancer Using Escharotics for 60 Years: 1896-1956

By the end of the 19th century, the successful use of es-charotics for the better part of a half century had become so widespread that various clinics and institutions began to spe-cialize in it. None that I know of is more noteworthy than the case of the Dr. Nichols Sanatorium of Savannah, Missouri. This institution cured more than 70,000 patients of cancer between 1896 and 1956, many of whom would have been regarded as untreatable by even today's best oncologists.[54]

this, coming from one of Hartwell's biggest fans. Chaparral was too widely used for Hartwell to not have been more familiar with its indigenous use in the treatment of cancer; Alma R. Hutchens, Indian Herbology of North America (Boston, Massachusetts: Shambhala Publica-tions, Inc., 1973), 82-84. The Indian nations of Papago, Pima, and Maricopa, among others, were users of the Larrea genus to treat a variety of ailments including arthritis, cancer, chronic backache, acne and other skin ailments, including skin cancer; kidney infection, leukemia, bronchial and pulmonary conditions, etc. Anthony J. Chichoke, D.C., Ph.D., Secrets of Native American Herbal Remedies, A Comprehensive Guide to the Native American Tradition of Using Herbs and the Mind/Body/Spirit Connection for Improving Health and Well-Being, (New York: Penguin Putnam, Inc., 2001), 35. Judith Sumner, The Natural History of Medicinal Plants (Portland, Oregon: Timber Press, Inc., 2000), 172, 213. Notes the historic use of Larrea to treat skin infections, but falls for the fallacious orthodox admonition about "acute" hepato-toxicity. Shame.

[53] Morris, 27-29.

[54] I have collected just seven of the Sanatorium's "annual yearbooks" over the years, the majority of each volume consisting of the name, home state, cancer type, and personal address of each cured patient -- something you would never see today. In just the few volumes I own,

I have received numerous references to the Sanatorium over the past 25 years. Nichols Sanatorium in Savannah, Missouri, would be the home of Nichols' operation for its last 44 years. I would have included more references to Perry when I wrote the first draft of *Meditopia* in 2004, but I lacked the material at the time.

In early 2016 I contacted the Andrew County Museum and Historical Society in Savannah and was surprised to find a wealth of material concerning the Sanatorium, which closed in 1956, the year I was born.

The specifics of the Sanatorium's beginnings are simple enough: its founder, Perry Nichols, was born in Benton County, Iowa, on March 20, 1863, worked with a clinic specializing in escharotic medicine in 1895, started up his own clinic in 1896 (hiring a physician to work with the patients), graduated from medical school himself in 1901, and later established a 200-bed hospital in Savannah, Missouri.[55] He incorporated the Sanatorium in June 1914, however, by this time he had already developed a widespread reputation of successfully curing cancer using his own techniques. "It was only after many years of research and diligent study that he discovered a safe and sane cure for the malignant disease of cancer without the use of the surgeon's knife and the miraculous cures that he has performed entitle him to the gratitude of thousands of patients and should give him eminent

there are thousands of cases, some of those are nothing short of miraculous.

[55] Williams, 1463-1464.

standing among the benefactors to mankind. His institution is modern in every
way, with skilled medical practitioners
and corps of trained nurses, and the
location of the building is in a section
where may be found every requirement
of health. Although Doctor Nichols has
built up this enormous business in but a
few years and has comfortable accom-
modations for many patients, coming
from every section of the country, at the
present writing (1915) he is comtem-
plating further extension, which means still further humanitarian usefulness."[56]

*Above: The phenomenal success of the Nichols clinic is a cautionary tale
about the frivolity of "acceptable" historical texts, or as the French philosopher,
Voltaire, so succinctly put it: "The history of humanity is a Mississippi of lies." In
this case, I would add "omissions." For the omission of the successful history of
the Nichols Sanatorium from any other meaningful text on the history of cancer
in the U.S. leaves a permanent black hole of deceit, intended to hide the ease with
which cancer was so easily and inexpensively treated more than a century ago.
The photo above is a photograph of the Nichols' staff, circa 1925.*

Those who might suggest that the success of the Nichols
Sanatorium would be based on some kind of personality cult
originating with its founder should know that the involvement of

[56] Ibid.

the founder was short-lived. Dr. Perry Nichols, a tireless work-aholic, died of a heart attack on August 29, 1925 at the age of 62.[57] Thereafter, his daughter, Mrs. Helen Nichols, took over the management of the Sanatorium, in accordance with his will.[58]

The successful work of the Sanatorium was represented in its annual "yearbooks," that the institution produced, year after year. (The photo at right shows seven volumes that I have managed to collect over the years.) Additionally, the Sanatorium managed to put out an enormous amount of catalogs and postcards. The voluminous amount of printed materials that the Sanatorium produced was, in part, an effort to overcome the conventional medical propaganda about cancer treatment, disinformation that has changed little over the past century. As the 1929 yearbook stated in its introduction, "Were it not for the fact

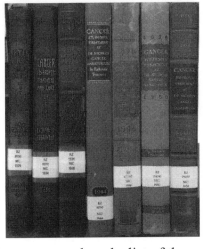

that a great many people are constantly making declarations that cancer cannot be cured; were it not for the fact that the majority of physicians and surgeons are advocating, as you will see published in popular magazines, that 'the knife, radium, and X-ray' are the only remedies, the publication of this book, which contains the proof that such declarations are false, would not be a necessity. We submit this book, with the facts as quoted, and a list of thousands of references, for your consideration. These are cured patients, and now living . . ." At the end of 1929, at the beginning

---

[57] Additionally, Dr. Nichols died following an operation. Though he succeeded in the budding world of alternative practice, the conventional procedure contributed to his undoing. See Perry Nichols Death Certificate: meditopia.org/images/Nichols_death_certificate.pdf

[58] See *Savannah Reporter*, Apr. 29, 1976. Also Nichols Perry appears to have drafted an informal will on the Sanatorium's letterhead, clearly indicating his intentions: pg. one, two, and three. Although the document does not appear to have been signed, it reflects that actual turn of events that followed his passing.

of the Great Depression, the Sanatorium experienced its greatest year ever, mailing out 13,000 catalogues to the public.[59]

Throughout the Depression, the Sanatorium continued to prosper. In 1942, at the start of America's involvement in World War II, the news of one mailing alone made it to the local paper: a mailout weighing 52,000 pounds. Four years later, in 1946, the Sanatorium produced a catalogue with over 350 pages and an "annual list of cured patients containing almost ten thousand names and addresses of recently cured patients." Given that the Sanatorium only reproduced the names and address of cured patients who formally gave their permission to have their personal contact information reproduced, one can only wonder what the Sanatorium's true impact was.[60]

Interestingly, I am not the only one who has found the Nichols Sanatorium story fascinating. His story has been summarized on *Whale.to* and in 2004, *Dermatology Times* ran a story by Andrew Bowser, M.D. about a dermatologist, Dr. Gary A. Dyer of St. Joseph, MO (just 13 miles from Savannah) who claims that he spent two years "piecing together a history of Nichols, interviewing nurses who worked in his institution, and scouring medical archives and local historical records. (I have) monitored eBay and Internet booksellers for surviving copies of yearbooks Nichols wrote touting his methods, patient testimonies, and cure rates . . ."[61]

Dyer traced Nichols' knowledge of the technique upon which he would later build his empire, to a visit to an Iowa clinic in 1895, where, at the age of 32, he learned about treating cancers escharotically from two doctors who ran the "Cherokee Sanatorium." By that time, many medical doctors, who at that time belonged to a fairly close-knot fraternity, were privately familiar with escharotics, many from the work of the men whose efforts are discussed above and others from the patent filings

[59] See: *Savannah Reporter*, Jan. 18, 1929. Comment about the success of the 1929 business year to be found at Savannah Reporter, Nov. 29, 1929.

[60] See: *Savannah Reporter*, July 5, 1942, followed by pages two and three.

[61] I've converted the article, also taken from *Whale.to*, into an easy-to-read Word file. Dyer did a more detailed article two years later (*Clinics in Dermatology*) (2006) 24, 458-460.

DR. NICHOL'S SANITARIUM, SAVANNAH, MO.
EXCLUSIVELY FOR TREATMENT OF CANCER.

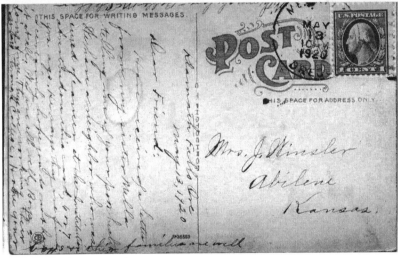

Above: Over the life of the Sanatorium, untold thousands of its post-cards were sold to the public and distributed through the U.S. Postal Service. I bought the one above in 2016 from CardCow. It's addressed to: "Mrs. J. Winsler (of) Abilene, Kansas." There is no other address information be-cause at that time, nothing else was necessary for letters sent to rural Ameri-ca. The postmark says May 13, 1920, and the writing on the back of the card is typical. "Have received a letter from my sister, Mella, telling me of your poor health. We have a neighbor who was cured of cancer at the institution advertised on this card, 6 or 7 years ago. He says they are fine. I certainly hope you do not have it (cancer) at all. We are all well. Boys are doing fine. They are working their way through college. Hope your boys and the family are well."

that had already been made in Washington. After spending time working at the Cherokee Sanatorium, Nichols set to work on his own escharotic formula and then opened his own clinic in November 1896.[62]

As to the burning question -- **what exactly was in Nichols' formula?** -- Dyers found a 1933 article in the *Journal of the American Medical Association* which revealed (probably through surreptitious acquisition) the results of its analysis: zinc chloride ($ZnCl_2$) and butter of antimony (antimony trichloride or $SbCl_3$). Dyers goes on to note: "Interestingly, in a skin pathology and treatment textbook published in 1895, Kaposi described a 'modified Landolfi's Paste' consisting of zinc chloride and butter of antimony." Then Dyers goes on to note that this is close to the initial paste used in Mohs surgery, consisting of zinc chloride and bloodroot.[63]

But the small formulary difference, and when you understand the effects of these different combinations, you realize they are quite close, was not the only thing separating Nichols and Mohs. Mohs "championed biopsy," a big industry money-maker, even though biopsies are inherently metastatic, thus guaranteeing future business. Nichols, on the other hand, understood, as did Hippocrates 2,300 years before him, that cutting into cancer aggravated and stimulated malignant growth.

Dyers ends his article by saying that if Nichols had gone a more conventional route, using an on-staff pathologist, he could have "made the discovery" that Mohs made later and been much more successful.

This is nonsense. It's nonsense because what Mohs did was co-opt an existing medical modality and attempt to make it more profitable for the profession. Dyers admits that from July 1931 to June 1948, the Nichols Sanatorium, which treated several thousand patients per year, was only averaging about 70 surgeries annually. If you treat 7,000 patients and subject 70 of them to surgery, that's 1%. That's a little bit less than the Mohs procedure, which calls for surgery 100% of the time. Which approach

[62] Ibid.
[63] Ibid.

is likely to be more profitable?

One thing I wasn't able to determine from any of the materials I read was the exact reason the Nichols Sanatorium closed in 1956. The Sisters of St. Francis, who moved in shortly thereafter to set up a nursing home at the hospital, were hardly the reason for the closure. What we do know is that by 1956, the public practice of escharotic medicine in the United States was clearly under attack. Given the public airing of Harry Hoxsey's travails, it is difficult to imagine anybody in the administration of Nichols' Sanatorium not knowing that the American Medical Association, Food & Drug Administration, and other minions of the medical-industrial complex were, even then, committed to putting Nichols' Sanatorium, and small organizations like it, out of business, taking them to court, fining them to death, hopefully imprisoning those in charge, etc.

It is thus most logical to surmise that a decision was made to close Nichols Sanatorium, concluding a 60-year period of uninterrupted and successful medical practice, in the most graceful and non-combative way possible.

And, as it turns out, that's exactly what they did.

I feel quite certain that these historical cases represent but a small sampling of the long list of practitioners who have used escharotic preparations. They were hugely successful and their clinical reports were most positive. So, why did escharotics fall into disuse?

Is it possible that the answers can be found in the "Ten Conditions" discussed in Chapter Four? Is there a logical explanation that would refute them? Even in the medical records of antiquity we find evidence of the ubiquitous practice of suppression towards those therapeutic practices that would pose the greatest threat to organized medicine.

Long before the escharotic publications and pronouncements of 1858, indeed, long before the miraculous cures of Paracelsus himself, the truth was evident to all who would investigate without vested interest. Paracelsus himself, in attempting to promote his accomplishments chose a namesake that would not refute the soundness of his escharotic protocols. "Paracelsus" is Latin for "above Celsus," so who would Celsus have been that Paracelsus chose him as a point of lofty comparison? Why not "Paragalen"?

Shortly after the invention of the printing press around 1450 by Johann Gutenberg, one of the first medical works to be published was "De medicina," by Aulus Cornelius Celsus, the first century Roman physician and medical writer.[64] Its initial publication in 1478, just fifteen years before Paracelsus' own birth, would lead to wide acceptance in the orthodox medical community. Divided into three parts, according to the type of treatment that various diseases demanded, dietetic, pharmaceutical, and surgical, Celsus' work laid the foundation for many of the components of the modern medical paradigm in ways even more fundamental than those of Paracelsus. Even Celsus believed that "caustics should be tried before knife or cautery."[65] Before him, "caustics" were used by early Arab and Roman physicians.[66] Viewed from a historical perspective this long, is it really possible that a truly effective way of curing cancer could so easily be suppressed?

Before you finish *Meditopia*, the answer will become self-evident.

As self-evident as the results of the suppressed cures themselves to those that have worked closely with them.

The legitimate, suppressed cures that orthodox medicine has worked so hard to eliminate.

---

[64] The New Encyclopaedia Britannica, 15th ed., vol. 3 (Micropaedia), "Celsus, Aulus Cornelius" (1986), 16.

[65] Ibid.

[66] Ibid.

Chapter 5

A Brief Commentary on Chapter 6

It has been almost 14 years since I authored this part of *Meditopia*, which in that online work is actually Chapter 4.[1] Even since that time I have been exposed to many different natural modalities, therapies, and products that are effective in the treatment of cancer such that even to me, parts of this chapter seem dated.

Nonetheless, there is sufficient foundation to show that, as the chapter title clearly states, "Suppression is the Medical Profession's Most Enduring Legacy." If I be accused of anything in the text that follows, let it be that I have failed miserably to characterize the true size and scope of just how scandalous, vicious, and truly evil the inner workings of modern medicine have been, for centuries.

People who are already familiar with *Meditopia* will ask why I skipped Chapter 3, which deals primarily with my "criminal case" in the U.S. The answer is simple: I cover my case to such an extent that its inclusion in this volume would, in my humble opinion, come off as annoyingly self-centered. There are so many other more important things to discuss here. Nonetheless, those who are really curious can still view Chapter 3 online.[2]

Lastly, it is worth noting that when certain portions of this chapter are compared to material written years later, contradictions become apparent and unreconcilable. A good example is my less than wholly sympathetic treatment of the anarcho-primitivists in the "book review" section of this chapter where I tackle the work of John Zerzan.

I clearly state that "I take issue with the anarchists on several fronts . . ."

Not anymore. My previous book makes this clear.[3]

Discrepancies such as this are attributable to the maturation not only in my work, but in my development as a thinker, as a philosopher -- if only unto myself -- and in my growth as a human being.

---

[1] Chapter 4 was written is four parts beginning with: www.meditopia.org/chap4.htm

[2] Chapter 3 of *Meditopia* begins at: www.meditopia.org/chap3-1.htm

[3] Greg Caton, The Joys of Psychopathocracy (Miami: Herbologics, Ltd., 2017).

Chapter 6:

Embarrassment of Riches

How I Learned Suppression is the Medical Profession's Most Enduring Legacy: A Quick Review of the Astonishing Number of Effective Cancer Cures; the Conflict This Poses to Our Common Narrative; and How it Contributes to Understanding the Defects in our Cultural Operating System.

Special Comparative Case Study: Short History of Scurvy And the Suppression of Hypoascorbemia

"[Oral tradition] is the method wherein the art of healing is preserved among the Americans [Indians] to this day. Their diseases, indeed, are exceedingly few; nor do they often occur, by reason of their continual exercise, and (till of late, universal) temperance. But if any are sick . . . the fathers immediately tell their children what remedy to apply. And it is rare that the patient suffers long; those medicines being quick, as well as generally infallible."

John Wesley -- (1703-91)[1]

---

[1] Virgil J.Vogel, American Indian Medicine (Oklahoma: University of Oklahoma Press, 1990), 74. The quote is preceded by the following introduction by Vogel: "A well-known figure who was as interested in the medical secrets of primitive peoples as he was in the folk medicine of the Old World was the evangelist **John Wesley** (1703-91), who preached in Georgia from 1735 to 1737. He was favorably impressed with the rugged health of the Indians and praised their health and medical practices in his book, Primitive Physic, (Andesite Press, 2017), which was first published at London in 1747. It enjoyed phenomenal popularity, going through forty-odd editions in the next hundred years. Simple knowledge, he believed, was once the property of people everywhere until 'men of learning began to set experience aside, to build physic [the study of proper health practices] on hypotheses, to form theories of disease and their cure, and to substitute these in place of experiments.' He held that physicians had estranged the practice of medicine from the people for their own advantage and maintained that lovers of mankind labored to reduce physic to its ancient

> *"While we haven't yet cured all cancers, the progress made in the past twenty years is phenomenal, and perhaps the greatest medical achievement of this century -- the cancer cure -- is now within sight."*

> **Edward Shorter**[2]

> *(**Author:** This represents the 'common narrative' of modern, orthodox medicine. This hogwash was written in 1989, but it could have just as easily been written in 1848, 1910, or 2006. If we continue to give the Medical Industrial Establishment a free pass, our descendents will be hearing this garbage 500 years from now.)*

> *"One of the most salient features of our culture is that there is so much **bullshit**. Everyone knows this. Each of us contributes his share. But we tend to take the situation for granted. Most people are rather confident of their ability to recognize bullshit and to avoid being taken in by it. So the phenomenon has not aroused much deliberate concern, nor attracted much sustained inquiry."*

> **Harry G. Frankfurt**[3]

> *"It's a bunch of shit."*

> **James Watson, M.D.**[4]
> *Nobel-Prize Laureate*
> *Co-Discoverer of DNA*
> *(Comment made in 1975 when asked about the National Cancer Program, after having served two years on the National Cancer Advisory Board.)*

> *"All [civilized] social organization consists . . . in neutralizing the disruptive and deregulating impact of moral behaviour."*

> **Zygmunt Bauman**[5]

standard, to 'explode out of it all hypotheses and fine-spun theories, and to make it a plain intelligible thing, as it was in the beginning.' No strange chemicals, exotics, or compound medicines were necessary, said he, 'but a single plant or fruit, duly applied.'"

[2] Edwards Shorter, The Health Century (New York: Doubleday, 1989), 211.

[3] Harry G. Frankfurt, On Bullshit (New Jersey: Princeton University Press, 2005), 1

[4] Barry Lynes, The Healing of Cancer: The Cures -- the Cover-ups and the Solution Now! (Marcus Books; 1989), 1, quoting Peter Barry Chowda, "The National Cancer Institute the the Fifty Year Cover Up," East-West Journal, January, 1978. Regular readers of my many posted articles on the Alpha Omega Labs web site, will remember this quote, since I began one of the prominent recommended reading pages with the longer passage by Barry Lynes, taken from the introduction of the above cited work.

[5] Taken from Bauman's Modernity and the Holocaust, as quoted in Whistleblowers (Cornell University Press; 1989), 97. I have added "civilized" to clarify the kind of social organization

W hat I found most intriguing during the time I developed Alpha Omega Labs and researched alternative cancer treatments was not the lack of effective approaches, but their abundance and how efficiently the forces of the medical establishment and their allies had been at suppressing the evidence.

My initial exposure to the outrageousness of this presumption on the part of Modern Medical Mythology, namely, that effective cancer cures are not already in abundance, came through escharotics. However, it is not simple chronological integrity that caused me to devote so much of the first part of the book to it.

Escharotics may have been the "path" by which I sought and found "enlightenment," but, if you will allow me to extend the metaphor, once having arrived I soon learned that there are many other legitimate paths to "enlightenment." And yet, as genuine Indian gurus are likely to tell you, paths to enlightenment may be abundant, but they are largely ignored.

Before we get into the mechanics of "how they got away with it," and continue to do so, it is important to cover the most outstanding approaches and the relevant evidence. Because the readers of this work will include a broad spectrum from novices in alternative health care to those rare practitioners who are already familiar with much of this material, I have tried to strike a compromise. There is plenty of bibliographical support below, however, I stick primarily to those approaches to which I have been an eyewitness.

With this introduction in hand, the purpose of this chapter thus turns on three objectives:

1. **Recite The Evidence** of the truly effective cancer remedies that the author worked with over the life of Alpha Omega Labs, evidence which is only the "tip of the iceberg."

---

that Bauman talks about. In great contrast, one will find quite the opposite among traditional indigenous groups. American Indians. One gets an extraordinarily poignant sense of this in Seton's Gospel of the Red Man (Doubleday, 1936).

2. **Analyze the Power of 'Common Narrative'** Show why most people so strongly resist believing that effective cancer cures have been with us all along and that modern medicine's most significant contribution to Western culture is not its development of effective treatments, but its successful suppression of them; and even worse, the adoption of practices that actually enhance immunosuppression and a multitude of disease states for the benefit of its profit and influence, which I cover in later chapters.

3. **Introduce the Underlying Cause: The Defect in Our "Cultural Operating System"** Show that the cognitive dissonance created between objective, empirical reality and modern medical mythology can only be cured by a study of Western civilization's "cultural operating system," setting the stage for subsequent chapters, where I will tie all the evidence together within a historical context. The chapter prepares the reader for this study by bookending this section with a study of hypoascorbemia, which is its most extreme state is known as "scurvy." This historical case study was chosen because it ties together the most important points outlined in this chapter: the use of the "suppression pattern" in dealing with effective, competing remedies; co-optation of competing healing systems or techniques when it serves the prevailing "profit model," the perverse use of common narrative to prevent people from acting in their own best, healthful interest; and, finally, the admission of a TRUE CURE only after a critical mass are already aware of a cure and further suppression can only prove bad for business or is otherwise politically untenable.

A Quick Word Before We Begin About Orthodox Medicine & 'Managed Maladaptation'

Before I expand the discussion of suppressed cancer remedies, I want to preface any further investigation by stating that in the thirteen years I operated Alpha Omega Labs, I was in contact, either in person, by email, or by phone, with literally thousands of cancer patients and their primary health care providers. Over this time, I came to believe that no treatment of any kind was a substitute for examining the underlying 'maladaptation' that was at the root of the problem.

Nearly all disease, but particularly cancer, has as its primary cause some condition to which the body, mind, or spirit has been subjected, which is in deviation from its natural state.[6]

Perfect health is man's natural state. Not disease. The body contains an unfathomably complex system of countermeasures to maintain its natural state (or "homeostatis") and is able to adapt to a wide variety of conditions. Those 'unnatural conditions' which take it outside the range of adaptable measures through which it can change and still maintain health, be they spiritual, emotional, or grossly physical, i.e., bad diet, exposure to toxic chemicals or harmful EM emissions, etc., are always examined first by a competent health care practitioner before the issue of 'treatment' is ever addressed.

If a nail causes you to have a flat tire, logic would dictate that you remove the nail before you attempt to patch the puncture. Orthodox medicine, as I will examine in more detail in coming chapters, is built upon an enormous edifice that holds that since there is more money to be made by applying the patch

[6] I have long known that disease is foreign to the natural functioning of the body and that civilization, as we now know it, has had a tendency to introduce environmental conditions, or "sickness by design," for the benefit of a specific, benefiting class. The idea, however, is not original, and can be recognized as derivative in the works of Rene Dubos, see Mirage of Health: Utopias, Progress, and Biological Change, Man Adapting (New Brunswick, New Jersey: Rutgers University Press, 1996) and A God Within (New York: Charles Scribner's Sons, 1972). If I were forced to truncate the concept of maladaptation to one pithy quote, I'd probably go with Szent-Gyorgyi: "More than sixty years of research on living systems have convinced me that our body is much more nearly perfect than the endless list of ailments suggests . . . (its shortcomings) are due less to its inborn imperfections than to our abusing it." (See Free Radical, New York: Paragon House Publishers, 1988, 253). Those with a more philosophical bent will find the same concept in Lao-Tzu:

> Those who flow as life flows
> Feel no wear, feel no tear,
> Need no mending, no repair.

See Mirage, p. 256, taken from the Tao Te Ching, (NY: Vintage Books, 1972) Taoism's most important work.

(i.e., treatment) and keeping the nail in the tire (i.e. ignoring the maladaptive cause, the better to promote repeat business), the notion of timely, preventive 'nail removal' is pure quackery. This position is part of a larger set of functions within orthodox medicine that I call "managed maladaptation," which I will get to later.

Among the thousands of ready examples is the determination with which orthodox medicine has fought throughout most of its existence to teach that proper diet has nothing whatsoever to do with disease. More than one honest physician in the U.S. has told me in private, "We don't have 'health care' in this country. We have 'disease care.' It makes more money."

This having been established, it is important to note that the examples below should not be considered in isolation of this understanding. Rather, the treatment approaches below are presented because they all follow a similar pattern, the same pattern that has to do with the Cansema issues that I have previously discussed. You will recognize most of the points below because most of them were included in the "Ten Conditions"[7] when this suppression pattern was first introduced. Specifically, each treatment I will talk about carries the following characteristics:

1. On balance, these treatments consistently work more effectively than the approaches currently offered by orthodox medicine for most serious internal cancers, to wit: surgery, radiation, and/or toxic, allopathic chemotherapy.

2. They are substantially cheaper than conventional treatment.

3. They are substantially safer than conventional treatment.

4. They cannot be patented, or if they have been patented, such legal protection has long since expired; and if they could be patented, they would be impossible to legally protect.

5. The majority lend themselves to self-administration, or

---

[7] See: meditopia.org/chap1.htm#ten_conditions

otherwise make the patient less dependent on a physician or care provider.

6. If these treatment approaches were ever widely employed by a critical mass of primary care practitioners, it would mean the wholesale bankruptcy of a huge segment of the health care industry in the industrialized West.

Successful Internal Use of Escharotics

During the very brief life of Lifeline Sciences, I was contacted by a 'distributor,' who claimed that she successfully used our zinc-chloride based escharotic preparation on her own stomach cancer.[8]

"You realize that 'Formula G'[9] is designed for topical use only, don't you?" I responded in surprise.

"Yes, I know," she retorted, "but it worked so well on my skin cancer, that it only seemed to make sense that it would work on the stomach."

"Yeah, but didn't it hurt like hell?" I responded, still amazed on hearing about this internal 'off-label' usage.

"For the first few hours, it sure did. It got pretty bad there for a while. Although it was much easier when I took it the second time."

"Second time?" I interrupted. "You swallowed the salve more than once?"

"Oh, yes. I took several teaspoons of it over the last six weeks. I would have called you sooner, but I wanted to get the results of my doctor's check-up before I got back to you."

"What were the results?"

"He says I must not have had cancer, basically, that the initial diagnosis was not correct."

"I don't understand."

"Well, he didn't find any sign of my having cancer. And since I hadn't received 'chemo' treatment yet, I guess he figures

---

[8] Harry M. Hoxsey, You Don't Have To Die (New York: Milstone Books, Inc., 1956), 45.

[9] Formula G was a forerunner to Cansema. Again, see: www.meditopia.org/chap3-1.htm

that it must not have been cancer in the first place."

"This doesn't follow. You mean your doctor reasons that because you didn't receive conventional cancer treatment, that this constitutes an initial bad diagnosis?"

"That's right."

Repeatedly over the next dozen years, I was to hear this same 'non sequitor' time and again, supposedly coming from men of high education. Nonetheless, it was not the most ridiculous. The most ridiculous comment from doctors of customers who successfully used our escharotics for internal applications was actually more honest. It went something like this: "Please go to the front desk and pick up your final bill. I refuse to see patients that take an alternative treatment or therapy without my explicit authorization."

I use the term "honest" in bringing up this last professional response, because it leaves nothing unrevealed in the motives of the practitioner, whereas the first 'non-sequitor' response does. The latter response is transparent. It's revealing. The physician might just as well have said, "Fuck you. You're here so I can make money. If you're going to go ahead and do something to help yourself, perhaps even cure yourself, then why am I wasting my time with you? What? So you can get away with just a $50 visit and use my experience to get a diagnosis?"

At the same time, quite paradoxically, the most successful applications and protocols for the internal use of the escharotics I produced did not come from end user/customer/ patients.

They came from practitioners, rare souls, including M.D.s, who risked their medical licenses by running 'evidence-based' practices that didn't mind experimenting with a proven alternative if it was safer and more efficacious.

A good example of this was a medical doctor in Chicago who used a catheter as an enema device to deliver his own diluted concoction of Cansema to specific colorectal cancer sites. It was out of this novel approach, one I had never heard of before, that we developed a suppository operation[10] to make a suppository version of Cansema. This was closed down shortly before

[10] See: www.altcancer.net/aosuppos.htm

the FDA raid in 2003.

Widespread reports of effective internal use of the original Cansema lead to internal versions in capsule and tonic form.[11]

The dramatic success of Cansema led to a cornucopia of anecdotal testimonials, accessible from its product page,[12] and the highlighting of specific cases in article form that were nothing short of miraculous, such as the case of Kent Estes[13] (who had tongue cancer so bad that his doctors told him his only hope was to have his entire lower jaw removed), or the advanced melanoma case of R.L. Banks.[14]

> *"We are convinced that cancer cannot be cured successfully as an isolated phenomenon, unrelated to basic body processes. We attempt to get at the roots of the disorder, rather than deal merely with its end result. Our primary effort is to restore the body to physiological normalcy."*

Harry M. Hoxsey, N.D. [15]

Successful Escharotics of an Earlier Generation: The Harry Hoxsey Story

Had I been more familiar with the work of Harry Hoxsey when I first started making escharotic preparations in 1990, I would not have been surprised with my introduction to its internal uses by the woman with stomach cancer.

In time, Alpha Omega Labs[16] would strive to educate its customers about the benefits of Hoxsey's earlier work, natural remedies, both escharotic and non-escharotic, by encouraging them to read his original book, You Don't Have To Die,[17] purchasing Kenny Ausubel's book (see below) and providing a

[11] See: www.altcancer.net/capsules.htm

[12] See: www.altcancer.net/cansema.htm

[13] See: www.altcancer.net/estes.htm

[14] See: www.altcancer.net/rlbanks.htm

[15] Hoxsey, 45.

[16] See: www.altcancer.com/

[17] See: www.altcancer.net/lysis.htm#book8

When Healing Becomes a Crime

The Amazing Story of the Hoxsey Cancer Clinics and the Return of Alternative Therapies

KENNY AUSUBEL
FOREWORD BY BERNIE SIEGEL, M.D.

free viewing of Ausubel's movie.[18] We later added an internal version that was made by a manufacturer in Canada, and provided articles concerning its history.

Though expensive ($3,500 per patient) by the standards set by Alpha Omega Labs, the clinic in Mexico which today carries on Hoxsey's work treats cancer patients at a fraction of the cost of conventional treatment and reports results that are no worse than those obtained conventionally. (Although the testimonial section for the Center is weak, especially compared to Alpha Omega Labs' Cansema product,[19] we attribute this far more to poor documentation than to the time-tested beneficial effects of the Hoxsey formulas themselves, which are sold at his clinic in Mexico).

In the final years of Alpha Omega Labs, before the September 2003 raid, I was frequently asked if the Hoxsey formulas "really worked." My reply was based on my consistent observation: "The external formula, close as it is to Cansema itself, works better than 95% of the time. And based on my knowledge of the internal formula,[20] I have no reason to question the clinic's contention that the 'success rate (is) as high as 80 percent,'"[21] that is, though it may be stretching the upper limits, it is certainly not the gross exaggeration of outcome one hears from proponents of orthodox cancer treatments. And by contrast, there are none of the toxic side effects of conventional treatment. Similarly, probably because of the astonishing parallels between the methods used to suppress them, I was asked about Essiac.

At Alpha Omega Labs, we never manufactured this prod-

---

[18] See: www.altcancer.net/vidgal.htm#hoxsey

[19] See: www.altcancer.net/cantest.htm

[20] Ibid., 45-46. Hoxsey's ingredient listing is simple, though absent the percentages: "It (the internal formula) contains potassium iodide combined with some or all of the following inorganic substances, as the individual case may demand: licorice, red clover, burdock root, stillingia root, barberis root, poke root, cascara, Aromatic USP 14, prickly ash bark, buckthorn bark."

[21] Kenny Ausubel, When Healing Becomes a Crime (Rochester, Vermont: Healing Arts Press, 2000), 4 . . . Incidentally, for a more condensed summation of the Hoxsey story, I recommend Haley's "The Hoxsey Story": see Politics in Healing, 13-47.

uct, and assumed that this herbal formula, promulgated to the world through a Canadian nurse, Rene Caisse,[22] was proprietary. As it turned out, another Canadian manufacturer made the product and we carried it on our website as well.[23] Though I was never able to obtain convincing clinical research to prove (to myself if no one else) that this product was effective in the treatment of cancer, I can attest to a substantial number of people over the years who, as in the case of Hoxsey's formulas and regimen, indicated that this approach helped or even "saved" them from the less effective, politically sanctioned treatment approaches of the orthodox medical community.

Stories about the suppression of effective herbal formulations exist in such abundance that my exploration got to the point where I was no longer surprised to hear it. When I discovered the series of events that led to the closure of Dr. Jonathan Hartwell's botanical studies group[24] at the National Cancer Institute, a weakly funded operation that was uncovering hundreds of promising plant-derived "medicines," I made mention of it on the Alpha Omega website.[25] At the same time I documented a suppressed, Ecuadorean herbal compound, named Ammatosin[26] that was railroaded by the same Washington bureaucrats. The same pattern of suppression was documented in the manner in which the pharmaceutical industry attempted to quash news of the cancer killing benefits of graviola[27] *(Annona muricata).*

Those Deadly Apricot Seeds:
When Suppression by "The Authorities"
Reaches Breathtakingly Obscene Proportions

Let me confess from the outset that, based on my work with cancer patients, I did not myself find enough evidence to become convinced that apricot seeds, or the isolated nutrient from

---

[22] Sheila Snow Fraser, et al., Essiac (Buffalo, New York: New Action Products Publisher), 1.

[23] See: www.altcancer.net/amer_trad1.htm#essiac

[24] See: www.herbhealers.com/index.php

[25] See: www.herbhealers.com/index.php#hartwell

[26] See: www.herbhealers.com/index.php#ferguson

[27] See: www.altcancer.net/hsi0101.htm

them, vitamin B17, were as effective as most of the escharotic preparations that I worked with. I say this, even though Alpha Omega Labs sold its own packaged apricot seeds .[28] But there are legions of recovered cancer patients who swear by them, and, in fact, a close personal friend, Jason Vale, founder of Christian Brothers, who was incarcerated for more than five years in the U.S. for selling apricot seeds, was cured of his Askins tumor and renal cell carcinoma through an almost exclusive commitment to this approach. He even goes so far as to provide links to his CAT scans to show his progress in defeating his cancer using apricot seeds. Moreover, in his brief career, Jason amassed an impressive list of testimonials, comprising thousands of cancer patients who experienced substantial benefit by taking his seeds.

By the time that I decided to add apricot seeds[29] to the Alpha Omega web site in 2002, Jason Vale was already in the cross-hairs of the U.S. Food & Drug Administration. Therefore, the "copy" I used in presenting the seeds was decidedly restrained. My approach was to make G. Edward Griffin's video available,[30] along with a recommendation to read his book, World Without Cancer.[31] This would allow people to make up their own minds.

An honest government that worked as serving the interests of its citizens and not a wealthy, medical elite, would do something similarly: it would allow those who make such products available to make known the documented evidence of its "possible" benefit. It would not attempt to suppress the compelling argument that cancer is, at least in part, a nutritional "deficiency disease," and that people can be aided by the regular ingestion of fruit seeds containing specific nutrilosides, like the vitamin B-17 found in apricot seeds.

I am now of the opinion that the "nutritional deficiency" argument is sufficiency strong that there is a decided benefit to including apricot seeds in one's regular diet. But the benefit to this approach and the arguments that support it will, no doubt,

[28] See: www.altcancer.net/apseeds.htm
[29] See: www.altcancer.net/apseeds.htm
[30] Go to: www.altcancer.net/video/wwc_DSL.wmv
[31] See: meditopia.org/biblio.htm#griffin

continue to be suppressed.

Why?

Because, as in the case of all plant-based examples provided above, such benefits nearly always fall into the target zone of our originally stated "suppression pattern."[32]

> *"Star Trek fans rejoiced when 'Bones' waved a little electrical device over Captain Kirk's ailing body and, seconds later, his wounds were healed. That's close to where we would be in healing practice [today] if it wasn't for the Rockefeller directed medical-monopolists who have been suppressing the entire field of electromedicine since the early 1900s."*

Dr. Leonard G. Horowitz[33]

The Astonishing Suppression of Electromedicine

Horowitz ascribes "electro-suppression" as occurring for a little over a century. But the record is clear that it has been going on for much longer than that. Paracelsus' healing techniques were closely tied to subtle electromagnetic influences and their properties, though not identified as such in his time.[34] Franz Mesmer's remarkable electromedicine devices and their capabilities, dating to the 1700s, have been so well suppressed that most people associate his name exclusively with hypnotism (as in the English, "mesmerize"),[35] and the medical applications of the work of Karl Von Reichenbach,[36] Antonio Meucci,[37] and Nikola Tesla,[38] dating primarily to the 1800s, have all been subject-

---

[32] See: meditopia.org/chap1.htm#ten_conditions

[33] Dr. Leonard G. Horowitz, Healing Celebrations (Sandpoint, Idaho: Tetrahedron Publishing Group, 2000), 105.

[34] Franz Hartmann, M.D., Paracelsus: Life and Prophecies (Blauvelt, New York: Rudolph Steiner Publications, 1973). The evidence of Paracelsus' understanding of electromedicine is evident throughout his work, but one gets a glimpse of this understanding in the second section of Hartmann's work, in a section called "Cosmology," p. 41-57.

[35] Gerry Vassilatos, Lost Science (Kempton, Illinois: Adventures Unlimited Press, 1999), 9.

[36] Ibid., 1-55.

[37] Ibid., 56-75.

[38] Examples of the medical benefits of applied science from Nikola Tesla's work abound. Speaking close to home, the Tesla Photon Machine, made for Alpha Omega Labs by Nova Lite Research, came almost entirely from the theoretical foundations laid down by Tesla.

ed to the "suppression pattern."

Nonetheless, the name that is probably most synonymous with the suppression of electromedicine in the outright cure of incurable cancers in our time is Royal Raymond Rife, about whom I wrote a "quick primer"[39] for the Alpha Omega Labs site. Excellent treatises on the pathetic treatment of Rife, easily one of the greatest scientists of the twentieth century, at the hands of the U.S. Government medical mafia is covered extensively elsewhere.[40] It mimics the suppression of Wilhelm Reich's discoveries concerning orgone energy, in time frame and criminal methodology. I have seen the inner-workings of this facet of the police state "up close and personal," so I recognize all the signs. In the case of Reich, his work that was considered so threatening to the medical establishment that a U.S. Federal Judge ordered not only Reich's books burned, but also other work that merely **mentioned** orgone energy.[41]

It is unfortunate, though probably inevitable given the na-

---

[39] See: www.altcancer.net/emag_rife.htm

[40] A small sampling of the Rife material with which the author is familiar (and this does nothing to include the experiential and research related materials which have yet to appear in print -- by anyone) includes Gerry Vassilatos, Lost Science (Kempton, Illinois: Adventures Unlimited Press, 1999), 137-168; Barry Lynes, The Cancer Cure That Worked! -- Fifty Years of Suppression (Ontario, Canada: Marcus Books, 1987); Fred Farly, Royal R. Rife, Humanitarian, Betrayed & Prosecuted (R.T. Plasma Publishing, 2001); there is an excellent section of Daniel Haley's book, entitled "What Became of the Rife Technologies?" that is worth reading, see Politics in Healing p. 93-121. Also, worth reading is Gallert's New Light on Therapeutic Energies (Ltd. London: James Clarke & Co., 1966), 39 and 51-55, where he posits that both Rife and Dr. Wilhelm Reich were prosecuted not only because they offered effective, low cost treatment approaches that were an embarrassment to the orthodox, medical 'greed machine,' but their respective positions, essentially naturopathic, were compelling refutations of the long-standing, Pasteurian "germ theory," an atrocious concept I brave to deconstruct later in this book.

[41] James DeMeo, Ph.D. The Orgone Accumulator Handbook, 6. Specifically, Case #1056, March 19, 1954, U.S. District Court, Portland, Maine; Judge John d. Clifford, Jr. Thereafter, the author lists a list of 'BANNED, until expunged of all references to the orgone energy,' followed by a list of ten of Reich's books, and then "BANNED and ORDERED DESTROYED," and there follows another list of items to be incinerated . . . So much for the mythology of **free speech.**

ture of our culture, that Rife's name has been associated with an endless stream of questionable electronic devices, whose only connection to Rife is that he also powered his apparatus with electricity.

Such co-optation has not been so effective in dealing with devices that employ the simple schematics of Robert C. Beck. A good friend, medical researcher, and fellow victim of the U.S. criminal justice system, Michael David Forrest, wrote a small, 69 page booklet, also free of charge, for those wanting more information on this subject, entitled, "The Investigation of Electromedicine: An Inquiry into Effectiveness of Electromedicine Devices Against Disease; The Best Electromedicine Devices Explained & Reviewed."[42]) Nor have heavy-handed tactics prevented the results of the life-saving research of Dr. Robert O. Becker or Dr. Daniel Kirsch from getting into the hands of the public.[43]

My belief in electromedicine was greatly enhanced by two incidents that occurred in my own immediate family: the complete cure of my own father from a crippling osteo-arthritic condition he had in both his knees by the Prologue 2D,[44] which I purchased wholesale while in Moscow, and which is a biomedical device used by quite a number of Russian physicians now. Secondly, was the cure of my own brother, Daniel, of Stage IV esophageal cancer, using Beck equipment which he modified for his own personal use, beginning with a study of Beck's electrical schematics.

Quite a number of people I have encountered over the last few years have indicated to me that on the strength of the illegitimate suppression of Beck technology alone, they have come to a realization of most of the aspects of the suppression pattern[45] on their own.

---

[42] See: meditopia.org/docs/Electromedicine.pdf

[43] See Haley, Politics in Healing (Potomac Valley Press, 2000), 171-211 for a good summation. In this area I find Becker's two books indispensable: The Body Electric (New York: William Morrow and Company, 1985) and Cross Currents: The Perils of Electropollution, The Promise of Electromedicine (Los Angeles: Jeremy P. Tarcher, Inc. 1990).

[44] See: www.altcancer.net/prologue.htm

[45] See: meditopia.org/chap1.htm#ten_conditions

William Frederick Koch & Glyoxylide

Shortly after I got out of U.S. Federal Prison in March 2006, I came upon a man, Mark Krissle, who indicated that he was working with a physician in Mexico who had perfected the lost science behind Dr. William F. Koch's "glyoxylide therapy," a highly effective therapeutic approach that had "worked miracles" in a host of advanced cancer cases, an approach that I had assumed passed on when Dr. Koch himself did.[46]

The theoretical foundation to Koch's work (not to be confused with the nineteenth century physician[47] who developed Koch's postulates)[48] is well understood. What plagued those who attempted to follow his work after he died is the precise method of manufacturing glyoxlide to Koch's original specifications.

What I discovered from researching Krissle's claims is that the methodology has, indeed, been kept intact. It is, however, being sequestered to keep those using and developing it out of harm's way. The group who now has Koch's technology are developing an impressive clinical record of proof to back up their future claims. They do not advertise or publicize in any way, and their funds come from very private sources. They will make their methods available to the public when the "time is right."

To the uninitiated, all this talk about superior technology (in health care, or any other field) being kept alive, out of the public domain, by a secret group of enthusiasts -- nay, I dare say "believers," may sound spurious. To those not in the know, this smacks of secret societies, unproven conspiracy theories and/or paranoid psychosis. But to those who have the truth behind our

---

[46] A few points are worth footnoting: first, I have changed the name of my contact to Mark Krissle to protect his/her real identity. Secondly, for those unfamiliar with the Koch treatment, as a lay summary I recommend Haley's "Birth of a Science -- or Death of a Science?" -- see Daniel Haley, Politics in Healing (Potomac Valley Press, 2000), 49-91. Thirdly, for U.S. Senatorial remarks on Koch treatment, read . . . and for those who want to read source material in Koch's own words, see The Survival Factor in Neoplastic and Viral Diseases (self-published by William Koch; 1958). Comments found in Haley's work and from a wide range of associates had led me to the conclusion that Koch's secrets passed with him when he died.

[47] See: en.wikipedia.org/wiki/Robert_Koch

[48] See: en.wikipedia.org/wiki/Koch%27s_postulates

culture's "common narrative" it is nothing if not unoriginal and commonplace.

This development, more than anything else I have been associated with, reminds me of Morris Berman's prescribed course for protecting our culture's most prized technologies from greedy, corporate powers who are determined to destroy whatever interferes with their profit agenda. More specifically, Berman talks about the need for those who find ourselves "strangers" in our own modern culture, where postmodernism has brought to the table not merely the denial of truth but also the denial of the ideal of truth,[49] where one places his life in danger for unwittingly promulgating effective disruptive technologies that threaten established profit models, to assist in maintaining an underground of useful technologies which will surface at the appropriate time, such as the monks of the 4th century did at the dawning of the Christian era to prevent the most valuable portions of Greco-Roman culture from dying forever.

Berman calls this course the "monastic option."[50]

The monastic option carries with it an understanding that our culture is unsustainable, that like similar resource-hungry, non-replenishing civilizations before it, it has an end point. It carries with it an understanding that history is not linear. It's circular. What will survive through this coming "ekpyrosis," or as William Catton would put it, this "die-off," will, in part, be determined by the various underground movements that sequester and protect sustainable technologies away from the present elite.

In 1898 the American essayist, John Jay Chapman wrote that "business has destroyed the very knowledge in us of all other natural forces except business" (Practical Agitation).[51] This tendency to fashion all unapproved facts through the rubric of corporate profit, to marginalize, ostracize, if not destroy all

---

[49] Morris Berman, The Twilight of American Culture (New York: W.W. Norton, 2000), 51.

[50] Ibid., 8-9; 81.

[51] Ibid., 130. There are countless ways of saying the same thing. In the same volume (to choose a more modern example) the author quotes Horkheimer and Adorno, "Utilitarianism is the real, and pervasive (if invisible) philosophy of American society, a society in which very little has value in and of itself." (p. 107 -- emphasis added).

that doesn't conform to the current global fascist agenda, and my tone, will only surprise those who don't understand that corporatism and fascism are synonyms, and are what makes the monastic option a necessity

Before I saw what had happened to Koch's work and what was being done behind the scenes, away from the prying eyes of Western corporate spies (particularly, U.S.; more specifically, U.S. Government acting on behalf of its corporate overlords, in this case on behalf of orthodox medicine), I had no idea the extent to which this approach was being put into practice, naturally, unwittingly, and without regard to any name, label, system, theoretical structure, or formal social movement.

The CanCell Controversy

In 2002, Alpha Omega Labs got involved with a company that was making what was reputed to be the most advanced formulas to come out of what I call "The Cancell Project," made popular by Louise B. Trull's book.[52]

I created a web page[53] to announce the product, its history, how it worked, etc.

Although I understand the theory behind Sheridan's formula,[54] I myself have no idea how to manufacture it, as I do most of the other Alpha Omega Labs' products. However, I mention it here, in this chapter, because it is a nutritional supplement that has a long history of helping cancer patients, and those with other degenerative diseases, where the government, acting on behalf of the medical industry, has impeded its makers from discussing clinical results with existing and prospective customers.

Yet more evidence of "the suppression pattern."

Stanislaw Burzynski & Antineoplastins

My wife (Cathryn E. Caton, N.D.) and I dated throughout

---

[52] Louise Trull, The Cancell Controversy (Norfolk VA: Hampton Roads Publishing Co., 1993).

[53] See: www.altcancer.net/protocel.htm

[54] A slide presentation on the formula begins at: www.altcancer.net/protocel_slide11.htm

1992 before getting married in June of the following year. There was a period there, of less than a year, where my wife maintained her apartment in Houston, while working as a lab technician for the famous cancer doctor, Dr. Stanislaw Burzynski.[55]

Cathryn never physically worked *at* the Burzynski Clinic proper, but rather at the research and quality control department, which was housed in a separate facility

Few phenomena within the orthodox medical community are considered as distasteful or even treacherous as a member from their own ranks coming up with a simple approach to treating cancer, who obtains results that are superior to what is officially sanctioned. It is, therefore, no surprise to anyone who is familiar with Burzynski's case that the orthodox community has labelled him a quack with false credentials,[56] seen to it that the voluminous amount of data he has produced is written off as controversial,[57] and prosecuted him criminally to marginalize his work in the mind of the public.[58]

I can relate to the tribulations of Dr. Burzynski, in particular the government's attempt to give him life imprisonment for a bogus charge of fraud[59] (my own plea agreement had a bogus charge of mail fraud).

Despite the U.S. government's attempt to label him a charlatan, Dr. Burzynski has repeatedly encouraged prospective patients, or even just interested parties, to "do your own research."[60]

My wife, who in the early '90s, did have some communications with members of the clinic, was aware of the general consensus that success for patients was somewhere in the neighborhood of "60%." As with the numbers that have come out of the Hoxsey and Essiac communities (discussed above), my attitude is that even if this figure were some what elevated, what justification is there for attempting to target a doctor and his clinic who is using a heavily researched treatment, persecute

---

[55] See: www.burzynskiclinic.com/

[56] See: www.quackwatch.org/01QuackeryRelatedTopics/Cancer/burzynski1.html

[57] See: en.wikipedia.org/wiki/Burzynski_Clinic#Stanislaw_Burzynski

[58] See: edition.cnn.com/HEALTH/9701/07/nfm/cancer.doc/index.html

[59] See: www.simstat.com/ralph-moss-on-cancer/

[60] See: www.ouralexander.org/burzynski.htm

him for fraud charges that prosecutors know he didn't commit, and mischaracterize this non-toxic alternative which now has many hundreds of grateful, healthy patients and customers?

We again see abundant signs of the "suppression pattern."

Whistleblowers:
Analyzing the Co-Optive, Imprisoning Power
of Our "Common Narrative"

"I have never been a whistleblower, and yet I've felt like one all my life. In my family, no one ever spoke the truth, so I thought I must. Of course, it wasn't the truth, just my truth, but that counts for something. In my profession, people tell lots of tiny truths, and so it seemed important to me to try to tell big ones, even if that makes it harder to get it right. The big difference between my situation and that of the whistleblower is that I work in a remarkably tolerant profession, practicing it in a remarkably accommodating academic department. I can say almost anything and be ignored. Perhaps this is why I became so interested in what whistleblowers learned when their truths were taken so seriously, when, in other words, their truths were experienced as a threat to power."

C. Fred Alford[61]

While imprisoned in Beaumont, Texas, I spent quite a number of hours contemplating how to replicate in the reader of *Meditopia* my own experience. That is to say, "How can I help the reader internalize the intellectual intensity, the clarity, of the experience of our world, our culture, as being nothing like we have been lead to believe? What tools can I use to get the reader to break through the bondage of our common understandings, the 'propagandistic fog,' and see that we truly *do* live, imprisoned, in a kind of 'Matrix'?"

It was not until I was later exposed to the work of C. Fred Alford that I found the missing piece that would seamlessly connect my experiences with a new vision. This would then be presentable to the reader in such a way that all the diverse elements

---

[61] C. Fred Alford, <u>Whistleblowers: Broken Lives and Organizational Power</u> (Ithaca, New York: Cornell University Press, 2001), 3.

of my observations, when placed in juxtaposition to the absurdities of the medical-industrial complex and its monolithic set of eminently deconstructable mythologies, would fit together. In this way, with the cognitive dissonance of our culture exposed and removed, I could take my reader to a new place, with a new vision of the world.

Instead of presenting Book I of *Meditopia* as an epiphany in my own life, with the reader acting as passive observer, I could assist the reader in having one of his own. I wanted to be able to provide an experience that was as potent and as life-altering as my own.

This would be an awesome challenge.

I understood this.

It would be like the authors of books I had read on the experience of botanical entheogens, like peyote, ibogaine, or ayahuasca, what the uneducated on this subject call psychedelics, attempting not merely to report their "other worldly experiences," but to actually impart that experience to the reader!

How would or could you even attempt such a thing?

To achieve this I have to momentarily digress to a place where others, such as myself, have been allowed, using the language of The Wizard of Oz, to "see the man behind the curtain."

Our next stop on the journey to *Meditopia* takes us to a place with which all are vaguely familiar, but only few truly understand. This is because the vast majority of world citizens are like television travel hosts, who talk about places they have never been. Their knowledge of things is only surface deep, and much of it incorrect.

I'm talking now about whistleblowers.

> *"Hell, I wasn't against the system. I was the system . . . I just didn't realize there were two systems."*

Bob Warren[62]

C. Fred Alford is a professor of government at the Univer-

---

[62] Ibid., 49.

sity of Maryland, a respected teacher and political scientist,and prolific author, primarily dealing in what he fashions to be "moral psychology."

In 2001 he published <u>Whistleblowers: Broken Lives and Organizational Power</u>, which deals with his own experience with people who "blow the whistle" on corrupt, illegal activities: on the part of the government, a large corporation, or other large organizational entity. In the vast majority of cases, it isn't money or fame or adventure that causes the whistleblower to step into the limelight. It is the deep affront against conscience that inaction would initiate, born of the most primitive sense of moral obviousness.

The impetus behind the book was that Alford's experience with whistleblowers was consistently contrary to the common myths that have been generated about them -- so contrary, in fact, that he was compelled to investigate how and why this disconnect originates in the first place.

On the one hand you have "almost twenty books on whistleblowing . . . available through Amazon.com, and more than a hundred articles . . . on the topic," he writes.[63] These largely represent a homogenous view of whistleblowers, as a group, and whistleblowing, as a phenomena, which reflect and reinforce our common mythology on the subject: that whistleblowers are noble people with strong morals "who stand up for what is true and just. They suffer substantial retaliation, and while most are vindicated, a few are not. But even those who are not triumphant in the end know they did the right thing. They are richer and better for the experience, even if it will always pain them. Almost all would do it again."[64] What resides in the common mythology of whistleblowing is that good usually wins in the end, the Rocky-esque figure rises above overwhelming obstacles, David beats Goliath, Phoenix rises from the ashes, Job beats the Devil, the Turtle beats the Hare, Count of Monte Cristo gets his revenge, Gladiator kills the evil Emperor (in hand-to-hand combat, no less), the sheriff in the white hat beats a hundred bad

[63] Ibid., 1.
[64] Ibid., 1.

100

guys wearing black hats -- with one hand tied behind his back -- and justice wins the day. The proposterously improbable only **seems** improbable -- so take heart, noble citizen!

Moreover, this archetype saturates modern civilization at every level: the leading religion of our culture may have helped make Christmas (the birth of a savior) its most prized commercial event, but its most compelling message is that the creator of the universe sent his only progeny to Earth to blow the whistle on original sin, and even though he was crucified on a cross,

he resurrected into heaven and now reigns supreme, offering eternal redemption to all accepting souls who scurry forth on bended knee. This isn't insouciant insolence by an unbeliever, it is Christianity stripped bare to its overwhelmingly ubiquitous archetype, loaded as it is with inspiration and hope, but largely co-opted for mass consumption and manipulation at every other level.

This construct may be good (or convenient) for maintaining social order and generating good feelings among the citizenry, but none of this comports with Alford's own investigations, and none of it squares with my own parallel experience, having seen "behind the curtain" of our common narrative.

Instead of conjunction with this archetype, what Alford found was that whistleblowers are deeply shattered by their experience, unable "to assimilate the experience, unable, that is to come to terms with what they have learned about the world. Almost all say they wouldn't do it again -- if they had a choice . . ." Alford presents a variety of diverse examples: the inordinately large percentage of whistleblowers who lose their spouse and children and find themselves bankrupt; those that consider committing suicide; the majority, who almost always find themselves having so short-circuited their career by "doing the right thing" that they make a fraction of their former, pre-whistleblowing paycheck; and then there are the unforgetable stories that shock the conscience (like the physicist who blew the whistle to prevent a nuclear disaster and has been so hounded by forces more powerful than himself that his life has been reduced to that of a pizza delivery boy).

Even at this point, the reader should be able to see the connection between the cracks of the myths generated by the medical-industrial complex and those perpetuated about whistleblowing. And yet even close friends of mine were perplexed when I told them about Alford's findings. After all, aren't there hundreds of laws protecting whistleblowers against retaliation? Oh sure, there are. All believeable mythology requires props. And Alford recounts a sampling of these laws.[65]

The problem is that, like the rest of the crown molding that lines the edges of our culture, even democracy itself, such window dressing exists for show. It has no substance. **Whistleblowers have, for instance, won only four of almost ten thousand cases to reach the federal courts under the Whistleblower Protection Act of 1989**, a dismal record when one considers that the very purpose of the act was to protect those who come forward with evidence of government or corporate wrongdoing.[66]

Alford details the many tools that large organizations have to destroy the lives of those who even attempt to let their wrongdoing be known outside the workings of the "inner circle." One only becomes acquainted with these tools and tactics *after* having crossed the line and entered into another world -- a kind of "Through the Looking Glass" dimension that only whistleblowers share.

This is what Maurice Blanchot calls knowledge as disaster. "Not knowledge of the disaster, but knowledge as disaster, because it cannot be contained within existing frames and forms of experience, including common narrative."[67]

To come to terms with what the whistleblower uncovers in his life and in his world, he would "have to give up what every right-thinking American believes in." And just what must the whistleblower forsake in order to "hear his own story?"

- That the individual matters.

[65] Ibid., 108.
[66] Ibid., 110.
[67] Ibid., 50.

- That law and justice can be relied on.
- That the purpose of law is to remove the caprice of powerful individuals.
- That ours is a government of laws, not men.
- That the individual will not be sacrificed for the sake of the group.
- That loyalty isn't equivalent to the herd instinct.
- That one's friends will remain loyal even if one's colleagues do not.
- That the organization is not fundamentally immoral.
- That it makes sense to stand up and do the right thing. (Take this literally: that it 'makes sense' means that it is a comprehensible activity.)
- That someone, somewhere, who is in charge knows, cares, and will do the right thing.
- That the truth matters, and someone will want to know it.
- That if one is right and persistent, things will turn out alright in the end.
- That even if they do not, other people will know and understand.
- That the family is a haven in a heartless world. Spouses and children will not abandon you in your hour of need.
- That the individual can know the truth about all this, not become merely cynical, cynical unto death.

Alford closes this litany by stating, "Not only is it hard to come to terms with these truths, but when one finally does, it seems that one is left with nothing . . . What is the satisfaction in being right if as a consequence one has to give up everything one believed in?"[68]

It is difficult to put into words what this transition feels like, if you've never been through it. I remember in February 2004, while I was still imprisoned in Lafayette, Louisiana, waiting to see what kind of charges the Federal Government would come up with, my wife sent me a letter from the Business Adviso-

[68] Ibid., 48-51.

ry Council, an arm of the National Republican Congressional Committee. In it, the announcement was made that I had been "chosen as Louisiana Businessman of the Year,"[69] and that, as such, I was to be honored and presented "with your award at a special ceremony . . . in Washington." Along with this came a four-color, signed, frameable picture of President and First Lady Bush,[70] a copy of an "agenda," and other Republican Party paraphenalia.

Now, of course, everyone knows that such gimmicks are part and parcel of political fundraising. This isn't unlike getting nominated for inclusion in a *Who's Who In America*, or some similar "vanity publication." I could have just insouciantly brushed it off, or maybe passed a joke to my "cellie" about "finally earning a weekend furlough outta here" (never happen), and in any other situation, something equally nonchalant would have been my response.

But it wasn't.

I was having to deal with something I wasn't prepared for. I spent the next twenty minutes after that mail call sitting on my prison bunk, going over the materials from that letter, attempting to come to grips with these new feelings, as if I were reading correspondence that belonged to somebody else, as if I had confiscated somebody else's mail and were naughtily reading the interception. It wasn't that I just couldn't relate to the disconnect between the way the leading political party, what had been my party, in my country, was treating me juxtaposed to the outrageous events that lead me to prison. It felt like I was another person. It felt like the damage to any faith I had in the common narrative had been so fully demolished that any reference to the person that lived in my body prior to my imprisonment wasn't even addressed to me. I was not the same person. I would never be the same person. And no matter how hard I tried, I could never go back.

However, there has been solace in knowing that I am not the only one to have this experience.

[69] See: meditopia.org/images/la_bus_of_year_L.jpg
[70] See: meditopia.org/images/bush_card.jpg

For those who find themselves in the crosshairs of the medical-industrial complex, as I did, or Jason Vale, Michael Forrest, James Kimball, Mike Witort, Dr. Marilyn Coleman, or any of my other friends and acquaintances who, as a result, have "seen behind the curtain," there's a new reality that is equally as challenging to reconcile with the common narrative as it is for Alford's whistleblowers. It leads to an internal conflict that is no less harrowing. And what must we forsake in order "to hear our own story?" To understand the truth about health care in the modern era, one must be willing to accept:

- That making money is the primary objective of health care, and even the most ennobling acts are filtered through the prism of a hidden profit agenda;
- That orthodox medicine, like most of the offspring of modern scientism, has been, will be, and must be resistant to empiricism and all reasonable attempts to make it truly "evidence-based";
- That modern medicine has maimed, poisoned, and killed more people than it has ever healed, with iatrogenesis being a leading cause of death in the West;
- That modern medicine is not superior to, more cost effective, or more efficacious than a wide variety of alternative approaches it has sought to marginalize, criminalize, or just write off as "pure quackery" -- nor could it ever be.
- That suppression of treatment systems, indeed, the suppression of entire fields of scientific inquiry, which it cannot control or sufficiently profit from, is modern medicine's most enduring legacy.
- That modern medicine lacks any self-correcting feedback loops that would lead it to reform itself, or that it is utterly incapable of rising to anything higher than a sophisticated system of financial servitude.
- That rather than controlling the self-serving excesses of a select medical elite, the U.S. Government, and to a lesser extent, most other governments of the industrial-

ized Western World, aid and abet their wanton corruption.

- That there is no such thing as truth if it interferes with business and its constructs of power. Or speaking more broadly and in Alford's words: "Modern society is marked by multiple centers of meaning . . . (and) meaning tends to follow power."[71]

- That medical science, research, or any medically related intellectual undertaking that a normal human being would consider reducible to commonly agreeable fact, are molded around the objectives of business. Never the reverse.

- That the history of medicine as taught throughout the industrialized world is a farce: it presents an agreeable version of the past that is persuasively told from the medical establishment's point of view, and not from that of the patients (victims) who lived it.

Co-Opting Our Human Need
for Purpose and Meaning

"How could these things actually be true?" you might ask.

Is it not the case that if Power actually functioned in this way it would be too difficult to conceal from the masses?

Hideous and morally repulsive, though it be, power works to harness our own basic need to find positive meaning and purpose against us. For those who understand mind/body connection, it goes without saying that the health of an individual is integrally connected to the individual's "sense of purpose," that good mental health is upheld by a deep-seated "meaning of life." It is this basic need, essential to healthful, human living, that those in power exploit and co-opt. They know that it is possible to create mechanisms of power and control that the people will be disinclined to believe exist, even if they see it with their own eyes. This is what makes it so easy to create a Matrix, a field of human energy that exists to be harvested by a select few.

[71] Ibid., 6.

The importance of finding "meaning" in one's life is brought to life in the account of Dr. Victor Frankl,[72] whom we touched upon in Chapter 3. Frankl, the famous psychiatrist who lived through the Auschwitz Concentration Camp during World War II, was struck by the one common thread that marked all those who survived: they all had a strong and enduring sense of purpose. They knew that they would survive because their lives had meaning.

Frankl went on to found "The Third Viennese School of Psychotherapy" (behind those of Freud and Addison), known as Logotherapy,[73] based on his lifelong personal and clinical findings. The most basic tenet of logotherapy is that the striving to find meaning in one's life is the primary motivational force in man.[74]

On the surface, this may seem self-evident. A more cynical mind might suggest that "meaning in life" is the stock-in-trade of the world's religions and most of its philosophical systems. But even Freud, an avowed atheist, wrestled with this question and came up with "love and work" as the meaning of life.

It is this position that Alford uses as his key to unlock the barred door that the Halls of Power attempt to keep closed: for "what happens (thusly) when the world (around us) becomes unlovable and our work impossible?" he asks. "If love is not just a psychic discharge but a way of being in the world, then that way of being 'demands that the world present itself to us as worthy of our love . . . If love is not just a feeling but the force that makes the world go around, as Freud speculated . . . then loving the world and being able to love the world because the world is lovable are two sides of the same coin. We make the world meaningful with our love, and the world makes our lives

---

[72] See: en.wikipedia.org/wiki/Viktor_Frankl

[73] See: en.wikipedia.org/wiki/Logotherapy

[74] Victor E. Frankl, Man's Search for Meaning (New York: Pocket Books, 1971), 119-157. ("Logotherapy in a Nutshell")

meaningful by being lovable. When one partner fails, both do. The meaning of life depends on our ability to remain in a love affair with the world. Like any long-term love affair, this means that the world must love us back, even if this only means re-maining worthy of our love."[75]

Only when one has seen "behind the curtain" does one learn that the world which a select elite has created is not wor-thy of our love. To what extent will the common man go to cling to a vision of the world that is artificially created, full of worn cliches, feel-good slogans, and heartfelt, misleading political sound bites, all intended to co-opt man's need for meaning?

Very, very far, so far, in fact, that even whistleblowers, who have seen first-hand what lies behind the theater curtains, are loath to believe in their own perceptions, to "hear their own sto-ry."

Such is man's ability to exclude from his field of vision that which would deny him a psychologically healthy sense of the world.

When Christopher Columbus first approached what are, to-day, the Bahama Islands, his men were surprised to learn that the local Arawaks could not see their ships. There was nothing wrong with their vision. They did not approach in the dead of night. The impediment was mental: the very existence of such sailing vessels was so out of touch with the natives' "common narrative" that they literally failed to see the ships. They weren't trying not to see them. They just didn't see them.[76]

As it relates to the current volume, my contention is that most citizens of the Western world are no different than the Ar-awaks: they cannot face what Modern Medicine really is. For contained therein are "vessels" that do not comport with their fabricated vision of what the world is supposed to look like. The soil of elite power out of which such a hideous vine grows

---

[75] Whistleblowers, 52.

[76] Candace B. Pert, Ph.D., Molecules of Emotion (New York: Scribner, 1997), 148. I have seen reference to this historical fact more times than I care to remember. At the time of writing this book, I could not find the proper reference within Columbus's own writings, though it's frequency of presentation by notable authors would suggest that is hardly a whimsical creation. I use Pert's reference here because she provides a biological basis for the phenomenon.

is not compatible with a healthy sense of meaning. Even worse, it suggests incorrigible perversions in the very foundations of our Western culture, the close examination of which requires a stoutness of intellectual, emotional, and spiritual courage which, I believe, few possess.

Confronting the Defects in
Our Cultural Operating System

Cultures are molded over time, and the course they take is determined by those most predisposed to impose changes upon the order of so-called consensual reality. In our era, such individuals are those who have best taken advantage of those assymetrical systems of accumulation such that a select minority can determine what is best for the majority.

Cash is king.

And yet I find such an obvious conclusion distasteful and even unhelpful, and not because I fear the wrath of those who might say that such language has unsavory political overtones. Somehow, I find that a deeper understanding is required that demands that we examine the roots if we really want to know why the flowers are dying.

Such a quest must be thoughtful and not given to premature conclusions. If you consult the anarcho-primitivists, they will tell you that the defect lies in civilization itself.[77]

That argument is not without merit, but it does not serve my present purpose.

While in prison, I happened to come upon Howard Zinn's A People's History of the United States: 1492 - Present.[78] It isn't

---

[77] A good introduction on this line of thinking can be found in John Zerzan's Running on Emptiness: The Pathology of Civilization (Los Angeles: Feral House, 2002) -- one of his more recent works, which I highly recommend. The opening, by Theresa Kintz, p. viii-xviii, is as eloquent, concise, and comprehensive as any I have seen on the major polemics of the anarchist movement. I don't agree with all their positions, but I do believe that you cannot be a well-rounded intellectual in any of the social sciences today and be unfamiliar with the anarchists' arguments.

[78] Howard Zinn, A People's History of the United States: 1492-Present (New York: Harper-Collings Publishers, 2005).

the tome provided by Barzun, documenting 500 years of decline in the West,[79] nor does it provide the vision of doom we get from Spengler.[80] This is not to say that Zinn wastes time with pleasantries: he begins the book straight away by recounting the atrocities of Columbus and his men, and his fellow Spaniards who followed. Mass genocide. The expunging of entire cultures, peoples, languages. The enslavement of entire populations of indigenous peoples.

Exploitation is central to accumulation.

Immediately, if you are not familiar with the work of de las Casas or other non-revisionist historians of that era, you are caught, like whistleblowers are, in a conflict with the "common narrative," for nothing Zinn presents is designed to feed a common mythology, with its blessed discovery of America and the consequent "civilizing" of two continents of barbarian hordes.

"History is the memory of states," Zinn states, stopping to quote Henry Kissinger and lay the foundation for the rest of his book. And then he lays forth his purpose.

*"My viewpoint, in telling the history of the United States, is different; that we must not accept the memory of states as our own. Nations are not communities and never have been. The history of any country, presented as the history of a family, conceals fierce conflicts of interest (sometimes exploding, most often repressed) between conquerors and conquered, masters and slaves, capitalists and workers, dominators and dominated in race and sex. And in such a world of conflict, a world of victims and executioners, **it is the job of thinking people . . . not to be on the side of the executioners.**"[81]*

It was at this point that I realized that any journey through *Meditopia* must take into account that the common narrative of medicine in our time is reinforced by a history that is the "mem-

---

[79] Jacques Barzun, From Dawn to Decadence (1500 to the Present): 500 Years of Western Cultural Life (New York: HarperCollings Publishers, 2000).

[80] Oswald Spengler, The Decline of the West (Abridged Edition) (New York: Vintage Books, 2006).

[81] Zinn, 8-9.

ory of the Medical State," and we, indeed, cheat ourselves if we "accept it as our own."

What would happen if the history of medicine were not told from the point of view of its financial promoters? What would it look like if it were told from the point of view of the patients? How much different would the history of medicine look if those recounting it were those who were footing the bill for the last few thousand years, instead of those pocketing the money?

I came to the conclusion that no reconciliation with this massive "Tear in the Matrix" could come about without providing a historical perspective for my most important conclusions, and this is the subject of the next section.

However, before beginning a study of "A People's History of Medicine," I feel it is important to bookend this chapter with one specific historical case that ties together the important lessons just covered: the richness of the "suppression pattern," the refusal of orthodox medicine to accept the best therapeutic approach(es) when it threatens its power, profit, or privilege; the co-optation of indigenous healing techniques, and the final acknowledgment of the true cure only after the truth is so self-evident to the public that further suppression can only be counter-productive.

I want to examine the perverse common narrative that we were taught as school children about another ailment with which there are numerous parallels to cancer: "scurvy."

Scurvy: The "Cancer" of a
Previous Era in Orthodox Medicine

I'm not sure I know of anyone who cannot remember the grade school version of scurvy; how it was a widespread affliction in the British navy "because sailors had no access to fresh food during the long sea voyages; how it was discovered that lime juice prevented, or was thought then 'cured,' the symptoms"; and how the discovery of ascorbic acid (vitamin C), made possible through the miracle of modern science, finally brought about the elimination of this deficiency disease.[82]

The basis for this deficiency is well-established: that humans are among a very small handful of mammals who, along with guinea pigs and fruit bats, share a "genetic defect," namely, the inability to metabolize their own ascorbic acid ($C_6H_8O_6$). In fact, the internal production of ascorbate is almost universal to animal life. We lack it.[83]

None of this really tells the story as it deserves to be told, of course. And as well-read as I thought I was, it wasn't until I myself went to prison and came across story after story that showed the startling parallels between the history of scurvy and the more recent history of cancer that I began to understand the importance of the parallels. Most notably:

- **Cures for scurvy, like cancer, are amazingly and breathtakingly bountiful.** They're everywhere. We may now be able to point to a single, isolated nutrient, ascorbic acid (or simply, vitamin C) as the cure for scurvy, but from a naturopathic point of view, the number of source materials that will cure scurvy are many and ubiquitous. So ubiquitous among fruits and vegetables, that for all intents and purposes, one could say that in a balanced diet, the cure as well as the prevention of scurvy was and is, food that is fresh. In fact, scurvy is possible primarily because an important "freshness factor" (vitamin C) degrades easily.

- **Suppression Evidence Equally "Everywhere."** Evidence of attempts by the orthodox medical community to suppress the obviousness of these bountiful cures are

[82] Morris Fishbein, Fishbein's Illustrated Medical and Health Encyclopedia, Volume 20 (Scurvy to Stretch Marks), (Westport, Connecticut: H.S. Stuttman, Inc., 1981), 2629-2631. I could have used any of hundreds of difference references for a quick summation on our school book understanding of "scurvy," but nothing is as rigid and uncompromisingly fixed in orthodox medical mythology as the mid-twentieth century work (and there's a boatload of it) by former AMA President, Morris Fishbein.

[83] There are many introductions to this subject, but I recommend Jonathan Wright's. See Dr. Wright's Guide to Healing With Nutrition, ("A Genetic Defect We All Share -- Hypoascorbemia"), (Emmaus, Pennsylvania: Rodale Press, 1984), 67 - 80.

equally bountiful, shameful, and self-serving. (Should we be surprised?) This is particularly galling, given the number of effective cures within a wide range of indigenous communities that have been deliberately suppressed.

- **Suppression Even AFTER the Cure is Found!** Even after cures have been found, the orthodox establishment has encouraged nutritional regimens that will cause the problem to resurface for an indeterminate period of time extending well into the future. In the case of scurvy, this is done by downplaying the very existence of hypoascorbemia, of which scurvy is only the most severe or advanced stage, including attempts to qualitatively downplay the human nutritional requirements for ascorbyl containing foods. In the case of cancer, it is done by discouraging the use, consumption, education concerning, and sometimes even the cultivation of, cancerolytic herbs like red clover, poke root, purple lapacho, violet (*viola odorata*), chaparral, bloodroot, cat's claw, mistletoe, aveloz, alzium, oleander, aloe vera, nitriloside- containing fruit seeds, etc.[84]

- **Cures for both are/were dietary.** Yet in both cases the medical establishments of the day take/took the position that diet has nothing (and then later, "very little") to do with the disease.

- **Cures for both are/were low in cost.**

- **Cures for both are/were widely accepted by people outside the orthodox medical community.** You'll find this no less galling, in a moment, when you read the "People's History of Scurvy," as you have my brief review of cancer cure suppression.

- **Cures for both are/were suppressed in their respective time periods largely because implementation will cost people in power a lot of money!** . . . or will

---

[84] One of the better books for the lay reader that gives some sense of the scope of the suppression of cancer-fighting herbs is: Herbs Against Cancer: History and Controversy, by Ralph W. Moss, Ph.D.

cause specific revenue streams related to the flourishing of the disease to become extinguished.

- **The cure** was publicly acknowledged and revealed (in cancer's case, we use future tense) when those in Power had milked the cow dry and there was nothing further to gain by allowing curative techniques and methodologies to become public knowledge.

- **Ultimate source: maladaptation.** Both diseases are caused, if not exacerbated, by maladaptive conditions that are entirely manmade and unnatural. Such maladaptations are almost always related to some profit-producing line of endeavor by a small, elite minority.

- **Both have a maladaptive zeitgeist:** By this, I mean that each disease, although potentially existing at any point in human history, finds its greatest number of victims during those periods in which the underlying etiological maladaptations are most widely manifest in human affairs.

- **Prevention** for both is/was simple and also suppressed, and in both cases easier to prevent than to cure.

I readily admit that there are places where the analogy breaks down. Most noticeably, cancer is a leading killer in our own time. It has, from the beginning of the nineteeth century to the present taken the lives of tens of millions of people. Scurvy, by contrast, claimed only a little more than 2 million victims during its heyday. It was never a serious contender with the most aggressive killers of the time, such as bubonic plague, smallpox, or malaria.[85]

Additionally, whereas scurvy is the most extreme manifestation of a single nutrient deprivation, cancer is considerably more complex. Many different malignant cell developments had to be lumped together, some 200 different, separate diseases, into a single disease that we call "cancer." This was an important

---

[85] Stephen R. Bown, Scurvy: How a Surgeon, a Mariner, and a Gentleman Solved the Greatest Medical Mystery of the Age of Sail (New York: Thomas Dunne Books, St. Martin's Press, 2003), 3, 4, 26. The astute reader will readily ascertain that I regard Bown's work with respec for its depth of historical reporting, even if I disagree with many of his conclusions.

economic development. In fact, medical authorities should be proud of themselves that there will NEVER be one single, one-size-fits-all cure for cancer. Why? Because unlike scurvy, the word "cancer" does not define a single disease. It defines many, some of which, like basal cell carcinoma and leukemia, are only tangentially related. But I'll get to that later.

Despite these differences, the similarities between the two and the methods of suppression are sufficiently and so surprisingly alike that they deserve greater attention. Additionally, suppression of the benefit that vitamin C poses in the prevention of cancer adds an additional and important causal relationship in the comparison.[86]

The time frame within which scurvy is usually thought in the West as having been an epidemiological problem is roughly from the sixteenth to eighteenth century, but many of the important parts of the story can be found outside that time period.

The grueling ordeal of the 16th century French explorer, Jacques Cartier, and his men in the bitter winter of 1535-36 is instructive.[87] His three ships were frozen in the St. Lawrence River, near what is now Montreal, Canada. With four feet of ice beneath them and the spoiling of fresh food within the ship holds, scurvy soon set in so severely that by mid-March, 25 men had died, and among the remainder, only "three or foure" men were not so ill as to be considered hopeless. However, with the help of a local Indian chief, Domagaia, who had once cured himself of scurvy, a questionable embellishment of the story, since

---

[86] See Irwin Stone's The Healing Factor: "Vitamin C" Against Disease (Putnam Publishing Group, 1974). Dr. Stone was a pioneer in vitamin C research, and like Dr. Linus Pauling, whom he greatly influenced, he preached vitamin C's protective effects against a variety of cancer-causing agents. It is Stone who originated the concept of "hypoascorbemia," and his critics attempts to discredit his findings have not worn well. As Jonathan Wright points out, the critics' arguments can be summarized as "no one thing could be capable of so much." [Translation: It's all about the money!]

[87] See Virgil J. Vogel, American Indian Medicine (University of Oklahoma Press, 1990), 3 - 4. Also, Jonathan Eisen, Suppressed Inventions & Other Discoveries (New York: Berkley Publishing Group, 1999), 7 - 8, quoting from Racketeering in Medicine. Fuller accounts are found in Bown (Scurvy), who tells his version (p. 27-31), as does Carpenter (The History of Scurvy and Vitamin C) (p. 8-10).

scurvy was almost unheard of among the Indians, "the juice and sappe of a certain Tree" saved the remaining men.

The branches from this "magical tree" were first gathered and then "boiling bark and leaves for a decoctain, and placing the dregs upon the legs." All those who were treated "rapidly recovered their health and the Frenchmen marveled at the curative skill of the natives." We now know that the cure used was nothing more than hemlock or white pine. Far from being an obscure story, it was the basis for the later work of James Lind, credited in the West with "discovering" the dietary basis for curing scurvy (which I'll review in a moment), who launched his own experiments after he read Cartier's account.[88]

The most amazing thing you discover when studying the cultural anthropology surrounding this phenomenon is that there were almost no indigenous peoples outside of "Civilized Europe"who did not know how to cure scurvy – if they ever had it at all. The issue is that much of a no-brainer.

Today we know the relationship between vitamin C and a host of fresh fruits and vegetables, so one would think that if anyone on earth would be susceptible to getting scurvy, it would be at the most northern latitudes. After all, surely people with no regular access to any fresh fruits or vegetables would be afflicted with this illness.

Weston Price found this not to be the case. During his travels in the Canadian north in the 1920s, he happened to ask an old Indian, through an interpreter, "why the Indians did not get scurvy." The Indian promptly replied, "That's a white man's disease." He told Price that Indians know how to prevent scurvy, but that white man does not. The secret? After killing a moose for game, the Indians would seek out the "two small balls of fat" at the back of the moose, just above the kidneys (adrenal glands), cut them up into small pieces and give them to their family members. It is a fact that the adrenal glands, even of moose, contain vitamin C.[89]

---

[88] Ibid., 4, 84-86

[89] Weston A. Price, D.D.S., Nutrition and Physical Degeneration (La Mesa, California: The Price-Pottenger Nutrition Foundation, Inc., 2000), 75. Bown concerns in Scurvy concerning

How many "civilized people" know this?

The most shameful and misleading aspect of the grade school version of the history of scurvy is, in my opinion, the suppression of critical facts more fundamental than this. How much does the story change when it is revealed that even among many Europeans, the cure for scurvy was well-known all along, but just not "officially acknowledged," (just as in the case with effective cancer cures today)? How much does the story change when it is revealed that even medical officials at the time knew the cure, but it was suppressed because to implement proven prevention, in an age when citrus and other fresh fruit were seasonal and refrigeration non-existent, was considered an intolerable inconvenience? How much does the story change when it is revealed that the official rallying cry to "find a cure for scurvy" was sounded by the elite only after extremely expensive war vessels had to be abandoned at sea because the death toll wasn't leaving enough sailors to navigate the ships -- thus, making the search a matter of profit and not human life?[90]

Scurvy, like cancer, is largely a manmade disease.

There is such an abundance of ascorbate throughout the vegetable kingdom, that one has to create a highly artificial condition to induce scurvy in the first place. It is no wonder the evolutionary process jettisoned the ascorbate manufacturing capability within man: why sustain a metabolic process that is redundant throughout the vegetable kingdom and readily accessible through one's natural diet?

Such an artificial condition is rare in the world, but it did exist with the emergence of larger ships in the 15th century, capable of transporting men over great distances through long journeys lasting for months. This advance in seafaring created

the Inuits. See p. 39.

[90] See Bown's Scurvy (New York: Thomas Dunne Books, St. Martin's Press, 2003). What comes to mind here is Lord (Commodore) George Anson's disastrous four-year voyage (1740-1744) that "historians have described as the worst medical disaster ever at sea. Most of the Anson's crew were killed by scurvy; and only one of the five warships that departed England in 1741 made it home." (p. 50, 51). The loss of the Gloucester was particularly hurtful, as it was "outrageously expensive" to build. Even the author (Bown) is lead to comment: "It was becoming apparent that even if the Admiralty placed little value on the lives of the sailors, it did place value on its ships." (p. 68). The official "search for a cure" began shortly after the Anson expedition's conclusion.

an unnatural condition, a "maladaptation," for which humans were not created. Disease, remember, is created when demands are placed upon the human body for which it is not naturally adapted, or for which the attempt to adapt brings disrepair. Applied to scurvy, we may restate this principle as a corollary: namely, that the farther foods are removed from nature, the more likely they are to create disease.

The unfortunate story of Jacques Cartier and his scurvy afflicted crew may have been one of the earliest of the modern era, but the disease was so rare and unknown to that point that it was not defined and popularized until much later. The disease was not well-known or widely experienced, because the maladaptation that created it, namely, having men live and work aboard ships for months on end without consuming fresh, ascorbate-laden vegetable foods, which are part of the natural human diet, was an unnatural rarity in the human experience. It was not until 1589 that Richard Hawluyt's <u>Principall Navigations</u> was published, where he makes mention of two men dying of "skurvie," one of the very first appearances of the word in an English publication.

Conjoining the increased demands upon sailors to subsist in unnatural habitats for months on end was a complete lack of regard for their general welfare. This is evident in examining their assigned diets, which set the stage for scurvy outbreaks. One must be careful not to be eating or drinking while reading Bown's sickening account of the standard naval diet, which varied only slightly over the centuries "and only slightly between the various European nations." Victuals were limited by what could be preserved or stored for many months at a time without spoilage, but the most influencing factor in the victualling process was, of course, money. Officers of the line were far less likely to get scurvy than were the poorly paid non-commissioned, because they could afford to bring their own provisions: dried apples, pears, berries, and the like, whereas the crew was subjected to an unnatural diet that even by modern, orthodox standards of nutrition, was devoid of most nutrients, even if ample in calories. Bown recounts the typical weekly menu for the average sailor:

Biscuit	1 lb. daily
Salt beef	2 lb. twice weekly
Salt pork	1 lb. twice weekly
Dried fish	2 oz. thrice weekly
Butter	2 oz. thrice weekly
Cheese	4 oz. thrice weekly
Peas	8 oz. four days per week
Beer	1 gallon daily

This might not sound too unappetizing until one realizes the condition in which it was served. The remarks made by James Patten, a surgeon aboard Captain Cook's second voyage, were par for the time: "Our bread was . . . both musty and mouldy, and at the same time swarming with two different sorts of little brown grubs, the circulio granorius (or weevil) and the dermestes paniceus . . . Their larvas, or maggots, were found in such quantities in the pease-soup, as if they had been strewed over our plates on purpose, so that we could not avoid swallowing some of them in every spoonful we took."[91]

Such was the low regard that the various national navies took for the diet of their sailors. And, yet, it was not because they couldn't have provided better. Quite the contrary, the authorities of the day often went out of their way to ensure that the sailors would not get what they needed. As late as 1736, William Cockburn, a noted physician and naval surgeon, wrote in his influential Sea Diseases[92] that scurvy had nothing to do with diet, but was the result of idleness. With added physical exertion, i.e., working harder for the Admiralty, "digestion and nutrition were better performed" and scurvy would be abated. Another influential voice, John White, opined that fresh fruit caused enteritis and that "one must, when ships reach countries abounding in oranges, lemons, pineapples, etc., ensure that the crew eat very little of them since they are the commonest cause of fevers and

---

[91] Bown, Scurvy, 13 - 19.
[92] William Cockburn, Sea Diseases (Farmington, Hills, MI: Gale Ecco, 2010).

obstruction of the vital organs."[93]

And yet the historical record is chockful of reports where it was apparent that wise sailors throughout Europe, not tethered to purse-conscious, national navies, fully understood the importance of proper diet in their seafaring activies. Both the Norse and the Chinese knew the value of including fresh cranberries, seaweed, or ginger in their victuals, common before the construction of larger ships and much longer voyages.[94]

In the early 1600s, the legendary sea captain of Elizabethan England, Sir James Lancaster, was well-known for taking lemon juice as a provision aboard his ship, Red Dragon, for the specific purpose of warding off scurvy among his men. When scurvy did begin to surface, Lancaster led his ships into port "to refresh our men with oranges and lemons, to clear ourselves of this disease." He even purchased thousands of lemons, then put his men to work, squeezing them to make a "lemon water" for his continuing journey.

Far from being considered the recommendations of a sea-going crank, Lancaster's methods were standardized in his day. In 1617, The Surgeon's Mate,[95] written by John Woodall, the surgeon general of the East India Company, wrote that lemon juice was often used as a daily preventative on company vessels. "There is a good quantity of juice of lemons sent in each ship out of England by the care of the merchants and intended only for the relief of every poor man in his need, which is an admirable comfort to poor men in that disease."

Likewise, the Dutch East India Company not only made frequent use of lemon juice on their voyages, but they went so far as to maintain citrus plantations at key stops along their routes, including Mauritius, St. Helena, and the Cape of Good Hope, where by 1661, they reportedly had 1,000 citrus fruit trees. These were influential companies, experienced at international trade and maintaining viable fleets. So, it is no wonder that by the early 1600s, long before any mention of an official

[93] Bown, Scurvy, 37
[94] Ibid., 39.
[95] John Woodall, The Surgeon's Mate (UK: Kingmead Press, 1978).

cure by orthodox medicine, and even long before scurvy's emergence as an epidemiological nightmare among the navies of the world, lemon juice was "well regarded as the universal solution to the scurvy problem."[96]

Francois Pyrard, who sailed two French ships to the Spice Islands in 1602, recorded his own ship's bout with scurvy and remarked that "there is no better or more certain cure than citrons and oranges and their juice: and after using it once successfully everyone makes provision to it to serve him when in need." Likewise, lemon juice was considered a cure for scurvy by early American colonists. Baron De La Warr, a governor at Plymouth in the early 1600s who came down with scurvy on a trip to the Caribbean, remarked, "There I found help for my health by means of fresh diet, and especially of oranges and lemons . . . an undoubted remedy for (scurvy)."[97] In neighboring Canada, the Hudson Bay Company from their beginning in the 1600s, shipped out small quantities of lime juice to prevent scurvy.[98]

The story of how purveyors and sutlers of citrus products came to be effectively labeled quacks, not unlike a host of herbal providers of effective treatments are today, is a common tale. Over the course of the next hundred years, slowly but surely, the use of citrus products was replaced by more expensive remedies with much better markups for their providers and the creation of an orthodox medical system to provide a theoretical foundation for their use. That these newfound remedies didn't work was beside the point. No one could explain how lemon water worked either. But medical personnel were trained to explain how oil of vitriol (alcohol and sulfuric acid) worked.

That made it legitimate.

A new theory, with official sanctions, was all that was needed to create a new onslaught of scurvy as a seagoing disease reaching epidemic proportions. The products that would replace lemon juice as a cure for scurvy proved to be as outlandish,

---

[96] Bown, Scurvy, 71-73. See also Carpenter's History, ibid., 23 (on the Dutch establishment of plantations), and 137, (on the Hudson Bay Company).
[97] Ibid.
[98] Ibid.

goofy, and baseless as the official products used today to treat cancer (i.e. chemotherapy, radiation, and radical surgery). One hundred and fifty years later, the British Admiralty ordered as standard antiscorbutic treatment: a daily ration of two ounces of vinegar, oil of vitriol, and a potent patent medicine called "Ward's Drop and Pill" (a "viciously strong purgative and diuretic"). Such remedies were taken because the authorities in charge ordered it -- not because they had earned any reputation of efficacy among those who were the intended recipients. "(I) gave a quantity of (these remedies) to the surgeon, for such of the sick people as were willing to take them; several did so; though I know of none who believed they were of any service to them," wrote Lord Anson.[99]

As one reads historical records of this period, it is evident that with the infusion of professional medicine comes the abandonment, not the embracing, of the obvious cure. As Carpenter notes, "(the medical profession) made the subject so complicated that a safe and effective treatment could hardly be chosen without sophisticated diagnosis. This was certainly of benefit to the medical profession -- if not to the patient. As a modern French scholar has written: 'When theoretical considerations prevailed over empiricism, treatment became more and more complex and less effective.'"[100]

Well before sailors like Sir James Lancaster were keeping their crews alive by committing themselves to the obvious cure for scurvy, orthodox medicine was busy at work, attempting to find a way to profit from it. But therein lay the challenge. How could a professional class of physicians and their allied apothecaries, i.e., pharmacists, profit from a disease if those outside their class could easily identify this disease and cure it themselves?

It couldn't.

What was required at this point was a state of dependency upon the medical professional. But how could orthodox medicine profitably insert itself into the newly emerging scurvy phe-

[99] Ibid., 58.
[100] Carpenter, History, 42.

nomenon without discrediting the already established cure?

It couldn't.

There was always the option of leaving well enough alone and letting the sailors continue to identify and cure, not treat, but cure their own malady. But then how could professional medicine assert its own authority in the affairs of society if one of the fastest emerging medical crises was being eradicated without them -- no doctor, no apothecary, no medical authority required?

It couldn't.

Could the status quo possibly continue without severely impacting the very legitimacy of established medicine?

It couldn't.

And so the stage was set, not for the acknowledgment of the cure for scurvy, though it was obvious, even in the absence of a vitamin C discovery, but rather its eradication. This would be a campaign so successful, executed wittingly and unwittingly, that it would not be until well into the 20th century that these efforts would finally be laid to rest; by which time cancer would take the limelight as the "disease du jour," and orthodox medicine would develop the audacity to take credit for the scurvy cure, a cure it had spent over three centuries suppressing and to a considerable and paradoxical extent, still suppresses to this day in its less extreme state: hypoascorbemia.

Because humanity's tragic experience with scurvy occurred during a time when modern medicine, as we now know it, was just emerging, its study provides especially keen insight into how culture creates patterns that become entrenched over time. These patterns contain the seeds of a civilization's demise, but not before exhibiting ghastly anomalies, like the out-of-control condition endemic to today's orthodox medical establishment.

For there to be any institutionalized medical infrastructure under the cultural operating system that now defines Western civilization, there have to be several indispensable components, all of which are interrelated: an authoritative hierarchical structure, an ideological foundation, a monopoly of force, and the resources to sustain these functions. Yet all of these are subservient to, and feed into, the most critical element of all: the need to "establish and constantly reinforce legitimacy." In this respect, the anatomy of institutionalized medicine is no different from that of any governmental state.

Hierarchy and complexity, as Joseph Tainter has noted, "are rare in human history, and where present require constant reinforcement. No societal leader is ever far from the need to validate position and policy, and no hierarchical society can be organized without explicit provision for this need."[101]

Hierarchy and social complexity naturally gravitate towards the creation of a center, not necessarily a geographical one, but certainly a "symbolic source of the framework of society. It is not only the location of legal and governmental institutions, but is the source of order, and the symbol of moral authority and social continuity. The center partakes of the nature of the sacred. In this sense, every complex society has an official religion."[102] Tainter goes onto to say this "moral authority and sacred aura of the center"[103] is critical not only to the maintenance of a complex society, but its emergence Tainter goes onto to say this "moral authority and sacred aura of the center" is critical not only to the maintenance of a complex society, but its emergence.

This demands not simply the manipulation of ideological symbols, but requires substantial resources. As it applies to medicine, how are these resources created? If it is the case, as I clearly postulate, that the cures for most diseases are simple, natural remedies that do not lend themselves to private ownership (via patent, proprietary process, etc.) or higher profit margins, then what primary condition would have to be put in place for a viable organized medical community to emerge?

The answer is obvious: it requires artificiality. It requires systems of thought, bordering on religion, that give artificial value to artificiality. And if disease can be thought of as unresolved maladaptation, it means creating complex, artificial, maladaptive approaches to treating maladaptation. To understand

---

[101] Joseph Tainter, The Collapse of Complex Societies (Cambridge University Press, 1988).
[102] Ibid.
[103] Ibid.

this principle as it applies to organized medicine is to understand why it is not possible for orthodox medicine to have ever
evolved into anything more, or other, than an extended crime
syndicate, parasitic on those it claims to serve, while devoted
to the suppression of legitimate cures. The simple, indisputable
fact of the matter is that value-added products and services, in
medicine as in every other field of endeavor, means taking what
Nature has provided, most often for free, and creating from it
something that is scarce. This isn't even medicine: it's a tauto-
logical given in microeconomics. To take what Nature has freely
provided and make something uncommon, scarce and perhaps
even difficult to replicate and expect this artifact, extrinsic to
nature, to improve what is intrinsic to Nature, is ludicrous.

Organized medicine is itself a disease, self-serving and malignant. It enters into the field of Nature, where of their own
accord, wounds heal, blood clots, pathogenic microbes are
overcome by natural immunity, and attempts to co-opt Mother
Nature and claims that using methods entirely unnatural that it
can improve upon the function of natural biological systems.
Modern medicine proposes the impossible: that through maladaptation, it can bring health, when health never exists outside
an organism's own adaptive boundaries. In this sense, Modern
medicine functions in ways that mimic the disease process itself.

Applied outside the realm of "direct aggression against
individuals," Ivan Illich calls this "social iatrogenesis," where
"medical bureaucracy creates ill-health by increasing stress, by
multiplying disabling dependence, by generating new painful
needs, by lowering the levels of tolerance for discomfort or con-
cede to an individual when he suffers, and by abolishing even
the right to self-care."[104]

We see this again and again in the unfolding of the scurvy
cure and the revisionist version that now passes for history. I can
think of no better example than James Lind and the "Salisbury
Experiment" of 1747. This was "one of the first controlled trials

---

[104] Ivan Illich, Limits to Medicine / Medical Nemesis: The Expropriation of Health (London,
UK: Marion Boyars Publishers, Ltd., 2001) 40-41.

in medical history, or in any branch of clinical science." [105] It deserves our attention not just because it proved conclusively that oranges and lemons contained something that cured scurvy, but also illustrates the inexcusable, long, painful suppression of scurvy's simple cure. The examination of its history is almost too painful too read. It would take another 48 years (1795), only after the loss of untold thousands of sailors, an indeterminable number of warships, the loss of the American Colonies, and then nearly England's own survival, until the lords of the British Admiralty would admit a more humiliating defeat and make citrus fruit standard issue on its ships of the line. Only when the life of the nation itself was at stake would those in authority admit the folly of their unproven remedies and allow sailors ready access to a cure that had been known for hundreds of years. (For those who would conclude from my commentary that indifference to the health of their charge was or is exclusive to British authority, I would present its American counterpart: after 30,000 soldiers came down with scurvy during the American Civil War, the U.S. Army finally adopted anti-scorbutic rations in 1895 -- another 100 years after the British adopted them.)[106]

> *"It must however appear clear to every reflecting mind, that the care of the sick and wounded is a matter equally of policy, humanity and economy. Independently of men being sentient beings and fellow creatures, **they may also be considered as indispensable mechanical instruments.**"*

> *Adm. Gilbert Blane[107]*

By any reasonable standard, James Lind's experiment aboard HMS *Salisbury*, beginning in May 1747, today hailed as a remarkable scientific accomplishment, was an exercise in common sense. At this time, Lind did not possess a medical degree, something which, in retrospect, probably gave him a decided advantage. He was a ship's surgeon, a position which, at

---

[105] Bown, Scurvy, p. 97.

[106] Irvin Stone, The Healing Factor: Vitamin C Against Disease (Putnam Publishing Group, 1974), 31.

[107] Ibid., 203. (Emphasis added)

that time, carried with it a level of respect, and pay, only slightly above the common sailor and well below that of the officers. What Lind did have aboard the *Salisbury*, a fourth rate ship of the line, was the confidence and permission of his captain to proceed with his experiment. Bown describes the simplicity of Lind's approach: he took twelve sailors, all with similar levels of advanced scorbutic symptoms.

He then ". . . hung their hammocks in a separate compartment in the forehold -- as dank, dark, and cloying as can be imagined -- and provided 'one diet common to all.' Breakfast consisted of gruel sweetened with sugar. Lunch (or dinner) was either 'fresh mutton broth' or occasionally 'puddings, boiled biscuit with sugar.' And for supper he had the cook prepare barley and raisins, rice and currants, sago and wine. Lind also controlled the quantities of food eaten. During the fourteen-day period, he separated the scorbutic sailors into six pairs and supplemented the diet of each pair with various antiscorbutic medicines and foods.

"The first pair were ordered a quart of 'cyder' (slightly alcoholic) per day. The second pair were administered twenty-five 'guts' (drops) of elixir of vitriol three times daily on an empty stomach and also 'using a gargle strongly acidulated with it for their mouths.' A third pair took two spoonfuls of vinegar three times daily, also on an empty stomach, also gargling with it and having their food liberally doused with it. The fourth pair, who were the two most severely suffering patients, 'with the tendons in the ham rigid,' were given the seemingly oddest treatment: sea water, of which they drank 'half a pint every day, and sometimes more or less as it operated, by way of a general physic.' The fifth set of sailors each were fed two oranges and one lemon daily for six days, when the ship's meagre supply ran out. The sixth pair were ordered an 'electuary' (medicinal paste), 'the biggest of a nutmeg,' thrice daily. The paste consisted of garlic, mustard seed, dried radish root, balsam of Peru, and gum myrrh. It was washed down with barley water 'well acidulated with tamarinds.' and on several occasions they were fed cream of tartar, a mild laxative, 'by which they were gently purged three or four times during the course.' Lind also kept several scorbutic sailors aside in different room and gave them nothing beyond the standard naval diet other than the occasional 'lenitive electuary' (painkiller) and cream of tartar."[108]

The results would probably not surprise many indigenous people, but they surprised Lind. The lucky pair who were fed the citrus fruit were nearly recovered after only a week. None of the other test subjects were to similarly recover. In fact, the citrus eaters ended up helping to nurse the other unfortunate scurvy victims who had not been so treated. Lind's conclusion was clear and concise, "the most sudden and visible good effects were perceived from the use of the oranges and lemons . . . Oranges and lemons were the most effectual remedies for this distemper at sea."[109]

The following year (1748) Lind retired from the Royal Navy, as hostilities between England and Spain diminished. He completed his medical degree at the University of Edinburgh and in 1750 was elected a fellow of the Royal College of Physicians in Edinburgh. He then got married and established a private practice.

It would appear, however, that Lind was a rare bird in the nascent field of modern medicine as we now know it. A contrarian not content with conventional thinking on scurvy that ran contrary to his own findings, he spent the next three years on work so comprehensive and bibliographical that it took into account every known desription of scurvy, from the earliest records to the most modern. Letters and documents were compiled and translated from places all over Europe.

In 1753, six years after the *Salisbury* experiment, Lind's treatise appeared in Edinburgh: _Treatise on the Scurvy, Containing an Inquiry into the Nature, Causes, and Cure, of That Disease Together with a Critical and Chronological View of What_

[108] Ibid., 96.
[109] Ibid., 97.

Has Been Published on the Subject.

This book is hailed by numerous sources and authorities as a landmark in the history of medicine. It was, of course, resisted by an inertial system of patronage that was every bit as grotesque as the one that infests the military establishments of most Western nations today.[110] But what is more revealing is how modern historians treat the matter. Harvie himself opens his treatise on Lind by remarking that scurvy killed "thousands of men, mainly sailors, every year for at least four centuries before a remedy was found."[111] Found by whom? For whom? Not the Eskimos. They had a cure. Not any of the native peoples of North America. They had their own cures. Not the Polynesians, or the Melanesians, or the Maori, or the Incans -- hell, try to name an indigenous people who were not contaminated by the sick cultural environment that gave birth to the modern abomination we call modern medicine that did not have a cure![112]

[110] David I. Harvie, <u>Limeys</u> (Phoenix Mill, UK: Sutton Publishing, 2002) 145.

[111] Ibid., 1

[112] Two things came to mind as I wrote this. First, Weston Price's study of the superb health and physical condition of people he found all over the world who had not (yet) been contaminated by Western dietary habits. See his <u>Nutrition and Physical Degeneration</u> (La Mesa, California: The Price-Pottenger Nutrition Foundation, Inc., 2000). The very idea of "searching" for a cure to a disease that is artificially induced by separating yourself from fresh food would strike indigenous peoples as tragically ridiculous.

Then secondly, my own personal experiences with the indigenous shamans of Ecuador and Peru.The *"ayahuasqueros,"* who utilize the ayuhuasca / chacruna formulations (the vine, *Banisteriopsis Caapi*, and the leaves of *Psychotria Viridis*) in their own quest to obtain healing knowledge from "the plant teachers," sound ludicrous to outsiders. And yet many tribes in South America, completely isolated from one another have this same understanding. See Schultes, <u>Vine of the Soul</u> (New Mexico: Synergetic Press, 1992) which although centered in Colombia, gives some sense of the ubiquitousness in the Amazon of this common knowledge.

My own ayahuasca journeys with shamans in the Amazon have taught me that plants do, indeed, have spirits that can be your personal teachers, in all matters of life, such that something as readily curable as scurvy could be grokked in that altered state, as if you'd ever put yourself in such a state that you'd really need it. This is not a "belief," as that term is used in the West, it is what I have directly grasped. Moreover, I think that most indigenous peoples, especially those who have preserved the use of of entheogens from their ancient cultures and are uncontaminated by a Western culture far removed from Mother Nature, intuitively have this sense. Plant teachers can be used in the wild to acquire knowledge about all things related to healthy living, and several shamans I know in Ecuador have used them to learn the proper use of many hundreds of medicinal plants. See Pinchbeck's <u>Breaking Open the Head</u> (New York: Broadway Books, 2003); Smith's <u>Cleansing the Doors of Perception</u> (CO: Sentient Publications, Boulder, 2003); the compilation, Robert Forte, (editor), <u>Entheogens and the Future of Religion</u> (San Francisco, California: Pine Forge Press, 2000); but especially any of the books by the late Terence McKenna, particularly <u>Food of the Gods: The Search for the Original Tree of Knowledge</u> (New York:

The entire Western-centric thinking in which the discovery of the scurvy cure is framed reminds me of the mainstream society's treatment of Christopher Columbus. He, too, is credited with discovering something: America. But how can you *discover* a place where over 55 million human beings are already living? A hemisphere which, as Las Casas recorded, was "teeming with people. . . like a beehive."[113]

Lind's contribution does not merit the use of the word "discovery." How can you discover something that people all over the world who are not connected to the intellectual convolutions of modern medicine already know and use and benefit from? Instead of noting the obvious: that Lind simply used Cartesian methods of observation to confirm what people in cultures all over the world already knew, he is instead, within the confines of modern medical history elevated to a position on his own private Mount Olympus. He is exalted for his "truly pioneering controlled clinical trial," while one eulogy of note contends that Lind is "one of the greatest names in the whole history of medicine," and, "the discovery of the cause and prevention of scurvy is one of the great chapters in all human history . . . largely the work of James Lind."[114]

What unmitigated rubbish.

For lost in the heady crediting of Lind with the initial "discovery of the scurvy cure," is the suppression of the good doctor's involvement in the suppression. Not content to leave well enough alone -- for what contribution to medical science is there in recommending the consumption of lemons? -- Lind decided to make his own contribution to medicine. Nature's cure wasn't

Bantam Books, 1992).

[113] Charles C. Mann, 1491: New Revelations of the Americas Before Columbus (New York: Alfred A. Knopf, 2005). It sickens me to think of how much the Baconian / Hobbesian view of indigenous peoples and their ways has worked to suppress our understanding of history. Mann recounts the conclusions of a generation of anthropologists who now conclude that in 1491 there were probably more people living in the Americas than in Europe, that the earliest cities in the Western Hemisphere were "thriving before the Egyptians built the great pyramids," that Mexico was the most densely populated place on Earth (p. 94). As to the actual numbers debate itself, a more focused source is William M. Denevan's The Native Population of the Americas in 1492 (Madison, Wisconsin: The University of Wisconsin Press, 1976) whose careful methodology comes up with a hemispheric total of approximately 57,300,000 (p. 291).

[114] Carpenter, The History of Scurvy and Vitamin C (Cambridge: Cambridge University Press, 1986), 72-73.

good enough. What respectability could there be in that? So he came up with the idea of producing a "rob" -- a concentrate of citrus fruit, made by boiling down the citrus fruit itself. The astute observer today will readily see the fault there: vitamin C, being subject to heat lability, would be destroyed in any such process.

Now surely, James Lind, the man credited with doing the first controlled medicine study, would test his rob to ensure that it worked as well as raw oranges and lemons. So that's exactly what he did, right? Of course not.

As time went on, Lind began making untested, untried, untrue, mindlessly ineffective recommendations that were no better than the other profit-producing recommendations of his peers. In 1779, his final work suggests that cream of tartar is an adequate substitute, and so it is confidently inserted among Lind's other stupendous recommendations for mitigating scurvy: including the fumigation of ships with burning tar. By diluting his initial finding with a plethora of ineffective nonsense, it has been noted that Lind "complicated, if not delayed, the successful management of scurvy in British and Western European shipping."[115]

Nonetheless, Lind never suffered the consequence of leveraging the publicity of his positive initial scurvy find into this series of worthless, untested scurvy recommendations. How could official opprobrium result when those in charge were backing proprietary scurvy treatments that were every bit as untested and void of any curative properties? (What comes to mind is Dr. John Pringle's position as President of the British Royal Society and his influence on the Admiralty to promote, for many years in the late 1700s, the continued use of "wort of malt," a completely worthless treatment.) Instead, Lind spent the rest of his professional life as a high ranking hospital administrator, and I believe it would be fair to say a member, though not of the highest stature, of the ruling aristocracy.

As we saw earlier, modern medicine requires ideological foundations to sustain its legitimacy and having become a full-

[115] Ibid., 74.

131

fledged physician and member of the establishment, it would have been unthinkable for Lind to conclude his treatise without introducing his own theory about its cause and cure. Not only are Lind's theories (too extensive to recount in full here) every bit as hare-brained as his contemporaries, but he actively criticizes the ideas of the one physician who, more than any other in his day, understood the true cause and cure of scurvy.

Johan Friedrich Bachstrom was a Dutch physician of this period who correctly identified scurvy as a dietary deficiency disease. He divided plants into three broad categories, ranking their strength as antiscorbutics (in fact, he coined the term). Though primitive and in need of alteration by today's understanding, the uncelebrated Bachstrom, unlike the highly celebrated Lind, correctly saw that "the most common herbs and fresh fruits excel the most pompous pharmaceutical preparations," and that "this evil is solely owing to a total abstinence from fresh vegetable food and greens, which alone are the true primary cause of the disease."

What? No proprietary formula? No special treatment or officially sanctioned remedy? Wrong answer.

For his impudence, Bachstrom was imprisoned and died in Lithuania in 1742, at the age of fifty-six.[116]

From this point the official story, depending on whose version of history you listen to, winds through the empirical success of Captain James Cook's arresting scurvy at sea and on to Gilbert Blane's ultimate success at getting citrus products back into fashion as a scurvy preventive and cure.[117]

This is where the story ends, according to the common narrative. Citrus fruit becomes accepted as the answer, later to be confirmed as containing the one true isolated cure, vitamin C. Scurvy is accepted as a deficiency disease. And now everyone gets to live happily ever after, once again, thanks to modern medicine.

But that is not at all what happened. Over the last 200 years,

[116] Bown, Scurvy, 82-83.
[117] Ibid., 133-162, and 163-184 respectively.

scurvy has repeatedly reared its head, and in nearly every case, it recurred where modern medicine, with and without assistance from its brethren in the processed food industry, couldn't resist the temptation to intervene with some twisted angle to make money from its recurrence. Carpenter's work is packed with nauseating examples, of which only a couple will be referenced here for brevity's sake.

Beginning with the summer of 1845, weather in northwest Europe took a nasty turn resulting in the loss of about half the potato crop, an important staple and a vital source of vitamin C. In July of the following year, a similar turn resulted in almost a total loss for the crop in Ireland and Britain. This period in history is referred to The Great Potato Famine (1845-1848).

Ascorbates would not be discovered for another eighty years, and yet despite a well-established Treatise on Food and Diet (Pereira, 1843), noting the "need for succulent vegetables and variety in the human diet," prominent voices obtained the imprimatur of the medical establishment to help introduce an array of new, zany theories about scurvy and the exciting new therapeutic possibilities.

In 1842, Animal Chemistry[118] was published, giving voice to the "protein theory" of nutrition by Justus von Liebig. Carpenter summarizes his three main points:

1. The proteins (as we would call them) are readily converted to each other in animal digestion because of their common fundamental character
2. The energy needed for muscular contraction is derived from the breakdown of the muscle proteins themselves.
3. The only function of the non-nitrogenous starches and sugars in foods is to protect the tissue from the destructive effects of oxygen, by themselves reacting with oxygen and, at the same time, giving out heat that keeps animals at their optimal working temperature.

---

[118] Justus von Liebig, Animal Chemistry, or Organic Chemistry in Its Applications to Physiology and Pathology (Classic Reprint) (U.S.: Forgotten Books, 2018).

This theoretical framework created what would become the nutritional wisdom of the day, lasting almost to the 20th century: that only nitrogenous foods (proteins) had true nutritional value and that other organic compounds (what we would call carbohydrates and fats) acted as "respiratory materials," providing the basis for thermal integrity. Drawing upon Liebig's work, Dr. Robert Christison, created a new theory that found "the main cause of scurvy" was a lack of milk. He drew his conclusions from observations made of scurvy outbreaks in British prisons, and his opinions on the matter were so influential as to what we might call "protein deficiency" that he got the diet of inmates altered to include skimmed milk, morning and evening, and half a pound of meat. Never mind that the indisputable cure to that point, citrus fruit, could not at all have been considered a "nitrogenous" food, common sense observations mentioned by a handful of Christison's critics, but insufficient to alter his influence.[119] Remember, protein-based foods have, since the earliest stirrings of capitalism, carried higher profit margins than foods from other food groups, undoubtedly an influencing factor and something I discuss in my first book.[120]

An equally hare-brained theory that became widely accepted in orthodox medical circles was the potassium theory, reasoning that by restricting succulent vegetables from the diet, the scurvy sufferer was subjected to a deficiency in mineral salts, primarily potassium. In time, this theory sank, too, with the sheer weight of common sense; to wit: if a deficiency of mineral salts has anything to do with scurvy, why does the mere act of dehydration, in which mineral salts are preserved, kill the anti-scorbutic value of fruits and vegetables? However, as late as 1862, the theory still had a following among the medically prestigious.

Gradually, interest in new scurvy cures subsided with the absence of scurvy as a problem on land. In the summer of 1848,

---

[119] The examples to this point concerning Liebig and Christison are taken from Chapter 5 of Carpenter, The History of Scurvy & Vitamin C, entitled "Land scurvy, potatoes, and potassium (1810-1905)", 101-107.

[120] My comment on profit margins for protein-based foods comes from The Lumen Book.

there was a normal potato harvest, scurvy subsided, and without a way to help "create" new scurvy cases, orthodox medicine had to look to other markets to peddle its goods and services, but not before issuing its final, inane, dietary recommendations for avoiding scurvy: "Avoid the use of uncooked vegetables, unripe, sour or stone fruit . . . and acid drinks generally."[121] The cure for scurvy would, of course, require ignoring this misguided medical advice, just as surely as curing cancer today would require the avoidance of nearly all chemotherapy, radiation, and invasive, radical, surgical techniques, which are the FDA approved modalities in the United States.

With this in mind, it shouldn't surprise the alert observer that scurvy has always been rare in areas where people live close to the land, not just because they are more apt to get fresh fruit and vegetables, ample in ascorbate, but because they are blessed with an absence of menacing medical authorities. A good example is Hudson's Bay Company,[122] the oldest commercial corporation in North America, with continuous operations going back to 1670. In all that time, scurvy has never been a "serious problem that hampered their development." Bypassing the many "theories du jour," Hudson's shipped out small quantities of lime juice to its employees during this period.[123] One can only ponder what scorbutic horrors would have awaited their employees in the New World had they followed orthodox medical advice.

Regardless, it is in the period that follows, a period for which any Western school child will probably tell you that the scurvy problem had already been solved, after all, it's in the common narrative, that scurvy reared its ugly head again and modern medicine came forth with yet another zany theory.

I'll call this period "The Age of the Ptomaine Theory."[124]

---

[121] Carpenter, The History of Scurvy, 109. This ridiculous medical advice was made by the Edinburgh Board of Health in 1848, the same year as the founding of the American Medical Association (AMA) in the U.S., and ten years before the announcement of a confirmed cancer cure in London in 1858.

[122] See: en.wikipedia.org/wiki/Hudson's_Bay_Company

[123] Carpenter, The History of Scurvy, ibid., 137.

[124] Ibid., 133-157. The section that follows is taken from Chapter 6 of Carpenter's book, entitled, "Problems in the Arctic and the ptomaine theory (1850-1915)."

I n 1876 a British naval expedition returned from the Arctic after just one year. Out of 120 men, half had suffered from scurvy, and 4 had died of it. A full-scale inquiry was called for by the House of Commons, leading to the development of an entirely new theory on the cause of scurvy, one that would become influential by 1900.

That scurvy should still be a problem for explorers, over 120 years after Lind's now famous publication and only slightly more time than this to the date of this writing, deserves examination. As stated earlier, Weston Price noted that despite a dearth of fresh fruits and vegetables, Eskimos and other peoples of the far north are rarely seen to suffer from it. They are in touch with the land and their relationship to it.[125]

But such observations clearly do not square with modern medicine's own common narrative, so a new theory in the age of polar explorations had to be created to explain why those who ate meat in the northern latitudes did not get scurvy, while those farther to the south who ate meat *did*. Out the window went over a century of proof that fresh citrus was already an established cure. And so came about "The Ptomaine Theory," which, as one of its main proponents, Frederick Jackson, unwittingly declared, required the dislodging of the already established cure, "the use of lime juice neither prevents nor cures scurvy . . . (it) is a disease developed through eating tainted food . . . a slow poisoning . . ."[126]

Modern medical historians act as apologists (they have no choice) for the re-sprouting of these periodic zany theories that orthodox medicine latches onto, excuses that do not comport with common sense. In this case, the escape is that Jackson observed crews taking their aged daily ounce of lime juice to no

---

[125] Ibid., 146. It is interesting to note that Carpenter cites a comment from the Admiralty Committee on Scurvy (1877) that Eskimos were not immune from the disease because "they had been seen to suffer from it when living in the Danish settlements in Greenland." This again brings to mind Weston Price's frequent observation (see <u>Nutrition and Physical Degeneration</u>) that indigenous peoples have always lost their immunity and generally good health when they associated with Western civilized peoples and adapted their diet. If Eskimos were seen at Danish settlements with scurvy, it was most likely that they had already begun to assimilate Western diet practices before acquiring the disease, a common phenomenon, historically.

[126] See: pdfs.semanticscholar.org/8175/47130e69824a11ee6d19eff30dacbab140a0.pdf, 982.

effect. Ergo, citrus fruit is of no value. Never mind the simple observation that nearly all foods degrade in value the greater the distance in time from their initial harvest.

Working with Vaughan Harley, a Professor of Physiological Chemistry in London University, Jackson sought to give life to his theory, which garnered credibility from the new acceptance of Pasteur's Germ Theory. The testing for the Ptomaine Theory is described by Jackson in a then respected 1899 monograph:

> "If meat is not properly preserved, micro-organisms contaminate it, and as a consequence it goes *bad* -- the bacteria chemically change the albumen, fat, carbohydrates in the meat, and the new chemical products formed (ptomaines) cause the change in colour, smell, etc . . . Before the meat has actually gone so bad as to be repugnant to the sense of smell and sight, bacteria may have done their work, and yielded their ptomaines . . . It is such *tainted* meat, and not bad meat, that one must look to as the **cause of scurvy**. The greater prevalence of scurvy in the winter -- which used to be argued in favour of the fresh vegetable theory of the disease -- is in support of this theory; for in summer, if meat is kept, the bacteria would proliferate with such rapidity that the meat would soon smell bad and be rejected. In winter it would not taint so rapidly, and might be cooked and eaten without thought of danger. It must be remembered that, although cooking will destroy bacteria, the ordinary heat so used would have no action on their chemical products, or ptomaines. Again, if the meat were putrid, eating it would cause acute ptomaine-poisoning, with headache, violent diarrhoea, sickness . . . if only slightly tained meat were taken, the dose would cause no immediate symptoms, and the disease would gradually develop itself as we know scurvy does."[127]

This theory wasn't considered hair-brained or on the fringe.

---

[127] Frederick George Jackson, A Thousand Days in the Arctic (New York: Harper & Brothers, 1899), 382-5, as cited in History, p. 147-148.

It had support from no less than Lord Lister, President of the Royal Society, representing the pinnacle of establishment respectability. Readers will remember that this is the same position held by Dr. John Pringle in the late 1700s, who, for financial gain, promoted his worthless wort of malt despite the clear evidence of citrus's effectiveness as abundantly articulated by Lind.

Monkey studies were crafted to support the theory, which is to be expected, because one of the most grievous flaws in the popular religion we call scientism is that experiments always carry a bias to the willed, established doctrine.[128]

That the smallest consultation with students of the East would have killed the ptomaine theory in its cradle didn't seem to matter. After all, in India scurvy had been observed with soldiers who didn't even eat meat. When hospitalized, their scurvy was cured "by the simple addition of fresh limes or potatoes."[129] Such observation, however, would run counter to orthodox medicine's efforts to unify and filter its constellation of medical observations, theories, and practices under the rubric of the now hallowed Germ Theory. It is, therefore, not surprising that two years later, in 1902, the British Medical Association opened its annual meeting with a report from its Inspector-General, a retired naval surgeon named Turnbull that pronounced, "From extensive . . . researches in the literature . . . I am forced to the conclusion that . . . the presence of some toxic material in the food is the cause of scurvy . . . also that lemon or lime juice has been erroneously accepted as a certain preventative . . . Fresh or pure provisions are the true antiscorbutic." *(emphasis added)* Such thinking, now established as medical, scientific fact by the Establishment for the early 20th century, is reflected in comments by Reginald Koettlitz, the senior surgeon on one of Jackson's arctic expeditions: "The benefit of the so-called anti-scorbutic is a delusion . . . that the cause of the outbreak of scurvy in so many polar expeditions has always been that something

[128] Thomas Kuhn, The Structure of Scientific Revolutions (Chicago: The University of Chicago Press, 1962), 35-38, Section IV. "Normal Science as Puzzle-Solving."
[129] Carpenter, History, 150.

was radically wrong with the preserved meats, whether tinned or salted is practically certain. An animal food is scorbutic if bacteria have been able to product ptomaines in it . . . otherwise, it is not."[130]

The disaster that followed, namely the death of Commander Robert Falcon Scott[131] (1868-1912) and his companions in his last Antarctic expedition (1910-1912), deserves our attention not because they died of scurvy. The medical wisdom of the day, which has not progressed that far in the last century, and in many ways has regressed, made it inevitable. What is important is the manner in which the information was suppressed.

That suppression became a necessity because the second and final Scott expedition is the most famous in British history, setting forth a flurry of historical reconstructions that were not published until the late 1970s.[132] That Scott lost out to Roald Amundsen in the race to the Antarctic, an irrepressible source of embarrassment to the British, is not as important as unearthing the true source of the Scott expedition's demise. The daily ration on Scott's expedition itself tells its own story: pemmican, biscuits, butter, cocoa, sugar and tea. Low in calories and deficient in vitamin C.

When one of the naval surgeons, Atkinson, filed a report on the conditions of Scott and his companions after the bodies were found, hunger and frostbite were mentioned, but not a word is said about scurvy. Huntford speculates, based on his own evidence, that "there are stray hints that he [Atkinson] might have been concealing evidence of scurvy, which could not be revealed because it would have reflected on the whole conduct

---

[130] A. Turnbull, (1902). Discussion on the prevention of scurvy. *Br. Med. J.* ii: 1023-4. Cited in History, Carpenter, 150-151.

[131] See: en.wikipedia.org/wiki/Robert_Falcon_Scott

[132] Carpenter cites three: Elspeth Huxley's Scott of the Antarctic (1977); David Thompson's Scott's Men (1977); and Roland Huntford's Scott and Amundsen (1979). The last book (Huntford) was the leading source work from which the television miniseries, *The Last Place on Earth* (1985) was derived. Some criticism has been leveled at Huntford for being too harsh on Scott. More recent and less controversial volumes include Captain Scott (2004) by Ranulph Fiennes -- himself a polar explorer; and Susan Solomon's The Coldest March: Scott's Fatal Antarctic Expedition. Any criticism leveled at me for using Huntford in coming to the conclusion that scurvy had a decisive role in the death of Scott and most of his crew I leave to my readers. Consider, if nothing else, the horrific scorbutic state of their diet (discussed above).

of the expedition." Considering comments made by surviving crew members, as well as the degree of editing of Scott's own posthumous diary, I would say that the "hints" become far more certain than suggestive.

Western civilization, as we have seen, has taken humankind far on the path of maladaptation, but few examples are as illuminating as that of infantile scurvy, a disease which is, first and foremost, rooted in the inability to accept mother's milk as a human infant's most perfect food. Since modern medicine proposes, in innumerable ways, that it can improve upon Nature herself, it isn't surprising that our civilization would introduce an array of baby formulas which provide nutritional deficiencies to infants that proceed right up to the present day.[133]

Late in the 19th century, infants who manifested the symptoms of scurvy were diagnosed as having what was then called Barlow's disease. An orthodox medical system that can't cure scurvy in adults, certainly isn't likely to do any better for infants, and such was the case, with prescriptions resulting for items such as potassium chlorate, iodide of iron, quinine bark, cod liver oil, etc. For well over forty years, medical doctors made money, of course, by visiting and prescribing a variety of compounds to treat a deficiency disease for which the real cure is unthinkable. For a weaning infant, the best antiscorbutic prescription is mother's milk. Imagine!

Infantile scurvy is rightly a "disease of affluence," a subset of the "diseases of civilization" from which earlier adult versions of scurvy are themselves prime examples. Boyden identifies the impact of civilization on the emergence of new diseases: "The majority of the disorders of which people complain in Western society are disorders of civilization, in the sense that they would

---

[133] One of my companies, Lumen Foods (soybean.com) became embroiled in controversy in the early 2000s over comments we made telling parents to avoid giving their children soy milk, because of evidence that this was a source of low level manganese toxicity that lead to an array of health problems for children as they aged. My position is that we cannot measure all the subtle ways that children are made deficient by our lack of appreciation for mother's milk.

have been rare or non-existent in primeval society."[134] We come to much closer grips with the underlying conditions under which infantile scurvy would surface when we realize that in modern civilization, the very mention of women's breasts do not, first and foremost, bring to mind either milk or the sustenance of small infants. Among certain cultural groups breast-feeding is associated with a certain backwardness or even perversity.

Again . . . maladaptation.

So it is not surprising, proceeding with this short review of scurvy's history, that the next development would lend itself to modern medicine's key specialty: addressing maladaptation, the source of disease states, with yet more maladaptation. This took the form of yet more reinforcement of the still nascent Germ Theory with the sterilization of milk. Carpenter's work is quite suggestive of "cooked milk," as the cause of the large number of infantile scurvy during this period. A speaker at a Royal Society meeting in 1898 sets forth the dominant medical thinking of the day:

> "The sterilization of milk is one of the greatest advances that has been made in infant feeding . . . The most important diseases which we have to deal with among infants are the digestive disorders in summer time. The sterilization of the milk offers more advantages in checking or preventing those diseases than any other method which has, as yet, been offered . . . Is it possible that sterilization of milk may injure its nutritive properties to a slight extent . . . but the injury done by this is far outweighed by the greater advantage offered in preventing disease."

Another paper considered by the Society at the same meeting is even more emphatic:

> "It does not seem fair to put into an infant's stomach

---

[134] Thomas McKeown; The Origins of Human Disease (Basil Blackwell, 1988), 143, quoting Byden's The Impact of Civilization on the Biology of Man (Canberra, Australia: National University Press, 1970)

a food containing thousands of bacteria in each drop, these bacteria being of unknown quality and very possibly dangerous and pathogenic nature."[135]

None of this squared with the papers going back to 1894 that raw milk was known to be anti-scorbutic, a quality that was lost during sterilization. But then, which was more important? Curing infantile scurvy? Or exalting information that supported, while suppressing information which discredited, any facet of the Germ Theory, the newest cornerstone of medicine's profit model?

By 1920 there existed, however, enough epidemiological support for the idea that breast milk had a unique value to infants not obtainable from the common substitutes of the day. In the 1920 edition of the *Index Catalogue to the Library of the Surgeon-General's Office* reports were compiled from twenty-two countries, including Australia, Japan, Norway and Brazil. In communities where adult scurvy was rampant, breast-fed children showed no evidence of Barlow's. Evidence was making it clear even to critics that Barlow's in children and scurvy in adults were, in fact, the same affliction.

With the publication in 1907 of Axel Holst's famous paper on the use of the guinea pig as an animal model for studying scurvy, it would only be a matter of time before the cure for scurvy would be expressed in a way that even modern medicine's most entrenched opposition would be hard-pressed to combat.

The discovery of vitamin C, its implications and the manner in which the "cure for scurvy" is still suppressed to this day are the subject of the fourth and final section of this chapter.

The Suppression of Hypoascorbemia

"The medical profession itself took a very narrow and wrong view (of the body's need for ascorbic acid). Lack of ascorbic acid caused scurvy, so (surely) if there was no scurvy, there

[135] Carpenter, History, 164-5. Both quotes are taken from this citation.

142

*was no lack of ascorbic acid. Nothing could be clearer than this. The only trouble was that scurvy is **not** a first symptom of lack but a final collapse, a premortal syndrome, and there is a very wide gap between scurvy and full health. But nobody knows what full health is! . . . "*

Albert Szent-Gyorgi[136]
Nobel Laureate (Medicine, 1937)
Discoverer, vitamin C

"More than sixty years of research on living systems have convinced me that our body is much more nearly perfect than the endless list of ailments suggests . . . (its shortcomings) are due less to its inborn imperfections than to our abusing it."

Szent-Gyorgi[137]

"We may ask why the physicians and authorities on nutrition have remained so lacking in enthusiasm . . . there seems to have existed a feeling that the intake of vitamin C should be kept as small as possible, even though this vitamin is known to have extremely low toxicity. This attitude is, of course, proper for drugs -- substances not normally present in the human body and almost always rather highly toxic -- but it does not apply to ascorbic acid. Another factor has probably been the lack of interest of the drug companies in a natural substance that is available at a low price and cannot be patented."

Linus Pauling[138]
Nobel Laureate (Chemistry, 1954)

"Having worked as a researcher in the field, it is my contention that effective treatment for the common cold, a cure, is available, that is being ignored because of the monetary losses that would be inflicted on pharmaceutical manufacturers, professional journals, and doctors themselves."

---

[136] Stone, The Healing Factor (New York: Putnam Publishing Group, 1974), xi. The remark is made in the opening paragraph of the second Foreword. There are two in this volume: the first by Linus Pauling; the second, by Albert Szent-Gyorgyi.

[137] Ralph W. Moss, Free Radical (New York: Paragon House Publishers, 1988), 253.

[138] Linus Pauling, Vitamin C and the Common Cold (San Francisco: W. H. Freeman & Company, 1972), 4.

Douglas Gildersleeve, M.D.
as quoted by Linus Pauling[139]

Although the common narrative, as it relates to scurvy, teaches that scurvy was cured hundreds of years ago, I maintain that Irwin Stone, Linus Pauling, and Albert Szent-Gyorgyi had it right: scurvy is only the most severe development in a broader deficiency condition which Stone called "hypoascorbemia."

It is a complete sham to maintain a published Recommended Daily Allowance of 60 mg. of ascorbic acid per day, when the evidence clearly suggests that an intake that is closer to 4 to 5 grams per day, perhaps 70 to 80 times the amount that orthodox medicine, and its legions of doctors and nutritionists recommend, is closer to what is required for optimal human health. To get an idea of the incredible breadth of research that has been published demonstrating the benefits of ascorbic acid in higher doses, I have long recommended a thorough reading of Stone's work,[140] not because it is current or comprehensive, but because it is concise, compelling, and written in layman's terms. Research on higher ascorbate intakes has clearly demonstrated benefits in a wide variety of modern illnesses and conditions, from colds and other viral infections, to bacterial illnesses, heart disease, strokes, allergies, ulcers, diabetes, wounds, even shock. The range of benefits has been proven to be so broad that Stone viewed ascorbic acid not as a micronutrient, but as something close to a macronutrient. He preferred to call it "The Healing-Factor," and it is only in compiling the broad range of studies showing its many benefits that he was able to enlist the help of Linus Pauling in drawing attention to the established fact.

When living in the wild, living as gatherers of fruits and vegetables, eaten fresh with its nutrients undiminished by exposure to time, heat, or processing, most humans don't ingest 60 mg. a day of vitamin C. They ingest ascorbic acid measurable in several grams per day, and not in one or two lump sums sup-

---

[139] Ibid., 48. In a footnote on the same page, Pauling adds, "This name (Douglas Gildersleeve, M.D.) is probably a pseudonym, assumed by the author for professional reasons. I maintain this only serves to make yet another point about the 'doctors who speak out'."
[140] See: meditopia.org/biblio.htm#stone1

plementally, but gradually throughout the day as they eat small meals. Even the average gorilla in the wild ingests approximately 4 grams per day of ascorbate. With the recent emergence of civilization, but most particularly with the ascension of *Homo industrialis*, such natural living has met a terminal, maladaptive end. In its place there is now "civilized living" that leads to processed foods, while those that are fresh are aged, and those that contained heat labile ascorbate are now nutrient deficient.

In the name of progress, *Homo sapiens* have created an array of modern lifestyles, which cut across sub-cultures and socioeconomic levels, but which uniformly lend themselves to mass hypoascorbemia, which itself is but one small by-product of humankind's adventures in maladaptation."

To educate the public as to the very existence of this development would create an unfathomable diminishment in the reputation, influence, and profitability of today's medical-industrial complex.

That is why the orthodox establishment fights so hard to suppress it.

D espite the fact that vitamin C was discovered as the "cure" for scurvy, the latter recognized to be a form of avitaminosis (deficiency disease); despite the discovery of vitamin C's chemical composition (in 1937 Albert Szent-Gyorgyi was given a Nobel Prize for asborbic acid's discovery and Sir Walter Haworth for his research on its chemical structure and synthesis), the scientific establishment has impeded further discovery of its benefits for the last 70 years.

It is not remotely an exaggeration to say that ever since the discovery of vitamin C, with the further unfolding of the many conditions that improve from higher vitamin C intake, established medicine has done everything possible to downplay clinical results.

In fact, the positive results are so voluminous (when you factor out the studies where the ascorbate amounts selected for test subjects are deliberately chosen at a level too small to produce a clinical impact), that I will have to be selective in what area of application I discuss in the remainder of this chapter.

Since cancer is a major focus of my work, it would be interesting to note what discoveries have been made about vitamin C, a relatively cheap, inexpensive nutrient, and cancer.

In 1969, Dean Burk and his associates at the National Cancer Institute published a paper showing that ascorbate is highly toxic to carcinoma cells. In fact, vitamin C caused profound structural changes in the cancer cells in their lab cultures. As Stone notes, the group wrote:

> "The great advantage that ascorbates . . . possess as potential anticancer agents is that they are, like penicillin, remarkably nontoxic to normal body tissues, and they may be administered to animals in extremely large doses (up to 5 or more grams per kilogram) without notable pharmacological effects."

This finding, alone, should have been cause to bring greater resources to bear on an area of research that could bring enormous benefit to the public. What was the U.S. government's response? The Cancer Chemotherapy National Service Center, tasked with screening new cancer-killing materials, refused to include vitamin C in its testing for cancer-killing properties. Their reason? Ascorbic acid was too nontoxic to fit into their program![141]

To be fair, no one has ever suggested that vitamin C is a cure for cancer. Dr. Szent-Gyorgyi himself was resistant to any claim to quick fixes. Correction of defects may take the better part of a year, he suggested. What he did state, unequivocally -- and this is not an interpretation of clinical data, it is now hornbook physiology: vitamin C is built into "the very heart of life's

[141] Stone, The Healing Factor (Putnam Publishing Group, 1974), 94. Additionally, Pauling himself notes that although as little as 5 mg. of ascorbate "is believed" to be enough to "prevent scurvy in most people," ascorbate is so non-toxic that people have been given "as much as 150 grams, one-third of a pound, of sodium ascorbate by injection or intravenous infusion by mouth without serious side-effects." See Cancer & Vitamin C (San Francisco: W. H. Freeman & Company, 1976),100. Additionally, see Vitamin C Under Attack (Ann Arbor, Michigan: published by author, 2000), 56, where authors of a 1969 study reported that nontoxic substances "have been largely if not totally excluded from consideration in the screening program." (as cited on p. 86): "L. Benade, T. Howard, D. Burk, Synergistic killing of Ehrlich ascites carcinoma cells by ascorbic acid and 3-amino-1,2,4,-trizole. Oncology 1969, 23:33-43.

machinery . . . we are constantly building and rebuilding this machinery all the time." On this basis, Szent-Gyorgyi felt that a continuous supply of ascorbic acid was very important.

Dr. Szent-Gyorgyi, to the end of his life in 1986 at the age of 93, felt that cancer research was misdirected and was overlooking the obvious. "The blindfold search for a cure for cancer seems a hopeless waste."[142]

But as is typical of the modern medical Suppression Pattern, the vitamin C / cancer connection doesn't end here. It is not enough for modern medicine to thumb its nose at vitamin therapy and thereby destroy the lives, not to mention the pocketbooks, of its patients. The primary approved methods of cancer treatment in the West not only deny additional vitamin C at a time when the body needs it most, but they utilize immune-suppressive therapies that do just the opposite: they deplete it.[143]

The position of the orthodox medical community vis-à-vis vitamin C intake that rises above the grossest manifestations of hypoascorbemia, namely scurvy, is particularly irresponsible when one considers that for at least two generations, we have known that "all of (the impartial evidence gathered to date supports) the conclusion that vitamin C is intimately involved in cancer as well as in scurvy."[144]

Going all the way back to James Lind's autopsy reports of scurvy sufferers (1753) one finds expressions such as "all parts were so mixed up and blended together to form one mass or

[142] Free Radical (New York: Paragon House Publishers, 1988), 253-254.

[143] Andrew Weil, Ask Dr. Weil: Vitamins & Minerals (New York: Ivy Books, 1997), 12-13. I admire Andrew for his attempts to press the boundaries of orthdox medicine's stodgy resistance to those proven contributions that emanate from the "alternative community," but too often he proves to be a "company man." He has to be. Again, "respectable people are loath to rock the foundation of the very system that is itself the source of their respectability." Nonetheless, in this brief monogram, Weil's brief comments on vitamin C were fairly in accordance with recommendations of other alternative physicians. He recommends 1,000 mg. of vitamin C twice a day "at a minimum." (Yes, that's 3300% of the U.S. Recommended Daily Allowance.) And he admits that "we need more of it when exposed to toxins, infection, and chronic illness." How much? "I'd go up to 2,000 mg. three times a day." (A whopping 10,000% of the U.S. Recommended Daily Allowance. Oh my!) What isn't mentioned is that the most common forms of orthodox cancer treatment (chemotherapy and radiation) are highly toxic, so he is inadvertently admitting that if you're going to go through conventional cancer treatment, you're going to place demands on the immune system that require higher ascorbate intake to counter the more rapid depletion these treatments create. Predictably, the vast majority of oncologists don't say a word to their patients about the effects of orthodox treatment on this vital nutrient.

[144] Ewan Cameron and Linus Pauling, Cancer and Vitamin C, (Menlo Park, CA: Linus Pauling Institute of Science and Medicine; New York: W.W. Norton and Co., 1979). 99

lump that individual organs could not be identified,"[145] to which Pauling was led to comment, "(this is) surely an 18th-century morbid anatomist's graphic description of neoplastic infiltration."[146]

More recently, in 1954 and 1959 Dr. W.J. McCormick, a Canadian physician, formulated the hypothesis "that cancer is a collagen disease, secondary to a deficiency in vitamin C. He recognized that the generalized stromal change of scurvy (changes in the nature of the tissues) are identical with the local stromal changes observed in the immediate vicinity of invading neoplastic cells., and surmised that the nutrient (vitamin C) that is known to be capable of preventing such generalized changes in scurvy might have similar effects in cancer. The evidence that cancer patients are almost invariably depleted of ascorbate lent support to this view."[147]

Supportive of this position is the observation that "anemia, cachexia, extreme lassitude, hemorrhages, ulceration, susceptibility to infections, and abnormally low tissue, plasma, and leukocyte ascorbate levels, with terminal adrenal failure, are virtually identical with the premortal features of advanced human scurvy."[148]

Those who think that this observation is circumstantial are not familiar with the enormous amount of clinical work that has been done over the years supporting the benefits of orthomolecular (high dosage) vitamin C in connection with cancer. Thousands of studies exist substantiating the benefits.[149]

---

[145] Ibid., 101

[146] Ibid.

[147] Ibid.

[148] Ewan Cameron and Linus Pauling, Cancer & Vitamin C, 99-107.

[149] H.L. Newbold, M.D., Vitamin C Against Cancer (New York: Stein & Day, 1981); Sandra Goodman, Ph.D., Vitamin C: The Master Nutrient (New Canaan, CT: Keats Publishing, 1991); Dr. Emanuel Cheraskin (M.D., D.M.D.), The Vitamin C Connection (New York: Harper & Row, 1983); The Vitamin Controversy (Wichita, KS: Bio-Communications Press, 1988); and Dr. Steve Hickey and Dr. Hilary Roberts, Ascorbate: The Science of Vitamin C (Steve Hickey, 2004). Dr. Cheraskin, alone, shared in approximately 1,000 clinical experiments, eventuating

And yet every bit as compelling, are the proven benefits of increased vitamin C intake in the prevention and treatment of heart disease.

Discovery: Most Heart Attacks & Strokes Are Rooted in Vitamin C Deficiency; Dr. Linus Pauling Passes The Torch

"Never forget that you are fighting one of the most import-ant battles for human health . . . (The battle) will be long and hard."

Linus Pauling[150]

One of the most shocking demonstrations of the Suppression Pattern at work in the orthodox medical community concerns the described physiological mechanism connecting ascorbate deficiency, arteriosclerosis, strokes, and coronary heart disease. Though obviously not the sole etiological factor in all cases, what is known is that all of these conditions are initiated or worsened by ascorbal insufficiency; the correlation and caus-ative factors are well-described, as are the profit motives that prevent these facts from being widely known to the public. The role of vitamin C as a potential "anti-atherogenic" is, or should be, an important debate in medicine, since atherosclerosis "and its clinical manifestations, particularly angina pectoris, myocar-dial infarction and ischemic stroke, is the single most important cause of morbidity and mortality in the Western World."[151]

The discovery itself appears to have been properly credited by Dr. Linus Pauling to a noteworthy understudy, Dr. Matthias Rath. The discovery was so amazing, that Pauling was moved to comment before his death in 1994 that, "(You should) never for-

---

in about 80 published papers in the technical literature. The Vitamin Controversy: Questions & Answers (Wichita, KS: Bio-Communications Press, 1988), 183-193.

[150] Matthias Rath, M.D., Ten Years that Changed Medicine Forever (Santa Clara, CA: MR Publishing, Inc., 2001), 15 (Introduction). The quote is, according to Dr. Rath, a comment that Linus Pauling made to him in 1994 in one of the last conversations before Pauling's death. This author, knowing Pauling through stories from his own mentor, Dr. Russell Jordan, believes the quote to be most probably accurate.

[151] Rath, Ten Years, Ibid., 72.

get that your discovery is one of the most important discoveries in medicine ever."[152]

That heart disease and circulatory conditions were connected to a lack of vitamin C had long been observed. How could they not be? The same breakdown in tissue structure observed in scurvy could be observed in all of the above mentioned diseases, only it was made manifest in the circulatory system. Signposts were occasionally reported, such as the observation that vitamin C converts cholesterol into water-soluble bile acids.[153] Still, no one was able to definitively put all the causative factors involving vitamin deficiency and heart disease together until Rath.

Before Rath, no one was able to provide a viable explanation for why animals don't get heart attacks, but people do.[154] Surely, it would seem likely that someone would have come along in the interim between Szent-Gyorgyi's discovery of ascorbate as the "cure for scurvy" and Rath's emergence, someone to press this issue. After all, by the time Rath started speaking out, with Pauling's backing and assistance, it had been well known for most of the 20th century that one of the primary differences in the physiology between animals, which don't get heart attacks, and *Homo sapiens*, who do, is that humans can easily suffer from ascorbate deficiency, whereas most animals do not. They make their own.

As can be expected, Rath has been the subject of numerous ad hominem attacks, and equally predictable is his branding as

---

[152] Rodolfo Paoletti, Vitamin C: the state of the art in disease prevention sixty years after the Nobel Prize (Italia, Milano: Springer-Verlag, 1998), 59. -- citing AJ Gotto, AJ Farmer (1988). Risk factors for coronary disease. In: Braunwald E. ed. Heart disease: a textbook of cardiovascular medicine, 3rd ed. (Philadelphia: Saunders), 1153-1190. As an aside, the deficiencies in many of the studies cited by B. Frei, and similar studies funded by orthodoxy, are addressed in Vitamin C Under Attack: Unfair trials bombard high-dose benefits [Stephen Sheffrey, 2000]. A thorough reading angers the impartial reader on the mere basis of outrageous suppressive tactics used.

[153] I was first exposed to the finding of Jacobus Rinse, Ph.D., in Dr. Morton Walker's How Not to Have a Heart Attack (New York: New Viewpoints/Vision Books, 1980), 116. Note that even in the work of Rinse and Morton, dealing with the effort to perfect a dietary regimen for heart disease patients, there can be observed the same tendency, a la James Lind, to complicate the matter and pull it into the realm of ineffectiveness.

[154] To accent his findings in this area, Rath even titled his book on the subject, Why Animals Don't Get Heart Attacks . . . But People Do!. (Fremont, CA: MR Publishing, Inc., 2003). A well-written and less technical treatise on this subject, however, is covered in his Ten Years.

a quack by the orthodox medical community.[155] He has been engaged in extensive litigation, criminal and civil,[156] which is standard operating procedure for any one who threatens the orthodox system with therapeutic systems or products that threaten profits in the orthodox system (high profile cases immediately coming to mind include Rife, Reich, Hoxsey, Wright, Koch, Naessens, and Burzynski).[157] But the relevant criteria with respect to Rath's work are not whether his antics have been respectable, his actions self-serving, i.e., he commits the unpardonable sin of actually selling his own brand of vitamins, or the delivery of his message less than elegant.

No, as contrasted with the orthodox medical system which loathes scientifically objective, evidence based research, the most relevant question with respect to Rath's work is: "Is what he says objectively true?"

Rath's initiation into the world of corrupt medicine goes all the way back to his last year in medical school when his father died of a heart attack. After graduation, Rath was hired on with a research project, sponsored by the German Research Foundation. The goal? To identify the mechanisms by which cholesterol and other fat particles "get stuck" inside blood vessel walls. By the time Rath began his research, cholesterol-lowering drugs were already a billion dollar a year industry, so there were plenty of research grants to go around to try and help support the "high cholesterol" juggernaut. At that time, medical research in cardiology was focussed on "bad cholesterol" or low-density lipoproteins. Not only was LDL acknowledged by medical orthodoxy

---

[155] By way of example, see his treatment in the online *Skeptic's Dictionary*, skepdic.com/rath.html, or Dr. Stephen Barrett's commentary in: chealth.canoe.ca/columns.asp?columnistid=3&articleid=2854. Obviously, it would take a separate book to do justice to the ongoing debate between Rath and his critics, and for the record, I do not agree with Rath on every point. By way of example, my belief is that although vitamin C contributes to an effective "anti-cancer" regimen, I would agree with Szent-Georgyi himself that it is not an effective treatment, after the fact. Rath crosses the line and says it can be, which I believe overstates the case and threatens the strength and legitimacy of his other statements and findings. For the purposes of this discussion, however, I wish to narrow the focus to the relationship between vitamin C and the above stated circulatory ailments.

[156] See: en.wikipedia.org/wiki/Matthias_Rath

[157] A sampling of this suppressive "legal" warfare on therapeutics that prove too threatening to vested interests can be found in Dan Haley's, Politics in Healing (Maryland, DC: Potomac Valley Press, 2000).

as the main factor causing atherosclerotic plaques, and therefore a primary and direct causative agent in the case of most heart attacks and strokes, but research funds were fueled by Big Pharma's lust to have yet another problem to fix.

Rath's career path took a dramatic turn when he began to question the role of a newly discovered risk factor in heart disease: "lipoprotein(a)." What followed is best told in Rath's own words:

" . . . Our own studies involving more than ten thousand research data and measurements left no doubt that in order for the 'bad cholesterol' to stick inside the blood vessel wall, it needs the biological adhesive lipoprotein(a). The results established together with my colleagues were an important milestone towards the understanding about the nature of cardiovascular disease. What we found was that everywhere cholesterol was deposited in the blood vessel wall there was the biological adhesive tape 'apo(a)'. It was clear that the deposits were not dependent on the amount of cholesterol but on the amount of 'adhesive' present in the body. At that point we did not know that this, also, would only be the partial truth and that heart attacks and strokes would turn out to be primarily the result of vitamin deficiencies.

"These discoveries on the 'sticky cholesterol' lipoprotein(a) were so new, that the American Heart Association (AHA) did not accept the presentation of these data at their annual convention in 1988. They simply did not believe it. It was not until one year later that the AHA invited me to give a presentation at their annual convention in Anaheim in November, 1998. At the same time the AHA accepted these findings in their official journal, *Arteriosclerosis*.

"Lipoprotein(a) turned out to be a ten times greater risk factor than cholesterol. More importantly, no drugs, not even cholesterol-lowering drugs were able to lower this risk factor in the blood. But by far the most intriguing question about this new risk factor for heart attacks and strokes was the fact that it was only found in humans -- but rarely in other living species.

"It was back in 1987 when I made the following decisive discovery that should change medicine forever: The sticky risk factor lipoprotein(a) was only found in humans and other species that had lost the ability to manufacture their own vitamin C. Apparently, there was an inverse relationship between the lipoprotein(a) molecule and the deficiency in vitamin C. I immediately started to do experiments on vitamin C and lipoprotein(a) and later conducted a clinical pilot study where vitamin C was shown to lower elevated lipoprotein(a) levels.

"Imagine the year 1987, vitamin C was considered quackery and no reputable medical institution was even willing to consider conducting clinical studies with vitamins. The knowledge about vitamin C as a carrier of cellular bio-energy was entirely lost in the medical education, and patentable pharmaceutical drugs were considered the only form of acceptable medicine . ."[158]

After having his findings reported in *Arteriosclerosis*, Rath sought out the counsel of Linus Pauling, who, subsequent to their initial meetings, recognized the enormous value of Rath's work and created a place for him at his marginally funded research organization, The Linus Pauling Institute.

Rath had already successfully established the principle behind the vitamin C - lipoprotein(a) connection and its relation to heart disease, but he needed something more definitive. He needed "more scientific proof." As so many of his fellow 20th century researchers in vitamin C research had done, he used guinea pigs to conduct the next phase of his investigation. He began with a theory that followed naturally from his findings to date: that guinea pigs, which, as we discussed early in this chapter, share the human genetic disorder of having virtually no vitamin C manufacturing capability in vivo, would devel-

[158] Matthias Rath, M.D., Ten Years that Changed Medicine Forever (Santa Clara, CA: MR Publishing, Inc., 2001), 56-58, in section marked, "How I got interested in cardiovascular research."

op arteriosclerotic deposits once they were put on a vitamin C deficient diet. He further conjectured that if one analyzed the "plaster cast" that was deposited in the arterial walls, he would find the sticky lipoprotein(a) fat molecules.

If medical science resembled anything close to a quest for truth; if profit motive were not the largest, mightiest, heaviest sphere in the scientist's constellation, whose gravitational field iss so great that it warps the orbits of all other objects in Scientism's galaxy, Rath might have had a chance. The truth would have leaked out and been embraced by an honorable medical tradition whose primary consideration was the welfare of its patients (i.e., customers, victims, and gullible 'tards') and not its own self-enrichment. But, alas, such is and was, not the case. As it turned out, Rath was able to show that a deficiency in vitamin C, which in humans would equate to levels far above the FDA's "Recommended Daily Allowance," caused a weakening of blood vessels, similar to scurvy. The fatty deposits, indeed, were composed of cholesterol, lipoprotein(a), and other risk factors in the blood. Cardiovascular disease developed "as an inevitable response of our body to repair the blood vessel walls weakened by vitamin deficiency."[159]

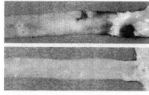

TOP: *Guinea pigs receiving too little vitamin C in the diet develop cardiovascular disease.* **BOTTOM:** *Guinea pigs receiving optimum vitamin C have clean arteries. Orthodox medicine, in its collusion with the pharmaceutical industry's multi-billion dollar cholesterol drug business, has no choice but to suppress this finding and its many implications. To have the public understand the underlying cause of coronary heart disease would cause the collapse of a huge profit center for organized medicine in the West.*

So how has Rath's miraculous finding been received by organized medicine? Was it received in terms that were anything close to Pauling's words to him? – "But no matter what happens, never forget that your discovery is one of the most important

[159] Ibid., 68-69.

discoveries in medicine ever."

Of course not.

Rath and Pauling, for all their collective genius, were still not able to see through the common narrative. Yes, they could see that, to use Rath's words, the medical community was guided by "economic greed of stratospheric proportions,"[160] and yet they held onto irrational notions of science's commitment to the quest for objective truth, like seasoned political scientists who, despite all evidence to the contrary, refuse to jettison the common narrative and accept that democracy is a co-opted tool of plutocratic power and has nothing to do with fulfilling the will of the people, but rather was created by the elite to give the people, the plebs, the illusion that they are the ones in charge.

What meaning could people of the caliber of a Pauling or a Rath, or anyone else who sacrifices themself in the quest to uncover life's deeper secrets, find in a world where science is recognized as little more than a co-optation tool for powerful, moneyed interests? Very little, it would seem.

And so, Pauling and Rath plodded along, achieving success in having their newest finding published in the *Proceedings of the National Academy of Sciences* in 1990.

The following August (1990), Pauling and Rath attended an arteriosclerosis meeting in Venice, Italy, where "the entire cream of medical researchers and medical opinion leaders in the area of cholesterol and heart disease were present."[161] Rath gave his presentation, noting in just a few sentences the discovery about lipoprotein(a), vitamin C deficiency and heart disease. How did the conference respond?

"From that moment on, the conference was not the same. The mood changed to that of a funeral . . ."[162]

Even within Pauling's very own institute, the mood termed somber. When certain researchers openly professed a desire to work with Rath on what, on the surface, appeared to be an exciting new area of scientific research, they were dissuaded by

[160] Ibid., 72.
[161] Ibid., 74.
[162] Ibid., 75.

their co-workers. "If you work with Dr. Rath, you will ruin your career," they were advised.[163]

Pauling and Rath should have gotten the hint, but they didn't. They continued under the illusion that science operates on a level playing field. After successfully publishing twice in the *Proceedings of the National Academy of Sciences*, Pauling himself attempted a third publication, under the title "Solution to the puzzle of human cardiovascular disease: its primary cause is ascorbate deficiency leading to a deposition of lipoprotein(a) and fibrin/fibrinogen in the vascular wall." After some mutually agreed modifications, the editor in chief, in a move that violated the rules of the academy, decided to send the manuscript to reviewers. They rejected the publication of the landmark paper with the argument, "Since there is no puzzle of cardiovascular disease, there can be no solution to this puzzle."[164]

Translation: "Alright, guys, you've had your fun. But now it's time for you to get your heads screwed on straight. Are you really that nuts? Do you have any idea what kind of economic impact our industry would suffer if this kind of material were to be positively received by common lay persons? Did you really think you would go very far with findings that would singularly torpedo the multi-billion dollar a year cholesterol lowering drug market, and injure many of our own personal incomes, as well? Get with the program!"

This is not to say that the medical-industrial complex did not at least attempt to profit from the Pauling/Rath finding. They did. On the only terms they knew how: with criminal price fixing practices on vitamin raw materials,[165] while simultaneously creating the "Codex Alimentarius" on the international level, which would ban any natural health claims in all U.N. member countries -- which is to say, throughout the world. (Interestingly, the decisive U.N. Committee on nutritional supplements is headed by the German government. "No wonder -- Germany is the world's largest export country for pharmaceutical products."

[163] Ibid., 75.
[164] Ibid., 76.
[165] Ibid., 73.

[166] And this battle is still ongoing.

Not everyone who has studied the "vitamin C research suppression phenomenon" fails to initially see through the common narrative. One such individual is Dr. Stephen Sheffrey, who self-published <u>Vitamin C Under Attack: Unfair trials bombard high-dose benefits</u>[167] in 2000. A dentist by trade with a keen interest in nutrition (like Weston Price),[168] Sheffrey decided to write about the suppressed benefits of high-dose vitamin C intake after he himself had taken 10 grams or more daily for several years, and 100 to 200 grams daily during signs of illness. He knew from personal experience and his own research that most of the warnings published on the dangers of high-dose vitamin C were overblown, if not deliberately misleading.

The author doesn't present his material without covering the necessary, well-established caveats. Most notably, orthomolecular intake levels of vitamin C (say, in excess of one or two grams at a time) are found to cause discomforting side effects with 20% of the population: diarrhea, intestinal discomfort, chapped lips, etc.[169] Some of those in the "20% camp" are able to negotiate their way through a high-dose regimen, but many are not.

But what 80% of the general world population that would benefit from higher ascorbal intakes are subjected to is massive misinformation. Sheffrey divides his study according to the tactic used to scare the public away from higher dosing: deliberately deceptive trial studies, inadequate dosing, faked data on "side effects and safety," etc.

On occasion, even in the face of well-orchestrated efforts to discredit higher dosages of a human nutrient that would adversely affect pharmaceutical sales, the truth gets through. Example: the National Cancer Institute's admission that of 46 epidemiological studies it examined, in 33 there was evidence of "statis-

---

[166] Ibid., 127.

[167] See: meditopia.org/biblio.htm#sheffrey1

[168] See: meditopia.org/biblio.htm#w_price1

[169] Stephen Sheffrey, <u>Vitamin C Under Attack: Unfair Trials Bombard High-Dose Benefits</u> (Ann Arbor, Michigan: published by author, 2000), 198.

tically significant treatment of cancers of the mouth, esophagus, stomach, pancreas, breast, anus, colon, and cervix."[170] But the vast majority of studies on the benefits of higher dose vitamin C, funded as they are by vested interests, utilize a consistent, predictable, menu of disinformation methods to prevent the public from realizing the benefits.

Summary: Hypoascorbemia and Cancer
As Metaphors For a Dysfunctional Art

Vitamin C is more than a singular molecular entity with known nutritional benefits. It is a metaphor for the natural world -- largely existing where foods that contain it are fresh, raw, and uncooked. It quickly diminishes in potency as it is removed from that world, and it is scorned and scientifically libeled because of the threat that a more complete understanding of its function and use would bring to moneyed interests. Its absence from the diet brings maladaptation and disease, not in an abrupt low-dosage-induced burst of scurvy as modern medicine would have us believe, but in gradual stages as we deviate from what nature has predetermined as optimal.

This is hypoascorbemia.

Cancer, like vitamin C, is also a metaphor, but in this instance, it stands for the converse: deviation from the natural world. A hodge-podge of loosely connected ailments, the very word itself represents the attempt to redefine nature and define a set of conditions from which an unsuspecting public can be bilked and not cured.

Studied fully and completely, we could, if so inclined, see the irreparable mess that medicine has become with just the study of these two metaphors, sitting as they do at opposite ends of a thorough gaze of civilization.

But then, we would lose the perspective that comes with comprehending our past, that comes with seeing the inevitability of that with which we currently live.

---

[170] Lynne McTaggart ed., The Cancer Handbook: What's Really Working (Bloomingdale, Illinois: Vital Health Publishing, 1997), 147.

Over the preceding pages I have reviewed my own personal experiences with approaches to cancer that met the "suppression pattern," and examined one of the most notable cases in recent history, one difficult to dismiss by even modern medicine's most staunch defenders.

In describing the "suppression pattern," I have identified a recurring social symptom, but where is the cause of the disease to be found?

This, I believe, as stated early in this chapter, extends far back in history, to the earliest stirrings of the known, historical civilizations. If there is a global "operating system" that has set the tone for humanity's course over the past 6,000 or so years (and I believe there is an abundance of evidence that there is), then have the cultural mimetics of this operating system made the medical atrocities we now witness inevitable?

Indeed, they have

More importantly, our quest leads us to a place where a clarity emerges as to "Civilization's End" as we know it. We can reach a point where we may understand why the system cannot be repaired.

It can only be destroyed and then be rebuilt.

In seeing this we can reach a point in our exploration where we, to borrow from Spencer, have a cognition of humanity, and it is not so much that we will not want history, rather, having distilled its essence, we will no longer need it.

Bibliographical Addendum to Chapter 6

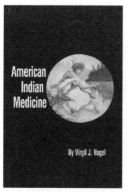

The following books, with my commentary, appeared in the original draft of Chapter 4 of *Meditopia*, in the chapter right-hand sidebar.

Because of the relevance to this and forthcoming chapters, this material is provided below:

The opening quote for this chapter is taken from Vogel's American Indian Medicine,[1] and is part of the University of Oklahoma Press's "The Civilization of American Indian Series."

One is struck by the widespread co-opting of indigenous American knowledge of the healing arts by established medicine, including its inclusion of large numbers of medicinal herbs in early *Materia Medica*, only to discard this treasure trove of medicinal knowledge once more profitable pharmaceuticals were developed.

The documentation that supports this historical phenomenon is voluminous and undeniable today, but even at the founding of the American republic, the reigning elite dared not admit their reliance on "Indian medicine" to treat their patients, a fact that is rooted in the respect that early colonists had for the healing techniques of the indigenous peoples. That physicians of that day could not even be honest with themselves is made obvious by the writings of Dr. Benjamin Rush (one of the signers of the Declaration of Independence), who was moved to write, "We have no discoveries in the materia medica to hope for from the Indians of North America," because "it would be a reproach to our schools of physic if modern physicians were not more successful than the Indians even in the treatment of their own diseases."[2] Such concern was well-founded, since it was the med-

---

[1] Vogel J. Virgil; American Indian Medicine (Norman, Oklahoma: University of Oklahoma Press, 1990)
[2] Ibid., 63

ical establishment that even well into the 18th century was still treating patients with mercury, blood-letting, and calomel; later to be replaced by today's preferred methods of poisoning the patient: chemotherapy, pharmaceuticals, and radiation therapy.

Those who have taken the time to study the historical record understand that modern medicine was largely the domain of "barber surgeons" before Indian influence.[3] Moreover, modern pharmacology has been shown to be largely a perversion of aboriginal phytopharmacology.

Thomas Jefferson's Criticism of Medicine More Valid Today And For The Same Reasons!

Thomas Jefferson warned about the dangers of the medical establishment and his criticisms are more valid today than when he voiced them. Vogel points out that Jefferson echoed a widely held sentiment in his day when he wrote to Dr. Caspar Wister, then professor of anatomy and surgery at the University of Pennsylvania, how he abhorred the changes in medical doctrines, "alleging that medical theories 'succeed one another like the shifting figures of a magic lantern. I believe we may safely affirm that the inexperienced and presumptious band of medical tyros let loose upon the world, destroys more of human life in one year, than all the Robinhoods, Cartouches, and Macheaths do in a century. It is in this part of medicine that I wish to see reform, an abandonment of hypothesis for sober facts, the first degree of value set on clinical observation, and the lowest on visionary theories.'"[4]

Put more simply, Jefferson was saying, "Let's forget all this theoretical nonsense. Medicine should, first and foremost, be about what works for the patient!" To borrow a phrase from

[3] Ibid., 112.
[4] Ibid., 114.

our own time, Jefferson was an advocate in the 18th century of the very thing that modern medicine fights hardest against in the 21st -- that is, clear and convincing benefit to the patient over and above the alternatives it attempts to suppress.

Jefferson's sentiments have been echoed by many famous American intellectuals. Oliver Wendell Holmes noted that the American medical mind "has clearly tended to extravagance in remedies, as in everything else." He despised its tendency towards over medication, adding that "nature heals most diseases without help from the pharmaceutic(al) art," calling medicine "a colossal system of self-deception . . ."[5]

Digressing from Vogel's work for just a moment, for those who might feel agitated by Jefferson's comment or think that it doesn't bear validity on the state of health care today, I offer my next exhibit. This is an important reference because it shows the degree to which modern medicine is devoid of any commitment to what is evidence-based.

The cover of the May 29, 2006 issue of *Business Week* announced a lead article, entitled "Medical Guesswork: From heart surgery to prostate care, the medical industry knows little about which treatments really work."[6]

The article itself was about the findings of David Eddy, M.D., a heart surgeon turned Ph.D. in mathematics and health care economist.

"The problem is that we don't know what we are doing," (Dr. Eddy) says. Even today, with a high-tech health-care system that costs the nation $2 trillion a year, there is little or no

[5] Ibid., 114-115.

[6] "Medical Guesswork: From heart surgery to prostate care, the medical industry knows little about which treatments really work," *Business Week*, May 29, 2006, 73-79

evidence that many widely used treatments and procedures actually work better than various cheaper alternatives.

Dr. Eddy's supporters, drawing from medical industry statistics, claim that the portion of medicine that has been proven effective is still "outrageously low -- in the range of 20% to 25%." *Business Week* quoted Dr. Stephen C. Schoenbaum, executive vice-president of the Commonwealth Fund and former president of Harvard Pilgrim Health Care, Inc., as stating that, "We don't have the evidence [that treatments work], and we are not investing very much in getting the evidence."[7]

Although Dr. Eddy emphasizes in the *Business Week* article that "what's required is a revolution called 'evidence-based medicine," it isn't capable of pointing out the obvious: it isn't possible for modern medicine to become 'evidence-based.' To preach this message to is demonstrate a lack of understanding about what modern medicine is: an organizational structure devoted to protecting higher profit therapies and treatments, while suppressing more effective, lower profit alternatives.

Modern medicine had, from its inception, this basic modus operandi hard-wired into the very fabric of its being. To move in the direction of "evidence-based medicine" would destroy the very means by which orthodox medicine is able to fund its competitive advantage. Dr. Eddy understands what's wrong with medicine (to this extent), but he fails to understand the economic and political dynamic that is the cornerstone of the industry in which he works.

To come to this understanding, he would have to be willing to step outside his industry's "common narrative." He can't do that. He's a respected physician. And respected physicians are

---

[7] *Business Week*, Ibid. All other quotations of Dr. David Eddy that follow in this chapter come from this same *Business Week* article.

loath to question a system which is the very source of their respectability.

A comparison of Jefferson's remarks with Eddy's findings provides insight into what's really wrong with medicine, the fact that orthodox medicine's proponents understand the problem, and why its defects are not fixable.

Since the early 1980s, Dr. David Eddy has been using the expression, evidence-based medicine, and his is an extraordinary, professional journey to come to many of the very same conclusions I did without working inside orthodox medicine.

Eddy comes from a family of four generations of doctors. He went to medical school in the 1970s; "picked cardiac surgery," he admits, "because it was . . . the glamour field." He tells a story of asking questions as a young physician, questions as to what evidence existed that certain treatments really worked. This, in turn, set him on a journey where he discovered that most treatments were based on "rules and traditions," and not on scientific evidence.

Still not content with these early findings, Eddy decided to use advanced mathematics and statistics to help make treatment decisions more reliable and "help bring logic and rationality to the medical system." He went back to Stanford to get a Ph.D. in a mathematically intense Ph.D. program in the Engineering-Economics Systems Department.

While going for his Ph.D. in math, Eddy got a job working at the legendary Xerox Corp.'s Palo Alto Research Center, where he created a program to model cancer screening. His Ph.D. thesis in 1980 made front-page news. The findings? That annual chest x-rays and yearly Pap smears for women were a waste of money; though he missed the underlying point: they aren't a waste of money for the people who matter: those in the medical field who administer them.

Continuing with his improbable story of rational disconnect, Eddy won the most prestigious award in the field of operations research, the Frederick W. Lanchester prize, causing the American Cancer Society to slightly alter its guidelines. Later he was appointed a full professor at Stanford, followed by an appointment as chairman of the Center for Health Policy Research & Education at Duke University. Over the past 26 years he has, repeatedly, passionately, compellingly, and over a broad range of ailments, shown that medicine, more times than not, acts not in accordance with what is best for the patient, but what is best for those who provide treatment.

But he still cannot confront the obvious. He cannot breach the very cornerstone of modern medicine: that it is born of exploitation, of political and economic asymmetry between doctor and patient, of monopolistic opportunism and captive markets, of medical tax collector and victim. If Eddy's advice were ever embraced by orthodox medicine, it would surely crash under the weight of its own inherent inability to provide what is in the best interest of the public's health. Modern medicine is, therefore, non-reformable; because the extinguishment of corrective feedback loops is built into the very fabric of its existence. If it were ever "evidence-based," it wouldn't be conventional medicine as we know it. It would be an entity we would scarcely recognize.

These are lines that Dr. Eddy simply cannot cross.

"I endorse this therapy even today for I have, in fact, cured my own cancer, the original site of which was the lower bowel, through Essiac alone."[8]

So wrote Dr. Charles Brusch, M.D., the personal physician of U.S. President John F. Kennedy; but then he was only one of many thousands of patients who claimed that Essiac cured their cancer. This should strike few as surprising. Its primary ingredients show a remarkable similarity to Hox-

sey's formula [in the case of Essiac, it is burdock (*Arctium lappa*), sheep sorrel (*Acetosella vulgaris*), turkey rhubarb *(Rheum*

---

[8] Cynthia Olsen, Essiac: A Native Herbal Cancer Remedy (Pagosa Springs, Colorado: Kali Press, 1996), 2.

palmatum), and slippery elm (*Ulmus fulva*)][9] in terms of its underlying botanically-based nutrients.

Nurse Caisse, the Canadian nurse who took this old Ojibwa Indian formula and made it popular, claimed a success rate of close to 80%, the same figure used by Nurse Mildred Nelson, who ran the "Hoxsey" clinic in Mexico for many years.

If actual success rates were even half this and a critical mass of patients in the West were aware of its benefits over the dismal rates of high-cost, conventional therapies, it would cause the collapse of a huge sector within the billion dollar "disease care" industry throughout the First World.

The governments of this world who are married to these powerful interests have so constructed political, economic, educational, and mass communications within society to ensure that this doesn't happen. So the medical "killing fields" continue unabated.

If there is no evidence that cancer is (at least in part) a nutritional deficiency disease, then why go to so much trouble to suppress the findings?

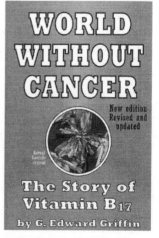

Does the answer have anything to do with the fact that if easily available nutrients were discovered that were effective in the treatment of cancer, and a critical mass of the citizenry were to discover this, the economic collapse of an entire trillion dollar health care system might ensue?

Even though laetrile and other forms of vitamin B17 therapies don't work for a substantial number of cancer patients, there is sufficient benefit to a large enough number that patients should be encouraged to examine this option.

If even one patient in ten obtains relief, the public should be made aware of it. As it is, Jason Vale documented a much higher percentage.

[9] Ibid., 45-54.

166

The response from the medical community and the mobsters who do their bidding at the U.S. FDA.?

Send him to prison!

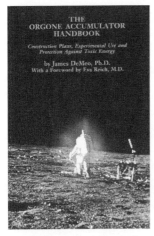

I discuss Wilhelm Reich and orgone energy elsewhere in this book, but I quote from James DeMeo's book in this chapter. It is one of the few simple, easy-to-read instruction manuals that show you how to make your own orgone accumulator.

I recommend this book because it includes a quick, historical summary of Reich's work and life, which ended in Lewisburg Federal Penitentiary, where "he died in 1957. His death in prison occurred two weeks prior to his parole date, at a time when he was happily anticipating his freedom, and a life in Switzerland with his new wife."[10]

James T. Kimball documents torture and killings in the Federal penal system, and based on what I saw myself in Federal prison in Beaumont. Texas, I have no doubt that select inmates are targeted for extermination.

It is easy to see that little has changed since Reich's death in 1957. There is every reason to believe that Wilhelm Reich was subjected to the highest level of suppression.

He was assassinated.

While I'm on the subject of suppressed electro-medicine, another monograph worth examining is the 1966 release of New Light on Therapeutic Energies by Mark L. Gallert, M.D., M. Sc. (Wilhelm Reich gets coverage in this volume, too,[11] as does Royal Rife[12]). It is amazing the number of unread books that

[10] James DeMeo, The Orgone Accumulator Handbook (Ashland, Oregon: Natural Energy Works 1999), 7.
[11] Mark L. Gallert, New Light on Therapeutic Energies (London: James Clarke & Co., Ltd. 1966), 57.
[12] Ibid., 51.

recount the incredible techniques that have been carefully document-ed that provide, in each of their re-spective niches, a measure of health benefit, at a much lower cost, than their conventional medical equiva-lents.

New Light on Therapeutic Energies

Compiled and summarized by

MARK L. GALLERT

One of the more amazing sto-ries in this work, which I had not seen well-documented elsewhere, concerned Dinshah Ghadiali and his use of Chromo-Therapy. Those who are familiar with color therapy know well its healing prop-erties, which, in the modern era were first made popular in 1877 with the publishing of Blue and Red Light, or Light and Its Rays as Medicine.[13] But it was Ghadiali who took compiled decades of research on light therapy and published -- in three volumes, no less -- his Spectro-Chrome-Metry Encyclopedia[14] in 1933, now out of print and extremely rare. Dinshah taught color ther-apy to thousands, including many doctors, and developed var-ious types of color-lamp equipment on which he obtained U.S. patents.

Modern medicine doesn't mind using sections of the elec-tromagnetic scale above and below visible light to burn and ra-diate their patients at high cost, but it won't allow the public to be educated in the very inexpensive way in which non-toxic, visible light rays can be used to heal.

The biggest reason for having Ghadiali's work suppressed, however, was the devastating implications of his conclusions. All visible colors have a vibratory rate in the range of 436 to 731 trillion oscillations per second. All elements (including, ob-viously, those making up the human body) have spectral lines

---

[13] Seth Pancoast, Blue and Red Light: Or, Light and Its Rays as Medicine; Showing That Light Is the Original and Sole Source of Life, as It Is the Source of All the Physical and Vital Forces in Nature; and That Light is Nature's Own and Only Remedy for Disease (Australia: Wentworth Press, Reprint, 2016).

[14] Dinshah Ghadiali, Spectro-Chrome-Metry Encyclopedia, (Malaga, NJ: Dinshah Health Society, 1997).

within that range, as well. Ghadiali was able to show that it is preferable to apply the color rays representative of chemicals rather than to treat with the chemicals or elements themselves in pharmaceutical form.

His arguments were well-thought out and compelling: "Thousands of drugs are used in medical practice. Is it wise to dump so many into the human body when they were not included in the natural composition of the body? . . . For example, there is no perceptible quantity of mercury in the human composition, yet this poison is administered in large quantities by doctors for syphilis and other ailments [editor: since Ghadiali's time, mercury has been employed in the amalgam used by dentists, to say nothing of its unscrupulous inclusion in vaccines] . . . Medicine ignores wholesale, the fundamental chemistry of the human body -- pouring into it many drugs containing compounds not found in the body, or in quantities far in excess of their natural proportion in the body. No part, not built for functioning in a machine, can be shackled into it without upsetting its rhythm. Chemicals are live potencies; their atoms have attractions and repulsions, and to endeavor to introduce haphazard inorganic metals into an organic machine, is like feeding a baby with steel tacks to make it strong." *(emphasis added)*

Because of his combined punch, exposing the cracks in the very foundations of modern pharmacology, together with a

cheap therapeutic approach that effectively treated a host of ailments, the medical elite made sure that Ghadiali was relegated to the dustbin of history.

The parallels existing between the "mythology" of whistleblowers (who report organizational malfeasance) and that of organized medicine are numerous and form the backbone of this section's content.[15]

[15] C. Fred Alford, Whistleblowers: Broken Lives and Organizational Power (Ithaca, New York: Cornell University Press; 2001), 3.

The standard story line that a brave, high-minded individual fights a soulless corporation or government entity, is persecuted, and yet triumphs in the end, is seductive and pervasive.

Here's the parallel story line by organized medicine and its military arm at the U.S. Food & Drug Administration: brave, high-minded medical authorities fight soulless, alternative practitioners and their allies who are only out to make a buck and bill you for their quack medicine. The quacks may win temporarily, but ultimately organized medicine wins and justice prevails. Hurray for the good guys!

Sound familiar?

It's complete rubbish.

Dr. Peter Rost (<u>The Whistleblower: Confessions of a Healthcare Hitman</u>) is a good example of a whistleblower who has yet to "hear his own story."[16] His situation is worth examining, first, because most of his professional findings are consistent with the current volume, but secondly, because he has had one of the best outcomes of a whistleblower I have ever heard: as a result of disclosing criminal activities by his employer,

THE WHISTLEBLOWER
CONFESSIONS OF A HEALTHCARE HITMAN
by Peter Rost MD

first Pharmacia, then Pfizer, he got what most whistleblowers only dream of: plenty of time to testify on Capital Hill [sic - mine], media exposure by the tonnage, accolades and words of praise from legislators, mainstream journalists and thousands of adoring fans, and honorable mention on too many Internet blogs to mention. The outcome? (Keep in mind this is about as good as it gets). He got slandered, then demoted, then fired by his employer. His book sits at #2,300 on Amazon -- admittedly better than Alford's #103,000 rating, but still a far cry from his paying all the bills. The Department of Justice has refused to take his highly meritorious case, and he's without medical insurance

---

[16] Peter Rost, <u>The Whistleblower</u> (Brooklyn, NY: Soft Skull Press).

(says he can't afford it), unemployed, and will probably never work in the pharmaceutical industry again. Okay, my mistake, maybe his life is ending on a upbeat note.) And the cause for which he made this great sacrifice? The right of U.S. citizens to have drug reimportation? Whatever happened to that?

Nothing.

The very goal for which Rost gave up everything is not one inch closer to becoming a reality.

The book itself ends reviling the current system as "not what our founding fathers envisioned," a slide from a democracy in to a "kleptocracy," and offers a prediction of the coming of a second American revolution. He, of course, fails to see that the current system is a result of the first revolution, or that the current system is exactly along the lines of what the Founding Fathers envisioned: plenty of class stratification, just as they intended.

Living on $13,000 a year unemployment, instead of his original $600,000 a year salary as a V.P. of Pfizer, Rost is one of the few whistleblowers who will tell you that "he'd do it again." (And, yes, I question the 84% figure in a "study of 233 whistleblowers" who say they would blow the whistle again. So opens Rost's book.)

Our libraries are filled with books that touch upon the fraud, greed, and corruption that saturate modern civilization at every level. The present volume touches upon that slice of the pie where the saturation impinges on health care. And even to this point the reader can see that my approach is more reformatory -- at least as it relates to working with a civilized, social structure. So are most of these other forementioned works. What is sought is a complete transformation; not across the board annihilation. Or, to put it another way, the sweeping away of an unfixable system of medical care is not the same as advocating the destruction of civilization in toto. Few health care reformers would sign on to this. Not so with the anarcho-primitivists, for whom I believe John Zerzan is currently the most eloquent spokesman.[17] For them reform is out of the question. You cannot have transformation of civilization without co-optation. So why would you even attempt it? Civilization, when examined with a cool, unbiased mind has brought nothing positive qualitatively to human evolution that rises above the life quality of early hunter gatherers; even worse, its contribution is socially and ecologically subtractive in the extreme. Not just our civilization.

Any civilization.

While the rest of us wrestle with issues of transformation, the anarchists have already made up their minds. They've thrown in the towel.

Reformers, like me, are naive, they would say.

I take issue with the anarchists on several fronts, but I am far more predisposed to give them the respect they deserve than are my brethren in the reformatory community. In fact, I go much farther: I do not believe that you can examine the reform of health care without taking into account the weight of their arguments. They bring a "gravitas," a hard edge to their polemics, backed by a strong, factual foundation, that makes it difficult for

thinking people to dismiss them out of hand. I have recommended the work of Zerzan to all of my associates, for I feel that if the positive goals addressed by the anarchists do not find themselves in the calculus of a final solution to our current crisis, the result will be temporary, co-optable patches that only delay the

---

[17] The book cited is John Zerzan's <u>Running on Emptiness: The Pathology of Civilization</u> (Los Angeles: Feral House, 2002); also pictured is the cover from a prior work that covers his major theses: <u>Against Civilization: Readings and Reflections</u> (Los Angeles: Feral House, 1999).

inevitable.

It is far more dangerous to ignore the anarchists than it is to seriously consider their diagnosis, even if you don't agree with their prescribed treatment. To consider another course could be the most serious suppression of all, intellectually dishonest and morally reprehensible.

The necessity of this approach is reinforced by elements that are evident in the current chapter; more times than not I find myself unwittingly reinforcing the anarchists' arguments. In fact, if I restrict myself, for a moment, to this chapter's presentation, it is easy to ask: when *has* civilization, as it has manifested itself in modern medicine, given more to humanity than it has taken away from more primitive, uncivilized human existence? That even I cannot come up with arguments that conclusively defeat their position shows how daunting the problem is. We are dealing with solutions on the level of some semblance that *could* exist, but hasn't existed. We are dealing with civilization as something that *could* be unexploitive, but hasn't been; as something that *could* be healthy to man's ecology, internal and external, but hasn't been. We are making recommendations that exist in theory, but have never existed in practice. Thus, we find ourselves -- or I find myself -- in the uncomfortable position of having to deal primarily in a theoretical framework, the same mindset to which I accuse medicine of excessively resorting. It will be up to my critics, and those who follow me to help implement the recommendations that come later in this book, to determine not only if a *Meditopia* has been achieved, but if it were ever possible for our species in the first place, at least in our current state of (under)development.

If Alford can be credited with decisively demonstrating that the "common myth" concerning whistleblowers is posterously out of touch with reality, then Zinn should be credited with something even larger:[18]

His deconstructive approach takes the reader to a place

---

[18] Howard Zinn, A People's History of the United States: 1492 - Present (New York: Harper-Collings Publishers, 2005).

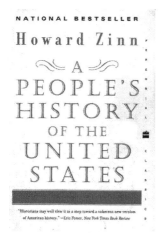

Howard Zinn

A
PEOPLE'S
HISTORY
OF THE
UNITED
STATES

"Historians may well view it as a step toward a coherent new version of American history." —Eric Foner, New York Times Book Review

where he realizes what an outrageous crock the conventional view (read: "the version they teach you in the American educational system") is concerning the History of the Americas. Euphemistic, self-serving, biased to the Elite; suppressive of the extent to which minorities, indigenous peoples, the working poor, and immigrants have been mistreated; these define the character of our "common narrative" as it relates to our history. We cannot be honest with the world, because we cannot be honest with ourselves.

One of the things that most struck me about Zinn's book was the degree to which, on close examination, democracy has been, throughout history, little more than a tool to control the public and provide some forum for deceptively convincing the common man that he has some control over his life, that government doesn't simply exist to serve a privileged few.

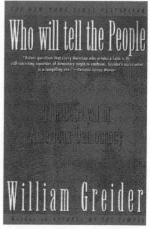

That democracy exists to "serve the people," turns out to be as mythological as the notion that modern medicine exists to serve the patient. In the U.S., to grasp the truth of the matter the serious investigator must return to the crime scene: the founding of the country and the creation of the national constitution. "When economic interest is seen behind the political clauses of the Constitution, then the document becomes not simply the work of wise men trying to establish a decent and orderly society, but the work of certain groups trying to maintain their privileges, while giving just enough rights and liberties to enough of the people to ensure popular support."[19]

[19] Ibid., 97.

This is why one can read something like William Greider's otherwise excellent volume, <u>Who Will Tell the People: The Betrayal of American Democracy</u>, and unless they have seen "the man behind the curtain," they will miss the point.[20] Greider opens his introduction by making clear the ubiquitous perversion of democracy. "The decayed condition of American Democracy is difficult to grasp, not because the facts are secret, but because the facts are visible everywhere," he says.[21] Greider then spends the majority of the next 400 pages showing just how head-spinningly grotesque representative government has become in America. But clearly Greider misses the point; a point that Zinn understands far more clearly.

Democracy is not failing to live up to its potential. In fact, today it is PERFECTLY living up to its potential. Democracy is doing exactly what it was designed to do: deliver the bounty to a select Elite and provide an "outlet" to the masses to deter revolution.

Greider, and millions of reform-minded people like him, believe in reform. They want to fix Democracy. But this isn't possible. You can't fix something if it is functioning precisely in the manner in which its designers intended. There isn't anything to fix.

Normally, one in the West associates this kind of dialogue as forged on the anvil of Marxist thought. And if it has anything to do with that merry band of leftist thinkers, there couldn't possibly be any truth to it, could there? And yet, even the most conservative, capitalist papers will occasionally fail to filter out the obviousness of this reality. I remember while I was in prison, I had my subscription to the *Wall Street Journal* mailed to me. In July 2005, an article appeared in the Op-Ed section, entitled, "The Export of Democracy." Written by Christopher Hitchens, the piece drew, no doubt, from the research of his own recent book, <u>Thomas Jefferson: Author of America</u>.[22] The disdain, even

---

[20] William Greider, <u>Who Will Tell the People: The Betrayal of American Democracy</u> (New York: Simon & Schuster, 1993).

[21] Ibid., 11.

[22] Christopher Hitchens, see: www.opinionjournal.com/editorial/feature.html?id=110006950. Tuesday, July 12, 2005. The cited work is his, <u>Thomas Jefferson: Author of America</u> (New

contempt that the founding fathers had for true democracy is revealed therein. And in quoting this piece, please keep in mind that Jefferson was probably the most "liberal-minded" (and I use that term in the 21st and not the 19th century sense of the term) of his fellow founding fathers. The reader may remember Jefferson's quote about the sorry state of medicine in his time on a previous page. And yet, as Hitchens points out, it is simply ludicrous to associate Jefferson with democracy.

"If hypocrisy is the compliment that vice pays to virtue," says Hitchens, "then the frequent linkage of the name 'Jefferson' with the word 'democracy' is impressive testimony, even from cynics, that his example has outlived his time and his place. To what extent does he deserve this rather flattering association of ideas?

"To begin with, we must take the measure of time. The association would not have been considered in the least bit flattering by many of Jefferson's contemporaries. The word 'democratic' or 'democratical' was a favorite term of abuse in the mouth of John Adams, who equated it with populism of the viler sort and with the horrors of mob rule and insurrection. In this, he gave familiar voice to a common prejudice, shared by many Tories and French aristocrats--and even by Edmund Burke, often unfairly characterized as an English reactionary but actually a rather daring Irish Whig. 'Take but degree away, untune that string,' as it is said in Troilus and Cressida, 'and hark what discord follows.' The masses, if given free rein, would vote themselves free beer and pull down the churches and country houses that had been established to show the blessings of order. **I cannot find ANY non-pejorative use in English of the Greek word 'democracy' until Thomas Paine took it up in the first volume of <u>The Rights of Man</u> and employed it as an affirmative term of pride** [in 1791]." *(emphasis added)*[23]

"We're not a democracy," former U.S. Attorney General,

York: HarperCollins, 2005).
[23] Ibid.

Ramsey Clark,[24] has stated, "It's a terrible misunderstanding and a slander to the idea of democracy to call us that. We're a plutocracy in the Aristotelian sense. We're a government of wealth. Wealth has its way. The concentration of wealth and the division between rich and poor is unequaled anywhere."[25]

This is not a recent development.

It goes back to the beginning of America's founding.

Perhaps to Hellenic times.

Or maybe anarchists are right after all: it began with the founding of civilization itself.

The evidence for it is, to borrow from Greider, "everywhere." We have only to look: it confronts us for the "embarrassment of riches" that it is.

If there is no true democracy, then in society's manifestations of health care there can be no political symmetry between those who provide care and those who receive it.

In such a society, medicine is incapable of ever rising above exploitation. Such a system cannot be fixed. It can only be overturned.

I use Kenneth Carpenter's work liberally throughout this section. His treatment of the subject is most comprehensive and focuses on scurvy itself instead of the biographies of those involved. It is less entertaining, but far more meaty. I also found Carpenter's work to be the most consistently quoted by other authors who rendered their own treatment of the subject.

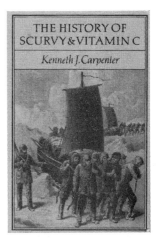

THE HISTORY OF
SCURVY & VITAMIN C

Kenneth J. Carpenter

---

[24] See: en.wikipedia.org/wiki/Ramsey_Clark

[25] Derrick Jensen, The Culture of Make Believe, 580. This quote is part of an interview between author Derrick Jensen, a leading author in the anarchist movement, and Ramsey Clark, former U.S. Attorney General during the Johnson administration. See pp. 576-584. The interview itself has been published elsewhere (an example is available online, courtesy of Derrick Jensen and *Sun Magazine*). It is a worthwhile read, and I highly recommend it, particularly to my friends in the U.S.

Typical of broad biographical works on the subject of Lind and the drama that unfolded in the aftermath of his treatise is Stephen R. Bown's <u>Scurvy: How a Surgeon, a Mariner, and a Gentleman Solved the Greatest Medical Mystery of the Age of Sail</u>.[26] (He is, by the way, referring to James Lind, the famous Captain James Cook, and Sir Gilbert Blane).

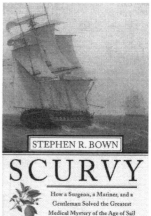

I use Bown's work because it gives a clear account of scurvy's history in Britain from the 16th century through the 19th. However, I do not at all subscribe to Bown's glowing account of this "miraculous discovery" on his terms. Bown is himself under the anesthesia of our common narrative and he appears careful to ensure that his account is concurrent with modern, orthdox treatment of medicine's history.

By way of example, Bown closes his opening prologue, gushing that "the defeat of scurvy was one of the great medical and socio-military advances of the era, a discovery on par with the accurate calculation of longitude at sea, the creation of the smallpox vaccination, or the development of steam power . . . How the cure for scurvy was found and lost and finally found again at an important juncture in the history of the world is one of the great mysteries of the age."[27]

No, it's not.

It's not a mystery.

It wasn't a mystery then and it isn't a mystery now.

When you understand the inner-workings of orthodox medicine and establishment power, there is nothing within the convoluted history of scurvy's history in the West that cannot be readily explained.

---

[26] Stephen R. Bown, <u>Scurvy: How a Surgeon, a Mariner, and a Gentleman Solved the Greatest Medical Mystery of the Age of Sail</u> (New York: Thomas Dunne Books, St. Martin's Press, 2003).

[27] Ibid., 7.

You simply have to be willing to step away from the propagandistic fog.

There was a point during my imprisonment in the U.S. when I realized that there was almost nothing in *Meditopia* that was original. The best that I could accomplish was to provide a fresh, current facade on a body of work, a veritable stream of wisdom extending through the Vedas, into the earliest Sumerian texts, and beyond into as yet unrecognized antiquities.

This thought is well represented in the Introduction to McKeown's The Role of Medicine: Dream, Mirage, or Nemesis?,[28] wherein McKeown opens with an unnamed historian's comment about the originality of "new ideas." "It is always earlier than you think," he says.[29] Given the time frame of my survey of the history of scurvy, I believe it is worthwhile to repeat his recounting of the long-held opinion of Montaigne (1533-1592), concerning the value of medicine.

". . . (A)t least from the time of Montaigne, the notion that treatment of disease may be useless, unpleasant, and even dangerous has been expressed frequently and vehemently, particularly in French literature. Molière's *Le Médecin Malgré Lui*, the famous operation in Madame Bovary and Proust's account of the psychiatrist's cursory examination of his mortally ill grandmother ('Madame, you will be well on the day when you realize that you are no longer ill . . . Submit to the honour of being called a neurotic. You belong to that great family . . . to which we are

---

[28] Thomas McKeown, The Role of Medicine: Dream, Mirage or Nemesis (New Jersey: Princeton University Press, 1979). A most interesting work, showing just how powerful Illich's Medical Nemesis has been. McKeown immediately opens the preface to the second edition (cited above) by attempting to distance himself from Illich, lest his work, too, be interpreted as "an attack on clinical medicine." McKeown, highly regarded in his field, proves in his defensiveness that we should follow Paracelsus' advice and be wary of respectable people. "For respectable people are loath to question the system which is itself the source of their respectability." Nonetheless, McKeown's own arguments paradoxically do damage orthodox medicine's credit-taking for a host of positive nutritional, environmental, and behavioral changes. In this respect, he is an unwitting aid to Illich. In either event, I think he doth protest too much. His work is, nonetheless, powerful, compelling, well-documented and quite relevant to the current volume.

[29] Ibid., xi.

indebted for all the greatest things we know') are examples of the irony and bitterness with which some of the greatest writers have expressed their conclusions about the work of doctors."[30]

> *"I have no difficulty in dating the origin of my own doubts . . . They began when I went to a London hospital as a medical student after several years of graduate research . . . there are two things that struck me, almost at once. One was the absence of any real interest among clinical teachers in the origin of disease, apart from its pathological and clinical manifestations; the other was that whether the prescribed treatment was of any value to the patient was often hardly noticed . . . I adopted the practice of asking myself at the bedside whether we were making anyone any wiser or any better, and soon came to the conclusion that most of the time we were not. Indeed, there seemed to be an inverse relation between the interest of a disease to the doctor and the usefulness of its treatment to the patient . . . Neurology, for example, was highly regarded and attracted some of the best minds because of the fascination of its diagnostic problems; but for the patient with [insert your neurological disorder of choice here], the precision of the diagnosis which was the focus of medical interest made not the slightest difference to the outcome."*

Thomas McKeown

But the Renaissance figures who wrote about the inherent problems of the medical profession were only expressing ideas that had already been observed in antiquity.

One salient example that helps make sense of scurvy's insane history comes down to the present day from Plato.[31]

---

[30] Ibid., xi.
[31] See: en.wikipedia.org/wiki/Plato

Neil Postman[32] opens his work, Technopoly,[33] by describing a story from the Phaedrus,[34] concerning the nature of technology. The failure of medical science, from its very beginning to the present day, to effectively address even the simplest of disorders becomes more clear in Postman's description of the issue of man's relationship to his technology:

"The story, as Socrates tells it to his friend Phaedrus, unfolds in the following way: Thamus once entertained the god Theuth, who was the inventor of many things, including number, calculation, geometry, astronomy, and writing. Theuth exhibited his inventions to King Thamus, claiming that they should be made widely known and available to Egyptians. Socrates continues:

"Thamus inquired into the use of each of them, and as Theuth went through them expressed approval or disapproval, according as he judged Theuth's claims to be well or ill founded. It would take too long to go through all that Thamus is reported to have said for and against each of Theuth's inventions. But when it came to writing, Theuth declared, "Here is an accomplishment, my lord the King, which will improve both the wisdom and the memory of the Egyptians. I have discovered a sure receipt for memory and wisdom.' To this, Thamus replied, 'Theuth, my paragon of inventors, the discoverer of an art is not the best judge of the good or harm which will accrue to those who practice it. So it is in this; you, who are the father of writing, have out of fondness for your off-spring attributed to it quite the opposite of its real function. Those who acquire it will cease to exercise their memory and become forgetful; they will

---

[32] See: en.wikipedia.org/wiki/Neil_Postman

[33] Neil Postman, Technopoly: The Surrender of Culture to Technology (New York: First Vintage Books, 1993).

[34] See: en.wikipedia.org/wiki/Phaedrus_(dialogue)

rely on writing to bring things to their remembrance by external signs instead of by their own internal resources. What you have discovered is a receipt for recollection, not for memory. And as for wisdom, your pupils will have the reputation for it without the reality: they will receive a quantity of information without proper instruction, and in consequence be thought very knowledgeable when they are for the most part quite ignorant. And because they are filled with the conceit of wisdom instead of real wisdom they will be a burden to society."[35]

Postman goes on to say that this story from the Phaedrus is no less relevant today than it was in the days of Plato -- in fact, more so. For **"we are currently surrounded by throngs of zealous Theuths, one-eyed prophets, who see only what new technologies can do and are incapable of imagining what they will undo."** *(emphasis added)*[36]

Such was the misguidance in constructing large warships to wage questionable wars, only to see more men and ships lost on account of disease and poor judgment than could ever be lost in battle.

Such is the centuries long detour that the cure for scurvy took when Lind introduced a "technology" for boiling and concentrating lemon juice ("rob of lemon"). The processing not only deactivated the ascorbate, but in the process of no longer seeing lemons work in the new, intended way, gave complete disrepute to any notion that citrus fruit was anti-scorbutic. The mistake would not be uncovered and understood until well into the 20th century.

Such is the fallacy in manufacturing vitamin supplements (including vitamin C) for the purposes of reinforcing devitalized, processed foods. For although the intended purpose is to make the food more nutritious, iit only keeps the consumer away from more natural, organic foods that possess the needed nutrients without having to have somebody add them, always producing results that are not as nutritious or healthy or life-supporting as the original foods they replace.

[35] Postman, Technopoly, 1-5.
[36] Ibid., 5

Such is the tragedy in allowing governmental bodies, such as the U.S. Congress, to create "protective" bureaucracies, such as the U.S. Food & Drug Administration, which is, itself, a kind of technology. For although its ostensible purpose is to protect Americans from harmful effects from improperly made or sold foods, beverages, cosmetics, etc., it is functionally and quite literally, a cruel mechanism to provide false assurance to the public that it is an organization that looks out for the public's best interest, when the brutal truth is that it whores for powerful pharmaceutical companies and others within the medical-industrial complex. The U.S. Food & Drug Administration's (FDA) policies are so malign, that for all anyone knows the many victims of its predictably ill-advised policies may exceed the number that have been killed by all wars in which America has ever been involved.

As the history of scurvy shows, "our inventions are but improved means to an unimproved end."[37] Postman makes this clear in discussing the implications of embracing technology as an end-all; medicine is today, as it was in the days of James Lind, all about analyzing disease and not curing the patient. What the patient knows is untrustworthy; but what the machine knows is reliable.[38] This is the tautology of modern science itself and it can never be made to comport with the needs of good health; for science itself is built on a foundation that dictates that the senses are not reliable, but the tools of the scientist are.

In 1748, the year that Lind performed his scurvy study on the H.M.S. *Salisbury*, a book was published in Europe entitled Man a Machine. It so scandalized the clergy that its author had to seek refuge in the court of the philosopher-king Frederick the Great. The essay opens by stating, "It is not enough for a wise man to study nature and truth; he should dare state truth for the benefit of the few who are willing and able to think. As for the rest, who are voluntarily slaves of prejudice, they can no more attain truth, than frogs can fly."[39]

[37] Ibid., 5.
[38] Ibid., p. 100.
[39] Julien Offrey De La Mettrie, Man a Machine (Open Court, 1992), 85.

The book wasn't written by a philosopher or student of political economy.

It was written by a physician.

A "truth for the benefit of the few" will always inure to those few at the expense of the many. For technology is and always has been a generator of the kind of social asymmetry of which an unbiased view of medical history provides an abundance of key, supportive examples. In the present instance I would say that my short history of escharotics is "Exhibit A." The truncated history of scurvy in the present chapter is "Exhibit B."

On a lighter note, readers wanting to get a closer look at James Lind's life and struggles would do well to examine Harvie's <u>Limeys</u>.[40] I used the work only lightly in my research because very early in the read I felt that Lind's contribution was excessively glorified. I take the position that in promoting his own worthless concoction, he became as much an impediment to promulgating the true cure for scurvy as the very forces and personages against which he fought.

James Lind is a wonderful, historical example of why someone who works in the system, for the system, and who must be held in respect by that system, is ill-equipped to be a reformer of that system.

I first learned this from Paracelsus.

It is a subject also covered by Kuhn in his study of scientific revolutions.

Few books in the history of science have created such a tumultuous response within the scientific community. I cover this briefly in the bibliographical insert for <u>The Structure of Sci-</u>

---

[40] David Harvie, <u>Limeys: The True Story of One Man's War Against Ignorance, the Establishment and the Deadly Scurvy</u> (Phoenix Mill, UK: Sutton Publishing, 2002).

entific Revolutions.[41]

I bring up Kuhn's work at this juncture, because no one else has done such a brilliant job of providing the conceptual framework that would allow a seeker of knowledge to understand why the scientific community is, and this applies in spades to orthodox medicine, so consistently wrong. Why what we call scientific fact so often changes fashion according to the intellectual (or anti-intellectual) tenor of the times. Kuhn also

provides us with more tools to help identify the hidden forces that make science undependable. The points below are taken from my prison notebook on Kuhn's work. They combine Kuhn's comments with excerpts from my unpublished prison notebook as it pertains to my reflections on Kuhn, and my own current commentary. These are the most salient concepts I learned from Kuhn, the inferences I drew from his thought in conjunction with all my other readings and reflections.

- Orthodoxists take the foundations of their field for granted, making them the least likely to uncover its cracks. (After all, acceptance of the prevailing foundation makes science, science!)[42] "Almost always the men who achieve these fundamental inventions of a new paradigm have been either very young or very new to the field whose paradigm they change."[43]
- The effect of a system where those who reconfirm the prevailing paradigm get more credit, praise, financial reward, etc. than those who uncover its flaws is hugely inhibitory to an impartial pursuit of knowledge or truth, by whatever standard you wish to define knowledge or

---

[41] Thomas S. Kuhn, The Structure of Scientific Revolutions (Chicago: The University of Chicago Press, 1962).

[42] Ibid., 21.

[43] Ibid., 90.

truth, as long as it isn't one controlled or dictated by modern science![44]

- The seeking of truth by the scientific method aims at confirming and upholding the prevailing doctrines. (Projects do not aim at "unexpected novelty" -- the missing variable in any research project leans to how to make the path fit the intended results.)[45]

- "One of the things a scientific community acquires with a paradigm is a criterion for choosing problems that, while the paradigm is taken for granted, can be assumed to have solutions. To a great extent these are the only problems that the community will admit as scientific or encourage its members to undertake."[46] By limiting their perspective, scientists are able to veer away from the interdisciplinary challenges that a true acquisition of nature's secrets would demand. Kuhn makes this clear by telling the story of an investigator "who hoped to learn something about what scientists took the atomic theory to be." So the investigator "asked a distinguished physicist and an eminent chemist whether a single atom of helium was or was not a molecule. Both answered without hesitation, but their answers were not the same. For the chemist the atom of helium was a molecule because it behaved like one with respect to the kinetic theory of gases. For the physicist, on the other hand, the helium atom was not a molecule, because it displayed no molecular spectrum. Presumably both men were referring to the same particle, but they were viewing it through their own research training and practice . . ."[47] An astonishingly good illustration of this, both current and relevant to my cancer/scurvy comparative study, are the findings of Gerald B. Dermer as discussed in his book, The Immortal Cell: Why Cancer Research

[44] Ibid., 26.
[45] Ibid., 35-36.
[46] Ibid., 37.
[47] Ibid., 50-51.

<u>Fails</u>.[48] Dermer was a pathologist doing studies on tumors removed from live cancer patients. What he found was a "vast and deadly gap between the reality of cancer, which strikes human beings, and the theory of cancer, which thousands of researchers are using in their [supposed] search for a cure."[49] It was the indifference to this fact that motivated Dermer to write his book: "Although some of my colleagues are aware of this gap, few are willing to risk their careers by discussing it openly. In the absence of public debate, cancer scientists around the country are free to propagate the myth of a productive 'war on cancer.' No one wants to admit that this so-called war has been a worthless investment of taxpayers' money and scientists' time. But as more and more money is spent, with fewer and fewer meaningful results, increasing numbers of patients and their familiers, taxpayers, and politicians want to know the reasons why . . . Although I firmly believe that research can and will produce practical and effective treatments for cancer, such advances will never come from the present research paradigm . . . it is an account of a scientific and medical scandal of the highest order."[50]

- The gist of Dermer's book, by the way, is that cancer researchers use cell lines that behave totally different from live cancer cells. Cancer researchers could use their current methods for the next 2,000 years and still never come up with a cancer cure -- guaranteed. Dermer, of course, fails to realize that this is the whole point! Viewed from the proper economic perspective, cancer researchers have been, are, and will continue to be successful! They are successful every day of their careers. For to find a cure for cancer would make them a failure: they'd lose their jobs and an entire industry

[48] Gerald B. Dermer, <u>The Immortal Cell: Why Cancer Research Fails</u> (Garden City Park, NY: Avery Publishing Group, Inc., 1994).

[49] Ibid. ix.

[50] Ibid. xi.

would be left in ruins!

AFTER FORTY YEARS OF LOSING THE WAR AGAINST CANCER ISN'T IT TIME TO ASK, WHAT IS SCIENCE DOING WRONG?

THE IMMORTAL CELL

WHY CANCER RESEARCH FAILS

DR. GERALD B. DERMER

It will be obvious to alert readers to this point that Dermer himself is operating without fully seeing through the common narrative. He cannot (or has not, perhaps because he has already bitten off enough of a controversy with his current work) admit that, like scurvy before it, the cure for cancer is already here. Knowledge about the forms of maladaptation that foster cancer and other diseases is half the battle. Any widespread knowledge that effective cures for cancer already exist and have since antiquity, if obtained by a critical mass of Western citizenry, would cause an unprecented economic collapse of the medical industrial complex, the loss of hundreds of thousands of jobs, the overnight evaporation of a huge source of income for politicians, and an unpredictable reshuffling of the political order.

- "Paradigms guide research by direct modeling as well as through abstracted rules." That "normal science can proceed without rules only so long as the relevant scientific community accepts without question the particular problem-solutions already achieved."[51] When you understand this, you understand why medical science has consistently, to this very day, downplayed the importance of ascorbate. Note that since scurvy cannot be denied as a dietary deficiency disease because the proof is too overwhelming, orthodox medicine has retreated to its next line of defense by denying that scurvy is only the most advanced stage of disease, a subset of a larger phenomenon called "hypoascorbemia." "To the extent that normal research work can be conducted by using (its own) paradigm as a model, rules and assumptions

---

[51] Kuhn, The Structure of Scientific Revolutions, 47.

need not be made explicit." . . . Orthodox medicine, or any other branch of establishment science for that matter, can create and sustain itself with the most ridiculous assertions because they create their own rules. This is why the path to understanding scurvy is lined with the lifeless skulls of the millions who died from it because there existed an establishment, an authoratative scientific body, which upheld the right to ignore the obvious. Above all else -- this is *science*. (I can think of no better example to demonstrate that the scientific establishment more closely resembles a brothel than it does an impartial body that seeks after truth than the current common narrative that has been created for AIDS. In a subsequent chapter I examine how preposterous it is that anyone could get away with proposing that the HIV virus has anything to do with AIDS; the very idea attempts to overthrow the establishment's own, long-established adherence to Koch's Postulates.)[52]

- Science involves assemblage of presentable fact into assimilated theory. What happens to the facts when the power elite control the acceptability of the theories?[53]
- The tendency of the human mind to take established fact and twist even the most anomalous information into a pre-established paradigm is well illustrated by the Bruner/Postman experiments, in which a series of playing cards was displayed, always with some anomalies, such as "a red six of spades and a black four of hearts," etc. "Even on the shortest exposures many subjects identified most of the cards, and after a small increase all the subjects identified all of them. For the normal cards these identifications were usually correct, but the anomalous cards were almost always identified, without apparent hesitation or puzzlement, as normal. The black four of hearts might, for example, be identified as the four of either spades or hearts. Without any

[52] Ibid., 88.
[53] Ibid.,. 55.

awareness of trouble, it was immediately fitted to one of the conceptual categories prepared by prior experience . . . With a further increase of exposure to the anomalous cards, subjects did begin to hesitate and to display awareness of anomaly. Exposed, for example, to the red six of spades, some would say: 'That's a six of spades, but there's something wrong with it -- the black has a red border. Further increase of exposure resulted in still more hesitation and confusion until finally, and sometimes quite suddenly, most subjects would produce the correct identification without hesitation. Moreover, after doing this with two or three of the anomalous cards, they would have little further difficulty with the others. A few subjects, however, were never able to make the requisite adjustment of their categories. Even at forty times the average exposure required to recognize normal cards for what they were, more than 10 percent of the anomalous cards were not correctly identified. And the subjects who then failed often experienced acute personal distress. One of them explained: 'I can't make the suit out, whatever it is. It didn't even look like a card that time. I don't know what color it is now or whether it's a spade or a heart. I'm not even sure now what a spade looks like. My God!'[54] This illustrates one of Kuhn's main points: "that novelty emerges only with difficulty, manifested by resistance, against a background provided by expectation." My problem here with Kuhn is that he fails to explore how economics both quantatively and qualitatively is consistently the 800-pound gorilla that weighs into that expectation. Another point he makes in this connection is worth observing: "In the development of any science, the first received paradigm is usually felt to account quite successfully for most of the observations and experiments easily accessible to that science's practitioners. Further development, therefore, ordinarily calls for the construction of elaborate equip-

[54] Ibid., 62-65.

ment, the development of an esoteric vocabulary and skills, and a refinement of concepts that increasingly lessens their resemblance to their usual common-sense prototypes. That professionalization leads, on the one hand, to an immense restriction on the scientist's vision and to a considerable resistance to paradigm change."[55] We see this repeatedly in the history of scurvy.

• The Bruner/Postman experiment is further reinforced by research conducted at the Hanover Institute.[56] A subject who "puts on goggles fitted with inverted lenses initially sees the entire world upside down. At the start his perceptual apparatus functions as it had been trained to function in the absence of the goggles, and the result is extreme disorientation, an acute personal crisis. But after the subject has begun to learn to deal with his new world, his entire visual field flips over, usually after an intervening period in which vision is simply confused. Thereafter, objects are again seen as they had been before the goggles were put on. The assimilation of a previously anomalous visual field has reacted upon and changed the field itself. Literally as well as metaphorically, the man accustomed to inverted lens has undergone a revolutionary transformation of vision . . . (Thus) what a man sees depends both upon what he looks at and also upon what his previous visual-conceptual experience has taught him to see."

• The support for an outmoded, disprovable theory requires the interjection of both complexity and money.[57] We saw this both in Tainter's work and now we see it in Kuhn's. This is why the multi-trillion dollar health care system in the West continues to suck in more and more money and produces diminishing results -- from the patients' point of view. (From orthodox medicine's point of view, spending more money to get worse re-

---

[55] Ibid., 64.
[56] Ibid., 112-113.
[57] Ibid., 69.

sults equates to success, just as long as this parasitic activity does not kill the host or pose a serious threat to its legitimacy or hegemony.) Excuses for this state of affairs on the part of establishment personages are only more predictable: the explanations just keep getting more and more ludicrous. Kuhn presents a replication of this same phenomenon in the field of astronomy in his The Copernican Revolution,[58] from which we are less than four centuries removed.

- More than one theoretical construct can always be placed over a collection of data.[59] However, Kuhn himself fails to consider that the scientific construct that yields the best monetary return to the establishment always has "the edge." A construct is made weaker not so much by its failure to live up to observation or a lack of repeatability or an insufficiency of any of the common narrative criteria that are supposed to substantiate good science. A construct or paradigm is made weaker because it fails to provide an economic return that is on par with a competing construct. The superior construct supplying better financial returns is usually abandoned only when it threatens the legitimacy of the scientific establishment that is backing it, and this phenomenon exists only because losing legitimacy itself is the ultimate threat to an establishment's economic hegemony.

- In the absence of crisis, a new paradigm doesn't surface. The most ridiculous concept prancing around as scientific fact will endure so long as it goes unchallenged. So a theory is declared invalid only if it has a suitable candidate to replace it.[60] The degree to which a suitable candidate poses economic or political loss will be a far more influencing factor than any of its underlying non-monetary merits.

---

[58] Thomas S. Kuhn, The Copernican Revolution: Planetary Astronomy in the Development of Western Thought (Cambridge, MA: Harvard University Press, 1992).
[59] Kuhn, The Structure of Scientific Revolutions, 76.
[60] Ibid., 77-79.

- Good paradigms leave "all sorts of problems (yet) un-resolved." Thus, there is a built-in prejudice against final solutions to which any further research is unnec-essary![61] Thus, there is a built-in prejudice against final solutions to which any further research is unnecessary.
- Science, by definition, demands consensus, or it lan-guishes in a pre-paradigm state.[62] The inference, al-though Kuhn is never bold enough to state it straight away, is that because science, by definition, is built on the consensus of a specialized body, it is always vulner-able to economic leverage. If a truth is or can be dam-aging to the financial welfare of the specialized group, then suppressing that truth becomes a needful activity of that group. For this reason, science is always vulner-able to be co-opted by those who represent it. Or, more to the point, scientific truth is dictated by those who pay the bills.[63] Linguistically, it is no coincidence that the word, real, in English, although etymologically said to be derived from the fifth declension Latin noun, *res*, (thing), is more accurately placed as a derivative of the third declension Latin noun, *rex* (*regis*), meaning king, which in the adjectival form is *regalis*. The meaning is clear and unmistakable: through all ages, that which is real or factual, that which has existence, that which has legitimacy, that which is acceptable as true, is consis-tently that which has secured the consent of the king (represented by a power elite which has secured its par-asitic position over the majority of the population over which it feeds . . . er . . . rules). It takes an idiot not to see that kings are loath to accept facts which limit the stream of wealth pouring into their coffers.
- By way of inference, paradigms provide scientists not only with a map, but also with some of the directions

---

[61] Ibid., 10.
[62] Ibid., 101.
[63] Ibid., 101.

essential for map-making.[64]

- Here it is three centuries after the discourses of Descartes and we still have no "pure observation-language," an agreed upon theory of perception and of the mind. This does not yet exist. But science has and does behave as if it does. It is part of its enduring mythology.[65]
- "It is hard to make nature fit a paradigm. That is why the puzzles of normal science are so challenging and also why measurements undertaken without a paradigm so seldom lead to any conclusions at all." Understanding the conflict between nature and the rise and fall of paradigms explains why orthodox medicine is, never has been, and never will be evidence-based. To be evidence-based is to commit oneself to the best outcome of the patient, even if you cannot explain how it came about. To be evidence-based is to pick what is empirically provable as the best therapeutic choice for the patient, regardless of whatever rules and regulations have been created by the medical establishment, themselves having been established by monetary incentives. In fact, to be evidence-based is to do what is best for the patient regardless of whether or not it makes any money at all. Orthodox medicine must co-opt evidence. It is in natural opposition to it. To take a cooperative position with the search for true evidence means sacrificing the monetary and political imperatives that an orthodox medical system requires to sustain its very existence.[66]
- The prevailing pharmaceutical paradigm, that the only true, authentic drug is one that descends from a single, pure, patentable molecular compound, usually one that is so original that one cannot find evidence of its existence anywhere in nature, must be destroyed to allow acceptance of more effective healing evidence and bring about anything close to an evidence-based system.

[64] Ibid., 109.
[65] Ibid., 125-128.
[66] Ibid., 135.

- "Textbooks ... being pedagogic vehicles for the perpetuation of normal science, have to be rewritten in whole or in part whenever the language, problem-structure, or standards of normal science change. In short, they have to be rewritten in the aftermath of each scientific revolution, and, once rewritten, they inevitably disguise not only the role but the very existence of the revolutions that produced them. Unless he has personally experienced a revolution in his own lifetime, the historical sense either of the working scientist or of the lay reader of textbook literature extends only to the outcome of the most recent revolutions in the field." The importance of this truism, as it relates to orthodox medical education, regardless of type or specialty, is that suppression of information that would support the notion that science, regardless of field, is constantly in flux in accordance with monetary and other unscientific inputs, that there are, in fact, few unchanging facts, is a requirement to sustain the respectability and integrity of each respective scientific field. At all costs the scientists in each field cannot be placed in a situation where they convey either to the lay person or to new, upcoming students who will become the field's new standard-bearers, "We do not really know any ultimate truth. But we represent that we do, and we change it from time to time, quite frequently as it turns out. And what we call truth today is based on the mythology that what we represent is the best, most accurate information available, obtained through impartial investigation using indisputable methods of observation. Moreover, although you may be aware of mistakes made in the past, it is important that you accept that we really have the truth this time! We work diligently to ensure that it doesn't occur to you that the information we provide in the future will, in great likelihood, look very different from what we call truth today. And what is the key determinant as to what that future truth will look like? Well, of course, it's the underlying political and economic incentives." That this key linchpin of Scientism's mythology is necessary for its credibility is demonstrated by the fact that scientific textbooks hide the very existence of these revolutions. To provide students with this historical foundation serves not only to discredit science itself, but it detracts from a key objective of the educational process: to communicate the vocabulary, syntax, respectability and believability of a contemporary scientific language and mode of thinking.[67]

- "Yet the textbook-derived tradition in which scientists come to sense their participation is one that, in fact, never existed. For reasons that are both obvious and highly functional, scientific textbooks (and too many of the older histories of science) refer only to that part of the work of past scientists that can easily be viewed as contributions to the statement and solution of the texts' paradigm problems. Partly by selection and partly by distortion, the scientists of earlier ages are implicitly represented as having worked upon the same set of fixed problems and in accordance with the same set of fixed canons that the most recent revolution in scientific theory and method has. No wonder that textbooks and the historical tradition they imply have to be rewritten after each scientific revolution. And no wonder that, as they are rewritten, science once again comes to seem largely cumulative. Scientists are not, of course, the only group that tends to see its discipline's past developing linearly toward its present advantage. The temptation to write history backward is both omnipresent and perennial. But scientists are more affected by the temptation to rewrite history, partly because the results of scientific research show no obvious dependence upon the historical context of the inquiry, and partly because, except during crisis and revolution, the scientist's contemporary position seems so secure. More historical detail, whether of

[67] Ibid., 137.

science's present or of its past, or more responsibility to the historical details that are presented, could only give artificial status to human idiosyncrasy, error, and confusion. Why dignify what science's best and most persistent efforts have made it possible to discard? The depreciation of historical fact is deeply, and probably functionally, ingrained in the ideology of the scientific profession, the same profession that places the highest of all values upon factual details of all sorts. Whitehead caught the unhistorical spirit of the scientific community when he wrote, 'A science that hesitates to forget its founders is lost.' Yet he was not quite right, for the sciences, like other professional enterprises, do need their heroes and do preserve their names. Fortunately, instead of forgetting these heroes, scientists have been able to forget or revise their works."[68]

Commentary: Going beyond Kuhn, I found the "mythology of history as progress" even better articulated by Hiram Caton (no relation) in his The Politics of Progress.[69]

"Until you have got a true theory of humanity, you cannot interpret history; and when you have got a true theory of humanity, you do not want history."

Herbert Spencer[70]

One of the primary theses of Hiram Caton's work is that the rendering of history since the 17th century has been fashioned to show consistent progress and make diminutive our primitive beginnings. "One fruit of the renovation of historiography was a view of the history of the human species as an advance from primitive conditions."[71] All the usual suspects are included in

[68] Ibid., 137-139.
[69] Hiram Caton, The Politics of Progress (Gainesville, Florida: University of Florida Press, 1988).
[70] Ibid., 3.
[71] Ibid., 21.

his coverage, of course, Kepler, Huygens, Locke, Newton, etc. But to juxtapose Caton's observations to Kuhn's we see that the suppression of historical information necessary to upholding current paradigms is not merely a tendency, but an absolute requirement to maintaining any semblance of legitimacy. So rooted is the myth that the history of science is a linear march of unending improvement that Kuhn is moved to write, "Does a field make progress because it is a science, or is it a science because it makes progress?"[72] Nonetheless, this is a myth which is indispensible to sustaining the respectability of science in the mind of the public. After all, with each successive scientific revolution, how could the victorious camp ever admit to something less than progress? "That would be rather like admitting that they had been wrong and their opponents right."[73] "When it repudiates a past paradigm, a scientific community simultaneously renounces, as a fit subject for professional scrutiny, most of the books and articles in which that paradigm had been embodied. Scientific education makes use of no equivalent for the art museum or the library of classics, and the result is a sometimes drastic distortion in the scientist's perception of his discipline's past. More than the practitioners of other creative fields, he comes to see it as leading in a straight line to the discipline's present vantage. In short, he comes to see it as progress. No alternative is available to him while he remains in the field."[74]

Those who hold that orthodox medicine has not been suppressing effective treatments for the entirety of its existence know nothing about the history of science itself!

- Each paradigm brings with it new puzzles. But the new paradigm may fail to solve problems that earlier paradigms handled easily.[75] One example that strikes me poignantly, because it involved the theoretical under-

---

[72] Thomas Kuhn, The Structure of Scientific Revolutions, 162.

[73] Ibid., 166.

[74] Ibid., 167.

[75] Ibid., 140.

pinnings for an Alpha Omega Labs product called Bone Builder,[76] is that of biological transmutation.[77] The product itself made use of a well observed fact that is completely denied by modern chemistry: that biological organisms have the ability to transmute elements. An abundance of further examples can be readily shown in the laboratory to prove that biological transmutation is a fact of everyday life.[78]

• One of the most ubiquitous defense mechanisms used by the orthodox establishment (and this equally applies to orthodox medicine) is the pejorative labeling of those who identify Elite misbehavior as conspiracy theorists, never mind that the very nature of maintaining the established order and preventing people from seeing through the mythology of the common narrative requires well orchestrated conspiracy. One of the best examples of this is demonstrated in the very historigraphical tools used to uphold a major tenet of scientism: that, as Hiram Caton has noted, history (be it the history of civilizations, the history of science, the history of medicine) is presented as progress to uphold the glory of the present system and make its precedessors (which have failed and are now dead) diminutive. Every civilization has followed this pattern -- without exception. In every empire and in every age, the reigning culture has attempted to inculcate the idea that it will succeed where all others have failed, irrespective of the fact that each successive civilization uses but a slightly different variation on its path to failure of the the many that preceded it. The famed historian, Arnold Toynbee, noted that not less than 25 prior dominant civilizations over the past 5,000 years have taken this path. He notes that sixteen are completely dead and buried, and all but one exhibit the distinctive characteristics of disintegration: Western

---

[76] See: www.altcancer.net/bb.htm

[77] C.L. Kervran, <u>Biological Transmutation</u> (Magalia, California: Happiness Press, 1988).

[78] Ibid., which I discuss at greater length in a later chapter.

Civilization.[79] My position is that Toynbee's close, personal association with the Elite prevented him[80] from seeing that Western Civilization has already passed the point of no return. The inevitability of this was not lost on Oswald Spengler.[81]

- A corollary to the notion that "history is the record, proof, reinforcement, source of common narrative, and propaganda major" of its prevailing Elite is the mythology of **cumulative acquisition** of unanticipated novelties, which "proves to be an almost non-existent exception to the rule of scientific development. The man who takes historic fact seriously must suspect that science does not tend toward the ideal that our image of its cumulativeness has suggested . . . cumulative acquisition of novelty is not only rare in fact but improbable in principle. . . . The man who is striving to solve a problem defined by existing knowledge and technique is not, however, just looking around. He knows what he wants to achieve, and he designs his instruments and directs his thoughts accordingly. Unanticipated novelty, the new discovery, can emerge only to the extent that his anticipations about nature and his instruments prove wrong. Often the importance of the resulting discovery will itself be proportional to the extent and stubbornness of the anomaly that foreshadowed it. **Obviously, then, there must be a conflict between the paradigm that discloses anomaly and the one that later renders the anomaly law-like . . . There is no other effective way in which discoveries might be generated.**" Examples throughout history abound, if objectively examined in this light: "only after the caloric theory had been rejected could energy conservation become part of science . . . Einstein's theory can be accepted only with the recognition that Newton's was wrong . . . It is hard to

---

[79] Arnold J. Toynbee, <u>A Study of History</u> (Oxford University Press, 1987), 244.

[80] Caroll Quigley, <u>Tragedy & Hope</u> (New York: The Macmillan Company, 1966), 7.

[81] Oswald Spengler, <u>The Decline of the West</u> (New York: Vintage Books, 2006).

see how new theories could arise without these destructive changes in beliefs about nature. Though logical inclusiveness remains a permissible view of the relation between successive scientific theories, it is a historical implausibility."[82] *(emphasis added)*

- The transition between an old paradigm and a new is rarely smooth. The parallels between upheavals in politics and in science are striking. "Political revolutions are inaugurated by a growing sense, often restricted to a segment of the political community, that **existing institutions have ceased adequately to meet the problems posed by an environment that they have in part created**. In much the same way, scientific revolutions are inaugurated by a growing sense, again often restricted to a narrow subdivision of the scientific community, that an existing paradigm has ceased to function adequately in the exploration of an aspect of nature to which that paradigm itself had previously led the way. In both political and scientific development the sense of malfunction that can lead to crisis is prerequisite to revolution . . . the parties to a revolutionary conflict must finally resort to the techniques of mass persuasion, often including force."[83] *(emphasis added)* The revolution, as I have been able to observe it in the U.S., is already running at full-steam. The FDA is presecuting, imprisoning, has even murdered, those who stand in the way of the money machine that fund their top management: primarily the pharmaceutical industry.

- It is hard to make nature fit into a paradigm. (It is my belief that this a logical corollary of Godel's Incompleteness Theorem in mathematics.)[84] "That is why the puzzles of normal science are so challenging and also why measurements undertaken without a paradigm so seldom lead to any conclusions at all. (To make a para-

[82] Kuhn, 96-98.

[83] Ibid., 92-93.

[84] For Godel's Incompleteness Theorem see glossary.

digm work you have to) beat nature into line."[85]
- Science can never be a reflection of truth, because it is limited by commonly held precepts and cultural memes -- but most importantly, political / economic forces that are the strongest and most durable forces in our current cultural operationg system -- a system which has ruled the majority of humanity for at least the last 8,000 years.

The prevailing pharmaceutical paradigm can never allow the acceptance of evidence-based medicine (which, to be effective, will almost always be derived from nature herself, since the physical system itself is an artifact of nature). Thus, the pharmaceutical paradigm must be destroyed to allow acceptance of effective healing evidence. But that cannot happen without the introduction of a more compelling, dynamic paradigm, hence the timely need for Meditopia.

Greg Caton

- Each paradigm brings with it new puzzles. But the new paradigm may fail to solve problems that earlier paradigms handled easily.[86]
- A scientist is much like a chess player. He will test millions of possible moves, but never the rules of the game.[87]
- The old must die off for a new paradigm to take hold. "A new scientific truth does not triumph by convincing its opponents and making them see the light, but rather because its opponents eventually die, and a new generation grows up that is familiar with it."[88]
- "The transfer of allegiance from paradigm to paradigm is a conversion experience that cannot be forced. Life-

---

[85] Ibid., 135.

[86] Ibid., 140.

[87] Ibid., prevailing paradigm, 144-145.

[88] Ibid., 151, see also Max Planck, <u>Scientific Autobiography and Other Papers</u> (Santa Barbara, California: Greenwood Publishing, 1968).

long resistance, particularly from those whose productive careers have committed them to an older tradition of normal science, is not a violation of scientific standards but an index to the nature of scientific research itself. The source of resistance is the assurance that the older paradigm will ultimately solve all its problems, that nature can be shoved into the box the paradigm provides. Inevitably, at times of revolution, that assurance seems stubborn and pigheaded as indeed it sometimes becomes. But it is also something more. That same assurance is what makes normal or puzzle-solving science possible. And it is only through normal science that the professional community of scientists succeeds, first, in exploiting the potential scope and precision of the older paradigm and, then, in isolating the difficulty through the study of which a new paradigm may emerge."[89] The exploitation of a paradigm and its eventual submission to a new replacement, as well as the direction of the paradigm's replacement, is more influenced by moneyed interest than any other factor.[90]

- For all its ballyhooed strict adherence to the hard, intellectually rigorous scientific method, modern science is as much influenced by feeling and emotion as it is anything objective. "Even today Einstein's general theory attracts men principally on aesthetic grounds, an appeal that few people outside of mathematics have been able to feel."[91] Or as Nobel laureate Paul Dirac put it, "it is more important to have beauty in one's equations than to have them fit experiment."[92] What logical or reasonable basis, for instance, can be seen in science in the famous exchange between Wolfgang Pauli and Neils Bohr? To

[89] Ibid., 152.

[90] Spencer Klaw's The New Brahmins (New York: William Morrow & Company, 1968), 168-227, which, although dated and focused on the scientific community in the U.S., clearly spells out the nature of this influence.

[91] Kuhn, 158.

[92] Kaku, Michio; Hyperspace: A Scientific Odyssey Through Parallel Universes, Time Warps, and the 10th Dimension (New York: Doubleday, 1994) 189..

recap, physicist Wolfgang Pauli gave a lecture on the Heisenberg-Pauli unified field theory with "many eager physicists in attendance." When he was finished, however, the lecture received a mixed response. Niels Bohr finally stood up and said, "We are all agreed that your theory is crazy. The question which divides us is whether it is crazy enough."[93] In this light, it is even easier to see how moneyed interests and high entropy solutions could influence the direction of science. After all, under the cultural operating system that civilization has been obeying for 8,000 years, what is more aesthetic or beautiful or motivating than money? Nothing.

- "The very existence of science depends upon vesting the power to choose between paradigms in the members of a special kind of community . . . The group's members, as individuals and by virtue of their shared training and experience, must be seen as the SOLE POSSESSORS *[emphasis added]* of the rules of the game or of some equivalent basis for unequivocal judgments. To doubt that they shared some such basis for evaluations would be to admit the existence of incompatible standards of scientific achievement. That admission would inevitably raise the question whether truth in the sciences can be one [won]."[94] As it relates to the health sciences, where evidence-based medicine has consistently shown that simple, low entropy therapeutic solutions that work in accordance with nature are superior to more complex, more profitable therapeutic approaches, this flawed feature of science becomes glaring. For as the sole possessors of the rules of the game, the dominant group, the assenting majority that constitute the acknowledged, authoritative, scientific community, must, of necessity, destroy its competitors. Suppression is not an option. It is a necessity. From this angle, we again see why modern medicine, holding sway over that area

---

[93] Ibid., 137.
[94] Kuhn, 168.

of science devoted to health care, could never come to an agreement with that stream of thought and practice that is evidence-based.

- It is on account of science's fundamental flaws, written into the very fabric of its being, that "we may have to relinquish the notion . . . that changes of paradigm carry scientists and those who learn from them closer and closer to the truth."[95]

- "We are all deeply accustomed to seeing science as the one enterprise that draws consistently nearer to some goal set by nature in advance. But need there be any such goal? Can we not account for both science's existence and its success in terms of evolution from the community's state of knowledge at any given time? Does it really help to imagine that there is some one full, objective, true account of nature and that the proper measure of scientific achievement is the extent to which it brings us closer to that ultimate goal?"[96] The fact is, science doesn't have any nature-specified goal, and the only common force that unifies all science as its one and only deficiency nutrient, the absence of which would starve any scientific enterprise, is *money*. Proofs of this that can be drawn from the medical community abound. In fact, the only way that modern medicine could ever have evolved into anything other than the current cesspool of corruption, payola, widespread death-by-doctoring, and iatrogenesis as the world's leading epidemic, is if there were a close conjunction between making money and curing patients. Because of the effectiveness of low entropy therapeutic approaches, such a conjunction does not, could not, and will not ever exist. Caught between the demands to return a profit and the demands of nature to cure the patient, it is the patient that will lose under our modern cultural operating system.

[95] Ibid., 170.
[96] Ibid., 171.

- The uniformity of education and grooming of scientists means that all who want to be in the "club" drink from the same, figuratively cyanide-laced punch bowl. Whatever virus or defect exists in the prevailing paradigm will therefore be magnified.[97]
- By having a paradigm, the scientific community, and this is so very evident in medicine, must have something to defend, but any phenomenon is inclined to align itself with economic benefit. The bigger the money, the stronger this centripetal force.[98]
- Sometimes the new paradigm employs new definitions or understandings of old terms. This section provides insight into why the medical-industrial complex must so viciously fight evidence-based health care. *Meditopia* doesn't replace the vinyl siding; it identifies a serious crack in the foundation that requires the destruction and rebuilding of the whole house.[99]
- As the discussion of the work of Dr. Gerald Dermer revealed, what is endorsed by one group of scientists in one discipline will be opaque to another.
- Kuhn takes the position that "practitioners of the developed sciences are . . . fundamentally puzzle-solvers. Though the values that they deploy at times of theory-choice derive from other aspects of their work as well, the demonstrated ability to set up and solve puzzles presented by nature is, in case of value conflict, the dominant criterion for most members of a scientific group."[100] I most strongly disagree. Since the very measure of success under our current cultural operating system centers around one value and one value alone -- making a profit -- it only stands to reason that consciously or unconsciously, the problem-solving process will always be biased towards a solution that affords

---

[97] Ibid., 177.
[98] Ibid., 179.
[99] Ibid., 179.
[100] Ibid., 205.

financial opportunity. Those who would disagree are not being honest with themselves. Take the very word itself: success. Now repeat it gently in the mind, as if it were a Hindu mantra. Is there anything other than financial prosperity that is evoked in the Western mind when this word is repeated? Of course not. To grasp the truism of this observation is to understand why modern medicine was, from its inception, doomed to be an abysmal failure, like so many other facets of Western civilization, from which it was born.

- Modern medicine does not represent a step forward in humanity's understanding and employment of healthcare. It is a dysfunctional step backwards. There are other parallels to be found in other scientific disciplines. For all the plaudits concerning its advancement in our understanding of physics, "Einstein's general theory of relativity is closer to Aristotle's than either of them is to Newton's."[101]

- There is a "relative scarcity of competing schools in the developed sciences."[102] The school that makes more money will, by application of pure common sense, be in a better position to quash its competitors. This insight shows, yet again, why modern medicine could never serve the best interests of the patient. That system which can skillfully extract the most money from a given pool of patients will have an enormous edge over a system which is purely devoted to the best outcome for that same patient pool.

- Kuhn closes by stating that "scientific knowledge, like language, is intrinsically the common property of a group or else nothing at all."[103] However, Kuhn fails to delineate the inherent, fascist condition by which the group imposes its view of the world on everyone else! In doing so, he fails to illuminate the effects of its pow-

[101] Ibid., 207.
[102] Ibid., 209.
[103] Ibid., 201.

ers of co-optation, the employment of cooperating state powers, and the suppression of its competitors.

Chapter 6

Brief Introduction to Chapter 7

"Seed Corrupted" was written in the 2007-2009 time frame, and was originally a revised Chapter 5 for what would have been a completely revised *Meditopia*, for which I wrote "prison notes" while incarcerated from September 2004 to June 2006.

It can still be found online.[1]

Before entering into a discussion of a history of orthodox medicine, I felt it was important to establish the roots of the current, corrupt, out-of- control global medical system. It naturally segues from the previous chapter.

---

[1] See: www.meditopia.org/chap5.htm

Chapter 7:

Seed Corrupted

"[The reigning] model of human history, carefully built-up by scholars over the past two centuries, is sadly and completely wrong . . . [It is something which we cannot] put right with minor tinkering and adjustments. What is needed is for the existing model to be thrown out the window and for us to start again with open minds and with absolutely no preconceptions . . ."

Graham Hancock[1]

W
hen I was in my early teens, in the early 1970s, I attended a Roman Catholic seminary. Think high school with no girls, pressed uniforms, strict rules, a campus marked with Roman Catholic symbolism everywhere, daily observance of innumerable elements of ritual: a matrix within the Matrix, if you will. Readers should not read disparagingly into my description, because my overall remembrance of the experience is far more positive than negative.

However, even in my own time, at that early age, I was able to witness how orthodoxy twists empirical evidence in amazingly convoluted ways to fit its own agenda. Specifically, I can remember one class where the lecturing priest attempted to reinforce a long held belief among strict creationists, namely that our planet, our solar system, our galaxy, indeed, the entirety of the Universe, was not only created in seven days, but that the Universe could not possibly have existed prior to 4,004 B.C.

And how would one explain recently developed methodologies, such as carbon-14 dating, which show that the Earth is -- at the least -- billions of years old? Well, that's easy, stated my

---

[1] Graham Hancock, introduction to The Hidden History of the Human Race, by Michael A. Cremo and Richard L. Thompson (Nadia, West Bengal: Torchlight Publishing, 1999), xiii. The comment is in reference to "prehistory," and not "modern history." I use it here because the cracked foundation upon which modern archaeology is built mimics the incorrible cracks found in orthodox medicine, and, as I show as *Meditopia* unfolds, a host of other areas of supposed "knowledge" held dear by the high priests of modern science. They have all been victimized by the unseen hand of our Cultural Operating System.

professor, brimming with confidence, "For all we know, a day at the time of Creation may have been equal to a billion years in our time."

As I glanced around the classroom, I was equally sure that I was not the only one in attendance not buying this nonsense. Years later I would remember this experience while contemplating Joseph Campbell's "chiding mother," who scolds her twelve year old son for writing a paper on evolution, sans Adam and Eve: "Oh, those scientists! Those are only theories![2]

Those who hold themselves as unyielding adherents to modern science have no cause to laugh or belittle, however. For a far greater discovery in my own life is the degree to which our own orthodox system of knowledge is caught in a vast fabric of cognitive dissonance. It exceeds by orders of magnitude the minor prejudice that ensnared my seminary professor.

As I discussed in the context of Thomas Kuhn's thought in Chapter 6, the fatal flaw in modern science is that it doesn't concern itself with a quest for truth, but to the power of consensus among a professional elite, who exist to tell the unwashed masses the truth that is acceptable for them to believe. Concurrent with this, they must do what they must to convey that financial and political success, the yardstick by which people of our age measure their worth, has no influence on the integrity of their work within their underlying disciplines. That people everywhere accept this absurd proposition is yet another example of doublespeak.

Although prevailing historical thought gazes at our Western mechanistic world view and places its origins at the foot of Descartes, or even Bacon,[3] I maintain that a more penetrating mind

---

[2] Campbell, Myths to Live By (New York: Penguin Group, 1972). 3-4. Incidentally, the notion of us living in a Universe that is scarcely more than 6,000 years old has been with us a while. The Archbishop of Armagh, James Ussher, "famously dated the creation at Saturday afternoon on 22nd October, 4004 B.C.E." Martin Rees, Our Final Hour (New York: Basic Books, 2003), 185. He was one of several over the past millennium to come up with a creation date of this proximity.

[3] I've read this in more places than I care to tell, but still notable are Rifkin, Entropy (New York: Bantam Books, 1980) 19-29, and Barzun, From Dawn to Decadence (New York: HarperCollins Publishers, 2000), 203-204. As a side note, Barzun interestingly doesn't come to the

will see that the seeds of our current predictament go back much farther. Toynbee himself, who ascribed to Western Civilization a position of "apparentation" from Graeco-Roman or Hellenic Society, was still able to see enough homogeneity in the twenty civilizations that have lived, breathed, and died before ours in the last 6,000 years to say that "(all) should be regarded hypothetically, as philosophically contemporaneous and philosophically equivalent."[4] For Quigley, in his count of "twenty civilizations which have existed in all of human history," there can be found one "common pattern of experience."[5]

I maintain that these common elements are particular to this age, but not prior ages, that there are, as it were, "Global Cultural Operating Systems" (GCOS) that operate inter-cataclysmically -- between truly severe mass extinction events. These, however, must not be confused with smaller cataclysmal phenomenon which are not sufficiently severe to cause the GCOS to be rewritten, only rebooted. Within the GCOS are numerous sub-cultures, some operating at various times within the life of a GCOS that are at considerable variance from one another. Those sub-cultures that are dominant, as "Modern, Western Civilization" is now, are those that play to the strengths of prevailing GCOS, as in the Prisoner's Dilemma game model I analyze later in this section.

It's not possible to understand the history of medicine in our own time, without understanding the GCOS under which it operates. A number of fundamental premises are key to attaining this understanding.

---

the defense of Bacon ("The master of those who know") in recounting the latter's recommendation to observe nature "free of preconceived ideas," a fundamental principle of the scientific method. (And yet, Stephen Wolfram's discovery of the highly complex forms derived from the simplest of rules, one of the greatest discoveries in my lifetime, was made by observing Bacon's edict and not that of traditional scientific methodology: A New Kind of Science (Champaign, Ilinois: Wolfram Media, Inc., 2002), 108. As Bacon himself noted, most great "scientific" discoveries are achieved by accident or serendipity.)

[4] Arnold Toynbee, A Study of History (Oxford University Press, 1987), 43.

[5] Carol Quigley, Tragedy of Hope (New York: The Macmillan Company, 1966), 3, 7.

Premise #1: History is Cyclical Not Linear; Made So Through the Convolutions of Numerous and Surprisingly Frequent Mass Extinctions on this Planet

A fundamental error that has dogged orthodox archaeology, as tenaciously as the theme of "chemotherapy and radiation treatment for good health" has dogged modern medicine, is that history is linear; that as my creationist history teacher implied: our civilization rides a linear wave of progress from our progenitors ascending fruit-laden trees butt-naked in the jungle to modern men ascending gleaming skyscrapers in fast-moving elevators. And whether the time span appointed for this alleged improvement is four thousand or four billion years, held within the grips of religious creationist thought or neo-Darwinism, is immaterial.

 The Ottosdal metallic spheres are made of such sophisticated material that they cannot be scratched by steel. Found embedded in pyrophyllite rock in the early 1980s, they appear man-made and yet predate any acceptable age for advanced life forms on Earth. They were made approximately 2.8 billion years ago, right here on Earth. Note: that's 2.8 billion, not 2.8 million.

"[We are besieged with the ignorant notion that] if facts do not agree with the favored theory, then such facts, even an imposing array of them, must be discarded . . . There exists within the scientific community a knowledge filter that screens out unwelcome evidence. This process of knowledge filtration has been going on for well over a century and continues to the present day . . .

" . . . Man disfigures the past to purge it of anything that violates his need to have harmony and stability, to have 'the heavens themselves, the planets, and this centre, observe degree, priority and place.'"[6]

[6] See Footnote #1. Cremo, <u>The Hidden History of the Human Race</u> (Torchlight Publishing,

They're wrong, and the catastrophists are correct, through the sheer weight of the empirical evidence.

Holding onto ideas that support an establishment's dogma is no more fitting today than assuaging the prejudices of Galenists of almost two thousand years ago. Those who wish to spend untold hours going through incontrovertible evidence without the pre-approval of the establishment might start with Michael Cremo, or even Immanuel Velikovsky.[7]

It is beyond the scope of this book to re-itemize the thousands of pieces of evidence that clearly show that human beings, or to speak more broadly, humanoids as intelligent as ourselves have lived on this planet for not hundreds of thousands of years, but for what would appear to be hundreds of millions of years. The unspeakable damage that such evidence would inflict on any of the variations of current neo-Darwinism thought is self-evident. What is not so self-evident is why something as simple as humanoid footprints that are 250 million years old cannot be properly addressed by modern archaeology, and are instead relegated to investigators on the scientific fringe.[8]

And yet it is not as if members of the orthodox scientific establishment have not come to similarly dismissive conclusions about some of the most hallowed tenets of our origins. What comes to mind are things like the late-in-life revelations of Francis Crick, the Nobel Prize winning co-discoverer of DNA. He capped his career preaching that the human race most probably did not originate on planet Earth, but was the result of pansper-

---

1999), first quote: p. xviii. The orbs are discussed on p. 120-122; 267. The second quote is taken from Mankind in Amnesia (New York: Doubleday & Company, Inc., 1982), 46 (the secondary quote Velikovsky takes from Shakespeare's Troilus and Cressida, Act I). Incidentally, I recommend Velikovsky's two prior works in cementing the obvious: that the catastrophicists are correct, and the uniformitarians should now be regarded as a relic of the past: Worlds in Collision (New York: Simon & Schuster, Inc., 1977) and Earth in Upheaval (New York: Simon & Schuster, Inc., 1977). In my own worldview, the uniformitarians of modern science are to the catastrophists what apologists for modern medicine are to alternative practitioners like myself, who are strictly empirical. For those not familiar with the difference, I recommend D.S. Allan's discussions in Cataclysm!, (Vermont: Bear & Company, Rochester, 1997), 17-18, 66; though, Velikovsky's treatises make Allan's appear narrower in scope. Nonetheless, the latter is more succinct.

[7] Velikovsky's exposition begins with Worlds in Collision (1950).

[8] Brad Steiger, The Philadelphia Experiment & Other UFO Conspiracies (New Brunswick, New Jersey: Inner Light Publications, 1990), 97.

mia -- that is, seeding from extraterrestrial origins.[9]

For readers who cannot accept this premise as a given, a more thorough reading of books in the footnotes of this chapter is recommended. Quite apart from footnoted, published sources, I can say from personal experience that numerous colleagues have told me through the course of their own journey that they have independently come to the conclusion that human history on Earth is far older than convention would have us to believe.

And if you believe that the human race, or something close to humans in morphology and intelligence, is hundreds of thousands, if not untold millions of years old, than you have to accept that there must have been cataclysmic events, lots of them, that have completely wiped out earlier cycles of civilization. As it turns out, there is plenty of archaeological evidence to support the contention that mass extinctions occur with a frightening regularity on this planet, far more than scientific convention would admit.[10]

Such evidence forms the backbone of my second premise.

Premise #2: Severe Global Cataclysms Create New, Distinctive Civilizational Ages & Rewrite the New Global Cultural Operating Systems (GCOS) That Mark Them

The archaeological evidence, most of it spurned by the orthodox community, showing that mass extinctions have taken place on Earth with a shocking regularity, is so voluminous that a host of theories have arisen to try to make sense of the data. Some cataclysms are mildly severe, such that the global operat-

---

[9] Francis Crick, Life Itself: Its Origin and Nature (New York: Simon & Schuster, 1981) Read the whole book. P. 73-88 provide his explanation of why there is such a small chance that life could have begun on Earth.

[10] Richard Leakey, et al., The Sixth Extinction (New York: Doubleday, 1995), 38-58, in a chapter entitled "The Big Five" details what convention would have us believe are the five previous mass extinctions on this planet that have preceded the one that is presently underway, mostly caused by Homo sapiens. I do not confuse a downfall of individual civilizations with something as drastic as a planet-wide extinction involving a cross section of all life on the planet, but my reading of current anthropological data suggests that there have been a great many more than five. Leakey makes mention of an average cycle of 26 million years on p. 57. But my belief is that it is far more frequent than this as suggested in the text that follows.

ing system has to reboot. Like your computer, the system starts anew, but with no fundamental changes having been made to the global operating system. Only when the cataclysm reaches serious mass extinction levels is the GCOS entirely rewritten, but I'll get to that later.

Richard Firestone, and his associates, have written about the relatively recent effects of a supernova explosion (their best candidate being called "Geminga") that caused mass extinction events on this planet in waves, at roughly 41,000, 34,000, and a longer wave that occurred 13,000 to 16,000 years ago. The effects of the first wave were so great that virtually all megafauna on the North American continent was destroyed (i.e. horses, camels, mammoths, masadons, etc.)[11]

The evidence is compelling and overwhelming.

Thought provoking is Firestone's approach in including indigenous stories which support and enlarge the evidence gathered -- (seventeen in all).[12]

As Firestone points out, supernova remnants move with incredible speed. One fragment from the constellation Sagittarius travels at more than 1.3 million miles per hour. The evidence suggests that a similar fragment hit Earth around 41,000 BCE. Because the life of an individual human is of such short duration, we are not able to appreciate just how dangerous our galaxy is and how frequently our solar system (and Earth specifically) encounters extraterrestrial objects.[13]

"Legend has one great foe to its perpetuation -- civilization. Civilization brings with it a contempt for everything which it cannot understand; skepticism becomes the synonym for intelligence; men no longer repeat -- they doubt,

---

[11] Richard Firestone, et al., The Cycle of Cosmic Catastrophes (Rochester, Vermont: Bear & Company, 2006).

[12] Ibid., Brule (Lakota), p. 152-153; Ojibwe, p. 154-156; Aztec/Atayala, p. 161-162; Arawak, p. 169-170; Hopi, p. 177-178; Maltamuskeets, p. 193-194; Iroquois, p. 209-210; Pawnee, p. 217-218; Aztec, p. 224-225; Navajo, p. 234-235; Toba/ Pilagá (South America), p. 252-253; India, p. 263-264; Wintu (California), p. 290-291; Greece, p. 299-300; Inca, p. 308-309; Kato (north of San Francisco), p. 324-325; Yurok, p. 337.

[13] Ibid., 175.

they dissect, they sneer, they reject, they invent . . ."[14]

Equally impressive is the work of D.S. Allan and J.B. Delair. They distill a host of archaeological findings, some of which overlay Firestone's comments concerning conditions evidenced after the Younger Dryas period. One of the results of this particular extraterrestrial cataclysm (which many believe to have been caused by the celestial body, Phaeton, popularized by Ovid) was "the flood." As it turns out, the resulting deluge is not an isolated story from the Bible. There are over 500 known stories, most from the descendants of indigenous survivors scattered around the world on all six populated continents that confirm the event -- which the authors estimate happened approximately 9,500 BCE.[15]

Where I live in South America, the legends of previous great civilizations are rampant. Harold Wilkins provided a connection between legends throughout Latin America and the fall of Atlantis.[16] Of more recent date, is the collection of essays brought together by J. Douglas Kenyon in his Forbidden History,[17] who introduces his work by reminding us of the myopic conditions that prevent us from recognizing the signs of our immense past that are all around us:

> "[For] after all, it is argued, if there had been an earlier, advanced civilization we would have discovered unmistakeable evidence of its existence. Presumably, we would have seen the remains of its highways, and bridges, and electrical wiring. We would have found its plastic bottles, its city dumps, and its CD-ROMS. Those are, after all, the things **we** will leave behind for future archeologists to

---

[14] D.S. Allan, J.B. Delair, Cataclysm!, 149. Taken from Donnelly, I., 1894, Ragnarok: The Age of Fire and Gravel (Echo Library, Fairford, UK, 2007), (New York), vi, 452; 117, as quoted by Allan/Delair.

[15] D.S. Allan, Cataclysm!, 150-151.

[16] Harold Wilkins, Mysteries of Ancient South America (Kempton, Illinois: AdventuresUnlimited Press, 1947).

[17] J. Douglas Kenyon (editor), Forbidden History: Prehistoric Technologies, Extraterrestrial Intervention, and the Suppressed Origins of Civilization (Rochester, Vermont: Bear & Company, 2005).

puzzle over.

"But could an ancient civilization have risen to heights similar to our own, yet have traveled a different road? What would we understand of a world that might have employed fundamentally different -- though no less effective -- techniques to harness the forces of nature? Would we, or could we, comprehend a world capable of, for example, creating and transmitting energy by means other than a power grid, traveling great distances without internal combustion engines, or making highly complex calculations involving earth science and astronomy without electronic computers?

"Do we have the grace to recognize and respect achievements other than our own, or must we take the easy way out and resort to crude stereotyping of our mysterious primitive ancestors, dismissing out of hand anything we don't immediately understand?"[18]

Kenyon goes on to note that Immanuel Velikovsky studied the issue of prior civilizations extensively and came to the conclusion that modern man is suffering from a collective amnesia, that traumatic events of the past have so scarred man's collective consciousness that a protective psychological defense mechanism prevents us from remembering events we cannot bear to remember. On the individual level we call this post-traumatic stress syndrome, but, as Kenyon notes, why could this diagnosis not apply to the culture of an entire planet?[19]

It is futile to grade the probability of the various theories that have emerged to explain the new archaeological data, and it is unnecessary for the purposes of this book. What is important is to recognize that evidence exists that entire world civilizations have fallen and been replaced by new ones. And it is at the juncture where cataclysm occurs, where nature has cleaned out the Petri dish, laid waste prior complex societies and ecosystems worldwide, and left advanced life forms to begin anew, that real change can occur, unhampered by huge inertial impediments of

---

[18] Ibid., 1.
[19] Ibid., 3; 53-68.

the prior age.

Any computer programmer knows that when he or she sits down to write code, the moment where the screen is bare and not one character has been set down holds infinite possibilities, limited only by the boundaries of the underlying hardware. With the first line begins dramatic limitation. Structure has begun. Functionality requires focus and limits. There may be 50,000 lines of code -- but none that so narrow the course of what follows as the first few lines.

An arrow may travel 200 meters to reach its target, but nothing so restricts the direction, range, and speed of the arrow as the conditions set by the archer before the arrow leaves the bow. I maintain that to uncover, through a process not unlike linear regression, what code was written at the beginning of one's age, one may, with a level of comprehension that borders on the metaphysical, grasp everything else that follows. You cannot understand the essence of your age, see through thousands of years of Orwellian doublespeak, or successfully navigate through a sea of cognitive dissonance and the unending disparities between common narratives and the understandings of elites, if you don't.

My journey in coming to this conclusion was greatly aided by the work of Stephen Wolfram. A prodigy in mathematics, Wolfram began at age twelve (1972) to study cellular automata and was surprised to find that formulas of immense simplicity gave rise to patterns of such unintended complexity that the outcomes were completely counter-intuitive. We live, after all, in a world culture where it is given that engineering a complex outcome requires the development of complex inputs.

Devoting himself, for the next 30 years -- first as an occasional hobby and then eventually with considerable effort -- to studying this phenomenon, Wolfram released his findings in 2002.[20]

---

[20] Stephen Wolfram, A New Kind of Science (Champaign, Ilinois: Wolfram Media, Inc., 2002), 17-22. By the way, this concept should not be confused with "entelechy," where something complex emerges when you put a large number of simple objects together. Such an idea has existed in the philosophy of science for many years. This complexity emerges from one very simple concept or "program."

Early on, Wolfram provides 255 "rules," or simple formulas to demonstrate his "new science." His question began with a simple idea, or as he himself explains:

> *New directions in science have typically been initiated by certain central observations or experiments. And for the kind of science that I describe . . . these concerned the behavior of simple programs.*
>
> *In our everyday experience with computers, the programs that we encounter are normally set up to perform very definite tasks. But the key idea that I had nearly twenty years ago . . . was to ask what happens if one instead just looks at simple arbitrarily chosen programs, created without any specific task in mind. How do such programs typically behave?*
>
> *The mathematical methods that have in the past dominated theoritical science do not help much with such a question. But with a computer it is straightforward to start doing experiments to investigate it. For all one need do is just set up a sequence of possible simple programs, and then run them and see how they behave . . .*
>
> *An important feature of cellular automata is that their behavior can readily be presented in a visual way. And so the picture below shows what one cellular automaton does over the course of ten steps.*[21]

The picture Wolfram points to is shown below. The precondition is simple: for each and every step, as in all cellular automata of this type, there is a definite rule determining the color of a given cell from the color of that cell and its immediate left and right neighbors on the step before.

Here, the formula is: **each cell on each row will be black where it or either of its neighbors were black on the step before:**

---

[21] Ibid., 23-24.

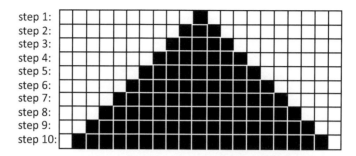

Simple, right? . . . We know what this pattern is going to look like 10,000 generations from now. But what happens if we introduce the tiniest variation -- still keeping the formula simple. Do we still get a predictable, intuitive result? In the 50 generation sample below, we see the pattern produced by "Rule 90," shown on p. 25 of Wolfram's book. The formula is as follows: **a cell should be black whenever one or the other, but not both, of its neighbors were black on the step before.**[22]

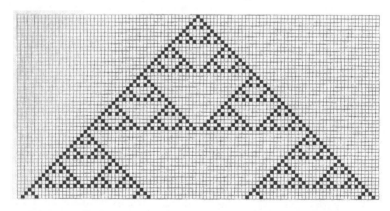

It's not all that complicated, but it still contains nested elements that would not have occurred to us without forethought -- namely, producing the automata for ourselves from the formula provided. The following example is the same formula taken out 500 steps. It is more complicated, but still just a larger version of the 50 step evolution of the same formula. Novelty has peaked.[23]

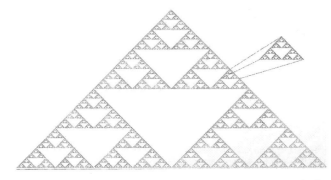

The last example I'll use from Wolfram's work is called Rule 30. The formula is: **Look at each cell and its right-hand neighbor. If both of these were white on the previous step, then take the new color of the cell to be whatever the previous color of its left-hand neighbor was. Otherwise, take the new color to be the opposite of that.** Given a moment of thought, this is still a very simple formula. Taken out 50 generations, yields the following.[24]

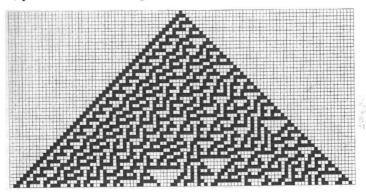

The result, on the surface, appears to be chaotic. There is neither discernible order nor clearly definable regularity. However, carrying out the automaton evolution to 500 generations, yields a completely different picture. Although chaos still occupies the right side of the pattern, a very regular set of patterns emerges on the left. The imbalance exists because even if it were not immediately apparent, even if it didn't appear intuitive at the onset, the originating formula contained within itself the requi-

[24] Ibid., 27.

site asymmetry.[25]

Wolfram was not the first to note the enormous, unforeseen complexities that can emerge from simple initiating conditions. The emerging field of chaos theory was built on this premise. Years earlier James Gleick had commented on a population biologist at Princeton University who in the early days of this discipline was "about to publish an impassioned plea that all scientists should look at the surprisingly complex behavior lurking in some simple models."[26] Seen, from a different angle, the impetus behind English author and biologist Rupert Sheldrake's work on "formative causation" was based, in part, on his observation that in terms of morphology, behavior, social structure, etc., there was far too much that could not be explained through conventional, mechanistic explanations of genetic predisposition. (In other words, how is it possible for all this complexity to emerge from such simple biological preconditions. We must be missing something).[27] Nevertheless, Wolfram's work is the most illustrative for my purposes.

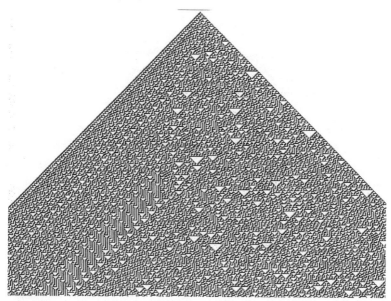

[25] Ibid., 29.

[26] James Gleick, <u>Chaos: Making a New Science</u> (New York: Penguin Books, 1988), 4.

[27] Rupert Sheldrake, <u>A New Science of Life</u> (Los Angeles: Jeremy P. Tarcher, Inc., 1981).

T he idea that marks my current premise is simple, but not novel. Moreover, it is hardly controvertible. In fact, the converse is ludicrous: that there are severe cataclysms that decimate people, their civilizations, the animal and plant life of the period, that the existing order undergoes breathtaking destruction, and then, as if by magic, the GCOS of the one dominant species continues on, unimpeded.

Cultural operating systems, once set in motion in earnest, are like tailor-made gloves. If you destroy the hands for which the gloves were made, you render the gloves useless. Someone else may wear them, albeit that they are ill-fitting. If my analogy appears awkward it is because it is, and I grope to find one that is better. Cultural operating systems are not tailor made; they grow as the new emerging age following a world cataclysm grows. Calcification begins to set in only a few centuries after inception, taking millennia to unfold until, to use the conceptual framework of futurist and entheogenic explorer, Terence McKenna, the novelty critical to the survival of that civilization approaches zero.[28]

What is more controvertible is the existence of a truly worldwide cultural operating system. Does enough commonality exist, as is alluded to by the earlier comments from Toynbee and Quigley? Surely, the records of cultural anthropologists are replete with stories of clashing civilizations that are not only distinctly different, but completely opposite in character. The most notable example for those of us who have lived most of our lives as North Americans, is that of native, indigenous peoples versus Western Civilization, characterized by waves of Europeans who sought not to co-exist with native cultures, but control, conquer, and subsume them.

Whereas European culture carried with it a concept of governance that served primarily monied interest, native cultures were primarily socialist, in the truest sense. European leadership was marked by what it could take from its people; native

---

[28] Terence McKenna, The Invisible Landscape (New York: Bantam Books, 1992). The point cannot be made without a lengthy explanation of McKenna's exposition of the I Ching as it relates to Rule 2(6) -- (the "I Ching" has 64 hexagrams, or two to the sixth power), and the resulting development of his Timewave Zero.

peoples in North America assessed leadership by what it did for its people. Europeans left medicine and the healing arts to a specialized class; native peoples felt that something so personal as healing should be owned by everyone in the tribe. Europeans spread with them law enforcement, prisons, and criminal laws; native peoples did not have law enforcement, prisons, or criminal laws because, living in an appreciation of life in its natural state, they never needed them, crime being rare. Europeans had a concept known as the mental institution; native peoples didn't have them and couldn't relate to them, because their people had no concept of mental illness, probably because their lifestyles don't lend themselves to producing people who are mentally ill.

Seton illustrates these distinct differences between these localized sub-cultures (as opposed to World Cultures) then quotes Dr. Edgar L. Hewett in his own comparison, "There can be no question that the Red man had evolved a better civilization than our own. Its one weakness was in the fact that it did not carry the mastery of metals . . . In esthetic, ethical, and social culture, the Indians surpassed their conquerors . . . it is to the glory of the American Indian race that it developed a type of government entirely different from that of the European, and more effective. The welfare of the people was the supreme end of government."[29]

Professor C. A. Nicols, reportedly a "profound student of Indian life," was quoted in the same work, saying: "I am afraid we have stamped out a system that was producing men who, taken all round, were better than ourselves."[30]

Surely, one cannot say that Western Civilization and the cultures of the hundreds of native tribes that occupied North America were similar. They certainly are not branches coming from the same tree.

So what can possibly be meant by a controlling or Global Cultural Operating System? The answer, strange as it seems, comes from examining what has become a widely accepted tenet of evolutionary biology: our selfish genes.

[29] Ernest Thompson Seton, <u>The Gospel of the Red Man</u> (New York: Doubleday, 1936), 31-32.
[30] Ibid., 32.

I t goes without saying that in our global Western culture, it is competition, and not cooperation, which provides the backdrop for our sense of healthy development, advance, and self-worth. For example, consider the implications of our ubiquitous sporting events as they reflect on our culture, with the single-minded objective of beating all opponents, and rendering them losers as compared to the one, unique, acclaimed winner.

It wouldn't seem right to see the scientific establishment, to which the current, dominant sub-culture within our GCOS gave birth, provide a self-definition that deviated from this outlook. "We are survival machines -- robot vehicles blindly programmed to preserve the selfish molecules known as genes."[31] And not just people: " . . . all animals, plants, bacteria, and viruses."[32] The problem I have with Darwinists like Dawkins is that, if -- truly -- we are reduced to nothing but machines exclusively committed to the four "F's" (feeding, fearing, fighting and fucking) does this not severely limit our cultural development possibilities? Are we not unnecessarily limited in seeing all our cultural development options through the rubric of our current, global Zeitgeist?

Richard Dawkins saw in an old game, the Prisoner's Dilemma, the opportunity to examine the possibilities.[33] There are

---

[31] Richard Dawkins, The Selfish Gene (Oxford, UK: Oxford University Press, 1976), xxi.

[32] Ibid., 21.

[33] In The Selfish Gene, 205, Dawkins explains the original: "'Prisoner comes from one particular imaginary example. The currency in this case is not money but prison sentences. Two men -- call them Peterson and Moriarty -- are in jail, suspected of collaborating on a crime. Each prisoner, in his separate cell, is invited to betray his colleague (DEFECT) by turning King's Evidence against him. What happens depends upon what both prisoners do, and neither knows what the other has done. If Peterson throws the blame entirely on Moriarty, and Mariarty renders the story plausible by remaining silent (cooperating with his erstwhile and, as it turns out, treacherous friend), Moriarty gets a heavy jail sentence while Peterson gets off scot-free, having yielded to the TEMPTATION to defect. If each betrays the other, both are convicted of the crime, but receive some credit for giving evidence and get a somewhat reduced, though still stiff, sentence, the Punishment for mutual defection. If both cooperate (with each other, not with the authorities) by refusing to speak, there is not enough evidence to convict either of them of the main crime, and they receive a small sentence for a lesser offence, the Reward for mutual cooperation. Although it may seem odd to call a jail sentence a "reward," that is how the men would see it if the alternative was a longer spell behind bars. You will notice that, although the 'payoffs' are not in dollars but in jail sentences, the essential features of the game are preserved . . . If you put yourself in each prisoner's place, assuming both to be motivated by rational self-interest and remembering that they cannot talk to one another to make a pact, you will see that neither has any choice but to betray the other, thereby condemning both to

many variations to this extremely simple two party game, but here is the original one, the one used by Dawkins in his book. At the center of the game is a "banker," who pays winnings and collects "fines" from the two players. Each side has but two cards in his hands. One is marked "cooperate" and the other "defect." Each holds the cards face down so that the other party cannot see or be influenced by the other's move. The players submit their playing cards and wait for the banker to turn them over.

The possible outcomes are very limited, or so it seems: twice two possible outcomes, or four. The outcomes, and their related payments and fines, are as follows:

Outcome 1 -- both cooperate: The banker pays each $300. This is the **REWARD** outcome.

Outcome 2 -- both defect: The banker fines each $10. This is the **PUNISHMENT** outcome.

Outcome 3 -- the first cooperates, the second defects: The banker pays the one $500 (the Temptation to Defect) and fines the other (the Sucker) $100.

Outcome 4 -- the first defects, the second cooperates: The banker pays the first the Temptation payoff of $500 and fines the second, the Sucker, $100.

		WHAT SECOND PLAYER DOES	
		COOPERATE	DEFECT
WHAT FIRST PLAYER DOES	C O O P E R A T E	Fairly good **Reward** (for mutual cooperation) $300	Very bad **Sucker's Payoff** (giving with no return) $100 fine
	D E F E C T	Very good **Temptation** (to defect) $500	Very good **Punishment** (for mutual defection) $10 Fine

The table above illustrates the relevant outcomes, with the respective monetary gains or losses.

The simplicity of the game and the surprising number of

heavy sentences." The 'iterated' version of this game, played out an indefinite number of times with the same players, produces, as Dawkins notes, a higher level of complication, and "in its complication lies hope."

possible outcomes when played through an extensive number of rounds is intriguing. When played repeatedly (called "Iterated" or "Repeated" Prisoner's Dilemma), there is a wide range of potential strategies. These strategies carry descriptive names like "Always Cooperate" and "Always Defect," where the latter will always defeat the former. "Tit for Tat," where the player cooperates on the first move and thereafter copies the previous move of the other player. "Naive Prober," identical to Tit for Tat, except that there are random moves where the player throws in a gratuitous defection and claims the high Temptation payment. "Suspicious Tit for Tat," identical to Tit for Tat, except that the player defects on the first move. "Remorseful Prober," like "Naive Prober" except that the player remembers whether it has just "spontaneously defected, and whether the result was prompt retaliation. If so the player 'remorsefully' allows its opponent 'one free hit' without retaliating, and so forth.

Dawkins leans heavily on the work of Robert Axelrod, who ran computerized competitions using a variety of submitted "strategies." Those strategies leaning in favor of cooperation were termed "nice"; those in favor of defection, "nasty." These strategies can be thought of in terms of localized cultures, or perhaps the culture of an entire civilization. The rules of the *Prisoner's Dilemma* game can be thought of as our Global Cultural Operating System, of which the strategies or localized cultures are but possible subsets. Stated another way, the GCOS can be seen as the set of over-arching global cultural conditions under which sub-cultures are strategies for playing, governed by the over-arching set of rules.

Statistically, but not intuitively, the "nice" strategies fared better overall. In fact, Dawkins entitles the chapter on this subject, "Nice guys finish first."

Such outcomes, however, do not translate into the real world. I suspect that this is largely because of the artificiality of the game: each player sees the move of his opponent as soon as it is played. The same rules apply to both sides. Knowledge is not bifurcated. Truth is not sequestered.

It goes without saying that today's "winning strategy" modern or "Western" civilization, is most decidedly "nasty." It is not by accident that an axiom of American business is the expression, "Nice guys finish last." It is with this self-evident observation that Harold Bloom could look at the expanse of history, find within it the unerring leaning to the forces of the demonic and proclaim, "Nature does not abhor evil; she embraces it. She uses it to build. With it, she moves the human world to greater heights of organization, intricacy, and power . . . Death, destruction, and fury do not disturb the Mother of our world, they are merely parts of her plan. Only we are outraged by The Lucifer Principle's consequences . . . for we are casualties of Nature's callous indifference to life, pawns who suffer and die to live out her schemes. One result: from our best qualities come our worst. From our urge to pull together comes our tendency to tear each other apart. From our devotion to a higher good comes our propensity to the foulest atrocities. From our commitment to ideals comes our excuse to hate. Since the beginning of history, we have been blinded by evil's ability to don a selfless disguise. We have failed to see that our finest qualities often lead us to the actions we most abhor -- murder, torture, genocide, and war." It is no wonder that in observing the effects of what was, even then, the winning strategy of our current global operating system, Descartes would come to the conclusion that the "basic categories of ethics are not good and evil, iniquity and righteousness, but, as in the natural world, power and impotence."[34]

The astute reader will not miss the application of this tendency in modern medicine. Stripped of its well-worn, thread-thin propaganda, we see an organism that creates diagnostic techniques that actually induce disease,[35] vaccines that confer more disease than they have ever prevented,[36] pharmaceutical

---

[34] Howard Bloom, The Lucifer Principle (New York: The Atlantic Monthly Press, 1995), 2-3. Comments on Descartes are taken from Hiram Caton's The Politics of Progress (Gainesville, Florida: University of Florida Press, 1988), 63.

[35] Lynne McTaggart, What Doctors Don't Tell You (New York: Avon Books, 1998), 15-41. The author states that most of the more than 1,400 different diagnostic tests have been shown not to work very well. (p. 17) She goes on to enumerate the more common tests and some of the related dangers. I chose this text as an example because McTaggart goes to considerable length to be balanced.

[36] Neil Z. Miller, Vaccines: Are They Really Safe & Effective? (Santa Fe, New Mexico: New

drugs with laughably lengthy side effect caveats that even at their best address one or more symptoms, rarely the underlying cause -- why? Because they are fundamentally toxic:[37] 1) scientific research elites who effectively create parameters that absolutely ensure that it will be impossible to find a cure for the disease for which taxpayers are paying them billions;[38] 2) regulatory agencies (think: U.S. FDA) that work to ban or make unavailable inexpensive vitamin and mineral products that threaten pharmaceutical profits[39] or even existing medications for indications when they threaten existing patent drugs;[40] 3) whore-like medical journals that admit that the research they are publishing make a "mockery of clinical investigation;"[41] to name just a few of the objectionable elements that form the cesspool that is modern, organized medicine.

Has it always been this way and must it always be? Bloom

Atlantean Press, 2002), 105-106. The book begins giving medicine every benefit of a doubt until the evidence is laid out, and organized medicine is forced to take it on the chin. The book concludes with the only possible position for those who can review the particulars without an interest in medicine itself: (1) Vaccines have largely not been the cause of a epidemiological decline in disease, (2) No vaccine is able to confer genuine immunity. (3) All vaccines can produce side effects. (4) The long-term effects of all vaccines are unknown. (5) Several of the vaccines (cited) are especially dangerous.

[37] Tonda R. Bian, The Drug Lords: America's Pharmaceutical Cartel (Kalamazoo, Michigan: No Barriers Publishing, 1997), 95. "Any drug without toxic effects is not a drug at all." -- Eli Lilly. I found particularly illuminating Andrew Weil, M.D.'s comments on p. 160, that medicine "lacks any clear concept of health." He adds: "I heard the word health mentioned very infrequently during four years of medical school . . . allopathic doctors gave lip service to preventative medicine . . ."

[38] Gerald B. Dermer, The Immortal Cell (Garden City Park, New York: Avery Publishing Group, Inc., 1994) ". . . I have learned that there is a vast and deadly gap between the reality of cancer, which strikes human beings, and the theory of cancer, which thousands of researchers are using in their search for a cure . . . it is an account of a scientific and medical scandal of the highest order." (p. ix - xi) So begins Dermer's account in a book that left me so pissed off at various intervals that I had to put it down. Everyone in the cancer researcher field should read this book, but, of course, they don't and they won't. And that is the entire point.

[39] Elaine Feuer. Innocent Casualties: The FDA's War Against Humanity (Pittsburgh, Pennsylvania: Dorrance Publishing Co., 1996), 65-79. I could have picked hundreds of sources for this footnote, but Feuer's chapter seven of this book, "The FDA -- As Dangerous As The Worst Disease," does an excellent job of covering the history of the FDA as it pertains to that agency's suppression of essential nutritional supplements.

[40] Jack Dreyfus, A Remarkable Medicine Has Been Overlooked (New York: Continuum Publishing, 1997). When someone as powerful as Jack Dreyfus spends 20 years and untold millions of dollars, helps produce over 10,000 studies from 38 countries, published in over 250 medical journals, and still can't get the FDA to move, you know how powerful the pharmaceutical company overlords are. The study itself begins on p. 297.

[41] John Abramson (M.D.); Overdosed America (New York: HarperCollins Publishers, Inc., 2005), 96-97.

closes with a glimmer of hope, stating "To our species, evolution has given something new -- the imagination. What that gift, we have dreamed of peace. Our task -- perhaps the only one that will save us -- is to turn what we have dreamed into reality."[42] I agree with Bloom's sense of urgency concerning our future, but I disagree with his assessment of our past.

Our age is Luciferian because it is so dictated by our current dominant Global Operating System, set in place at the close of the last major catastrophe, the Deluge, an event that was not the last major global catastrophe, but certainly among its most severe.[43] Evidence abounds of a Golden Age, one preceding the current run of 26 civilizations, where peace dominated, life was simple, and the Luciferian principle did not hold sway. "The malaise has apparently been perceived in all civilizations," notes Hiram Caton, "for none lacks a mythology of yearning for the golden age and the simple life."[44] Steve Taylor's recent work combs through considerable recent anthropological evidence to show that throughout the world, indigenous peoples tell of a "Golden Age," where war was virtually non-existent, in patriarchy's place stood an equality and mutual respect between the sexes, greed and exploitation were unknown as they are now, and predominant was a 'strong attachment to the natural world' and a deep reverence for it." He calls the transition to our current GCOS, The Fall[45] -- which is the title of his work.[46]

"It sounds like paradise, and in a way . . . it was. In fact . . . this is exactly how it seemed to later peoples, who remembered this pre-Fall period of history in their mythology, as a Golden Age or an era when 'The men of perfect virtue' lived. No human groups invaded other groups' territory and tried to conquer them and steal their possessions. There were no wandering bands of marauders who raided villages, and no pirates who lived by at-

---

[42] Bloom, The Lucifer Principle, 331.

[43] Immanuel Velikovsky, Worlds in Collision (New York: Simon & Schuster, Inc., 1977).

[44] Hiram Caton, The Politics of Progress (Gainesville, Florida: University of Florida Press, 1988), 11.

[45] Steve Taylor, The Fall: The evidence for a Golden Age, 6,000 years of insanity, and the dawning of a New Era (Hampshire, UK: The Bothy, John Hunt Publishing, Ltd., 2005).

[46] Ibid., 29-49.

tacking coastal settlements. Everywhere the status of women was equal to that of men and nowhere were there any different classes or castes, with different degrees of status and wealth . . . a spirit of natural harmony seems to have filled the whole planet, a harmony between human beings and nature and amongst human beings themselves. Human beings may have been oppressed by nature to an extent, but they were free from oppression by other human beings. Human groups didn't oppress other groups, members of the same groups didn't oppress each other, and men didn't oppress women."[47]

Heinberg, writing 16 years earlier, with less access to the recent findings, notes, "The evidence of anthropology and archaeology may not prove (though it certainly does not deny) the former existence of a Golden Age -- that is, of a unitary culture in which people were universally and continually telepathic, lived close to Nature, and possessed miraculous powers. But . . . anthropological and archaeological discoveries have shown, almost beyond a doubt, that two of the most destructive aspects of civilization (the use and justification of violence as a means of ordering society and the desire for dominance over other human beings and over Nature) were acquired only recently. The findings of archaeologists show that in the past human beings did live -- and therefore in principle are capable of living -- in peace and harmony both among themselves and with Nature."[48]

It has been a grand quest through the ages to determine what caused this "Golden Age" to come to an end. Taylor has no problem locating a point of decline, which he attempts to show is connected to environmental causes in an area which James DeMeo calls "Saharasia." What resulted were resource wars, or just plain wars, which resulted in man's devolution into an "ego explosion" which has plagued our species and Nature ever since.[49] But Heinberg is not willing to commit to any one theory, *"What caused the Fall? Why and how was the Age of Innocence*

---

[47] Ibid., 49.

[48] Richard Heinberg, <u>Memories and Visions of Paradise</u> (Wheaton, Ilinois: Quest Books, 1989), 239.

[49] Steve Taylor, <u>The Fall</u> (Hampshire, UK: The Bothy, John Hunt Publishing, Ltd., 2005), 50-51 and 104-124.

brought to an end? These questions have perplexed theologians and philosophers for millenia . . . the myths themselves do not present a straightforward, unified explanation, rather, in describing what seems to be a shift in the fundamental polarity of human consciousness, they employ a variety of images that seem to be metaphors for some subjective, spiritual event." From the orthodox Christian, who believes that the Fall took place in the Garden of Eden, to the similar myths recounted by Heinberg, one thing is undeniable: the common elements that unite them all. Such stories are regarded as myth, but it is the contention of researchers like Heinberg that they are meant to convey real events. Velikovsky notes that the prophets of the Old Testament speak incessantly about global catastrophes, which although they are more recent than those which caused the Fall, are equally the victims of discounting: "(they all) speak insistently about these catastrophes (but despite their clear intent and concreteness of testimony they have gone) unnoticed. The texts are read and looked upon as mere metaphors or allegories of political events."[50]

Were the exact cause of The Fall crucial to *Meditopia*, assuming it comes down to just one cause, I would extend my own argument.

It is not.

Were the exact, chronological location of the spiritual demise of our race crucial, I would extend my own argument.

But it is not, for it matters not one whit whether, to use Taylor's language, we have subjected ourselves, our environment, our planet, to 6,000 years of insanity, or to 8,000 years, or if I am to use D.S. Allan's chronology going back to the last major Deluge in 9,500 B.C., to 11,500 years. It matters little whether or not the deluge was created because of a pole shift, the gravitational effects of a large, passing, extraterrestrial object, a supernova explosion outside our solar system, like Geminga, or some

---

[50] Immanuel Velikovsky, Mankind in Amnesia (New York: Doubleday & Company, Inc., 1982), 43. The quote from Heinberg is taken from Memories, p. 82. The entire exposition on the cause of the fall is contained in Chapter 5, "The Saddest Story," pp. 81-111.

combination thereof.

The point is, it happened. The record is too replete from too many sources to pretend that it didn't.

Contained within those same records are the stories of altered life that follow cataclysm -- and here is where common sense must override the incessant need to justify everything from the archaeological record, as if we have all lost the ability to reason the obvious: cataclysm brings with it a breakdown of the established order. Mass extinction comes, and with it ecosystems and societies are remade. I regard this as self-evident, though the record is clearly supportive. In the scientific realm, Kuhn's <u>Structure of Scientific Revolutions</u>[51] makes clear that paradigm shifts (a microcosmic example of what I'm talking about) never occur on their own. They are a result of crisis posed by a new and compelling theory or stream of thought. The old thought is not destroyed unless a new and compelling "cataclysm" arrives to remake the discipline. Rebirth does not occur without destruction.

In the act of a GCOS rewrite, not a reboot, but a rewrite, the rules of the Prisoner's Dilemma change. Using the example of Wolfram's analysis, the global operating system gets to start fresh, as it were, with a new cellular automata formula. In that delicate moment when life begins anew, opportunities emerge to take the world in a direction that may be at complete variance with the dictates of life in the prior age. The Petri dish called Earth is a new, fresh culture, ready to accept the first few lines of a new operating code. What new program will be introduced to run the new Earth? Will it be anything close to what we have now, where a variation of "Always Defect, Especially When You Deceptively Can Make It Look Like You're Cooperating" has been employed now for thousands of years to give the greatest spoils to the one who does the best job of pillaging, raping

---

[51] Thomas S. Kuhn, <u>The Structure of Scientific Revolutions</u> (Chicago: The University of Chicago Press, 1962). This book is hugely important. The internalization of its major concepts should be considered elemental to being an educated person in the 21st century. Known for having coined the expression "paradigm shift," the book is a highly damaging critique of scientism. Even one of its fiercest critics, Steven Weinberg, has remarked, "Structure has had a wider influence than any other book on the history of science." It is not enough to know that truth is not a criterion of scientific theory. It is more important to know why.

and bombing, while perfecting internal and external propaganda to justify such benign behavior? Will the new program allow organized medicine to continue as it is now, creating more disease than it relieves? Underwriting a health care holocaust that rivals the most vicious of declared wars?

I hope not.

But then it is my argument that we risk making the same mistakes in "writing" the new program, unless we aggressively go back to the first few lines of code from the existing GCOP, the one that was written 6,000 or 8,000 or 11,500 years ago and examine the cultural DNA that created our world. Ours is the product of corrupted cultural seed, and we will not succeed in creating a new world unless we can fully understand the one we leave behind. Moreover, we coincidentally now find ourselves with an emerging urgency to do so.

People like Ervin Laszlo believe we are approaching the "tipping point," and the time to make changes to our global operating system is now, because as dire as things appear on the surface, it's not yet too late (though he doesn't use those exact words.) Yes, despite all the evidence that the inertial factors that hold our unsustainable ways in place are implacable, Laszlo pleads for a miracle within the near future.[52] Sir Martin Rees argues that our species is approaching its "final hour," and is "more at risk than at any earlier phase in its history,"[53] an opinion seconded by Sir James Lovelock, who popularized the concept of "Gaia."

"I am not a pessimist," James Lovelock writes, "and have always imagined that good in the end would prevail. When our Astronomer Royal, Sir Martin Rees, now President of the Royal Society, published in 2004 his book, Our Final Century, he dared to think and write about the end of civilization and the human race. I enjoyed it as a good read, full of wisdom, but took it as no more than a speculation among friends and nothing to lose sleep over . . . I was wrong, it was prescient, for now the

---

[52] Ervin Laszlo, The Chaos Point (Charlottesville, Virginia: Hampton Roads Publishing, 2006), 84-87

[53] Martin Rees, Our Final Century (London: Arrow Books, 2003), 188.

evidence coming in from the watchers around the world brings news of an imminent shift in our climate towards one that could easily be described as Hell: so hot, so deadly that only a handful of the teeming billions now alive will survive."[54]

Given the timing of the current global malaise, I am moved to wonder if it is severe cataclysm that brings an end to the GCOS and causes it to be rewritten, or whether the GCOS contains the seeds of imperfection that invite the next cataclysm?

Premise #3: Characteristics of Our 6,000+ Year Civilizational Age and the "Winning Strategy Sub-Cultures" That Have Defined It Provide Clues To The Opening Lines of our GCOS

What initial conditions could possibly have been written in the opening code of our age such that we would get, as a programmed outcome, the hellhole we have now? Can we work backwards to decipher the initial code by studying a sampling of its many outcomes, or as Ludwig Wittgenstein states in commentary to the second "line of code" in his own exposition on the philosophy of knowing, "In logic, nothing is accidental: if a thing can occur in a state of affairs, the possibility of the state of affairs must be written into the thing itself . . . If things can occur in states of affairs, this possibility must be in them from the beginning."[55]

Theories abound; from orthodox Christians we would hear that this world, and everything in it, belongs to, or is the dominion of, Satan. The opening code has in it the plucking of the apple from the Tree of the Knowledge of Good and Evil, an open defiance of God, and only with a cataclysmic outcome (Armageddon) and the return of Christ will there be a more wholesome

---

[54] James Lovelock, The Revenge of Gaia (New York: Allen Lane (Penguin Books), 2006), 147-148. When I contemplate the effects that the enormous global warming to come will have, I cannot help but reflect on an old Burmese traditional saying, "When luxury prevails, fire consumes the world and water washes it away . . ." Harold T. Wilkins, Mysteries of Old South America (Kempton, Illinois: Adventures Unlimited Press, 1947), 24.

[55] Ludwig Wittgenstein, Tractatus Logico-Philosophicus (London: Outledge Classics, 1921), 6. Taken from proposition commentaries 2.012 and 2.0121.

direction, where the Kingdom of God rules, a positive change in the operating system.

For Steve Taylor, the opening code might include his "ego explosion," such that the changes to the code are the result of changes in humankind collectively. There are certainly plenty of books on the market now that preach that the only way out of man's current dilemma is a change of heart, a collective change within humankind.[56]

For those who want something more structured, I recommend Terence McKenna's Timewave Zero It's done a pretty good job of deconstructing history so far, but the initial conditions are ambiguous, nor is it clear that we have the ability to change them.[57]

Then again, we can use the mind to build more creative, many would say outrageous, possibilities: marry together the translated Sumerian texts of Zacharia Sitchin with the psychological analysis of Immanuel Velikovsky, then toss in the observations of a handful of related authors and here's the result -- forget Francis Crick, panspermia, and being seeded from outer space -- it's much worse than that: Homo sapiens is a designer species created by a nefarious, sadistic, exploitative, extraterrestrial group called the Anunnaki, who will come again when the planet Nibiru does a fly-by in the near future. We've had a "War on Terror," in some form or fashion, for some 6,000 years now, but it's what the Anunnaki left behind that ails us: a world governing "Elite," whose tentacles are the influential secret societies whose members can be found in every corner of the world. This Elite, whose members and their forebears were once victimized by the Anunnaki and Earth disasters, now emulate them. We could remember some of this past trauma ourselves, but are collectively prevented from doing so as a self-protective mechanism of the psyche.[58]

---

[56] Taylor, 114-115.

[57] McKenna, 161, 170-175

[58] In the order mentioned in this paragraph. Few people have time to read all seven books that Zacharia Sitchin has written on this subject. Fortunately, there is considerable overlap, so if you don't have time to begin with Sitchin, The 12th Planet (New York: HarperCollins, 1999) (originally published in 1976). and work forward, at least read the summation in the

Wow, talk about defying the common narrative!

Well, forget other people's theories. Let's build our own. If we were to create a formula, with the simplicity of those used by Wolfram in his cellular automata, how would it read?

Stated in plain language, not mathematical symbolism, perhaps it would read something like this:

1. My thoughts are separate from others.
2. "I" is separate from "not I",
3. Mine (possessions) are separate from not mine.
4. Aid "not I" only if materially beneficial to "I".

That's it. Remember, any initial program must be simple.

Right away, we see that the opening code contains elements of Taylor's "ego explosion," but this is not an original idea. Richard Maurice Bucke proposed over a century ago that man must pass through self-consciousness on the way to higher states of collective evolution, ending in cosmic consciousness, first for select individuals, and then for the entire species. Bucke makes clear that passing through this stage means experiencing the "ego" in ways inaccessible in prior stages of development.[59]

What these first few lines of social reality code reveal is a collective

move to atomisation, fragmentation, individual benefit at the expense of the collective polity and not societal wholeness. There is asymmetry. There is a zero sum struggle which must inevitably develop between the "I" who has and the "not I" who does not. From this originating operating code there develops a natural bifurcation in assets, social standing, and knowledge.

Yes, there are peoples, like most of the native American tribes who flourished in North America before the European in-

---

seventh and final installment of his Earth Chronicles series: Sitchin, The End of Days (NY: HarperCollins, 2007). The self-protective mechanism of the psyche is the subject of: Immanuel Velikovsky, Mankind in Amnesia (NY: Doubleday & Company, 1982). The balance of the thoughts are taken from diverse sources such as Marshall Masters, David Icke, Jon Rappaport, Jim Marrs, Jim Keith and Ralph Epperson, to name but a few who speak along these lines in sources too numerous to list here.

[59] Richard Maurice Bucke, Cosmic Consciousness: A Study in the Evolution of the Human Mind (New York: E.P. Dutton & Co., 1969), 61-82.

vasion, playing out cultures that seem counter to the opening code. But they do not survive. Variants of "Always Cooperate," are not winning strategies. They are not Luciferian. They will not make it and, indeed, they haven't.

For any of the indigenous cultures of the Americas to have winning strategies, the GCOS would have had to read something like this:

1. My thoughts spring from a Collective Unconscious.
2. "I" is not separate from the collective.
3. My life is woven into the fabric of community -- the collective.
4. Aid the community that is an expression of the wholeness of Life.

Such an initial set of operating conditions represents almost an antithesis of what mankind has been witness to for the last 6,000 years.

What you would get if you took the first set of operating code and in Wolfram-esque fashion fast-forwarded through 300+ generations of human existence can be seen permeating every area of human life.

But this is *Meditopia.*

So I'll stick to the effects, the history, of just one area for now.

Medicine.

Bibliographical Addendum to Chapter 7

Something went wrong in the aftermath of the last cataclysmal episode, such that the resulting GCOS (Global Cultural Operating System) of our current civilizational period ended up giving greedy, self-centered, "Always Defect -- But Make It Look Like Cooperation" gaming strategies a decisive survival edge, to the disadvantage of living strategies that are community-based, Earth-friendly, balanced in their relationship to Nature, and joyful to everyday people.

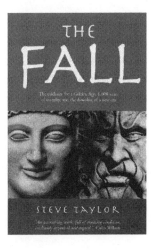

Our era is one where the GCOS --- the Seed --- was corrupted at its inception. Our current world, screwed up ecologically, socially, and politically, ravaged by war, pollution, unending Elitist-centered propaganda and divorced from the natural world, is the devolutionary end result.

This is the position I am taking in this chapter. The end result is supported by the general conclusions of Steve Taylor in THE FALL: the evidence for a Golden Age, 6,000 years of insanity, and the dawning of a new era.

Taylor makes the case that "after 6,000 years of psychosis, we may finally be regaining our sanity,"[60] drawing from recent historical developments and current events. It may not be that easy. Judging from the past, it may entirely be the case that only a major mass extinction event sufficient to cause a rewriting of the GCOS will bring an end to the insanity." The inertial factors of the current operating system are too great.

Taylor's recounting of what was lost from an earlier Age, is expanded on in an earlier work by Richard Heinberg, Memories and Visions of Paradise: Exploring the Universal Myth of

---

[60] Steve Taylor, 303.

a Lost Golden Age.[61] There are many common elements between Heinberg and Taylor's approach. Both see a "return to the Garden," and present evidence that a sea change is underway. Heinberg quotes from Bucke's Cosmic Consciousness, using an argument that I used myself in Lumen,[62] namely, that our entire species is involved in an expansive evolutionary trend from self-consciousness to cosmic consciousness.

I now regard any notion that such a change can take place without cataclysm as provincial.

Edited by J. Douglas Kenyon, Forbidden History,[63] a collection of 42 essays dealing with the "suppressed origins of civilization," covers a broad swath. Most notable because the important thesis in *Meditopia* is that modern science has been far more about the suppression of knowledge and/or its sequestration to the benefit of a select Elite, than it is about the open quest for truth.

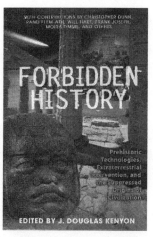

Forbidden History is but one of a slew of works to recently surface that are supportive of Premise #1 in this chapter: that history is not linear. It's circular, or as an old Indian proverb teaches, "There is nothing new under the sun."

---

[61] Heinberg, Richard; Memories and Visions of Paradise: Exploring the Universal Myth of a Lost Golden Age (Quest Books, Wheaton, IL; 1989).

[62] Greg Caton, Lumen: Food for a New Age (Lake Charles, Louisiana: Calcasieu Graphics, 1986), 136-150.

[63] J. Douglas Kenyon, Forbidden History: Prehistoric Technologies, Extraterrestrial Intervention, and the Suppressed Origins of Civilization (Vermont: Bear & Company, Rochester, 2005).

The fields of modern, orthodox archaeology / anthropology / history are still dominated by the uniformitarians. The entire notion that the Earth regularly undergoes crustal displacement and the north and south poles change positions is still considered dubious. To admit that this is the case would be a wholesale admission of defeat by orthodoxy and a statement of victory for the catastrophists.

But given the weight of evidence at hand, which has only been enhanced since Charles Hapgood wrote Path of the Pole,[64] just when will orthodoxy throw in the towel?

"A great many empirical data indicate that at each point on the earth's surface that has been carefully studied, many climatic changes have taken place, apparently quite suddenly. This . . . is explicable if the virtually rigid outer crust of the earth undergoes, from time to time, extensive displacement over the viscuous plastic, possibly fluid inner layers. Such displacement may take place as the consequence of comparatively slight forces exerted on the crust, derived from the earth's momentum of rotation, which in turn will tend to alter the axis of rotation of the earth's crust . . . I think that this rather astonishing, even fascinating, idea (of crustal displacement) deserves the serious attention of anyone who concerns himself with the theory of the earth's development."[65]

Such a pronouncement was not made by a cataclysm fanatic. Albert Einstein wrote this in the foreword for the first edition of Hapgood's work, three years before he died in 1955. This only reinforces lessons gained from the trials of Linus Pauling in Chapters 4 and 6: no matter how high you ascend the ladder of success in orthodoxy's world, you risk having your ideas, if not your reputation, besmirched by your colleagues, if you don't

---

[64] Charles Hapgood, Path of the Pole (Kempton, IL: Adventures Unlimited Press, 1999).
[65] Ibid., xiv-xv.

strictly adhere to orthodoxy's statement of reality.

Immanuel Velikovsky's <u>Worlds in Collision</u>[66] (1950) was the first of four books written by this esteemed physician on the subject of his view of catastrophism.

Taken together, the reader is presented with such a dizzying array of evidence -- archaeological, historical, and from a surprising number of indigenous sources, that one has to wonder how orthodoxy has been able to hold out for so long.

The answer, by now should be easy: after all, if the orthodox medical community can convince the public that radically toxic therapies like chemotherapy and radiation therapy are actually good for them, they can convince a naive public to believe anything.

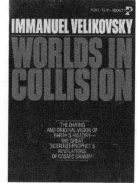

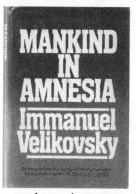

Mankind, in Velikovsky's theoretical framework,[67] is the victim of untold planetary destruction in remote antiquity. Collectively, we subconsciously seek to relive our trauma, while paradoxically seeking to hide the truth of the obvious. This explains, in part, why our race so doggedly sticks to a worldview that world cataclysm is extraordinarily rare. Velikovsky's position is not wild conjecture. Widely regarded as one of the greatest psychiatrists of the 20th century, Velikovsky was merely extrapolating from what psychiatrists observe in trauma victims all the time. The only debatable point is: could humanity be acting, through its collective unconscious, as an amnesia victim? Could this explain the wholesale destruction of the planet's life-support systems?

Velikovsky's position is quite possible, nor is it exclusive

---

[66] Immanuel Velikovsky, <u>Worlds in Collision</u> (New York: Simon & Schuster, Inc., 1977)
[67] Immanuel Velikovsky, <u>Mankind in Amnesia</u> (NY: Doubleday & Company, 1982)

to, or a rejection of, the theory of a current, self-centered, suicidal GCOS as the foundation for our current civilizational era.

Velikovsky drew primarily from written records -- most of them ancient -- to make his point about the frequency of cataclysmal events on our planet. Drawing from an array of more recent archaeological evidence, Richard Firestone demonstrates that just one cosmic event, which he attributes to the explosion of supernova Geminga approximately 43,000 years ago, is the cause of not one, but three distinct and separate cataclysmic eras as described 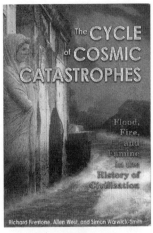 in his book, The Cycle of Cosmic Catastrophes.[68] He then overlays the recent archaeological evidence on matching indigenous stories which concur with his scientific find.

These events, all sufficient to rewrite the GCOS in their respective times, are the subject of numerous indigenous stories. Strangely, all of the stories bear the same common elements: 1) The Creator warns of trouble. 2) Almost everyone ignores the warnings. 3) The few people who listen take action to save themselves and others. 4) Fire, stones, and/or ice soon fall from the sky. 5) Thick clouds form, heavy rains fall, and flooding begins. 6) Many people, plants and animals perish. 7) Some survive to build and repopulate the world.[69]

Cataclysm![70] makes the most compelling case I've seen for a cosmic catastrophe over 11,000 years ago. It closely corresponds to "the Flood," as depicted in Genesis. Phaeton is the candidate of choice for D.S. Allan and J.B. Delair, but for my

---

[68] Richard Firestone, Allen West and Simon Warwick-Smith; The Cycle of Cosmic Catastrophes: Flood, Fire, and Famine in the History of Civilization (Vermont: Bear & Company, Rochester, 2006).

[69] Ibid., 154.

[70] Allan, D.S.; J.B. Delair; Cataclysm! Compelling Evidence of a Cosmic Catastrophe in 9500 B.C. (Vermont, Bear & Company, Rochester, 1997).

current thesis, the cause is quite irrelevant. More important is the presentation of an astonishing amount of evidence of the degree to which this one catastrophe remade our world, its topography, and undoubtedly it's GCOS.

The notion that whatever operating system runs our Matrix decidedly favors evil over good will not surprise most. Howard Bloom doesn't say exactly that, you have to connect the dots for yourself, but he does make clear that what we call evil is a by-product of the creative process.

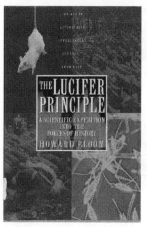

The idea, and conclusion, is old and well-worn. Bloom himself opens with the story of Marcion, an "influential Christian heretic" who, circa 200 A.D., took a look at the world around him and came to the conclusion that "the god who created our cosmos couldn't possibly be good. The universe was shot through with appalling threads -- violence, slaughter, sickness, and pain. These evils were the Creator's handiwork. Surely he must be some perversely sadistic force, one who should be banished from influence over the minds of men."[71]

Nonetheless, I have, of late, heard this same refrain from a surprising number of sources. Last year, I happened to read Kurt Vonnegut's final work before his death. His closing words are telling: "When the last living thing / has died on account of us. / How poetical it would be / if Earth could say, / in a voice floating up / perhaps / from the floor / of the Grand Canyon. / 'It is done.' / People did not like it here."[72] He does little to give any

---

[71] Howard Bloom, 1.

[72] Kurt Vonnegut, A Man WIthout a Country (New York: Random House, 2007), 137.

indication in his final composition that in his 82 years, he found anything distinctly "good" about humanity.

Evolution can go to hell as far as I am concerned. What a mistake we are. We have mortally wounded this sweet life-supporting planet . . . with a century of transportation whoopee.[73]

Yet he is even closer to the "mark," (as in Twain) in making mention of one of Samuel Clements last works, a curious short story entitled, *The Mysterious Stranger*.

" . . . if (one doubts) we are demons in Hell, he should read *The Mysterious Stranger*, which Mark Twain wrote in 1898," Vonnegut writes, " . . . In the short story he proves to his own grim satisfaction and to mine as well, that Satan and not God created the planet earth and the 'damned human race.' If you doubt that, read your morning paper. Never mind what paper. Never mind what date."[74]

Twain closes his story quoting the character representative of "God," as telling the protagonist: "Strange! that you should not have suspected years ago -- centuries, ages, eons ago! -- for you have existed, companionless, through all eternities . . . (that you have resided in a dream with) a God who could make good children as easily as bad, yet preferred to make bad ones; who could have made every one of them happy, yet never made a single happy one; who made them prize their bitter life, yet stingily cut it short; who gave his angels eternal happiness unearned, yet required his other children to earn it; who gave his angels painless lives, yet cursed his other children with biting miseries and maladies of mind and body; who mouths justice and invented hell -- mouths mercy and invented hell -- mouths Golden Rules, and forgiveness multiplied by seventy times seven, and invented hell; who mouths morals to other people and has none himself; who frowns upon crimes, yet commits them all; who created man without invitation, then tries to shuffle the responsibility for man's acts upon man, instead of honorably placing it where

[73] Ibid., 9.
[74] Ibid., 111-112.

it belongs, upon himself; and finally, with altogether divine obtuseness, invites the poor, abused slave to worship him!"[75]

Such dissonance comes from the oddest places. I remember re-reading the Book of Ecclesiastes (Old Testament) while in prison and coming to the conclusion that if King David (the alleged author) could pen something so nihilistic, what conclusions should come to the rest of us. "I have seen all the works that are done under the sun; and, behold, all is vanity and vexation of Spirit. That which is crooked cannot be made straight; and that which is wanting cannot be numbered . . . I gave my heart to know wisdom and to know madness and folly. I perceived that this also is vexation of spirit. For in much wisdom is much grief; and he that increaseth knowledge increaseth sorrow."[76]

Such words hardly come from the mind of a man who believes that the world rests on a foundation of good.

From the time I was a small boy, well before I became a meditator at the age of 15, or even entered the seminary around the same age, I had the impression, the feeling, the unmistakeable sense that I was living through a time of enormous imbalance. And yet this crookedness, this monumental defect that was imbued in all facets of human existence, was a temporary state, and not a statement of man's permanent condition.

That the teachings of indigenous peoples from around the world tell of a Golden Age preceeding this one, confirms my own sense. It tells me that Bloom's Luciferian World is a statement of our age and not humankind's potential.

It tells me that with the right GCOS set in motion in the aftermath of the next cataclysm, we can return to the Golden Age. We can create a global society where joyful variations of "Always Cooperate" have a chance.

We can create a world in complete, utter contrast to this one, a world that is not Luciferian.

Steve Wolfram's A New Kind of Science provides the foundation for my belief that the model of a GCOS (Global Cultural

---

[75] Ibid., 252-253.

[76] Bible, 505, Ecclesiastes, 1:14,15,17,18.

Operating System) is a useful tool in understanding the current state of the world.[77]

And what or who sets a GCOS in motion? Many authors hint that a GCOS exists, but no one provides a satisfactory answer. Perhaps we can never know with certainty. Zacharia Sitchin might say that ancient Sumerian texts provide the answer: that we are a slave race, the result of advanced genetic manipulation

(which, would, of course, explain the inexplicable "missing link" that has dogged anthropologists now for the entirety of the discipline's existence) -- that the greed and selfishness of our age is the leftover remnant of extraterrestrial forces that came to the planet eons ago, not to live in harmony here with its other inhabitants, but to exploit it for minerals.

I have a very difficult time dismissing Sitchin, or the Sumerian scribes who composed the ancient works that are the well-spring for Sitchin's material. It isn't simply that Sitchin's theses are radically at variance with, or even defiant of our common narrative, but that they have an air of authenticity. My primary reservation rests in the fact that Sitchin describes an Anunnaki that co-existed with humans over eons, in fact, trans-cataclysmi-cally through multiple GCOS rewrites. Strangely, I acquired a renewed respect for Sitchin's work when I considered the impli-cations of Cleve Backster's work with plants. (The connection is not immediately intuitive, so I explain below.)

Nonetheless, this, or any other theory which attempts to solve the riddle as to what could have set our current GCOS into motion, is bound to be contentious. Our quest to find an initiat-ing condition or causative agent may always be conjectural. We are left to wonder (1) what agent wrote, created, or otherwise

---

[77] Stephen Wolfram, A New Kind of Science (Champaign, Illinois: Wolfram Media, Inc., 2002).

cast those first few sensitive lines of GCOS code that gave birth to our Luciferian world, and (2) under what conditions was that GCOS candidate able to blossom -- crushing other possible candidates in its wake. This quest is, to my mind, both unknowable and irrelevant. We know from its blossoming result that it exists -- even if we are shielded from knowing the exact particulars with certainty.

I am not embarrassed by this position.

Astrophysicists argue the very same kind of questions in debating the particulars of the Big Bang. Even with the relatively recent inclusion of String Theory, I have found most explanations for events before and during the Big Bang to be as wildly conjectural as any I may make for the originating conditions of our GCOS.[78]

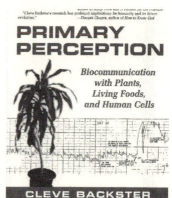

I first became familiar with Cleve Backster's work as a teenager with Peter Tompkins' The Secret Life of Plants.[79] The 2003 update on Backster's work, Primary Perception greatly expanded on the small section devoted to Backster in the earlier work.[80]

Perhaps every reader who en-

---

[78] Michio Kaku, Visions, (New York: Doubleday, 1997), 350-353. I could pick numerous examples, but those who study physics -- even like myself, a complete amateur, out of my field, settling for layman's predigested texts sans the advanced mathematics -- know that in the Big Bang we are dealing with a vague theory that exists simply to help us piece together the evidence. I find it fitting that Kaku has quoted, not in one or two of his books, but three, the following well-worn story (which does nothing but enhance my argument, even though it deals with the Unified Field Theory): "In 1958, physicist Jeremy Bernstein attended a talk at Columbia University where Wolfgang Pauli presented his version of the unified field theory, which he developed with Werner Heisenberg. Neils Bohr, who was in the audience, was not impressed. Finally, Bohr rose up and said, 'We in the back are convinced that your theory is crazy. But what divides us is whether your theory is crazy enough." Parallel Worlds, (New York: Doubleday, 2005), 186-187.

[79] Peter Tompkins, with Christopher Bird; The Secret Life of Plants: a fascinating account of the physical, emotional, and spiritual relations between plants and man (New York: Harper & Row, 1973).

[80] Cleve Backster, Primary Perception: Biocommunication with Plants, Living Foods, and Human Cells (Anza, CA: White Rose Millenium Pres, 2003).

counters these works comes away with a different impression. Here's mine, the short version, of course, and here's the relevance to the current chapter: modern, "civilized" man, *Homo industrialis*, pick the name of your choice to describe our kind, is an extreme aberration, so completely divorced from Nature and the workings of this planet, that it is in no way inaccurate to say that we are vastly inferior to ordinary plants.

Backster's work repeatedly points to a world of plants where organisms communicate telepathically, sometimes over extraordinary distances. Whereas we experience the limits of five senses: seeing, not as good as eagles; smelling, not as good as dogs; hearing, touching, and tasting, not as good as too many animals to name; plants in their world have approximately twenty senses. The innumerable ways in which plants are rooted in the earth, communicate with their surroundings, and share empathy with other organisms, even on the cellular level, makes me question by what measure of insanity we have gathered the audacity to call ourselves *sapiens* -- an intelligent species.

Zecharia Sitchin's rendering of Sumerian texts sounds positively loony, but only in relation to the common narrative. If we are not the aberrant result of genetic tinkering by extraterrestrial creatures more intelligent than ourselves, a mutant humanoid race, a parasitic virus to this planet, than why do we behave as if we are?

And, yet, condemning of my own kind as I may sound, I am moved, when I read indigenous stories of life before the Fall, to believe that contained with our current GCOS is the power to reduce us to such primitive, industrial savages. On the other side of the next cataclysm will be a new GCOS, one that will recognize the folly of our current path, one that will allow us to regain what we lost before the Fall.

I decided to use a section of Dawkins' The Selfish Gene[81] to illustrate the various strategies that an operating system (in this case, the rules of a game called "Iterated Prisoner's Dilemma")

---

[81] Richard Dawkins, The Selfish Gene (Oxford: Oxford University Press; first published in 1976, but this is the 30th anniversary edition, 2006).

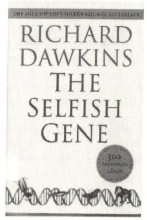

can make. The rules of the game will ultimately determine which strategies are most successful under the dictates of those rules, just as there are hidden within Wolfram's formulas, the outcomes, some quite unintended, that must blossom from them.

I am no expert at Game Theory, though I felt the employment of the Prisoner's Dilemma was important to demonstrate the relationship between the rules of an underlying set of conditions (operating system) and those strategies that will best exploit it.

Dawkins' book is very poor as a primer, so, for a more thorough introduction to this area of game theory, its history, and the life of one of its early innovators, John von Neumann, I recommend Prisoner's Dilemma.[82] Essential, too, are the more recent volumes on "cooperation" by Robert Axelrod.[83]

James Lovelock was, for many years, the promoter of the concept of "Gaia" (the idea that Mother Earth, with its extensive control systems, exhibits characteristics that using even the strictest criteria in biology constitute evidence of a distinct living orgasm). With The Revenge of Gaia he has thrown in the towel.[84] Oh sure, he provides the salutary, "Go team, go! We can win!" In fact, it's on his book cover, "We can still save humanity."

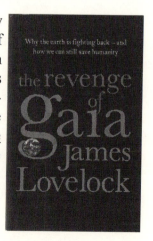

However, underneath the bravado, if you read the book

[82] Williams Poundstone, Prisoner's Dilemma (New York: Doubleday Books, 1992).

[83] Robert Axelrod, The Complexity of Cooperation (Princeton, NJ: Princeton University Press, 1997). Axelrod, The Evolution of Cooperation (New York: Perseus Publishing, 2006).

[84] James Lovelock, The Revenge of Gaia, (New York: Allen Lane (Penguin Books), 2006).

through in its entirety, is the distinct sense that the football score is 36-0; your team is losing; there are two minutes left in the fourth quarter; but what are you going to do? You can't very well cheer for the other team, can you?

Ervin Laszlo sees through the bravado, as well, and notes Lovelock's position as an acknowledgement that we have passed a "point of no return."[85] In his The Chaos Point, he argues that it is not too late[86] but even in its beseeching ("Seven Years to Avoid Global Collapse . . .") I detect a faint-heartedness.

More importantly, I think that Laszlo misses the point: he wants renewal, but he refuses to acknowledge that when things are this --- well . . . what can I say? Nothing short of the vernacular will do here --- when things are this totally, completely, and irreversibly fucked up, you cannot have renewal without cataclysm.

You can't have life without rebirth, and you can't have rebirth without death.

You can't save this global system; it's beyond repair. The unspeakably decadent state of modern medicine is but a microcosm of the failing system, which, as I'll show later, shares its virulent characteristics throughout the full spectrum of what we call civilization.

We need a complete overhaul of our GCOS; unfortunately, we don't get that without cataclysm.

And there are unmistakable signs that Mother Nature, which has just about had her fill of humanity, has no qualms about accommodating.

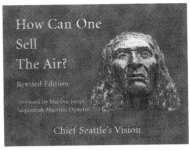

Jared Diamond is incorrect in asserting that the Native peoples of the Americas lost to superior European forces merely because they were technologically inferior. Ostensible technical

---

[85] Ervin Laszlo, The World at the Crossroads (Seven Years to Avoid Global Collapse and Promote Worldwide Renewal) (Charlottesville, Virginia: Hampton Roads Publishing, 2006), 31
[86] Ibid., 84-85.

deficiency in warfare was a symptom of something much more fundamental. Native Americans' inability to murder, plunder and steal at a pace, even when they learned how the European game is supposed to be played, that could compete with their counterparts, was born of deficient operating cultures that did not play well in the current GCOS.

This disparity is apparent in a famous speech given by Chief Seattle of the Squamish tribe in what is now Washington State. The value it places on man's connectedness with his environment stands in stark contrast to the values of our GCOS's winning strategy. The excerpt, below, enunciates this chasm:

Every part of this earth is sacred to my people. Every shining pine needle, every tender shore, every vapor in the dark woods, every clearing, and every humming insect are holy in the memory and experience of my people. The sap, which courses through the trees, carries the memories of the red man.

The white man's dead forget the country of their birth when they walk among the stars. Our dead never forget this beautiful earth, for it is the mother of the red men. Our dead always love and remember the earth's swift rivers, the silent footsteps of spring, the sparkling ripples on the surface of the ponds, the gaudy colors of the birds. We are a part of the earth and it is a part of us. The perfumed flowers are our sisters: the deer, the horse, the great condor, these are our brothers. The rocky crests, the juices in the meadows, the body heat of the pony, and man all belong to the same family. So when (Washington) sends word that he wishes to buy our land, he asks much of us . . .

(But) we will consider your offer . . . It will not be easy. This land is sacred to us. We take our pleasure in the woods and the dancing streams. The water that moves in the brooks is not water but the blood of our ancestors. If we sell you the land, you must remember that it is sacred to us, and forever teach your children that it is sacred. Each ghostly reflection in the clear water of the lakes tells of events and memories in the life of my people . . .

If we sell our land, you must remember, and teach your chil-

dren, that the rivers are our brothers, and yours, and you must henceforth give the rivers the kindness you would give to any brother. The white man does not understand. One portion of land is the same to him as the next, for he is a wanderer who comes in the night and takes from the land whatever he needs. The earth is not his brother, but his enemy, and when he has won the struggle, he moves on. He leaves his father's graves behind, and he does not care. He kidnaps the earth from his children. And he does not care. The father's graves and the children's birthright are forgotten by the white man, who treats his mother the earth and his brother the sky as things to be bought, plundered, and sold, like sheep, bread, or bright beads. In this way, the dogs of appetite will devour the rich earth and leave only a desert.

The white man is like a snake who eats his own tail in order to live. And the tail grows shorter and shorter. Our ways are different from your ways. We do not live well in your cities, which seem like so many black warts on the face of the earth. The sight of the white man's cities pains the eyes of the red man like the sunlight that stabs the eyes of one emerging from a dark cave.

The air is precious to the red man, for all things share the same breath -- the beasts, the trees, and man, they are all of the same breath. The white man does not mind the foul air he breathes. Like a man in pain for many days, he is numb to the stench.

If we sell you this land . . . I will make now this condition: You must teach your children that the ground beneath their feet responds more lovingly to our steps than to yours, because it is rich with the lives of our kin. Teach your children what we have taught our children, that the earth is our mother. Whatever befalls the earth befalls the sons of the earth. If men spit upon the ground, they spit upon themselves. We know this. The earth does not belong to the white man; the white man belongs to the earth. This we know. All things are connected like the blood that unites our family. If we kill the snakes, the field mice will multiply and destroy our corn.

All things are connected. Whatever befalls the earth befalls the sons and daughters of the earth. Man did not weave the web of life; he is merely a strand in it. Whatever he does to the web, he does to himself.

Tribes are made of men, nothing more. Men come and go, like the waves of the sea. The whites too shall pass, perhaps sooner than all other tribes. Continuing to contaminate his own bed, the white man will one night suffocate in his own filth.

But in his perishing the white man will shine brightly, fired by the strength of the god who brought him to this land and for some special purpose gave him dominion over this land. That destiny is a mystery to us, for we do not understand what living becomes when the buffalo are all slaughtered, the wild horses all tamed, the secret corners of the forest are heavy with the scent of many men, and the view of the ripe hills blotted by talking wires. Where is the thicket? Gone. Where is the eagle? Gone. And what is it to say goodbye to the swift pony and the hunt? The end of the living and the beginning of survival.

If we sell you our land, it will be filled with the bold young men . . . Your dead go to walk among the stars, but our dead return to the earth they love. The white man will never be alone unless, in some distant days, he destroys the mountains, the trees, the rivers, and the air. If the earth should come to that, and the spirits of the dead, who love the earth, no longer wish to return and visit their beloved, then in that noon glare that pierces the eyes, the white man will walk his desert in great loneliness . . .[87]

---

[87] Eli Gifford and R. Michael Cook, <u>How Can One Sell The Air?</u> (Summertown, Tennessee: Natives Voices, 2005), 49-61. This excerpt is taken from the Ted Perry's version of Chief Seattle's 1854 speech.

256

Chapter 7

Brief Introduction to Chapter 8

"Primitive Medicine" was written, like the previous chapter, in the 2007-2009 timeframe. It was originally a revised Chapter 6 for what would have been a completely revised Meditopia, for which I wrote "prison notes" while incarcerated from September 2004 to June 2006. It can still be found online. [1]

Following the principles laid down in the previous chapter ("Seed Corrupted"), this chapter makes it clear that under the rules of the current GCOS (Global Cultural Operating System), the only possible outcome is the corrupt system that prevails today. Our present world is the genetic expression of the underlying conditions that have been previously articulated.

---

[1] See: www.meditopia.org/chap6.htm

Chapter 8:

Primitive Medicine

Simple, Effective Systems of Healing Would & Could Not Prevail Under the Current GCOS

"Occasionally, begrudging recognition is given the fact that the Indians taught the early arrivals to these shores what to eat, how to farm, and how to survive in the harsh, cold woods. And nowadays, because of the recent work of groups attempting to protect the rainforests of the world, we are hearing about forest Indians' knowledge of medicinal plants. We are beginning to grasp that modern pharmacology is rooted in the ancient knowledge of forest plants, and that we have barely begun to tap the Indians' full knowledge of these matters. And yet that knowledge is on the verge of being totally lost as the forests are destroyed and the Indians are killed or removed from their lands."

Jerry Mander[1]
(emphasis added)

"Intuition from traditional science and mathematics has always tended to suggest that unless one adds all sorts of complications, most systems will never be able to exhibit any very relevant behavior. But the results so far . . . have shown that such intuition is far from correct, and that in reality even systems with extremely simple rules can give rise to behavior of great complexity . . . (this) implies that there is never an immediate reason to go beyond studying systems with rather simple underlying rules."

Stephen Wolfram[2]

---

[1] Jerry Mander, <u>In the Absence of the Sacred</u> (New York: Sierra Club Books, New York: 1992), 230.
[2] Stephen Wolfram, <u>A New Kind of Science</u> (Champaign, Ilinois: Wolfram Media, Inc., 2002), 110.

"The fascinating feature of primitive medicine is that it represents a medical system utterly different from our own, yet one that functions satisfactorily."

Erwin H. Ackerknecht, M.D.[3]

"The believer in truth . . . is bound to maintain that the things of highest value are not affected by the passage of time; otherwise, the very concept of truth becomes impossible . . . (Nonetheless) let us remember all the while that the very notion of eternal verities is repugnant to the modern temper."

Richard M. Weaver[4]

While imprisoned in Beaumont, Texas I happened to be introduced to a Native American from Mexico. He was from the Carro tribe that lives in the Sierra Occidental where the states of Nayarit and Jalisco meet. He described the place as quite indigenous, where Mexican federales knew better than to enter. As he said this to me he drew a pointed index finger from one side of his throat to the other. "The land is not their home. It is ours."

At the time, I spoke little Spanish, and my Carro friend spoke no English, only his native language and Spanish.

When I brought up the subject of native medicine, "Juan" was always decisive on any given treatment. He knew the plant, insect, or in the case of deadly snake bites, the excrement, that was used, the protocol, contraindications, not to mention extensive stories of anecdotal case histories.

"You are a doctor or shaman?" I inquired, very early in our relationship."

"No," he replied. "There are many people in my tribe who know these things."

"And what do you do if you need to use a white medical doctor?" I then inquired.

"Except for traumatic accidents, that is almost never," he

---

[3] Erwin H. Ackernecht, M.D., <u>A Short History of Medicine</u> (Baltimore: The John Hopkins University Press, 1982), 10.

[4] Richard M. Weaver, <u>Ideas Have Consequences</u> (Chicago / London: The University of Chicago Press, 1948), 52-53.

replied. "Our medicine works better."

One of the most remarkable things about living in a place like Ecuador, where indigenous ways have not been entirely exterminated, and in many ways are actually cherished, is you get to see, firsthand, the effects of authentic shamans. The common people have access to knowledge of their environment sufficient to sustain basic good health, but there is a level above that, which seeks to sustain not just the physical well-bring of members of the tribe, but the psychological, emotional, and spiritual well-being, as well. The shaman practices his craft openly, using amulets, herbs, incantations, etc. No secrets. No patented medicines. The authentic shaman doesn't even charge for his services, but, from what I have observed in the Amazon, lives largely on the voluntary donations of what his fellow man (the word, patient, seems ill-fitting), provides.

This is the all-encompassing role of the shaman.

You must seek them out, of course, because none of the effective shamans I have met are given to catering to tourists. In fact, nowadays, it is common to find charlatans among those claiming to be shamans. Common, yes, but the real deal is there for those who seek with sincerity, a pure heart, and an open mind. In one of John Perkins' books, he discusses his eyewitness account of a 103-year-old Otavalan shaman and his miraculous healing powers. He even records his experience in watching someone brought back from the dead.[5]

I have seen authentic shamans in action, and I can boldly attest to their healing abilities. They are not systems of recent development. To speak to the shamans of South America of their traditions, they will tell that they *are* the purest, modern representation of ancient medicine. They are the true representatives of ancient systems of healing that are our birthrights, birthrights that, I believe, were forsaken with the executed unfolding of our current GCOS.

I have read the antiseptic and sterilized accounts of paleop-

[5] John Perkins, The World is as You Dream It (Rochester, Vermont: Destiny Books, 1994), 88-95. On the shamanic power to bring people back from the dead: 71-74.

athology and paleomedicine, which attempt to take archaeological accounts of ancient medicine, pass them through the rubric of modern science, and produce an accounting of worthless, wannabe medical practice.[6] I could give more credence to orthodox accounts if I had not witnessed such shocking attempts to suppress scientific truth in my own time.

I am a living, breathing person. So are my associates. We have worked with thousands of people and cured diseases, primarily cancer, that orthodox physicians had claimed were hopeless. If the orthodox establishment can do such an effective job of squelching what I know, if they can suppress an effective cancer cure that was actively published as such in 1858, what power do they have over cultures, peoples, and archaeological sites that passed on thousands of years ago? At least I have some limited ability to speak and write. I can talk to people. I can photograph results and reproduce hundreds of testimonials. What power, in this present age, do ancient cultures have, aside from their descendants in the shamanic community, where no one is present who can know fully what they knew and represent their knowledge as relevant in our own time?

I open this chapter by recounting my experience simply because if we draw from strictly orthodox accounts, we must take into account the bias that all modern, authoritative sources have built into their story-telling, because as I have shown, our historical accounts are brimming with breathtaking levels of fudging. After all, no respectable historical accounts are allowed to travel far from the all-consuming, centripetal force of the common narrative.

Truly, we have not strayed far from Hobbes' portrayal of

---

[6] Lois N. Magner, A History of Medicine (New York: Marcel Dekker, Inc.1992), 1-13. Examples abound, so I will pick just one. Magner closes her opening chapter on early medicine with the following: "we should remind ourselves that the ingredients in many traditional remedies are so exotic, nauseating, or toxic that the prescriptions were more likely to scare people out of their illness than to cure them. When faced with the choice of consuming 'boiled black bugs and onions,' or pleading guilty to good health, many marginally ill patients must have chosen the latter course . . . (the) vestiges of these actions remain in the 'old wives' tales' told by people entirely too sophisticated to believe such stories any more than they would worry about a broken mirror or Friday the thirteenth."

the lives of primitive peoples as "nasty, brutish, and short."[7] And yet, contrary to the way in which indigenous peoples are portrayed, in any aspect of their lives, including health care, I am always struck by how relatively satisfied they are. It reminds me of famous comment by Richard Weaver, in the best known work of his trilogy:

> " . . . modern man has not defined his way of life . . . (so) he initiates himself into an endless series when he enters the struggle for an 'adequate' living. One of the strangest disparities of history lies between the sense of abundance felt by older and simpler societies and the sense of scarcity felt by the ostensibly richer societies of today. Charles Péguy has referred to modern man's feeling of 'slow economic strangulation,' his sense of never having enough to meet the requirements which his pattern of life imposes on him. Standards of consumption which he cannot meet, and which he does not need to meet, come virtually in the guise of duties. As the abundance for simple living is replaced by the scarcity of complex living, it seems that in some way not yet explained, we have formalized prosperity until it is for most people only a figment of the imagination . . ."[8]

Premise #4: Cleaving Wholeness for Fragmentionalism Was The First Step in the Development of Modern Medicine. It Manifested As a Demand for Elite Specialization. It is the First Predictable Outcome in the Unfolding of Our Current CGOS.[9]

The majority of works I have read on the history of medicine, and I have read over a dozen, can be broken down into two sections: primitive medicine and so-called civilized medicine.

---

[7] See: www.phrases.org.uk/meanings/254050.html

[8] Weaver, Ideas, 14-15.

[9] As a matter of continuity, the first three premises before this one are clearly laid out in the previous chapter.

The first one or two chapters are devoted to the primitive: paleo-medicine, paleopathology, perhaps some space to early ethno-botany, etc. The bulk of the remainder goes to so-called civilized development.[10]

Great effort is made to construct a smooth, linear history, such that time, progress, and technical achievement are overlaid in perfect conjunction. That this approach appears to be universal does not surprise, after all, it utilizes the myth of unending, linear progress in our time that was set in motion by Francis Bacon, refined with contributions by Descartes and Newton, and sealed with the evolutionary principles of Darwin and commentaries of Herbert Spencer.[11]

No one questions this because these are the evolved rules of the game, for as Kuhn notes, scientists in any era, and apparently those who write about them, ply their craft like chess players. They are allowed to construct endless strategies for winning the game as long as they don't question the underlying game rules.[12]

Contained within this approach, however, is a huge deception. By measuring medical advance through chronology, the earliest systems of human health care, those which are, yes, the simplest, but also the most time-tested, the most employed as a result of empirical observation, are unwittingly castigated as elemental and unworthy of serious consideration by the modern mind. Such prejudice is embedded in the etymology of the very words used, primitive meaning first born (L. *primitivus*) and civilized referring to urbane citizens (L. *civilis*), as opposed to soldiers, foreigners, and, as if it needs repeating, so-called savages.

What is missed is the homogeneity and striking efficacy of ancient systems, some of which I have used myself, encountering them, as I have, as a result of first traveling to, and then

[10] Marshall D. Sahlins, Evolution and Culture (Ann Arbor: University of Michigan Press, 1960), 36. In noting the study of cultures as integrated into the Darwinian mindset, he notes, "The social subsystem of cultures is especially illustrative of progress in organization, and it is often used to ascertain general evolutionary standing. The traditional and fundamental division of culture into two great stages, primitive and civilized, is usually recognized as a social distinction: the emergence of a special means of integration, the state, separates civilization from primitive society organized by kinship."

[11] Jeremy Rifkin, Entropy (New York: Bantam Books, 1980) 19-29.

[12] Kuhn, The Structure of Scientific Revolutions, 144-145.

living in close proximity to, the Amazon rain forest, which is home to over 80,000 species of plant life. In the Amazon there are shamans who have used the very same effective methods, formulas, and practices for countless generations. And that's the rub. The modern mind is immediately outraged by this apparent dissonance. After all, how could medicine be effective unless it was progressing? It has to progress! After all, there can't be excellence in any field without progress, can there? There can't be progress without change. But change cannot be embraced as a critical component of progress without an unwitting refusal to accept universal verities. (Such a worldview consistently over-looks the obvious throughout Nature. Natural healing is instinc-tual in higher life forms. Even Fielding Garrison, an outspoken critic of primitive medicine in his own treatise, noted that "a dog licks its wounds, hides in holes if sick or injured, limps on three legs if maimed, tries to destroy parasites on its body, exercises, stretches, and warms in the sun, assumes a definite posture in sleeping, and seeks out certain herbs and grasses when sick."[13] One requires a modern temper to not see that primitive medicine follows along the same lines that other fellow mammals have been following, with surprising success, for millions of years, unchanged. When Garrison continues, quoting John Burroughs, he fails to grasp the full meaning of his observation. "Man has climbed up from some lower animal form, but he has, as it were, pulled the ladder up after him.")[14]

It is an incontestable fact that the modern mind is at odds with the notion, to borrow from Weaver, that "the things of highest value are not affected by the passage of time."[15] As re-cent as the age preceeding the Enlightenment, the possessor of highest learning was still thought to be the "philosophic doc-tor." Such an individual "stood at the center of things because he had mastered principles. On a level far lower were those who had acquired only facts and skills. It was the abandonment of

---

[13] Fielding Garrison's An Introduction to the History of Medicine (Philadelphia: W.B. Saun-ders Company, 1929).

[14] Ibid., 19.

[15] Weaver, Ideas, 52.

metaphysics and theology which undermined the position of the philosophic doctor, a position remarkably like that prescribed by Plato for the philosopher-king. For the philosophic doctor was in charge of the general synthesis. The assertion that philosophy is queen of studies meant more to him than a figure of speech; knowledge of ultimate matters conferred a right to decide ultimate questions."[16]

So it is in the world of practicing shamans, whose practices and concepts are shockingly similar all around the world.[17] Despite their diminishing numbers and the manner in which their world has been diluted and poisoned by the encroachment and dominating influence of our GCOS's winning strategy, we see in the authentic practitioners the blossoming of the philosopher-king, a political concept to Plato, but a living reality to those indigenous communities that have not yet lost their way in the torrential undertow of modernity. More importantly, we see a kind of wholeness that is almost incomprehensible to the modern mind, whose more objective anthropologists have attempted to define the healing shaman with a smorgasbord of specialized terms, functions, and corresponding occupational name tags: composite physician, pharmacologist, psychotherapist, sociologist, philosopher, lawyer, astrologer, priest, and creator of tribal order.[18]

Modern science cannot view the shaman in his wholeness, because its very act of observing and interpreting what he is requires that the study itself be filtered through the psychotic, fragmented filter that is born of a genetically-altered, artificial world that we call modern civilization. This, in turn, is nothing more than our GCOS run out 200 or 250 or 300 generations (as if an exact number really matters), and observing the manifest results of the winning (i.e., dominant) strategy (i.e., subculture).

This is not a critical excoriation of division of labor. Even the smallest bands of indigenous peoples exercise division of

[16] Weaver, Ideas, 53.

[17] Mircea Eliade, Shamanism: Archaic Techniques of Ecstasy (Princeton, New Jersey: Princeton University Press, 1972), 50

[18] Jeremy Narby, The Cosmic Serpent: DNA and the Origins of Knowledge (New York: Jeremy P. Tarcher/Putnam, 1999), 14-17.

266

labor. It's the unavoidable denotation of division of mind -- one rooted in artificial constructs leading to an artificial world that is at war with the Nature that gave it birth.

It is a worldview that is an early manifestation of the greed and selfishness at the heart of the GCOS. It is the basis for the human experience of "the bicameral mind."[19] It is the foundation for a modern medical system that creates more disease than it could ever eradicate. How can it be otherwise? If disease is the manifestation of maladaptation, and modern civilization (i.e., the current winning strategy) is inherently maladaptive to Nature, it is the only possible outcome. It is the basis for Chief Seattle's comparison of modern "civilization" to a "snake who eats his own tail in order to live. And the tail grows shorter and shorter." Modern man seems surprised that the snake is quickly approaching the consumption of its own head. Indigenous people I know are not.

We see how this division of mind must, by its very nature, ultimately glorify those systems of health care that best serve dysfunctional division by making the most money (i.e., a proxy for energy, the power to do in the physical world) for those most committed to the fragmented, Luciferian side of the bicameral mind, while simultaneously doing whatever is necessary to suppress wholeness.

U ntil recently, the unanimous civilized view of the common practitioner of primitive medicine, as represented by the shaman, was that the entire lot were "neurotic, epileptic, psychotic, hysterical, or schizophrenic." Such is our modern world's view of a practitioner who would cure his patients through the knowledge and insights of non-locality gained

---

[19] Julian Jaynes, The Origin of Consciousness in the Breakdown of the Bicameral Mind (Boston: Houghton Mifflin Company, 1976), 84-99. I could do an entire chapter on my proposed modifications to Jaynes' work, but sufficient to state, for the purposes of keeping within the confines of this chapter's subject matter, that Jaynes' "executive part" and "follower part" -- the components of the "bicameral mind" -- are, in my opinion, rooted in the bifurcation of the part of us which seeks unity with the Whole and the sequestered, fragmented part of us that is the universal meme created by our current GCOS. Using language with which Christians are accustomed, acquainted, and comfortable, we might call this the Higher and Lower Selves. Using language with which psychiatry is acquainted we might call this the Super Ego and the Ego.

through altered states, eschewing the aid and assistance of a corporately-produced and funded Physicians' Desk Reference (PDR).[20] The common view of anthropologists is best summed up by George Devereux, an authority on the matter, "In brief, there is no reason and no excuse for not considering the shaman as a severe neurotic and even a psychotic. In addition, shamanism is often also culture dystonic . . . Briefly stated, we hold that the shaman is mentally deranged."[21]

Less pejorative descriptions and portrayals of shamanism have been developed in the past four decades, but as Narby notes, ". . . the difficulty in grasping 'shamanism' lies not so much in the concept itself as in the gaze of those who use it. The academic analysis of shamanism will always be the rational study of the nonrational -- in other words, a self-contradictory proposition or a cul-de-sac."[22]

Even when the powers of shamanism are confirmed through the work of other disciplines, modern academics don't make the connection. I remember one passage by Russell Targ, one of the celebrated developers of so-called remote viewing, which had original backing by the U.S. Central Intelligence Agency. He discusses at some length the "amazing" developments in "intuitive medical diagnosis" and "distant healing" that are now offspring of this extensively researched psychic phenomena. His writing, and the references in his book, do little to nothing to make clear that these modern, scientific discoveries are but a crude rehashing of a handful of shamanic techniques that have been in regular practice for untold thousands of years.[23]

---

[20] Narby, The Cosmic Serpent, 15. With four bibliographical citations of support, p. 167.

[21] Ibid., 15. Running commentaries on the sick state of ancient practitioners of medicine -- regardless whether the term "shaman," or "medicine man" or "indigenous healer" is used -- abound. Indeed, they are too numerous to list fully. A typical example is one provided by Albert Buck, who characterized the genesis of early "medicine men," as occurring when "some member of the tribe who had displayed special skill in the treatment of disease, and who at the same time was liberally endowed with the qualities which characterize the charlatan, was chosen.

[22] Narby, The Cosmic Serpent, 18.

[23] Russell Targ, Limitless Mind: A Guide to Remote Viewing and Transformation of Consciousness (Novato, California: New World Library, 2004), 105-150 This level of arrogance, reminds one of the historical robe used to dress Christopher Columbus, "discoverer of America," as if anyone could claim to "discover" a land where 55 million people had already been living for countless generations. This great, historical tribute is given to a man who, as native

This, in turn, is but a subset of a larger pattern of denial wherein modern technology draws vitality, creativity, and sustinence from "the primitive," only to denigrate or ignore it in turn. "Seventy-four percent (74%) of the modern pharmacopoeia's plant-based remedies were first discovered by 'traditional' societies -- (and yet), only two percent (2%) of all plant species have been fully tested in laboratories, and the great majority of the remaining 98 percent are in tropical forests -- the Amazon, alone, home to half of all the plant species on Earth -- [much of which as been decimated over the past century to make more land for cattle and monocultural food crops]."[24]

This mindset is not newly developed. The very first *Materia Medica Americana*, published in Latin in 1787, was the work of Dr. Johann David Schöpf. He came to America as a physician with German troops in the British service during the Revolutionary War. He remained after the war to catalog more than 400 medicinal plants and therapeutic substances. A close examination of *Materia Medica Americana* reveals that America's first pharmacoepia was an aboriginal *materia medica*. Rather than give credit for the source of this medicinal largesse, Schöpf makes it a point to criticize the very source that is the basis for his work: "(In the matter of Indian remedies) I see no reason to expect anything extraordinary or important, and I am almost certain that with the passage of time nothing will be brought to light."[25] The author of America's first *materia medica* leaves his readers with the preposterous notion that he most probably figured out all his information on his own.

The social, political, and financial goals behind such denigration, stolen authorship, and overlooked potentialities have not been without transparency -- "(for only) after we have thoroughly routed the medicine men from their entrenchments and made them an object of ridicule (could whites) hope to bend

American activist, Russell Means, told me " . . . thought he had found India. You cannot be on this planet and be more WRONG than to think you have found a place whose true location is on the opposite side of the globe!" I mention this because it is emblematic of the convoluted mindset used by modernity to denigrate the primitive.

[24] Ibid.

[25] Narby, The Cosmic Serpent, 38. Bibliographical support: p. 170; the passage on Dr. Schöpf from p. 66.

and train the mind of our Indian wards in the direction of civilization."[26] With this savage attack on native healing systems, it is no wonder that as early as the 1850's, Henry David Thoreau would write, quoting a "wise, old Indian," that "the present generation of Indians had lost a great deal" [of practical medical knowledge].[27]

Declaring war on the natural world is the only way in which modernity could have possibly held victory over subcultures which did not possess the winning strategy under the current GCOS. How could subcultures, particularly in the area of medicine, particularly in the area of medicine, endure when they exhibited "general readiness to produce, without reward, their manifold roots, barks, and herbs for the (relief) of those needing aid . . . they show at least no selfish and mercenary views which are the commonest motives among the no less numerous mystery-usurers of more civilized and enlightened nations."[28]

To see this development with more clarity, we have to return to its early lines of code.

I maintain that the opening lines of the current GCOS's code, maintaining as they do, a rigidity in separateness between "I" and "not I," "mine" versus "not mine," and performing acts that benefit "me" as opposed to "not mine," can be used to explain the history of any facet of the current civilizational era: in this case, medicine. Run out over hundreds of generations, humanity's "cellular automata" produce a "modern man (that) is suffering from a severe fragmentation of his world picture."[29]

In medicine, the first step on the road to separating oneself from the rest of Creation would manifest itself in the hoarding of knowledge (authorized knowledge versus unauthorized knowledge), the creation of a medical caste (authoritative use of that knowledge versus those incapable of acting without it),

---

[26] Virgil Vogel, American Indian Medicine, (Oklahoma: University of Oklahoma Press, 1990), 35.

[27] Ibid., 119.

[28] Ibid., 67, quoting from "Travels in the Confederation (1783-1794)". ed. Alfred J. Morrison, I, 284-87.

[29] Weaver, Ideas, 59.

the development of schools to train select candidates eligible for admittance into the caste (to separate the initiated from the uninitiated), and the creation of a system of practice that favors a moneyed versus an impoverished patient base. Bifurcated self thus yields a bifurcated expression in health care. Since good health is of vital interest to any citizen in any society, it would only stand to reason that those with some inclination to working in the area of medicine would find a rich field in which to help the GCOS express itself.

Thus the doctor becomes the one with knowledge. His patient, the one without. The doctor, teacher; the patient, student. The doctor's opinion, an expression of authority; the patient's opinion, an expression of ignorance. The doctor, collecting fees for what is "mine"; his patient, the paying party who represents what is "not mine." The relationship is not and cannot be symmetrical, because the GCOS cannot express itself if the doctor is acting on behalf of what is best for the patient. Drawn out to the point of GCOS system crash, the doctor becomes torturer and the patient is the victim.

Medicine now must exist to benefit itself -- represented by its high priests. Even the underlying knowledge upon which the medical high priest relies is twisted to conform to the game rules provided by the GCOS. "The excessive love of self is in reality the source to each man of all offenses; for the lover is blinded about the beloved, so that he judges wrongly of the just, the good, and the honorable, and thinks that he ought always prefer his own interest to the truth."[30]

If the lines of code we have chosen for the GCOS are correct, we should see a consistent, increasing, unyielding movement in this direction over time, over the last six, or eight, or ten thousand years since it was first set into motion.

Using the information provided by conventional history itself, self-serving though it be, it should surprise no one that as we leave primitive medicine for its supposedly civilized variants, that is precisely what we see.

---

[30] Ibid., 71. Weaver takes the quotation from Plato.

Bibliographical Addendum to Chapter 8

"Our lips shall tell them to our sons,
And they again to theirs . . .
That generations yet unborne
May teach them to their heirs."

Isaac Watts
(1674-1748)

A wide variety of texts exist which provide a brief overview of the history of medicine. Some are encyclopedic and daunting (Garrison Fielding's <u>Introduction to the History of Medicine</u> comes to mind).[31]

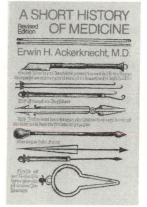

In the end, I choose <u>A Short History of Medicine</u> by Erwin H. Ackerknecht, M.D.,[32] as a chronological guide for the balance of Book II of *Meditopia*. Although not as detailed -- and certainly filled with conventional views that are not consistent with my own views, it, nonetheless, provides a comprehensive, yet succinct, overview of the most important developments that mark the history of medical practice.

John Perkins is, of late, better known for his writings in the political arena. <u>Confessions of an Economic Hit Man</u>[33] made him an international celebrity, a darling of those opposed to the excesses of U.S. foreign policy, and placed him in the same league as Noam Chomsky and William Blum.

But his earlier work, much of it drawn from his earlier ex-

---

[31] Fielding Garrison's <u>An Introduction to the History of Medicine</u> (Philadelphia: W.B. Saunders Company, 1929).

[32] Erwin H. Ackerknecht, <u>A Short History of Medicine</u> (Baltimore: The John Hopkins University Press, 1982).

[33] John Perkins, <u>Confessions of an Economic Hit Man</u> (San Francisco: Berrett-Koehler Publishers, Inc., 2004).

periences in the shamanic community in Ecuador, is, in my opinion, more valuable.

The World Is As You Dream It[34] is as good an introduction as any to the world of authentic shamans and their surprising healing abilities that modern medical practitioners do not understand, let alone attempt to duplicate.

I remember the first time I went on a shamanic journey: the night of August 25, 2006 in a forest retreat in Ecuador. I was 50 years old.

There were many revelations that came to me that night, but one thing I realized with surprising clarity: there was such an abundance of snakes, appearing in such concrete vividness with a life all their own, that I realized that if there were no snakes on Earth, not now and not in any time in the past; if I had never heard of them, even in fiction; if I had never had any contact, through any of my senses, with anything that even looked like a snake, they would still exist in the Universe. They must stand for some kind of universal archetype. They are, after all, even found prominently on the ancient caduceus, symbol of medical practice.

It would appear that I am not the only one who has had this revelation. Narby makes clear in his work that he, too, recognizes how unseemly an ever present visitor this universal archetype is to the sincere participant in the ayahuasca ritual.

Users with many more years of experience with ayahuasca than I report its sacred place as a "plant teacher." I have met with three shamans in the Amazonian region of Ecuador who claim that their entire body of botanical knowledge came

[34] John Perkins, The World is as You Dream It (Rochester, Vermont: Destiny Books, 1994).

from the spirit world. What makes this a remarkable statement is that these same teachers could acquire indigenous medical knowledge from their elders. But it would not be the same. To learn from a "teacher plant" is to be on the path to "owning the knowledge." Knowledge acquired from others is not the same as knowledge acquired from within.

The book, <u>Vine of the Soul: Medicine Men, Their Plants, and Rituals in the Colombian Amazonia</u>,[35] was written by two of the most respected ethnobotanists of the 20th century, Richard Evans Schultes (1915-2001) and Robert F. Raffauf (1916-2002). I know from a mutual friend that Schultes, in particular, became quite engrossed in the properties of ayahuasca towards the end of his life.

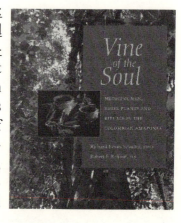

Although the focus on the book is the Colombian Amazon, the section on ayahuasca, from my experience, relates to many indigenous, botanical cultures running from Colombia south through Peru.

<u>Ideas Have Consequences</u> is the first in a trilogy of books that Richard M. Weaver wrote from 1948 to 1964. [36]His thoughts play prominently in the development of *Meditopia*.

This chapter draws heavily from Chapter 3 of Weaver's first book, <u>Fragmentation and Obsession</u>, which is, in this author's opinion, the most important of the book.

---

[35] Richard Evans Schultes, Robert F. Raffauf, FLS; <u>Vine of the Soul: Medicine Men, Their Plants and Rituals in the Colombian Amazonia</u> (New Mexico: Synergetic Press, 1992).

[36] Richard M. Weaver, <u>Ideas Have Consequences</u> (Chicago / London: The University of Chicago Press, 1948).

While Weaver does a superb job of identifying the ills of Western civilization, I found his recommendations less than satisfying. Absent an understanding of the current GCOS, one may blather endlessly about solutions to the current malaise so well described by John Zerzan, but this is the point: there is no solution, simply because an unintended consequence of the current GCOS, something built in to the very opening lines of its code, is humanity's self-destruction and the demand for an Operating System rewrite.

This becomes glaringly apparent in later chapters.

Ralph Moss's <u>Herbs Against Cancer: History and Controversy</u> contains a variety of simple relics of "primitive medicine."[37] It includes chapters on the work of Harry Hoxsey, Essiac, escharotics and it closes with an afterword that is well worth reading, on the life of Jonathan L. Hartwell, the patron saint of Alpha Omega Labs.[38]

Consistent with the legal and political milieu of our time, the author opens with a strongly worded "Important Note to Reader," a disclaimer stating that the author's work is for "historical and critical analysis" only. "It is not a book of instructions for cancer patients on how to treat themselves . . . it would be tragic if any reader were to misunderstand the author's or the publisher's intentions and attempt to use such information to self-medicate for any indication or condition . . ."[39]

Tragic, indeed.

I can attest to the effectiveness of many of the formulas and methods stated in Moss's book. I have no doubt that many

---

[37] Ralph W. Moss, <u>Herbs Against Cancer: History and Controversy</u> (Sheffield, UK: Equinox Press, 1998).

[38] See: www.altcancer.com/hartwell.htm

[39] Moss, <u>Herbs Against Cancer</u>, "Important Note to Reader" is an unnumbered page facing the title page.

of Moss's readers know the game, to wit: that there must be a wink and nudge when discussing any aspect of cancer treatment that would or could conceivably be used to direct market share away from the orthodox cancer community. Hence, the author's hearty admonition, "Readers with cancer should seek out the help of skilled oncologists, other physicians, and trained herbalists."[40]

Well, I suppose one out of three isn't bad.

Evolution and Culture[41] stands as one of the 100 most influential books in the development of *Meditopia*. It was my first exposure to Elman Service's "Law of Evolutionary Potential," which plays an important role in chapter 15 below. The book (at a mere 131 pages) is a compilation of four essays presenting the authors' thoughts on evolutionary theory as applied to cultural anthropology. Some readers may find it contradictory that I would

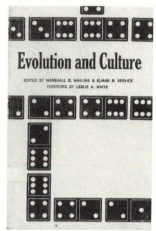

embrace a system of thought that leans towards linearity, even within cultural anthropology, not recognizing that even within a multiverse that churns in endless, repetitive rises and falls, there can be "subroutines" that demand progress and development, and create the "appearance" that such upward movements can be traced in a straight line back to the beginning of the universe. (Is it not the case that entropy [the rule of the Second Law of Thermodynamics] co-exists with laws where order is sought at the expense of chaos?)

The relevance of Evolution and Culture to the current chapter centers on David Kaplan's "Law of Cultural Dominance" -- which can be summed up as such: " . . . the cultural system which more effectively exploits the energy resources of a given environment will tend to spread in that environment at the

---

[40] Ibid.

[41] Marshall D. Sahlins, et al. Evolution and Culture (Ann Arbor: University of Michigan Press, 1960).

expense of less effective systems."[42] Parallel to this is a central principle of cultural anthropology, that "thermodynamically more versatile (cultures) . . . effective in a greater variety of environments . . . are able to drive out less advanced types."[43] I maintain that this is the governing rule under the current GCOS, but, regardless, the implication for primitive medicine is unmistakeable. As Kaplan points out: "The great reduction through recent millennia of the hunting and gathering societies of the world is a good case in point. Once the sole occupants of the cultural scene, they have tended to recede before later types that utilized new and more varied means of harnessing energy and putting it to work. The spread of these more advanced forms has pushed the hunting and gathering cultures deeper and deeper into more marginal areas."[44]

Kaplan emphasizes that "dominance," in this instance, relates to command over the environment. "(This law) underlies the fact that generally higher cultures have greater dominance range than lower forms, which is to say that it is also relevant to the understanding of general dominance. Higher forms characteristically exploit more different kinds of resources more effectively than lower; hence, in most environments they are more effective than lower, thus their greater range."[45]

Applied to primitive medicine, we see how the "Law of Cultural Dominance" has corrupted and perverted health care within the presiding GCOS. The human body is an artifact of nature, not technology. The healing systems, approaches and techniques, indeed, entire modalities, that work best are those that tend to be simple and most removed from the artificial creations of a dominant culture.

Interestingly, Kaplan doesn't omit the primary method that is used by a "dominant culture" to kill off the competition: "It would seem, then, that the spread of a dominant culture type almost invariably involves some sort of pressure being brought

---

[42] Ibid., 75.
[43] Ibid., 76-77.
[44] Ibid., 74.
[45] Ibid., 77.

to bear on less advanced types. Often this pressure takes the extreme form of outright military conquest with the conquered society being exterminated, driven off, or colonized and transformed. The mechanics of this process are easily understood. In most cases, an advanced cultural system can marshal a greater and more powerfully equipped military force, enabling it to take, and hold against encroachment or revolt, areas where its exploitative techniques are more effective than rival systems."[46]

But the mechanism behind it all, the real source of the power to suppress, if not exterminate, is something Kaplan never advances, and yet, it is readily apparent.

Money.

If the most effective methods of healing tend to be simple, inexpensive, easy to learn, easy to share, easy to employ, then what must an orthodox medicine system do within the dominant culture to eradicate these effective methods and fuel the source of their exterminating power (i.e., money)?

It must: (1) create less effective, artificial systems that play to the inherent asymmetrical relationship between a medical elite and the majority who live and work outside this select group; (2) it must destroy the competition by insuring that its superior resources gained through the employment of the first principle are used to establish a common narrative that discredits primitive medicine; and (3) it must solidify this disinformation

through an educational system that sustains the bias against supposedly lower form healing systems.

Question: Can the con job that is modern, orthodox medicine be sustained indefinitely?

Answer: Not on your symptom-treated, radiation-tested, pill-popping, toxically vaccinated, surgically-altered, chemotherapied life!

For, orthodox medicine is cursed with the same baggage that weighs down all complex, high entropy organizations. "A complex society is seen as impelled along a path of increased complexity [i.e. hence, the health care budgets of Western countries that are currently spiralling out of control], unable to switch

---

[46] Ibid., 88

directions, regress, or remain static. When obstacles impinge, it can continue in only the direction it is headed, so that catastrophe ultimately results."[47]

---

[47] Joseph A. Tainter, The Collapse of Complex Societies (Cambridge: Cambridge University Press, 1988), 59.

Brief Introduction to Chapter 9

This chapter introduces a set of principles, central to the original *Meditopia* composition, before revisions began in 2006, that cover the last half of that initial work. This was written in August, 2004, and is still online.[1]

Ten more chapters follow, taking the reader up to and through Chapter 19 ("Technological Development in a Meditopia: Protecting Lower Entropy Technologies.") Each one of these chapters deals with a different principle. I have made changes to the original text because there were "growing pains" that made certain things incomprehensible. For example, in the original text of the chapter you're about to read, I state "I have divided the Unifying Principles into five chapters, devoting one chapter to each principle." What follows is a list of SEVEN chapters, and then in actuality on the original site, you find THIRTEEN.[2]

These inconsistencies arose out of the conditions that gave rise to *Meditopia* in the first place. I was released from prison in May, 2004 for three months by the U.S. federal court in Lafayette. I was sentenced to 33 months incarceration on August 24, and then ordered to report back to prison on September 24. Again, I cover all of this in exhaustive detail online.[3] The initial idea to do *Meditopia* came to me at the end of May, and from the very beginning I knew I would have to work quickly to produce something cogent and complete before I was incarcerated yet again.

Three months time wasn't enough to finish *Meditopia*. Neither was it sufficient time to clean up a host of typos and other errors. When I continued writing again in 2006, after being let out of prison, I decided to do a rewrite. All of these "start-and-stops" operated behind the scenes for the entire time that *Meditopia* was being composed.

All these errors and inconsistencies are resolved in the present volume.

---

[1] See: meditopia.org/old/chap4_2004.htm

[2] See: meditopia.org/sitemap.htm

[3] Again, the fun begins at the following link for those who are really interested: www.meditopia.org/chap3-1.htm

Chapter 9:

Introduction To
The Unifying Principles

"In this world, there is nothing so sublime and pure as
transcendental knowledge. Such knowledge is the mature fruit
of all mysticism. . . "

Bhagavad-Gita 4:38

Meditopia, the title of this section, is intended to convey a very specific meaning. From an etymological standpoint, meditopia comes from the Latin "meder" (to heal) and the Greek "topos" (a place). One loose translation might be "a place of healing." My use of the term, however, is not intended to convey geographic location.

Meditopia is about a state of mind that brings about healing and optimal physiological function, indeed, optimal "human" functioning, body, mind, and spirit.

Meditopia is about conditions of mind in the person who seeks treatment, and in the healer who is capable of providing relief. It has objective and subjective components; it can be known through the understanding of certain "unifying priniciples," a largely intellectual pursuit, but its more powerful nuances can only be accessed through an expansion in consciousness.[1] In fact, from a higher level of consciousness the "unifying principles" of *Meditopia* become self-evident. Nonetheless, growth can be obtained by working the process in reverse: if you strive to understand the "Principles," you will, in time, grow in the state of consciousness that correlates to them.

These "unifying principles" are universal natural laws, really, that are greatly at variance with the prevailing paradigms

---

[1] This line of thought mimics the teachings of many great religious figures; one of prominence that comes to mind is Patanjali, who saw all "higher powers" (Siddhis) as accessible through "transcendence." See: Russell Targ, Limitless Mind: A Guide to Remote Viewing and Transformation of Consciousness, (Novato, California: New World Library, 2004), 21

that are the very foundation of modern medicine.

I decided to write this book because I was unable to find anyone who had connected these principles together in a cohesive, coherent way, so that people could understand the "Source of Cures" and make use of it. Some mental effort will have to be applied to understand these principles, but once understood, you will never view your health, or any system of "health care," in the same way again. My inclusion of autobiographical material serves merely to provide some situational context for the principles as it relates to me personally. If you understand the principles, it doesn't matter one whit what you think of me, my life, my work, or my opinions. Ultimately, they are irrelevant.

The Unifying Principles have a life, a power, and a force of their own. The focus should be on that.

Running Alpha Omega Labs for twelve years[2] taught me that if you understood these principles and found ways of employing them in your work, you would open yourself to a world of healing possibilities that bordered on the divine -- a mystical, magical force that is at the very basis of Life itself.

I focused on the Nine Causes in Chapter One to set the tone on how askew we are in Western Society from employing these Principles. I wanted you to hunger to uncover these secrets I have discovered, and so I laid out for you the enormous cognitive dissonance that the study of escharotics' suppression elicits.

If you want to know the Truth, intellectually, you will find it only in your realization of these Unifying Principles.

In the subsequent chapters of this section (Book II), I have divided the Unifying Principles into seven chapters, devoting one chapter to each principle:

Chapter 10: "Entropy & Caton's Exosomatic Axis"

Chapter 11: "Occam's Razor & The Power of

---

[2]Given the time at which this text was written, I am referring to a period roughly running from 1991 to 2003.

Simple Solutions"

Chapter 12: "Gresham's Law:
Its Treacherous Application"

Chapter 13: "The Matrix: As Applied to Medicine"

Chapter 14: "Healing Thoughts & The Power of
M-Fields"

Chapter 15: "Medicine & The Law of
Evolutionary Potential"

Chapter 16: "Organized Medicine: A Terminal Disease.
Corollaries of Parkinson's Law"

This powerful knowledge equally equips the practitioner
or the lay person to gather to him or herself all the other needed
tools to know what treatments are best.

Internalizing these Principles opens the door of Knowledge. Once opened, it can never be closed again.

It brings both the patient and the healer one step closer to
escaping the cycle of victimhood that is an endemic part of the
orthodox medical establishment.

Brief Introduction to Chapter 10

I feel this is one of the most important of the "Unifying Principles" in *Meditopia*. It immediately follows the "Introduction to the Unifying Principles" in the previous chapter. This chapter is so important that I included it as an appendix in my previous book.[1]

An entire worldview or general philosophy of humanity could be developed based on the content of this one chapter. The original is still online.[2]

---

[1] Caton, The Joys of Psychopathocracy, (Miami, USA: Herbologics, Ltd., 2017), 2017 – Appendix A

[2] See: meditopia.org/old/chap5_2004.htm

Chapter 10:

Entropy &
Caton's Exosomatic Axis

"[Classical thermodynamics] is the only physical theory of universal content which I am convinced, that within the framework of applicability of its basic concepts will never be overthrown."

Albert Einstein[1]
(1879-1955)

"All the evidence suggests that we have consistently exaggerated the contributions of technological genius and underestimated the contributions of natural resources."

Stewart L. Udall[2]

T he very manner in which intelligence is defined is integrally linked to the use of tools; the human ability to take objects from the surrounding environment and use them not only to survive and expand the range of human influence, but to reorder Nature and create contorted artificialities of which no other known species on Earth is capable.

As it pertains to the field of medicine, this has turned out to be more than a mixed blessing.

Anthropologists use endosomatic to describe the organs, extremities and other physical components of the human body. They use exosomatic to describe the tools, instruments and other physical objects that are not a part of the human body that humans use to reorder their environment. The expansive distinction between the purely endosomatic and the purely exosomatic

---

[1] G. Tyler Miller, Jr., Energetics, Kinetics and Life: Ecological approach, (Belmont, California: Wadsworth Publishing Co., 1971). 46.

[2] William R. Catton, Jr., Overshoot: The Ecological Basis of Revolutionary Change, (University of Illinois Press, 1980), xv. I. Catton's book is now considered a classic in ecological sociology, and the quote cited is taken from the "Foreword" by Stewart L. Udall.

provides, in my opinion, a perfect metaphor for what guides us to, or away from, optimal healing.

That metaphor is the purpose of this chapter.

My first exposure to the concept came a quarter century ago (1980) in my initial reading of Rifkin's Entropy. But I did not realize the importance of how entropy affects our lives until I saw its effects close up, relative to the corruption of organized medicine.

For those who may not know, entropy is a concept of physics which simply says that in any closed system (excepting the intake of sunlight from 93 million miles away, and the miniscule influence of various celestial bodies, planet Earth is a fairly closed system), the amount of energy available to do work (be it in the form of oil, coal, timber, etc.) is finite, and so without the infusion of additional, usable energy from outside the system, deterioriation results. Within the system, orderliness (high energy state) becomes disorderliness (low energy state); organization becomes chaos; action becomes inaction; efficiency becomes inefficiency; life (high energy state) becomes death (low energy state), etc. Most of what is considered "progress" (negative entropy), or what could be thought of as a defiance of entropy, is nothing more than an acceleration of it through an increased rate of energy resource usage. Increasing order, wealth, opulence, high society (the so-called "good life") come into being by creating disorderliness somewhere else. Entropy can be minimized by living in harmony with the environment, what ecologists call "sustainability," but physical science holds that entropy can never be completely circumvented.

Entropy is an immutable law of the universe.

This concept is derived from the laws of thermodynamics, which Rifkin summarizes with: "The total energy content of the universe is constant, and the total entropy is continually increasing."[3]

---

[3] The classical definitions of the two classical laws of thermodynamics are: (1) "Energy can be changed from one form to another, but it cannot be created or destroyed. The total amount of energy and matter in the Universe remains constant, merely changing from one form to another. The First Law of Thermodynamics (Conservation) states that energy is always conserved,

The relationship that exists between low entropy (greater energy and orderliness, lower rate of consumption in the use of surrounding energy) and higher entropy (less energy, more disorderliness, higher rate of consumption in the use of surrounding energy) has a direct correlation between what I call endosomatic-dominant and exosomatic-dominant systems of work. For example, if I walk down the block to buy some orange juice at the convenience store (endosomatic), I use a tiny fraction of the energy, measurable in ergs, that I would use if I got into my car (exosomatic) and made the same round trip.

> *"Man has 'wants' which he likes to regard as 'needs.' He has basic physiological needs for food and drink. He has other elementary wants for clothing and heating. Finally he has, as it were, 'high standard' wants, like reading, listening to music, travelling, amusing himself. Human wants have no upper limit, but they have a lower limit – the minimum food necessary to maintain life."*

> **Carlo M. Cipolla**[4]

Modern civilization has been made possible by a movement away from endosomatic solutions for life to those that are exosomatic. Modern civilization is only possible due to massive tool use, and at the present rate of resource consumption to create, use, service, and replace those tools, modern civilization is rapidly approaching a roadblock unlike anything the world has ever seen before; a conclusion that can be readily drawn just on the basis of the global dependence on non-renewable petroleum, the lack of any reasonable technology on the drawing board that will cost effectively replace it in time, its ubiquitous use in personal transportation, commercial shipping, energy production, manufacturing (steel, plastics, chemical, etc.), agriculture

---

it cannot be created or destroyed. In essence, energy can be converted from one form into another." When my father was in school, this was also referred to as Humboldt's Law (1848); and (2) what is often called "The Entropy Law," namely, "that in all energy exchanges, if no energy enters or leaves the system, the potential energy of the state will always be less than that of the initial state."

[4] Carlo M. Cipolla, The Economic History of World Population, (Baltimore, Maryland: Penguin Books, Inc., 1974), 35.

– well, just about every facet of daily life; and then there's the irrefutability of Hubbert's Peak,[5][6][7][8][9] the greatest implication of which is, humanity will begin to run out of food relative to the world population "load," concurrent with running out of oil.

But let's get back to medicine.

In a society with a cultural infrastructure devoted to a highly specialized, highly entropic, highly exosomatic orientation, the one area that most rebels against "the machine" is people, the person, the human body itself!

A human being is not a car, a house, a television, or a cellphone. All those things are exosomatic. So they can be improved by using exosomatic methods. But the human body is not an exosomatic tool. It is flesh and blood. It is a well-crafted creation of Nature, not an artificial construct created in a laboratory or manufacturing plant. In no other area has modern civilization failed more miserably than in the area of medicine, and the power elite has used all its powers of advertising, persuasion, regulation, education, and obfuscation to try and convince one and all that exosomatic methods employed on Nature's most perfect endosomatic specimen are the only right way.

Upon what scientific, or moral, or ethical, or legal meat doth this, our Medical Establishment, feed that it is so corrupt?

[5] Richard Heinberg, The Party's Over: Oil, War and the Fate of Industrial Societies, (Gabriola Island, Canada: New Society Publishers, 2003). I could list 50 more references I have on this subject, all of them good, but since this is tangential and not terribly relevant to our current focus, I'll just list this one reference, plus the next four, since they approach the issue from slightly different angles.

[6] Kenneth S. Deffeyes, Hubbert's Peak: The Impending World Oil Shortage, (Princeton, New Jersey: Princeton University Press, 2001).

[7] C.J. Campbell, The Coming Oil Crisis, (Brentwood, Essex, England: Multi-Science Publishing Com- pany & Petroconsultants, S.A., 1997).

[8] Justin Lahart, "Oil-Price Forecasts Seem to Miss Upward Trend," Wall Street Journal, May 19, 2004, C-3. In case you think the oil shortage issue is a far-fetched doom and gloom issue, this Wall Street Journal article is an intellectual dose of ephedra. Deffeyes, a former Princeton geology professor, who spent more than 30 years studying Hubbert's Peak, believed that world oil production "is set to peak on Thanksgiving Day, 2005, give or take a few weeks." His colleague, Tom Petrie, head of Petrie Parkman, a Denver investment bank specializing in energy, said, "I spent the first 12 years of my career thinking Hubbert was wrong, and I spent the next 20 realizing how right he was." This didn't spell "doom" in 2005. But it did signal that the era of cheap oil was over. We're now down to "resource wars." Want to know why we really went to Afghanistan and Iraq? Read Michael T. Klare's Resource Wars: The New Landscape of Global Conflict (New York: Henry Holt & Company, 2001).

[9] Thom Hartmann, The Last Hours of Ancient Sunlight, (New York: Harmony Books, 1998).

The answer is, it feeds on the supremely misguided notion that you can achieve perfection by forcing exosomatic methods on an endosomatic system.

And for all the modern medical apologists who would attempt to argue that increased longevity, or decreased infant mortality, or falling rates of infectious disease, are a sign of unqualified success, there is an even more powerful argument that modern medicine and its allies in the industrial sector have created untold ecological destruction, financial servitude, marginally functioning immune systems, limited moral, ethical and social vision, and a disconnectedness from the natural roots and wisdom that humanity can only obtain and sustain through a communion with the Earth and her natural bounty.

It is not possible to understand what this means without grasping the nature of the continuum, which I call the Axis, which progresses from the endosomatic to the exosomatic, and the inherent trade-offs that result from that progression.

In the table below, there are four categories that mark changes in properties, attitudes and approach in the progression from Pure Endosomatic to Pure Exosomatic. Reading through the table provides an intuitive "gist" of this reality to the point where other possible categories readily spring to mind. It is only important to get the basic concept, because, together with the material on Occam's Razor, this material forms core building blocks that are needed to understand the material in later chapters.

Conventional medical thinkers will find portions of the Table quite offensive.

Tough.

The key thing is to "get" the concepts; agreeing or disagreeing with any one or more particular positions or attributes I ascribe to any part of the table doesn't really matter.

You will only internalize and accept what your consciousness allows you to anyway.

Caton's Exosomatic Chart begins on the next page.

Caton's Exosomatic Axis

Axial Progression	Pure Endosomatic	Endosomatic dominant / Exosomatic subordinate	Exosomatic dominant / Endosomatic subordinate	Pure Exosomatic
Definitional Overview & Basic Properties				
Seed Concept	Me. My body, mind & spirit -- and my connections to the non-physical world. The greatest, most valuable tools I use are those that are within myself -- and in my relationship with the non-physical, be that identified as God, an unmanifest Supreme Good, etc.	The emphasis is on my person. The "tools" in my environment are utilized in a sustainable way, because consciousness at this level respects the interconnectedness between "me" and the environment that is "not me."	The emphasis is on the objectified outer world -- but there is a still a knowingness of the value of the subjective.	Man is defined by his ability to maximize the utility of his "tools." The Inner Man, the subjective value of humanity, is most suppressed at this stage.
General Orientation	The answer is within us. Whatever problem that can arise from within, can be solved from within. A failure to recognize this emanates from ignorance and a lower state of consciousness.	The answer to our problems starts from within. The solutions outside of us must take the "inner" into consideration.	The solution resides outside of us, but it is helpful not to forget that the inner component is a contributing factor.	Man defines his very intelligence -- indeed, his superiority over apes -- by his ability to use tools. Our solutions clearly reside in objective reality. Science and technology, regardless of discipline, theoretical or applied, dictate that we find solutions by mastering Nature, which is clearly external to whatever we define as "ourselves."
Consciousness	Highest level of consciousness or "self-actualization." Highest level of spiritual development. Spirit -- rarified.	Lower level of consciousness. More density in physical matter.	Still lower level of consciousness. Man's absorption in the physical world is high, and his consciousness of non-physical worlds is lower still.	The lowest level of consciousness. This level of consciousness has given way to our current mechanistic worldview, as well as our twisted systems of legal, moral, and ethical relativism.
Complexity	Tend to be simple.	More complex.	And still more complex.	Most complex.
Cooperation versus Competition	Cooperative. At this end of the axis, the fabric of unity that ties all humanity together is self-evident. Competition is seen as selfish and unnecessary.	Less cooperative with some competition, but cooperation is dominant.	More competitive with some cooperation, but competition is dominant.	Most competition. Even "apparent" co-operation has competitive overtones.

Caton's Exosomatic Axis

Axial Progression	Pure Endosomatic	Endosomatic dominant / Exosomatic subordinate	Exosomatic dominant / Endosomatic subordinate	Pure Exosomatic
Definitional Overview & Basic Properties				
Specialization	Least specialized. Most generalized. Comfortable operating in the abstract. Mimics an Indian proverb about the process of becoming 'enlightened': "A man who controls a fortress automatically controls all the paths leading up to the fortress. Focus on controlling the fortress and not the paths!"	More specialized. Not quite as generalized. Slightly more concrete. Here there is still the understanding that great healing draws from the wellspring of the great generalist. Another Indian proverb: "Water the root to enjoy the fruit."	Still more specialization. Even less generalized. Still more concrete.	Maximum tendency towards specialization. Least generalized. Everything is concrete and there is discomfort operating in the abstract. In a highly mechanistic environment, everything must appear in great detail, every 't' crossed, every 'i' dotted. A generalist is a specialist wannabe.
Thermodynamic Effect	Low entropy. Takes the least energy away from its environment, and puts the most back in.	More entropic.	And still more entropic.	Most entropy. Exosomatic systems of healing steal the most from their environment and put the least back in.
Ultimate Source of Healing: Inner to outer; subjective to objective; mind to matter.	Man is, above all things, a spiritual being. The ultimate source of healing resides INSIDE him. Whatever healing tools are employed, they are extensions of what is within us.	The spirit and mind of man must be taken into primary consideration. Healing cannot take place if the mind of the patient is not properly predisposed — without observing this principle, a doctor is only addressing gross physical symptoms.	The mind of man is a concern — after all, do not many illnesses have a psychosomatic component? Nonetheless, the tools of healing largely stand on their own merit, independent of what the patient does or does not think.	Everything that is necessary to heal man's ills resides OUTSIDE him. Science tells us that we can only know reality by adhering to the truth of objectivity — for subjectivity can only fail us.
Modalities: Systems of healing, methods, products, and protocols as they reside along the Exosomatic Axis.	Faith and 'psychic' healing practices, power of positive thinking, Reiki, therapeutic massage, chiropractic and osteopathic subluxation manipulations, 'psychic surgery'; exercise, hatha yoga, and related practices.	Nutrition and diet; natural vitamin / mineral supplementation; herbology (phytopharmacology / ethnobotanical medicine), iatrochemistry (involving naturally occurring minerals and compounds), balneology, bio-oxidative therapy, etc.	Artificial diet supplementation (or compound not as readily assimilated as from natural sources); minor surgery, pharmacologicals involving compounds that are close to those of natural sources (i.e. phytopharmacology, etc.)	Those farthest from man's natural origins: this would include most of the drugs now on the market in the West; chemotherapy with chemical compounds not found in nature, radiation treatment, radical surgery, etc. Those in this group tend to be immunosuppressive in some way; not immunosupportive — a propensity to work one's will ON nature instead of work WITH nature.

Caton's Exosomatic Axis				
Axial Progression	Pure Endosomatic	Endosomatic dominant / Exosomatic subordinate	Exosomatic dominant / Endosomatic subordinate	Pure Exosomatic
Between Unmanifest & Manifest				
Relationship Between Spiritual & Material Describe using set theory.	The spiritual (God) is the master set. All things in the material world are a subset of this reality -- for all things in the material are given birth by the Divine. 'As above -- so below.' All members of the material set are contained in the spiritual set.	The material world is subordinate to the spiritual. But the material is its own reality. I try to work in the 'intersection' set.	All things spiritual are a subset of a much larger Universe where the laws of nature are both material in nature and paramount. There is no intersection set.	The laws of science are the "master set." Things that appear to be spiritual can all be explained in strictly scientific terms. The mechanistic view of the Universe reigns supreme. Not only is there no intersection set; there is no spiritual set.
Role of Spirituality: On the part of patient or practitioner, what role belief in the Divine or Higher Power or Spirituality contributes to the healing process.	Central to the healing process. Heavy reliance on the 'innate intelligence of the body' by practitioner, and usually patient. 'Man does not live by bread alone, but by every Word that comes from the mouth of God . . . ' 'If you but had the Faith of a mustard seed . . . ' 'By Faith you are healed . . .'	Still a primary component of the healing process, followed closely by the right material means outside the body and observance of the scientific method.	May or may not have some influence. But our true faith must exist in science and the discovery of the helpful, mechanistic forces that exist outside the body. For science, by definition, we know -- and our spiritual beliefs are only conjecture.	Exists for those who believe in quack medicine. God is dead. Religion is the opium of the masses. Only gullible people believe in such things. Nutrition is unimportant or over-emphasized by quacks. Science will cure all our ills. A Higher Power exerts influence over my medical outcome? Oh please!
Human In Relationship With the Divine	We're spiritual beings having a human experience. [Deepak Chopra]	We're human beings, where the spiritual should matter more than the material.	We're human beings -- material (the seen) by nature. The spiritual (the unseen) is a secondary part of our nature.	We're material beings. Spirituality, at its best, is mere unprovable conjecture.

Caton's Exosomatic Axis

Axial Progression	Pure Endosomatic	Endosomatic dominant / Exosomatic subordinate	Exosomatic dominant / Endosomatic subordinate	Pure Exosomatic
Between Unmanifest & Manifest				
Role of God In Healing Process: Our 'relationship" with that role.	"GOD is my partner in the healing process. There is nothing I do that does not come from the spiritual. I carry this view if I am a practitioner ... or I am a patient."	"GOD is important in my life, and my attention on the spiritual component of the healing process works closely with the material."	"GOD or the spiritual element plays a part, but science is the most critical component in the process."	"GOD has nothing to do with healing. Healing is a science, pure and simple. I'll go this far and no farther: If the patient 'thinks' that his or her outlook, or spirituality, or some other non-scientific mumbo-jumbo is helping them, it's fine with me."
Good Vs. Evil	Pure Goodness.	Goodness has the upper hand over Evil.	Evil has the upper hand over Goodness.	At its extreme, Evil reigns supreme. After all, can we even say that goodness exists? Isn't goodness an artificial, subjective value? [Moral relativism].
Mind Vs. Matter	Mind (spirit) over Matter. The physical universe follows causatively from the Word (thought).	Mind can influence Matter.	Mind and matter can influence each other. The role of Mind is just one among many.	The laws of science are immutable. Matter over mind.
Light Vs. Darkness	"I work from the Light. I see Darkness as an absence of Light."	"I draw from the Light. But I am adept at working in the many shades of Grey."	"I work in the Dark, because the Earth resides in Darkness, with occasional help from the Light."	"There is only Darkness. It is the Light that is an illusion."
Form Vs. Substance	Substance follows Form. Form is acknowledged as the all-powerful causative factor.	More attention on Form -- and Substance follows.	More attention on Substance -- and Form follows.	Substance is all that matters. Form is an illusion used to control our objectives.

Axial Progression	Pure Endosomatic	Endosomatic dominant / Exosomatic subordinate	Exosomatic dominant / Endosomatic subordinate	Pure Exosomatic
Caton's Exosomatic Axis				
The Medical Intermediary				
Physician's Subjective View of His Role	"I am at my best when I am in tune with the Divine Healer within me." "I am but an Instrument, a Facilitator of Spirit." . . . "Not my will, but Thine be done."	"I draw inspiration from intuition and other subjective components of Mind that aren't taught in medical school."	"Adherence to proven medical principles is paramount, though I admit that some 'help from above' doesn't hurt."	"I am God."
Physician's Attitude To Compensation	"Helping my patients is paramount. If I devote all my attention to the wellness of those under my care, God will take care of my needs. I am uncompromising in doing what is best for my patient -- for my aid to my fellow man is part and parcel of my relationship with the Divine" . . . "As ye do to the least of my Brethren, so you do unto Me . . ." My best work DOES make me wealthy -- but with a wealth that cannot be measured merely in bank deposits.	"Helping my patients is what is uppermost on my mind. The products, services, and protocols I employ must benefit the patient or I will not use them. I charge my patient a fair rate for what I do. I need to be properly compensated for my talents and abilities, but I put the welfare of my patients over my desire to make money. In fact, I would give up my practice before I would allow a regulatory or other authorative body to force me to use methods that I suspected were not beneficial to my patients."	"Getting paid comes first. I do whatever I can to help my patient, but regardless of the outcome, practicing medicine is a business -- and those who foolishly forget this will not have a successful practice. Nevertheless (and secondarily), I will not use a product or protocol if I have any reason to believe it will harm the patient."	"Medicine is a business. You are in it to make money. The diagnostic techniques we use, drugs we prescribe, services we render, must earn a profit. If I make a referral, I expect a fee. There are recommendations I make that I know will not help some of my patients, but as long as 'it's legal' and I've covered myself to the letter of the Law, I'm fine with it. I use techniques on my patients that I wouldn't think of using on members of my own family. I would never take the risk of saving a patient's life if it meant that I would lose money ... or risk my license."

Caton's Exosomatic Axis

Axial Progression	Pure Endosomatic	Endosomatic dominant / Exosomatic subordinate	Exosomatic dominant / Endosomatic subordinate	Pure Exosomatic
The Medical Intermediary				
Medicine & The Role of Profitability	Marginally profitable compared to exosomatic approaches -- simply because money is not where the focus is . . . "I put the mission before the commission . . ." Again, the wealth that a practitioner obtains through adhering to endosomatic practices cannot be measured in money alone.	Always self-supporting -- because money still makes the world go round. But the best rewards, for both practitioner and patient, are still well outside the domain of money.	Probably quite profitable, because earning a profit is a primary concern. But the welfare of the patient is still important.	Very profitable. After all -- you don't support a medical product unless it has the potential to make money. Good medicine and good business go hand in hand. And good business, by definition, means you're earning good money. The relationship is linear: you make MORE MONEY because good business becomes better business. And better business means better medicine -- a kind of monetary biofeedback.

Caton's Exosomatic Axis

Axial Progression	Pure Endosomatic	Endosomatic dominant / Exosomatic subordinate	Exosomatic dominant / Endosomatic subordinate	Pure Exosomatic
Law, Politics & Other Artificial Constructs				
The Source Of Authority Centralized vs. Localized	The ultimate source of authority is the individual, the endosomatic wellspring. So authority is localized -- what is closest and most empowering to the individual. All endosomatic, low entropy cultures share a decentralized political system.	Movement towards more centralization. As we move along the exosomatic axis, the specialization of tools brings the opportunity to create 'power cells,' and these can only be consolidated through progressive centralization. Localized, dominant; centralized, subordinate.	Some authority is localized, but the emphasis is on centralization. Centralized, dominant; localized, subordinate.	Centralization rules -- in political structure, standards, laws, etc. Localized authority exists but is dwarfed by the power and dominance of centralized authoritative entities.
The Role Of Law In Healing	Natural Law is the foundation of healing in its purest form. We can only degrade healing when we depart from Natural Law.	Doing what's right takes precedent over the 'letter of the law.'	The 'letter of the law,' unfortunately, is still the law. You have to follow the Law even if you know it isn't right. Life is about compromises.	Medicine is business. Business needs protection. Law provides protection. What is "right" is not the issue, because rightness is subjective.
Patents & Proprietary Claims	Endosomatic methods of healing, by their nature, are not patentable. No one, but God, can claim ownership. When healers do their best work they are still just borrowing something they know belongs to no mere man. True healers know that real medical knowledge rests in a realm that is beyond money, patents, proprietary claims, monopolies, and, indeed, all manner of commerce. Such things belong to artificial, economic and political constructs that WE create. They are foreign to Nature and to Natural Law.	Various medical practitioners or groups may have their 'formulary secrets,' or elements of their work not in the 'public domain,' fleeting and temporary though these claims may be. Nonetheless, every conscientious practitioner knows that the source of their best work resides in a field of life and thought that is beyond the gross material plane. It resides in the "collective unconscious" for all to see, if they merely develop their Inner Vision.	Good medicine is rooted in progress and you promote progress by providing incentives to protect proprietary invention. That goes for every area of technology, not just medicine. That the source of such inventiveness may come from areas of life that reside outside commerce and the more practical areas of human endeavor doesn't marginalize the need to enforce effective, proprietary systems that make progress possible.	Again, medicine is business. You cannot have good business without respect for intellectual property rights. Great medical inventions come from people -- not God, angels, faines, or other unseen forces. Strictly enforced patent law makes medical progress possible. If a medical product or procedure isn't patentable, it is, no doubt, inferior. Medical progress -- the forward march of scientific achievement through time -- moves us forward, not backward. And the incentive to make money by providing proprietary protection cannot be divorced from good medicine.

Caton's Exosomatic Axis				
Axial Progression	Pure Endosomatic	Endosomatic dominant / Exosomatic subordinate	Exosomatic dominant / Endosomatic subordinate	Pure Exosomatic
Law, Politics & Other Artificial Constructs				
Imputations To Time	Natural Law exists outside linear time, as we know it. As the old proverb states: "There is nothing new under the sun" – capturing the limitations of a linear view of time, discovery, and evolution that a less expansive view can only truncate. A highly evolved healer knows that by tapping into the collective unconscious, the akashic records, call it what you will, he operates outside of time. He draws from the same inspirational sources that healers did 3,000 years ago, assuming they had the same level of awareness. Discovery, advancement, evolution, or well-being cannot be measured in time; they are rooted in pure consciousness which knows no time.	Although medical advances have appeared to accrue over time, we still adhere to those practices that work. Our allegiance is to what helps the patient. Just because something is old, doesn't mean it isn't effective; just because it's proprietary doesn't make it better. Just because it makes more money, doesn't mean we should employ it. Conversely, just because a medical technique is new, doesn't mean it is superior to a tried and true method that is over 1,000 years old.	Emphasis should be placed on using the newest and best. Medical progress IS linear. We get better at what we do all the time. We are better healers today than our brethren one hundred years ago. They were better than those one hundred years before them, and so on. History clearly reflects that the advancement of medicine has occurred over time. Nonetheless, a real healer is still an empiricist: he doesn't ignore older healing techniques if a newer one fails to benefit the patient.	Since medicine is business and good business demands progress, it only stands to reason that all regulatory and legal forces should be deployed at protecting the latest medical developments. These developments occur over time. Time is the ubiquitous foundation for how we measure our work, evaluate our advances, and determine quantatively our profitability. All good things come from a strict adherence to linear time. The absence of this adherence brings chaos.

Brief Introduction to Chapter 11

The application of Occam's Razor logically follows from the previous chapter, discussing the relationship between the endosomatic and exosomatic. It, too, was written in August 2004, and is still online.[1]

On close examination, one can see how the development of the central concept put forth in this chapter manifests in an earlier chapter in this book, which was originally written four years later: Chapter 7 – Seed Corrupted. The work of Stephen Wolfram plays a vital role in both chapters.

Additionally, Occam's Razor also plays a vital role in the unfolding of the upcoming chapters.

---

[1] See: meditopia.org/old/chap6_2004.htm

Chapter 11:

Occam's Razor & The Power
Of Simple Solutions

"A theory is more impressive the greater is the simplicity of its premises, the more different are the kinds of things it relates and the more extended its range of applicability."

Albert Einstein[1]

"Plurality should not be posited without necessity" (translation of "Pluralitas non est ponenda sine neccesitate"), or alternatively, "Entities should not be multiplied more than necessary" (i.e. "the fewer assumptions an explanation of a phenomenon depends on, the better.") This is a translation of "Entia non sunt multiplicanda praeter necessitatem."

William of Occam[2]
(1285-1349)

"The more perfect a nature is the fewer means it requires for its operation."

Aristotle[3]

The simplest explanation is usually the correct one. There are few people who have not heard that pithy saying, though there are variations of this same seed thought that even originated from its namesake, William of Occam (also spelled "Ockham").

---

[1] G. Tyler Miller, Jr., Energetics, Kinetics and Life, (Belmont, California: Wadsworth Publishing Co., 1971), 46.

[2] See: www.iep.utm.edu/ockham/.

[3] Occam's Razor (definition) from a "website for skeptics." An alternative translation, where Occam's Razor is applied to the field of logic is: "What can be done with fewer [assumptions] is done in vain with more." See: www.bartleby.com/65/wm/WmOcm.html, or, "It is vain to do with more what can be done with fewer." This is just an extension of Aristotle's own thoughts on parsimony of explanation: "Entities must not be multiplied beyond what is necessary." See: www.2think.org/occams_razor.shtml . . . A further reduction: "The simplest model is more likely to be correct--especially when we are working with unusual phenomena."

The basic concept is so simple that it eludes many. It has many corollaries, but the basic concept is the same -- simple, intuitive, and sublime. By whatever name you call it, "Occam's Razor," "The Rule of Economy," "The Principle of Parsimony of Hypothesis," "The Law of Parsimony," or even "The Law of Least Complex Postulation," it doesn't matter. The principle is the same. Writings on this topic go back at least to Aristotle, and probably much farther.[4]

When interpreted as an immutable law for fashioning scientific theory, or made into a centerpiece for rigid methodological reductionism, a debate can be expected to ensue. Wasserman, among others, argues that Occam's Razor "is an arbitrary convention, (which) turns out, on closer examination, to be an absurdity."[5] He projects his long flames of intellectual vitriol, proclaiming its failure "in the case of many of the most prominent scientific hypothetico-deductive theories." Considering the layers of complexity that exist in Quantum Mechanics or even Classical Electromagnetic theory, my reading of Wasserman is that the poor man is missing the point. Physics itself provides one of the most glaring examples of the perfection of Occam's Razor in "the Democracy of Paths."[6] In a universe with systems that are inherently differing in their level of complexity, it would seem that Occam's Razor itself should be applied at varying quantum levels to fit the systems which are the subject of examination. Furthermore, Wasserman and others fail to take into account the many elements of human nature that provide a propensity to make things more complicated than they really are, for reasons that are self-evident from the prior chapters of this work. Others, like Wolfram, note that the urge to discard Occam, is often attributable to a lack of depth of examination, for "what appears complicated may actually be produced by very simple

---

[4] The simplest explanation is usually the most accurate. Though this holds in the majority of cases, naysayers are quick to try to point out exceptions.

[5] Gerhard D. Wasserman, From Occam's Razor to the Roots of Consciousness -- 20 Essays on Philosophy, Philosophy of Science and Philosophy of Mind, (Hants, England: Avebury, Ashgate Publishing Limited, 1997 Chapter 3, p. 36-38.

[6] Discussion of the "Democracy of Paths" in layman terms: www.natural-law.org/ideal_administration/ch01.html

underlying programs -- which perhaps occur because they were the first to be tried, or are the most robust."[7] Like Sheldrake's morphogenetic fields,[8] Wolfram's "cellular automata" show that the universe is based on amazingly simple rules that generate counter-intuitively complex results.[9] My position is that optimal healing is based on insights into, and practical application of, very simple rules of healing. Our attempts to make these rules more complicated serves the interests of commerce and politics well.

It does not serve the interests of healing.

Putting the applications of Occam's Razor to theoretical modeling aside, my experience over many years in the alternative health care field has taught me that, with rare exceptions, the ideal medical solution tends to be remarkably simple, cost effective and natural, without the need for further complexity on the part of the practitioner or the patient. My experience in running into this phenomenon again and again became a source of inspiration for "Unifying Principles."

I already covered in some detail within Chapters Four and

---

[7] Stephen Wolfram, A New Kind of Science, (Champaign, IL: Wolfram Media, Inc., 2002), 1025. In this one instance, the entire quote on Occam's Razor is worth repeating: "Simplicity in scientific models: To curtail absurdly complicated early scientific models Occam's razor principle that 'entities should not be multiplied beyond necessity' was introduced in the 1300s. This principle has worked well in physics, where it has often proven to be the case, for example, that out of all possible terms in an equation the only ones that actually occur are the very simplest. But in a field like biology, the principle has usually been regarded as much less successful. For many complicated features are seen in biological organisms, and when there have been guesses of simple explanations for them, these have often turned out to be wrong. Much of what is seen is probably a reflection of complicated details of the history of biological evolution. But particularly after the discoveries in this book it seems likely that at least some of what appears complicated may actually be produced by very simple underlying programs -- which perhaps occur because they were the first to be tried or are the most efficient or robust. Outside of natural science, Occam's principle can sometimes be useful -- typically because simplicity is a good assumption in some aspect of human behavior or motivation. In looking at well-developed technological systems or human organizations simplicity is also quite often a reasonable assumption -- since over the course of time parts that are complicated or difficult to understand will tend to have been optimized away."

[8] Rupert Sheldrake, A New Science of Life: The Hypothesis of Formative Causation, (Los Angeles: Jeremy P. Tarcher, Inc., 1981).

[9] Steven Levy, "The Man Who Cracked The Code to Everything," Wired Magazine (June 2002): 132-137, 146-148.

Five, my creation of Cansema and the history of escharotics that formed the underpinnings of that development. Now I will re-examine this phenomenon in terms of Occam's Razor and the Exosomatic Axis.

It is hard to imagine a formulary process that is any simpler than one employing water, a zinc halide salt, and one or a handful of dried, ground herbal components.

The product is simple and inexpensive.

The process is simple . . . uncomplicated.

I defy anybody to come up with a product that works better and more consistently than Cansema on skin cancers, or cancerous growths of the dermal region. Internal results using variations of Cansema worked on an astonishingly high percentage of cases, better than highly expensive, high entropy, exosomatic chemotherapy, radiation, or surgical approaches. (For one shocking case study in this regard, see Kent Estes.)[10]

Another case study of note involves Heart Drops.[11] We did not create this formula at Alpha Omega Labs, but we created our own variation, for which we got excellent feedback from heart patients, something I was just beginning to work on when I was arrested in September 2003 by the FDA. In examining this case, it is important to note that the Strauss formula literally has thousands of end users who have reported more favorable results than any of the treatments they have received from conventional cardiologists.

The formula is remarkably simple (aged garlic oil, cayenne, bilberry, hawthorn berry, olive leaf extract, white willow bark, bio-energized in an aqueous alcohol base), easy to make, easy to use, relatively inexpensive (we charged $19.95 for our 120 ml. product, less than the cost of an office visit in the U.S. to a general practitioner).

How does the purchase, over time, of two or three bottles of this product compare with the expense of triple-bypass surgery? Or, as John McDonall once noted, "Research completed over the past eighty years not only supports the role of diet and life-

[10] See: www.altcancer.net/estes.htm

[11] See: www.altcancer.com/heartdro.htm

style in the cause and prevention of disease, but clearly shows that most of these same diseases can be treated more effectively by removing the causes than by using any of the drugs and surgical practices available today. Sad to say, the choice of therapy is often based on the profit margin tied to that therapy. Compare $100 worth of vegetables and a $25 pair of walking shoes to a $20,000 coronary bypass operation. The probability of positive results at one month and continuing positive results five years later are better with the $125 approach, but how many victims of heart disease know about this alternative approach?"[12]

Yet another case study that demonstrates the evidence of Occam's Razor at work in the realm of human health is the role of clay.

That's right: raw earth.

In my travels I encountered many indigenous groups and healing traditions. I was surprised to find out just how many native people used raw clay to cure a variety of different ailments, dermatological as well as gastrointestinal. The suppression of this entire area of study, which comprises an entire medical discipline, called "geophagy," is most illustrative. (I set up a special page for my own inexpensive, simple clay formulas, called Enchanted Ruins Healing Clays[13] to tell the story, introduce the products, and summarize a leading book on healing clays for lay people.)[14]

Outside the physical "walls" of the body, for any being on Earth, nothing is more endosomatic than clay. The uses of clay to cure such a variety of ailments has been well established, and yet very few medical doctors are aware of its properties or would ever think to use it in their practice.

It isn't complex.

It isn't proprietary.

You can't patent it.

All the research in the world isn't going to make it work

---

[12] John A. McDougall, M.D. & Mary A. McDougall, The McDougall Plan, (Piscataway, New Jersey: New Century Publishers, Inc., 1983), 4, 5.

[13] See: www.altcancer.com/e_ruins.htm

[14] Ran Knishinsky, The Clay Cure: Natural Healing from the Earth, (Rochester, Vermont: Healing Arts Press, 1998).

any better or improve its performance than to use it as Nature has provided.

And that leads to the worst indictment of all in modern medicine: it isn't profitable.

Once again, we fight Occam's Razor and end up with more costly, less effective, more expensive solutions.

Make no mistake about it: this is the source of the problem. The very nature of optimal healing, leaning as it does on Occam's Razor, sitting on the far left end of the Exosomatic Axis, not existing to make money, or provide proprietary protection, or bring power, or assist in enforcing economic servitude, is itself the source of the conflict.

Organized medicine, by its very nature, must, out of necessity, declare war on the most effective methods of healing. It cannot but do otherwise. Its inherent desire to insert itself in place of Mother Nature to extract maximum profits is not compatible with the very laws that determine the health of the human subject. Organized medicine is the attempt to enforce exosomatic solutions into an inherently endosomatic world.

Shackled by its own inherent corruption and self-centered agenda, organized medicine, without a radical makeover that divorces medical practice from political lobbying and the eternal fight for market share, can never be a part of the solution.

For the time being, it will remain part of the problem, as will its sycophants and co-conspirators at the pharmaceutical companies and its henchmen at the FDA.

Chapter 11

Brief Introduction to Chapter 12

Continuing with the original *Meditopia* chapters written in the summer of 2004, the treatment of the application of Gresham's Law to complicate consumer access to legitimate, efficacious, low entropy products is the subject here. It presents a converse situation to the proposed direction to creating better health care presented in previous chapters.

The original post was Chapter 7 of the original *Meditopia* draft, and it is still online.[1]

---

[1] See: meditopia.org/old/chap7_2004.htm

Chapter 12:

Gresham's Law:
Its Treacherous Application

This chapter, like all the chapters in this section, starts with an immensely simple idea: in this case, the simple observation (and fundamental principle in economics) that "bad money drives out good." Expanded to assume a more interdisciplinary utility, diluting "the good" in any system by allowing the introduction of "the bad," succeeds in getting rid of the good altogether, in varying degrees and in proportion to the bad that is allowed to flourish.

A good example of this might be the Internet. Email has become a vital tool of business and industry, not to mention what it has done for personal communications. In the early days of the Internet, I found it to be an enormous benefit. Then, over time, with the introduction of more and more "spam," many users now feel overloaded in attempting to "extract the good messages." I myself got to the point where even with advanced filtering methods, I was overwhelmed and urging my associates to call me on the phone if their message was important. I could not take the chance that an important message might be missed awash in all the unsolicited garbage. No one likes spam. And the laws to try to reduce or eliminate its overgrowth in cyberspace do not appear to be working. There are, however, far more sinister applications of Gresham's Law, involving far more deliberate attempts to drive out the good. And despite arguments that the converse of Gresham's Law holds historical accuracy, there is no evidence that the role of organized medicine, at any of its levels of operation, has served to use the good to drive out the bad.[1]

---

[1] See: www.columbia.edu/~ram15/grash.html The twelfth and final section ("Conclusions") of this Columbia University essay attempts to make just such an assertion. To wit: "The catchy phrase, 'bad money drives out good,' is not a correct statement of Gresham's Law nor is it a correct empirical assertion. Throughout history, the opposite has been the case. The laws of competition and efficiency ensure that 'good money drives out bad.' The great international currencies – shekels, darics, drachmas, staters, solidi, dinars, ducats, deniers, livres, pounds,

Because I am an herbalist, people are sometimes shocked to hear me say that at least 90% of the herbal products on the market are, at best, marginal. Most products are, to use the vernacular, just garbage.

How FDA Officials Assisted in the Production of Counterfeit Versions Of My Product

After the FDA closed down our Louisiana operation in September, 2003, one of our former distributors, Toby McAdam, began selling his own version of our product, stealing the name, the web page information --- virtually everything about our product off our site.

All this began while I was in prison, and with the FDA having confiscated virtually all our assets, it was impossible for us to respond to this counterfeiting activity.

At the same time, Mr. McAdam, began telling our customers that he was working WITH FDA officials to continue selling his "legitimate version" of Cansema for sale to the public.

It is now one year since the FDA raided our facility, and we have had the chance to analyze Mr. McAdams product. Is it anything like what the label claims it to be? Not at all. Although the label clearly indicates that Toby's Cansema contains zinc chloride, chapparal, bloodroot, galangal root, ginger root, graviola leaf, bitter melon seed, and glycerine, we found that it contains N-O-N-E of the active ingredients of Cansema.

No zinc chloride.

No chapparal.

No bloodroot.

No galangal.

What it does appear to contain is corn oil and a couple of herbal components that are NOT listed on the label.

dollars--have always been 'good' not 'bad' money."

It is both an adulterated and mislabelled products.

But it has the blessings of the FDA.

Skeptics might ask, "Why would the FDA do such a thing?" Our answer is simple: with thousands of this worthless counterfeit product being shipped all over the U.S. -- product that does not work AT ALL -- can you think of any better way for the FDA to prove to the public that Cansema doesn't work as we have promised? After all, didn't the FDA insist in testimony in my own criminal case that Cansema was a worthless, "unapproved drug." It absolutely did. I know. I was there.[2]

Postscript: The FDA eventually went after Toby McAdams and the various websites he created to copy our materials and sell counterfeit products.[3] I suspect this because of the fuss I made beginning in 2004 over the agency supporting this kind of treachery. Nonetheless, as I document elsewhere in this volume, it is a common tactic of this governmental criminal enterprise.

Herbology, well practiced with an eye towards maximizing the desired effect on the customer, is an exacting science. Depending on the herb and its use, and in varying degrees, the efficacy of a given herbal product will be based on when it is picked, how it is processed, the proven efficacy of the mixed ingredient formula itself (where applicable), and the validity of the protocol provided, etc.

Good manufacturing practices should be enforced to ensure the very best herbal products are sold on the market. But such standards are not used or enforced, and the reason is simple: the FDA doesn't recognize herbal supplements as anything more than a dietary supplement. Herbal manufacturers get to hide behind the DSHEA disclaimer. After all, if they tell the customer up front, "This product is not designed to diagnose, prevent, treat or cure any disease," and then market a medicinally worthless product, how can they be held accountable?

They can't.

Officials at the FDA know this. They know that the mar-

---

[2] See: www.altcancer.com/fake_cansema.htm; and: www.altcancer.com/docs/fda_emails.htm

[3] See: montanapioneer.com/fda-fine-livingston-man-85000/.

ketplace is awash with worthless herbal products that do not benefit the customer. They like it that way. The pharmaceutical companies like it that way. And most physicians like it that way. By turning a blind eye to having near non-existent standards for medicinal herbal products bad products inevitably drive out the good. In other words, consumers stay confused and distrustful of good herbalism in general.

For every customer who has tried a product like Cansema and had a spectacular result, there are 20 who honestly believe that herbs don't work. And why shouldn't they believe this? They bought some cheap $4.00 bottle of product from WalMart, took it home, tried it, got no result, so what conclusion should they draw?

Another good example of this phenomenon is the regulatory posture towards homeopathic preparations. Although the FDA takes a conciliatory position towards homeopathy on its web site.[4] its lack of enforcement of good manufacturing practices has lead to an unusual chasm in how homeopathy is perceived in the U.S. versus other countries that are more open to alternative health care practices.

A close associate of mine in New York is a native of India who came to the U.S. many years ago to get his MBA. He has indicated to me that he knows physicians in Mumbai (Bombay) who use homeopathic preparations regularly, along with ayurvedic, herbal, and more conventional drug therapies. He has told me, "I didn't realize why Americans didn't think more highly of homeopathic remedies until I came to understand that because of unenforced standards your homeopathics don't work as well, if at all."

Now, I have to regard this commentary as hearsay at this point. In all our work at Alpha Omega Labs, despite the fact that we manufactured, in part, most of the 350 different products we carried, we never manufactured any homeopathics. So this is not my area of specialty.

Nonetheless, given my experience in other areas where Gresham's Law runs amok, I regard this as another example of

[4] This piece was abstracted from the December 1996, issue of *FDA Consumer* magazine.

a phenomenon where the FDA, in allegiance to the pharmaceutical industry, turns a blind eye to encouraging the worst alternatives to flourish in the market, simply because by allowing the bad to dilute the public's confidence in the good, consumers are left only with the choice of going with more expensive pharmacological therapeutic options.

Brief Introduction to Chapter 13

Previous chapters point to the bifurcation between real knowledge and "fake knowledge," real objective reality and wholesale manufactured propaganda on a grand scale. So at this point I use metaphors created by the popular movie, *The Matrix*, to further enhance this.

The original post was Chapter 8 of the original *Meditopia* draft, and it is still online.[1]

---

[1] See: meditopia.org/old/chap8_2004.htm

Chapter 13:

The Matrix:
As Applied to Medicine

*"You've felt it your entire life. That there's something
wrong with the world. You don't know what it is, but it's there,
like a splinter in your mind, driving you mad . . . The Matrix is
everywhere. It is all around us, even in this very room . . . It is
the world that has been pulled over your eyes to blind you from
the truth . . . a prison that you cannot smell, or taste, or touch. A
prison for your mind."*

Morpheus
The Matrix

*"If you love wealth more than liberty, the tranquility of
servitude better than the animating contest of freedom, depart from us in peace. We ask not your counsel nor your arms.
Crouch down and lick the hand that feeds you. May your chains
rest lightly upon you and may posterity forget that you were our
countrymen."*

Samuel Adams
(1722-1803)

*"You have the honor of the king's favor; but you know
nothing about liberty, what relish it has and how sweet it is. For
if you had any knowledge of it, you yourself would advise us to
defend it, not with lance and shield, but with our very teeth and
nails."*

Étienne de La Boétie[1]

T he idea that we live in a 'land of illusion' which provides
the backdrop for our physical reality flourishes among
humankind's oldest religions and philosophies. It is best
known in the East under the Vedic concept of **maya**, or illu-

---

[1] Etienne de La Boetie, The Politics of Obedience: The Discourse of Voluntary Servitude,
(Montreal, Canada: Black Rose Books, 1997), p. 63.

sion.[2] This concept becomes anthropomorphic with the arrival of maya as goddess.

From my mid-teens I had a thorough intellectual understanding of maya, largely gained through a study of comparative religion. It is a recurrent theme and yet no study of classical texts is adequate preparation for the paradoxical realization that the Grand Illusion is more real than one might think. At one level it seems obvious that everything around us is temporal; life is brief; and no one can be certain what came before or what comes after this short walk. It even seems intuitive that a human life is a "blink in the eye of Brahman," or, as the Apostle Peter notes, ". . . with the Lord one day is like a thousand years and a thousand years like one day." -- (2 Peter 3:8 NAB)

There are, however, aspects of maya far more concrete than vague references to time, space, or temporary circumstance, and these are more immediate, specific, and sinister.

Those who are so bold as to peer behind this curtain of illusion come face-to-face with the undeniable certitude that, as in the film, *The Matrix*, they do live in a society where humans are a captive source of energy (i.e., through myriad systems of taxation, some apparent and some quite hidden), that human beings do live in a form of financial servitude that is, in truth, the most salient feature of so-called Western democracy, and that, in terms more pertinent to my book, the role of organized medicine is one of "agent," an evil gatekeeper that attempts to prevent people from knowing or using the true source of healing.

That our physical universe may be as illusory as a fist (which promptly turns into non-existence when the hand is opened) appears to be only the most outer skin on the cosmic onion. A universe of illusions, like an onion, has innumerable layers to traverse, and after passing "through" them all, the question remains: "Where is the core?"

Aside from descending into a universe of mirage that effectively lies out of human control, it has been proposed that humankind uses myth as a way of negotiating the hidden meanings of the collective unconscious. "Through a dialogue conducted

[2] See: encyclopedia.thefreedictionary.com/Maya%20(illusion)

with these inner forces through our dreams and through a study of myths, we can learn to know and come to terms with the greater horizon of our own deeper and wiser, inward self. And analogously, the society that cherishes and keeps its myths alive will be nourished from the soundest, richest strata of the human spirit."[3]

I understood these creative forces and the power of symbolism long ago. What I was not prepared for (and you'd never know it to read the work of writers like Campbell) is that modern society has powerful forces at work (at least on this physical plane) that are not at all benign. In fact, these forces are evil, manipulative, and corrupt to a degree that may exceed the average person's capacity to comprehend.

Organized medicine embodies these forces, but even it, as I shall shortly show, is but a subset of yet larger, more sinister forces.

The outline of those forces, in its broadest generalities, can be found in Niccolo Machiavelli's The Prince, who describes in terms quite comfortable to modern civilization, the ways of acquiring and sustaining power. His words of advice, admonition, and comfort are addressed to the tyrant.

But another sixteenth century writer, Étienne de La Boétie,[4] addresses the same forces and provides advice, admonition, and comfort to the victims of that tyrant. As such, de La Boétie provides a libertarian framework that has proven a source of inspiration for Thoreau, Ralph Emerson, Tolstoy and Gandhi. He doesn't detail so much the forces that create the dog collar, instead, he describes the forces that would help us understand why we would allow it be put our around our necks in the first place. In Book III of this work, it will provide a source of inspiration for us as well, but let's dissect his magnum opus first.

Politics of Obedience is divided into three sections, cover-

---

[3] Joseph Campbell, Myths to Live By, (New York: Penguin Group, 1972), 5.

[4] Étienne de La Boétie, Politics of Obedience: the discourse of voluntary servitude, trans. by Harry Kurz (Montréal, Canada: Black Rose Books, 1997), 2. De La Boétie was a close friend of the eminent essayist, Michel de Montaigne, and is remembered as "one of the seminal political philosophers, not only as a founder of modern political philosophy in France but also for the timeless relevance of many of his theoretical insights."

ing the following themes:

Part I -- The fundamental political question is: why do people obey a government? The answer is that they tend to enslave themselves, to let themselves be governed by tyrants. Freedom from servitude comes not from violent action, but from the refusal to serve. Tyrants fall when the people withdraw their support. [And this is why those in the alternative healing community are such a threat to the established order. They choose to withdraw their support from a system of organized medicine that is only intended to enslave them.] Therefore, governments expend great energy in attempting to convince the masses that they need government. "Legitimacy is the belief of the populace and the [lesser] elites that rule is proper and valid, that the political world is as it should be. It pertains to individual rulers, to decisions, to broad policies, to parties, and to entire forms of government. The support that members are willing to extend to a political system is essential for its survival."[5] To those who suggest that we live in a land of freedoms, that if we lived under tyranny, our oppression would be more obvious, the force of economics cures the ignorance and provides the answer as to the importance of the illusory veneer. "Coercion, though, is a costly, ineffective strategy which can never be completely or permanently successful. Even with coercion, decline in popular support below some critical minimum leads infallibly to political failure. Establishing moral validity is a less costly and effective approach."[6] (I can find no other instance of a complete lack of moral validity than our government's support of a system of organized medicine that suppresses effective medical cures so that a select elite of political supporters can make more money. That this has been ongoing, as we saw in Chapter 2, in its most egregious form since the 1840s only adds salt to the wound. In its own sick, twisted way it is the social equivalent of Nazi death

---

[5] Joseph A. Tainter, The Collapse of Complex Societies, 2003 reprint (Cambridge. England: Cambridge University Press, 1988), 27.

[6] David Easton, A Framework for Political Analysis, (Englewood Cliffs, NJ: Prentice-Hall, 1965), 220-4.

camp soldiers rummaging through the bodies of dead Jews to extract their gold teeth. And that is why the FDA is so strict in helping to support this cruel veneer of illusion. To have the truth exposed strikes at the very heart of legitimacy of the government, of any government.)[7]

Part II -- Liberty is the natural condition of the people. Servitude, however, is fostered when people are raised in subjection. People are trained to adore rulers. While freedom is forgotten by many, there are always some who will never submit. [Might we include those who don't want to die unnecessarily from a dangerous FDA-approved chemotherapy treatment, so that the local hospital and oncologists can make more money? So, instead, they seek out natural, effective remedies?]

Part III -- If things are to change, one must realize the extent to which the foundation of tyranny lies in the vast networks of corrupted people with an interest in maintaining tyranny. [And as it pertains to the Medical Industrial Complex, one can see intuitively the forces that work against giving freedom back.]

Every reformer has a different take on how to break this cycle of enslavement. As it pertains to reform of "the health care community," former U.S. Presidential Candidate for the Libertarian Party, Harry Browne, recommended the abolition of the FDA. "Let people decide for themselves, with the help of their doctors and private testing agencies they choose for themselves, which medicines are safe enough for them. Let people decide for themselves what risks they're willing to take. Let people with fatal illnesses choose any therapy they want in hope of beating the odds. No one will be left on his own unless he wants to be. You and your doctor can use any testing and certification company you want -- including one staffed by former employees of the FDA. Let drug manufacturers prove to you and your doctor the safety of their drugs. That way they won't have to run up the

[7] Tainter, ibid.

cost of the medicine -- as they do now to get the FDA to act."

What Browne, and reformers like him, fail to realize is that the system is endemically corrupt. The Matrix cannot be changed by human action. You can only reach the point where you realize the importance of becoming unplugged.

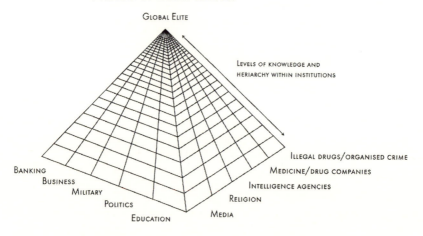

PYRAMID OF MANIPULATION

GLOBAL ELITE

LEVELS OF KNOWLEDGE AND
HERIARCHY WITHIN INSTITUTIONS

ILLEGAL DRUGS/ORGANISED CRIME
MEDICINE/DRUG COMPANIES
INTELLIGENCE AGENCIES
RELIGION
MEDIA

BANKING
BUSINESS
MILITARY
POLITICS
EDUCATION

All the mayor institutions and groups that affect daily life on the Earth connect with the Illuminati, who decide the coordinated policy throughout the pyramid. People in the lower compartments will have no idea what they are part of.

I didn't realize the degree to which the system had become immutable until I began to see correlations between the mechanics of the system as it pertains to the alternative health care system and those writers who have carefully, and in great detail, documented the history, nature and structure, the morphology, if you will, and behavior of the real "power elite."

The Matrix is just a metaphor. After all, machines aren't really running things. Beyond a certain point the metaphor breaks down. Or does it? Is it possible that the system follows a mechanistic set of rules that is so insidious, that we might as well be governed by machines? Is it really possible that, given the manner that our lives are devoted to 'working the system,' (as opposed to the lives of hunter / gatherers who work, on average, just ten to fifteen hours per week), that the power elite could not possibly create a system that is more parasitic than it is now and still get away with it?

Even if you discard, out of hand, the leading books in this genre over the last 30 years -- Epperson,[8] Cooper,[9] Marrs,[10] Icke,[11] Desborough,[12] Constantine,[13] Keith,[14] and Rappoport[15] come most immediately to mind -- you cannot help but notice the accuracy of their collective descriptions about "how" the system operations. You may not agree with the causes to which they point. You may not agree with all their specifics -- (Icke's repetitive work on the reptilian bloodlines, taking up where Horn[16] left off, will strike the uninitiated as over the top -- which is why I have advised friends to read, read, and read; accept what you are ready for and just put the rest aside for the time

[8] Ralph Epperson, The Unseen Hand: An Introduction to the Conspiratorial View of History, (Tucson, AZ: Publius Press, 1985). And secondly, see his New World Order, (Tucson, AZ: Publius Press, 1990).

[9] William Cooper, Behold a Pale Horse, (Sedona, AZ: Light Technology Publishing, 1991). Cooper was, by all accounts, an unusual individual. Frankly, I don't care one whit about a person's private life if their writings are true, complete, and accurate. My personal belief is that Cooper's exposure to government corruption was beyond any threshold of tolerance and he became jaded, over time, to a level that simply pushed him over the edge. An account of the bizarre circumstances that lead to his death at the hands of police in 2001 is rendered at: www. bibliotecapleyades.net/sociopolitica/esp_sociopol_cooper10.htm. See also, www.konformist. com/2002/cooper/cooper-terror-murder.htm. RIP: 1943-2001.

[10] Jim Marrs, Rule by Secrecy, (New York: Harper-Collins Publishers, 2000). An aside: Marrs' book, Crossfire, is the definitive, unbiased, and "unofficial" account of the JFK assassination. It formed the basis for Oliver Stone's film on the same subject.

[11] David Icke, Tales from the Time Loop, (Wildwood, MO: Bridge of Love Publications, USA, 2003). I list just this one book, because Icke's style is such that with each new book he gives a summary of much of the previous work. Previous volumes include: And the Truth Shall Set You Free, I am Me, I Am Free, Lifting the Veil, Children of the Matrix, and The Biggest Secret.

[12] Brian Desborough, They Cast No Shadows: A Collection of Essays on the Illuminati, Revisionist History, and Suppressed Technologies, (Lincoln, Nebraska: Writers Club Press, 2002).

[13] Alex Constantine, Virtual Government: CIA Mind Control Operations in America, (Los Angeles: Feral House, 1997). Other volumes include: Psychic Dictatorship in the U.S.A., and The Covert War Against Rock.

[14] Jim Keith, Mind Control, World Control, (Kempton, Illinois: Adventures Unlimited Press, 1998); also The Octopus: Secret Government and the Death of Danny Casolaro, (Los Angeles: Feral House, 2004. Keith died under suspicious circumstances, though not as openly and blatantly as William Cooper. RIP: 1949-1999.

[15] Jon Rappoport, The Secret Behind Secret Societies, (San Diego, California: Truth Seeker, 2003). Several of Jon's previous works, in the same genre, are worth reading as well, including Ownership of All Life, Oklahoma City Bombing, and AIDS, Inc.

[16] Dr. Arthur David Horn with Lynette Anne Mallory-Horn, Humanity's Extraterrestial Origins: ET Influences on Humankind's Biological and Cultural Evolution, (Montezuma, AZ: A & L Horn, Lake 1996).

being). Nonetheless, it is difficult to argue that the net effect is not as they portray it.

I speak from first-hand experience. There is a force which enforces its "will" from above -- a will that is not all at in accordance with what is best for the common good.

Becoming "unplugged," **is**, therefore, one of the first orders of priority in attaining to *Meditopia*. You cannot be a free and healthy person unless you free yourself of the Matrix -- from within and from without.

Chapter 13

Brief Introduction to Chapter 14

Morphogenetic fields are alluded to in Chapter 10, where I first introduced what I call "Caton's Exosomatic Axis." To understand that chapter is to realize that healing with the use of the mind alone is the purest form of healing. It is also the most natural.

The original post was Chapter 9 of the original *Meditopia* draft, and it is still online.[1]

---

[1] See: meditopia.org/old/chap9_2004.htm

Chapter 14:

Healing Thoughts & The Power of M-Fields

"Since the earliest of times, communities of people have recognized certain individuals in their midst who possessed a special gift for healing, from Native American shamans to Hindu gurus. The founders of the world's great religions, Buddha, Jesus, and Mohammed, were all reported to have been gifted healers. Jesus was the best known of all spiritual healers, and he inspired the first generation of Christians to practice healing in community. Jesus said that any who were willing to surrender to a higher power could learn to become healers, whether or not they were Christians."

Russell Targ[1]

T he first law of thermodynamics is the "conservation law" -- that matter and energy are never created, never destroyed, but simply transfer from one form to another. At a sublime level of human experience -- one that no amount of mathematical formulating or other intellectual modelling can possibly prove, no more than I can prove to you that when I look up into the sky on a clear day I see the color blue -- you get to add something else. Matter and energy are viewable, measureable, attribute-identifiable realities only because of something else: consciousness. That consciousness itself is never created and never destroyed and simply transfers from one form to another smacks of scientific heresy. What, on earth, do you do with such lunacy in a society so committed to the mechanistic? But there it is, if you have the inner vision to understand it, in all its elegant, wondrous, and, yes, simple self-evidence.

The role of consciousness and its manifestation as "thought," is an irrelevancy in the rigid halls of Darwinian evolutionary "science." Never mind that Darwin himself had seri-

---

[1] Russell Targ, <u>Limitless Mind</u>, (Novato, California: New World Library, 2004), 125-126.

ous doubts about his own theory, bringing to mind the "second thoughts" of his intellectual, nineteenth century, theorist cousin, Karl Marx: "I am not a Marxist!" The latest battleground in this area, a cornerstone in biological sciences, pits traditional Darwinists against those who argue for "intelligent design." Their primary contentions include: that there is no proof that life springs from randomness, increasing specialty and orderliness from chaos, natural selection from non-selection, natural law from no law, origination from non-origination, consciousness from unconsciousness, all without a higher ordering principle. Indeed, in its strictest interpretation, Darwinism is a rejection of the most basic laws of physics, it is a celebration of the idea that you can obtain something for nothing, from nothing.

Cracks in the mechanistic egg have come from several sources all at once; insufficient, of course, to change how organized medicine does business or infuse any logic into the profit-based edicts of the FDA; such as the latest piece of front page lunacy: that lower priced pharmaceuticals in Canada that are made by the same U.S. multinationals, same drugs, same labs, same labels, same protocols, same everything, are unsafe. Nonetheless, the cracks are there, and they are growing daily.

One of the most serious challenges to the mechanistic mindset of the hardened, orthodox biologist is presented by the intriguing phenomenon of biological transmutations. Although far more respected in Europe and Japan, the work of Professor C. Louis Kervran is now an indisputable fact of scientific life. His discovery that biological organisms are able to literally transmute elements in ways we cannot begin to understand was a blow to Lavoisier's law and the dogma of "the invariability of elements."[2] Outside the U.S., transmutations are recognized in medicine. They have "opened the door to new treatments and therapeutics for reputedly 'incurable' disease. There are solutions already projected for curing arteriosclerosis, rheumatism, excessive arterial tensions, decalcification, kidney stones, hor-

[2] C. Louis Kervran, Biological Transmutations (The movement of life stems from the constant change of one element into another). translation and adaptation by Michel Abehsera, Jacques de Langre, Ph.D., editor, second printing (Magalia, CA: Happiness Press, 1988), 4.

monal deficiencies, etc. in a natural way, without danger to the patient. Agronomists are already practicing Kervran's findings on a large scale."[3]

That scientists of the mechanistic order would have to acknowledge that life is capable of manipulating and changing elements in ways that inorganic systems, at least from what has been observed so far, are incapable of is indignity enough. Then along came Rupert Sheldrake and his hypothesis of formative causation, a theoretical system for explaining the unexplainable by attributing to life forms the ability to reorganize morphology and function over time. Have the immutable Laws of Science always been there, or have they been "developed" over time by the imprint of consciousness, by habits that, in effect, "evolve" into laws? Studying the effects of morphogenetic fields or "M-Fields," one begins to realize that much of what is regarded as "reality," as in *The Matrix*, are just constructs. In this world, as in *The Matrix*, some laws can be changed; others broken. Do repetitive thought forms make impressions within the universe that change these constructs, these so-called "immutable laws"? It has been decades since Sheldrake's ground breaking book was published, yet I have found no compelling arguments that the form, development, and behavior of living organisms is *not* shaped and maintained by M-Fields generated by members of that species.

Taking the journey along the Exosomatic Axis to the Endosomatic leads not only to an acceptance of transmuting elements and reality-altering M-Fields, but into realms of parapsychology devoted to healing.

The "power of prayer" is an acknowledged phenomenon in all major world religions. Many accept, even if they think that the effect is just occasional, or that it only works for "certain people," that prayers, or healing thoughts, can change the outcome in a person's health. And yet few will take the time to learn how such practices, like all human endeavors, can be improved upon and perfected further. It is the urge to reach for an exosomatic solution that holds many people back. But the answers are

---

[3] Ibid., xi.

within, beckoning for attention.

One of the great anomalies of modern science is that it accepts the mind-body connection when it suits its situational need, be it that of an academic, public relations, or most commonly, commercial nature. And if it doesn't suit its purposes, it discards the obvious.

As a young practitioner of meditation in the early 1970s, I could see the effects of changes in thought, in my own life and health. I remember attending a Jose Silva Mind Control course in 1973 in Hollywood, California. At that point, I had already been practicing deep meditation for well over a year; and TM for several months. At one point the instructor used a device to show that when participants had their eyes closed and were in a settled state, their brain waves were in "alpha wave" frequency, instead of beta. When the mind was quite active, the device registered "beta. I could sense and control the difference whether I had eyes open or not, whether I was actively "thinking" or not. When the instructor handed me the device, I stared at him while maintaining "alpha." He gave me some math problems to solve, at which point I understood what he was trying to do. I solved the problems while still maintaining "alpha." He took back the device and minimized my participation for the remainder of the course.

But maintaining specific brain frequencies at will is not the same as consciously and willfully influencing deeper bodily function, let alone treating serious disease.

One vanguard in the thick of endosomatic healing is Russell Targ. I talked about him in a previous chapter, but his work bears repeating here. A physicist and pioneer in the field of remote viewing, Targ now gives courses on remote viewing and distant healing. Psychic abilities in this area, like the CIA-funded programs for teaching remote viewing, can be learned. Rigorous testing can be performed to show that individuals can develop extraordinary powers to diagnosis disease and treat the problem.[4]

---

[4] Targ, 105-150.

Targ, a true physicist and classically trained scientist, is very emphatic about the empirical aspect of his work. His testing protocols consistently produce results. It can be readily shown that these training programs are effective, and in varying degrees from individual to individual, no doubt influenced by the fact that we all have different degrees of innate psychic talent, and they work.

Even more exciting is their cumulative effect. As more and more people master remote healing abilities, this activity, in and of itself, will create its own M-field. And this presents the opportunity to create an inherited, species-wide ability, much as Bucke noted in the growing "cosmic sense," over one hundred years ago.[5]

Western culture and society have for centuries viewed progress through the lens of exosomatic development, ignoring the infinite possibilities that reside, unexplored, within the confines of humankind's own internal universe. That universe, in the present age (or yuga) is just now being tapped, and through circumstances that will perhaps have more to do with necessity than volition, it will be developed further. It is the inevitable direction in which humanity will move.

---

[5] Richard Maurice Bucke, M.D., Cosmic Consciousness: A Study in the Evolution of the Human Mind. (Secaucus, NJ: Citadel Press, 1961). I make reference above to the primary thesis of Part II of his book, entitled, "Evolution and Devolution."

Brief Introduction to Chapter 15

Here I use Elmer Service's "Law of Evolutionary Potential" to clearly show how and why modern medicine, fragmented as it is into innumerable specialties, is actually anti-evolutionary, if not wholly devolutionary. This chapter draws upon arguments made in previous chapters. It further paints the picture of what perfect health care should look like, viewed from another angle.

The original post was Chapter 10 of the original *Meditopia* draft, and it is still online.[1]

---

[1] See: meditopia.org/old/chap10_2004.htm

Chapter 15:

Medicine & The Law
Of Evolutionary Potential

"The more specialized and adapted a form in a given evolutionary stage, the smaller its potential for passing to the next stage."

Elman Service
'Law of Evolutionary Potential'[1]

Having examined the contributions to the science of optimal health from the standpoint of entropy and the exosomatic axis (thermodynamics), Occam's razor (logic), Gresham's law (economics), The Matrix (philosophy) and M-Fields (quantum physics, some would say metaphysics), we place them under the umbrella of evolutionary potential (arguably both biology and sociology), with which they all share one or more tangents.

A host of books now crowd the market that place the corruption of organized medicine at the feet of politics and greed.[2] Alpha Omega Labs' own byline clearly reflects our understanding of this from our inception. But I propose that politics and greed are only symptoms or subsets of larger conditions that run much deeper in a system as complex and specialized as the present day, monolithic, monocultural, monopolitical, monopolistic system of health care.

Elman Service's 'law of evolutionary potential' provides insights as to why.[3]

Specialization is a hallmark of civilization. Indeed, Adam Smith emphasized division of labor as a key component of

---

[1] Elman R. Service, The Law of Evolutionary Potential. In Evolution and Culture, eds. Marshall D. Sahlins and Elman R. Service (Ann Arbor, Michigan: University of Michigan Press, 1960), 93-122.

[2] See: www.altcancer.net/lysis.htm

[3] Joseph A. Tainter, The Collapse of Complex Societies, (Cambridge, England: Cambridge University Press, 1988), 56.

wealth in the life of the nation. "The division of labour, however, so far as it can be introduced, occasions, in every art, a proportionable increase of the productive powers of labour . . . This separation, too, is generally carried furthest in those countries which enjoy the highest degree of industry and improvement . . ."[4] The explosive growth of specialization in graduate medical education of late is a clear sign that, wittingly or unwittingly, the "productive powers" of the expanding medical establishment are committed to the idea that specialization is good, more specialization is better, and maximized specialization is what's best for business, I mean for medicine, I mean for the patient!

Just who the real beneficiaries of this monumental conjoining of medicine, corporate interest, and higher entropy therapies are is debatable. I won't speculate on how the battle lines are drawn because I already know that the polemical combatants will be found in accordance with from where they derive their paychecks. That the exosomatic side of things delivers the heftier paychecks explains why the message of endosomatics is so faint and confused in the competition for mind share and market share, everywhere.

I can, however, surmise how such an exosomatic system will fare if the surrounding infrastructure were forced to subsist on a lower entropy diet. The outcome clearly falls into Caton's "die-off" category.[5]

Service's theory postulates that "specific evolutionary 'progress' is inversely related to general evolutionary 'potential.' Within this view, success at adaptation breeds conservatism; dominant polities are less able to accommodate change. Successful complex societies [i.e. high entropy, highly exosomatic] become locked into their adaptations, and are easily bypassed by those less specialized [i.e. low entropy, more endosomatic]."[6] R. N. Adams believes this rigidity and conservatism "result from investment in controlling major energy sources," which would

---

[4] Adam Smith, An Inquiry Into the Nature and Causes of the Wealth of Nations, as re-published in The Great Books, Volume 39 (Chicago, IL: Encyclopedia Britannica, Inc., 1952), 8.

[5] William R. Catton, Jr., Overshoot, (Urbana, Illinois: University of Illinois Press, 1980).

[6] Service, 97, as quoted in Tainter, 56.

follow because a high entropy culture, by definition, requires a high energy diet.[7]

Tainter continues to comment on the long-term viability of more specialized social structures. "So by having greater flexibility, less complex border states gain an increasing competitive advantage, and are thus able ultimately to topple older, established states."[8] The implications of this development are easy to draw from current news reports from the war on terrorism, and I will get to them later, but for now I want to focus on two important extrapolations on Service's observations.

Life for humans, or any other species on this planet, entails an unending stream of adaptations as the environment undergoes constant change. The deadly microbes of one era give way to those of another. Ecological challenges that may impinge on the health of one community at one time or place may be unknown to any other. Optimal health care, if it could speak on its own behalf, would choose a healing, therapeutic paradigm that maximized its potential, not restricted it. It would choose to be iconoclastically committed to seeking out the most empirically efficacious healing modalities, not narrow in its rigid adherence to peer review, maximum profiteering, and the nasty business of pseudo quack-mongering.

Human evolutionary potential is minimized by rigidly specialized structures not because they fail to serve their needful, specialized function, but because people give them a life of their own that rejects the notion that generalized and specialized forms can co-exist in cooperation and not competition.

The second point worth mentioning in connection with Service's law is the disservice inherent in 'tunnel vision' medical specialization. As I mentioned in the Entropy chapter, the human body is an endosomatic creation to which modern medicine insists on applying exosomatic solutions. Even Tainter falls into the trap of thinking of medical technology advances in the same

---

[7] R.N. Adams, Energy and Structure: a Theory of Social Power, (Austin, Texas: University of Texas Press, 1975). Quoted in Tainter, 56.

[8] Tainter, 56.

terms as you would think of advances in chemistry, metallurgy, or astronomy. "As more generalized knowledge is established early in the history of a discipline, only more specialized work remains to be done. This tends to be more costly and difficult to resolve, so that increasing investments yield declining marginal returns . . . Modern science is becoming less productive overall (there are always countervailing trends in some fields) because it has become increasingly specialized and expensive."[9] Tainter than goes on to quote a principle close to the heart of physicist Max Planck, one that Rescher calls 'Planck's Principle of Increasing Effort' which states that ' . . . with every advance [in science] the difficulty of the task is increased.'[10] This is where Tainter's otherwise brilliant observations break down, just as Newton's seemingly imperturbable laws break down under the microscope of quantum mechanics. My experiences exploring various healing traditions at Alpha Omega Labs taught me that the best solution is, more times than not, the simplest one, the inexpensive one, the one that isn't specialized or complicated, the one that proud men of esteemable learning would be most likely to overlook. ("What the builders have rejected has become the cornerstone.")

Simplicity and having one's eye on the endosomatic does something more than allow one to 'pass to the next stage,' it allows one to attune to the miracle of life, to stand in awe of its wonder, to realize that it's alright to acknowledge one's ignorance and allow a creative intelligence that the highly specialized mind will never grasp to reveal the whole, to manifest the wondrous possibilities of the whole, to make whole what needs healing in us, and in everyone and everything around us.

Only in that light is real evolutionary potential possible.

---

[9] Tainter, 114

[10] Nicholas Rescher, <u>Scientific Progress: a Philosophical Essay on the Economics of Research in Natural Science</u> (Pittsburgh, Pennsylvania: University of Pittsburgh Press, 1978), 80. As quoted in Tainter, 114.

Chapter 15

Brief Introduction to Chapter 16

I had been playing with and revising this text since 1996 when I finally posted it in 2000. Its most recent incarnation is still online.[1]

It developed out of an earlier online posting called "Cancerolytic Herbs: A History of Suppression."[2] A shortened version became Chapter 11 of the first *Meditopia* draft.[3]

I felt that the arguments behind this posting were so powerful that I incorporated them into *Meditopia*.

They can also be found in my most recent book.[4]

---

[1] See: www.altcancer.net/lysis5.htm

[2] See: www.altcancer.net/lysis.htm

[3] See: meditopia.org/old/chap11_2004.htm

[4] Caton, <u>The Joys of Psychopathocracy</u>, (Miami, USA: Herbologics, Ltd., 2017).

Chapter 16:

Organized Medicine: A Terminal Disease. Corollaries of Parkinson's Law

One night I came home from work; I had been corresponding with a number of people about the latest incident involving suppressed technology; in this instance, a brilliant piece of research that was going on in Utah, the application of which cures AIDS; no, it doesn't treat AIDS, it cures it.

I was so upset emotionally by all the tumultuous events at Alpha Omega Labs that day that I decided to put my latest thoughts about the suppression of valuable technology "on paper." Since I "write" in raw HTML and style-sheet code, that meant yet another web page.

Well before I saw the applications of "the entropy law," or Occam's Razor to a true and valid assessment of the state of our "health care" system, I saw it clearly in managerial terms. Having been a student of business administration, this made the most sense to me at the outset.[1]

I will not repeat the entirety of that page here, because you can read the footnote link below. (I authored the piece under my Alpha Omega pen and correspondence pseudonym, James Carr.) However, suffice it to say that in light of the Unifying Principles, my "corollaries" of Parkinson's Law, which I have called "The Impossible Mandate Principles," yield even more profound insights. Chief among these is that organized medicine is not about "curing people." It is devoted to keeping them diseased and then killing them. Making money is, above all, the prime directive.

Fighting words? Sure, they are.

But quite accurate, and provably so.

---

[1] See: www.altcancer.net/lysis5.htm; I also cover these principles in Chapter 1 of my book, The Joys of Psychopathocracy.

I received a number of comments on the phone concerning our having posted just this one page. The funny thing, however, is that I never once received a worthy attempt to try and dispute my Corollaries on the basis of argument. No polemic ever came my way that would cause me to have a second thought about what I wrote, or alter its content or tone.

It has remained essentially unchanged since I first posted it in 2001.

The Impossible Mandate Principles

The initial tenet which our arguments set out to explain is: "Why certain fundamental principles of organizational management work to: (1) ensure that the cancer research and clinical establishment NEVER COME CLOSE to providing any meaningful cancer cure, and (2) guarantee that each and every dollar donated to cancer research is unwittingly used to suppress REAL effective cancer remedies."

First Corollary: "In only the rarest of circumstances can an organization succeed if the fulfillment of a singular assigned mission means an end to the purpose which created it. If not provided with a subsequent mission, the organization will actually impede the goal(s) for which it owes its very existence."

Second Corollary: "Organizations assigned to 'finding a cure' - for anything, regardless of what it is, will always lean towards those treatments which are the most expensive, the most complicated, and least accommodating to self-administration. Only in this way can the organization justify its propensities for greater growth and funding requirements, restrict competition by raising the thresholds of specialized education and knowledge, and filter out potential rivals by setting large capital requirements as a 'sine qua non' to even participating."

Third Corollary: "The lack of a 'deadline' will always infect an organization on a mission as obscure as finding a 'cure' with structural elephantiasis. Parkinson's original law also stated 'Any project assigned without a deadline is likely never to be completed.' The fact that the organization itself, out of survival, will band with like organizations to suppress rivals who would suggest that the mission is completed and the deadline past, only puts this principle on steroids and produces yet greater obstruction to the original mission."

Fourth Corollary: "If you want to make your organization bigger (and all of them do) then you must make the problem bigger. Big budgets cannot be sustained in the presence of easy solutions. That means that survival demands that you use whatever means are at your disposal to suppress alternatives by rivals that would prove compellingly contrary. You cannot sustain an illusion in the public mind that the problem is bigger than it really is if you aren't willing to squelch those capable of undoing the big lie that forms the cornerstone of your operation. Advancing your cause requires a maximum, sustained effort to destroy those capable of providing an end to your grand 'raison d'être' and the many growing, demanding, and expensive projects which it consequently spawns."

As powerful and as defensible as The Impossible Mandate Principles were, I never took them to the next step. Despite its obviousness, I dared not proceed to put the pieces together and present the 'final conclusion.' Perhaps I felt that I had already done my part, going out on a limb, as it were, with the most detailed information on escharotics to be found anywhere on the Internet, or in print. So why aggravate the evil Power Elite even more? Besides, people would put two-and-two together and draw the ultimate conclusion for themselves anyway. Wouldn't they? I mean, people aren't *that* obtuse, are they?

I wrote this site to present just such a conclusion. I have nothing to lose. Federal agents have used perjurious statements and a breathtaking collage of fraudulent activities to come after me. They confiscated nearly all my property, going so far as to pocket whatever cash, most of it foreign, that they were able to find in my home. I had little more to lose, but my life, which, by even optimistic calculations was roughly half over naturally anyway. And, in fact, as you read this, I will have already served time in Federal Prison.[2]

If this is not a time to call a spade for what it is, there is no such time.

I remember sitting in my cell at the Lafayette Parish Correctional Center in Lafayette, Louisiana, one morning in May 2004. I was in the middle of Derrick Jensen's <u>The Culture of Make Believe</u> and I came upon a section, where the author tells of a woman, an ecologically-minded activist, who came up to him after a lecture and said in resigned exasperation, "I'll tell you something I've never told anyone: I don't think our culture is salvageable. I think we're doomed."

In a quiet moment of reflection, as the author is remembering these words, he hears the same thought echoed from a close friend. "I don't think we're going to make it," she says.

"I've been waiting for you to say that," he replies.[3]

As I sat in my cell, reflecting on the obvious parallels to my own work and the same sick fundamental forces in my life as an herbalist that Jensen recounts as an ecologist, I wept quietly. Not for myself -- I had already exhausted my tear glands in thinking about the horrors of what had already befallen myself and my family, but for an outcome I could do nothing to prevent. I wept because in my own brief moment of self-reflection, I realized that I could no longer call myself a reformer. A reformer is someone who believes that the system can be reformed. A reformer is still someone who believes that the system is not beyond being fixed.

I have lost that faith. And I am not alone.

I could readily chide you, if, by now, you have not pieced

<hr />

[2] Keep in mind this part of *Meditopia* was written before reporting to the U.S. Federal Prison system in September, 2004.
[3] Derrick Jensen, <u>The Culture of Make Believe</u>, (White River Junction, Vermont: Chelsea Green Publishing Company, 2002), 237.

together the elements of the Unifying Principles and applied it to where we go as a people, as a culture, and as a society.

But I'm not going to.

I will present my summation in the simplest terms I know. I do this because I have lost all reason and motivation to render pretense, literary or otherwise, be it for self-preservation by submission, to garner friendship or alliance, to avoid criticism, or to justify a more worthy end.

We're not going to make it.

Whether or not you are well-read; whether or not you have taken the time to hear out the views and voices of a hundred noble thinkers who have spent a lifetime contemplating where we are currently headed; whether or not you are even versed in the likes of Danilevsky, Spengler, Toynbee, Kroeber, Coulborn, Gray, Ortega y Gasset, Hubbert, Weber, Tainter or, as in the example above, a more contemporary writer like Jensen, it doesn't matter. It is something you must feel; it is a knowledge that must arise from within you.

Just because I am not a reformer, doesn't mean that I don't think we have work to do. But that work must be devoted to creating systems that will work, systems that make optimal healing possible, where those who devote themselves to the betterment of others can accomplish their ends without the rapacious interference and gleeful molestation of Federal agents.

Brief Introduction to Chapter 17

Here I present the seed concepts that would eventually form the backbone of my previous book, <u>The Joys of Psychopathocracy</u>. This was years before I encountered Marshall Sahlins' book, <u>Stone Age Economics</u>, and his "reciprocity chart." The short version forms my last book's subtitle, namely, that criminality is essential for effective modern government. This posting focuses on the medical side of things, but it's true of government at large.

The original post was Chapter 12 of the original *Meditopia* draft, and it is still online.[1]

---

[1] See: meditopia.org/old/chap12_2004.htm

Chapter 17:

Democratic Infrastructure
& Political Vortices
Why It is Absolutely Impossible
For the FDA to Serve the Public Interest

"Unless we put medical freedom into the Constitution, the time will come when medicine will organize itself into an undercover dictatorship . . ." [Greg Caton's note: medical freedom did not get put into the Constitution, and Dr. Rush's comments have come to be prophecy fulfilled.]

Dr. Benjamin Rush[1]
a signer of the Declaration of Independence

"We must free science and medicine from the grasp of politics." [Greg Caton's note: was he intoxicated or did he just slip?]

Bill Clinton[2]

I covered very briefly in the Entropy chapter, the relationship between localized and centralized authority and control on the Exosomatic Axis. A highly centralized government, or control mechanism, goes hand-in-hand with a highly exosomatic system. This chapter discusses the end result of having one of those highly centralized centers of authority oversee the making, labeling, buying and selling of foods, beverages, medicinal substances, and just about every product a human would internally consume. The U.S. FDA, an agency that brags that it oversees "items accounting for 25 cents of every dollar spent by consumers," oversees this very basic area of human life for a population approaching 330 billion, from Miami, Florida to the northern tip of Alaska (excepting the passage through Western Canada),

---

[1] Peter McWilliams, Ain't Nobody's Business If You Do: The Absurdity of Consensual Crimes in a Free Society, (Los Angeles, CA: Prelude Press, 1993), 561.
[2] Ibid., 566.

from San Diego, California, to the northern tip of Maine; and influences through political maneuverings the very same function for the rest of the planet's 7.5 billion humans.

The FDA is a vast enterprise with an annual budget of about $1.7 billion. The reason for its existence is sensible enough. On its own brief history page, the FDA recounts its emergence with the passage of the Federal Food & Drugs Act in 1906. This act was spurred by the exposé, The Jungle, written by Upton Sinclair, which exposed the meatpacking industry for unsanitary and adulterated practices that would make any person of conscience shudder. In a capitalistic system where food producers are motivated to cut costs in order to save money, often in ways that are injurious to the customer (by its nature it is already inherently injurious to the animals), there will need to be regulatory oversight. For the rest of this discussion, I exclude FDA practices of inspecting food and drug producers to make sure their facilities meet good manufacturing practices and kindred actions that would aptly be described as a function of good governance.

What a highly centralized organization like the FDA does, and its structure, I will argue, is endemically corrupt beyond any chance of reform, is define what is and what is not a drug; what therapies are approved for commerce; who gets to sell those drugs and from what approved sources; what is and what is not "adulterated" or "mislabeled." I have a rude awakening for those who think the definitional lines are clear cut. Despite the very girth and specificity of the ruling Title 21 in the Code of Federal Regulations, they are not, and, in fact, depending on what a given threat might pose to an FDA "client" in the pharmaceutical industry, the definition can be extremely arbitrary, conflicting with all law, custom, or reason. In my own personal case, the FDA had me plead guilty to selling "unapproved drugs" which were clearly herbal products whose labels and corresponding web pages clearly stated, **"To U.S. Users: This product is not intended to diagnose, prevent, treat, or cure any disease."** It was not, in the end, enough for them to not use coercive tactics to eliminate products that clearly worked better than their pharmaceutical equivalents, at a fraction of the cost, and with no toxic side-effects (specifically, H_3O and Cansema Tonic III).[3] This underscores the heart of the matter and helps us understand why the FDA cannot serve the public interest; expressed in its simplest terms, the FDA cannot serve two masters. It can either serve the interests of the public, or it can serve the interests of the pharmaceutical companies it was originally designed to oversee. Long ago, the FDA, as an institution, made its decision.

If the system in the U.S. were to lean close to the endo-somatic end of the axis, it would be the states (or even small political divisions) that regulated food and drugs "through local health codes, honest-weight restrictions, and other local regulatory laws."[4] Using interstate commerce as the leverage to strip states of this responsibility (which is the exosomatic thing to do), the FDA has assumed the lion's share of those tasks, to the immeasurable detriment of the American people.

The vast sea of corruption that the sequestering of this much power has wrought is the subject of many books, many of which I posted on the Alpha Omega Labs web site. For some unexplainable reason, most Americans are able to understand the basic concept behind tyranny and too much centralization, but not the ways in which it might threaten them. When Oliver Wendell Holmes said, in an oft-cited quotation, that "power corrupts and absolute power corrupts absolutely," he did not add a caveat that this principle did not apply if standing in a U.S. government jurisdiction. This appears to allude to the unwashed masses, or perhaps it is that they know how powerless they are to change it. That the master of the FDA is the AMA, the medical research industry, and the pharmaceutical companies, the very corporate entities they are supposed to oversee, and not the American people, has been discussed ad nauseam, but to what resulting reform? "The Food & Drug Administration is intimately connected with the American Medical Association and the handful of pharmaceutical companies that create and manufacture the vast majority of prescription drugs," echoes McWilliams. "Working

---

[3] See Chapter 3 of the online book *Meditopia*: meditopia.org/chap3-1.htm
[4] Ibid., 561.

at the FDA, being on the board of the AMA, and working for one or another of the large pharmaceutical companies, is like playing musical chairs. The high-paying jobs -- the gold ring on the merry-go-round -- are at pharmaceutical companies. The best way to get a raise is to become a 'public servant' for a couple of years and spend some time at the FDA or AMA."[5]

Patronage costs money. Lots and lots of money. And as I showed in my Chapter 5 online draft, huge profits can only be generated at the exosomatic end of the axis, in the exact location where health care is ultimately most absent, to the competitive exclusion of more effective endosomatic solutions.[6] To attempt to do so is to fight nature. In its simplest terms, that is precisely what the FDA is: an institution with an unwritten, declaration of war against Mother Nature. No wonder there are so many "forbidden cures" that, like Cansema, are so highly effective, inexpensive, and non-toxic that the FDA has no choice but to place them on its "list" of effective products that it must exterminate. The high cost of patronage requires it.

The dangers inherent in centralized government were not outside the purview of the founding fathers. It was a nagging problem for Thomas Jefferson, such that his nemesis, Alexander Hamilton, a grand apologist of federal overreach, was moved to make such inane justifications as, "Allowing the utmost latitude to the love of power which any reasonable man can require, I confess I am at a loss to discover what temptation the persons intrusted with the administration of the general government could ever feel to divest the States of . . . authorities. The regulation of the mere domestic police of a State appears to me to hold out slender allurements to ambition. Commerce, finance, negotiation, and war seem to comprehend all the objects which have charms for minds governed by that passion; and all the powers necessary to those objects ought in the first instance to be lodged in the national depository."[7]

[5] Ibid., 568.

[6] The original Chapter 5 draft is at: meditopia.org/chap5.htm.This chapter has been rewritten and exists as Chapter 7, "Seed Corrupted," in the current volume.

[7] Alexander Hamilton, *Federalist* No. 17, *The Federalist Papers*, edited by Clinton Rossiter (New York: New American Library, First Mentor printing, 1999), 86.

The problem with the FDA isn't the people who now work there, or the laws they are entrusted to enforce (over which they ride roughshod as they please anyway), and certainly not the basic principles under which it was constructed. The road to hell is paved with good intentions -- and $1.7 billion a year will give that road a pretty thick gold plating.

The problem is that the very structure itself makes untold corruption predictable, inevitable, multiplicitous, and unbearably egregious. That millions of people over the last century have endured painful deaths at the hands of FDA-approved chemotherapy, radiation, and radical surgery, when there existed more endosomatic dominant treatments that would have worked effectively, inexpensively, and without toxic repercussion, means nothing if the mechanism behind this FDA-approved holocaust cannot be identified.

I believe it can.

Or I would not have written this book.

Going back to Justice Holmes' simple observation that "power corrupts and absolute power corrupts absolutely," what does that mean in terms of the endosomatic-exosomatic axis? What it means is that lateral movement to the right on the axis, towards highly centralized, exosomatic, profit-oriented, high entropy policy, regulation and government in general, is an open invitation to the "undercover dictatorship" of which Dr. Rush forewarned.

To have a true democracy in which power is in the hands of the ordinary citizen, the "power center of gravity" has to be shifted towards that citizen. Governmental power carries with it a certain kind of gravitational force; money and power are the attractors of that force. If you concentrate that power in one location, you magnify the force and you make money and power the dominant "be all and end all." If you shift that power towards the locality of the individual, you diffuse the potential powers of misuse that are inherent to highly centralized power.

Every political unit, be it the governing entity behind a city, state, or nation, comprises a dynamic vortex, much like a black hole. A number of factors provide the elements that enlarge or reduce the "gravitational field" of that vortex proportionally. These include territory, resources (including financial where-withal), and people -- all interrelated. The larger the vortex, the more inherently corrupt it becomes. You can see this inherently in Icke's Pyramid of Manipulation, because from the view within the pyramid looking up, all "lines of power" flow to a center, a point, the capstone, the one all-controlling eye at the peak. (It is both ironic and synchronous that this Masonic image should appear so prominently on the currency issued by the Federal Reserve Bank of the United States.)

This is exosomaticity at its extreme. This is the pendulum of life when it has moved to the far right and it can move no farther, when it cannot avoid the need to restore equilibrium and move back to the center. Humans will always have some need for the exosomatic. Otherwise everyone would be naked breatharians without the need for tools. Perhaps the purely endosomatic exists in spirit form only. But there is a state of equilibrium. There is such a thing as balance. It exists when there is real democracy, not the political "theater of the absurd" that now operates in the U.S. and merely "pretends" to be real democracy. It exists when everything possible has been done to marginalize the power vortices so that government serves the common people, and not the other way around.

The FDA is an inherently defective polity simply because it cannot forsake its exosomatic roots. It is corrupt because it is not capable of being otherwise; it is in its nature, as surely as a carnivorous cheetah cannot forsake its need to hunt, kill and eat game.

The FDA is a creature of the Matrix. It cannot be reformed. Escape from its vastly corrupt influence cannot be accomplished by changing it. Escape is possible only by committing to un-plugging from it. And to become unplugged you must want it more than anything else in the world. You must fight for your liberty "not with lance and shield, but with your very teeth and nails."

Chapter 17

Brief Introduction to Chapter 18

This is an extension of observations made in the previous chapter. What is touched upon here is the importance of "minimizing sectorial distance" in human relationships. I don't use these terms here, and, in fact, it would be several more years before I made use of them, but, again, the seeds of what would become <u>The Joys of Psychopathocracy</u> are clearly evident.

The original post was Chapter 13 of the original *Meditopia* draft, and it is still online.[1]

---

[1] See: meditopia.org/old/chap13_2004.htm

Chapter 18:

Networking Politi-Cells:
Political Structure of a Meditopia

*"The decayed condition of American democracy is difficult
to grasp, not because the facts are secret, but because the facts
are visible everywhere. Symptoms of distress are accumulating
freely in the political system and citizens are demoralized by
the lack of coherent remedies. Given the recurring, disturbing
facts, a climate of stagnant doubt has enveloped contemporary
politics, a generalized sense of disappointment that is too diffuse
and intangible to be easily confronted. The things that Americans were taught and still wish to believe about self-government
-- the articles of civic faith we loosely call democracy -- no
longer seem to fit the present reality."*

William Greider[1]

T hose who are inclined to ponder the state of our current
political climate -- and few citizens appear to do so anymore with any depth -- generally fall into three distinct
camps. There are those who are generally happy with the status
quo and feel that whatever shortcomings arise, they can be fixed.
In other words, they have faith in the self-healing mechanisms
now in place. Secondly, there are those who feel a far more radical approach is required. The system has not been fixed, cannot
be fixed, and will never be fixed, and, therefore, the "People"
will never be properly represented unless they clean out the Petri
dish and start over. The third group are even more "radical" in
the current understanding of the term, and we call them "anarchists." Advocates of anarchism come in many flavors, but it
would probably be fair to say that their position represents the
same cleaning out of the Petri dish. But then they **keep** it clean.

This sounds good in principle, but it represents a swing-
ing of the pendulum too far in the other direction. *Meditopia* is
not about **no** government. It's about good government -- gov-

---

[1] William Greider, Who Will Tell The People, (New York: A Touchstone Book, 1993), 11..

ernment that provides responsiveness and accountability to the common citizen, rather than mythological theater.[2] It's about government that observes Natural Law and acts with a knowledge of the importance of endosomaticism. It's about acknowledging the dangers inherent in the centralization of power and authority and realizing that in any endosomatic-leaning society, people make decisions for themselves. It's all about community, and when you put all the pieces together, the best government comes from the networking of many communities, where the center of power is still localized. It's about creating a body of civic law that is so minimalistic, that the thought of so-called "consensual" crime (which abounds in the over 13,500 criminal laws now on the books in the U.S., and that's just on the Federal side)[3] is acknowledged for the absurdity it is.[4]

The Cruel Illusion of 'Entitlements'

The conventional minded will argue that the large portion of the U.S. budget that goes to "entitlements" (i.e., Social Security, Medicare, etc.) is proof of the beneficence of the system. Those who make this argument are careful not to mention that "social security" is a Ponzi scheme, that it is a mechanism to support what Tainter calls "legitimacy of government," but as with all systems that are parasitic, it must, by its nature, take more away from it than it gives back. The U.S. social security fund has been so rapaciously plundered that, as with Greider's observation about the facts of American democracy as a whole, the signs of its eventual collapse are "visible everywhere."

I liken social security as it is known and practiced in our Western democracies to a "generous robber." As you insert your key into the driver side lock on your car, you are accosted by a masked thief at gunpoint who tells you to give him your wallet.

---

[2] I no longer feel this way. In fact, I firmly believe that "good government" is an oxymoron. I passionately articulate my current views on government in my previous book, The Joys of Psychopathocracy (2017).

[3] David Novak, Downtime: A Guide to Federal Incarceration, mentions the "13,500" criminal laws now on the books. (David Novak Consulting, Inc., 2003)

[4] McWilliams, ibid. references the absurdity of consensual crimes.

You instantly comply, as you have no real choice. He opens the wallet, takes out five "twenties" -- but instead of running off with his $100 gain, he must convince you that he's not really all that bad. So he takes two of the twenty dollar bills and hands them back to you. He may even take a few seconds to tell you that he did what he did out of necessity, for food, family, or to complete the metaphor, shall we add national defense, space exploration, huge corporate subsidies – you get the picture. Then he leaves, and you look into your hand at your $40 "entitlement," and as you watch your assailant slip into the night, you notice that the back of his shirt is imprinted with something eerily familiar.

It says, "Uncle Sam."

A beginner's understanding of the "cost ineffective" nature of centralized government can be obtained by reading any of a number of works by Nobel prize-winning economist, Milton Friedman. A good starting point is: <u>Free to Choose</u>, though Friedman leaves the problem bereft of anything extending the boundaries of "laissez faire."[5] Apparently, his genius will not allow him to see the structural defects of "competitive capitalism," especially in the presence of a pseudo-democratic political system that will never, ever allow a real "free market" -- nor has it ever. Nonetheless, he will help crack your egg of illusion, if you still hold to the thought that our government is a bargain. The truth is, it is rapacious in its employment of myriad "systems" of taxation, most of them never appearing in any form on your tax return.

What is needed are discrete, localized "politi-cell" structures, where the center of political gravity is decentralized. The advantages of public works in economy of scale could still be accomplished through networking, but no centralized authority would have the power to exert itself over all the other communities. What would be helpful is a pre-existing model of political, endoso-

[5] Milton and Rose Friedman, <u>Free to Choose</u> (New York: Harcourt Brace and Company, 1979)

matic-leaning success that we can draw lessons from, and as it turns out, just a model already exists. The Iroquois Confederacy, the world's oldest living participatory democracy, has been operating successfully since August 31, 1142 A.D.. However, in terms of the maintenance of eco-sustainable, Earth-friendly, endosomatic culture, the Iroquois claim that Native North American Indians "can probably lay claim to a tradition which reaches back to at least the end of the Pleistocene, circa 30,000 B.C., and which, in all probability, goes back much further than that,"[6] perhaps to the Precambrian.[7] Many elements of Iroquois democratic rule are almost recognizable when compared to our own twisted version of democracy, for instance, all decisions affecting all tribes have to be agreed upon unanimously. (Although the founding fathers were influenced by Iroquois law, it appears to have played a small role – I believe an unfortunately insignificant one.)

In the oral tradition that tells the history of the Iroquois Confederacy or "Six Nations Confederacy," a Huron prophet, Deganawida, was inspired with a plan "to end human beings' abuses of other human beings." This oral tradition, "Gayaneshakgowa," or "Great Binding Peace," tells of the founding of the Confederacy at a time of immense warfare and bloodshed between the various tribes. Although my knowledge of the tradition is inadequate to know all its nuances as it pertains to the

---

[6] See: www.ratical.org/many_worlds/6Nations/#BCtC. Taken from the "A Basic Call to Consciousness, The Hau de no sau nee Address to the Western World," Geneva, Switzerland, Autumn 1977.

[7] Michael A. Cremo and Richard L. Thompson, The Hidden History of the Human Race, 4th printing (Los Angeles, CA: Bhaktivedanta Book Publishing, 2002), 120-122, 267. Graham Hancock calls this "one of the landmark intellectual achievements of the late twentieth century." I have to admit, the idea of men living in the Precambrian era sounds insane -- and the 2.8 billion year old fossil evidence (again, that's billion, not million), found in pyrophyllite, of what is clearly of human (or higher) intelligence is just one instance: and in South Africa, no less. Nonetheless, the dating method would appear to yield an accurate approximation of age. (As an aside: my use of the phrase "or higher" would probably mean extraterrestrial -- which got me thinking: you notice that in all the variations we discuss in our pop culture, ETs are never less intelligent, or less technically sophisticated than we are. In light of our poor husbandry of this planet, I suspect that on a deep level even we know that in the universal scheme of things, we are not one of the Creator's more intelligent species. A good introduction to "this deeper level of truth" is Dr. Arthur David Horn's Humanity's Extraterrestrial Origins: ET Influences on Humankind's Biological and Cultural Evolution (Lake Montezuma, Arizona: A & L Horn, 1996.)

use of resources, I suspect that, as in most conflicts, an "exoso-matic leaning" relative to the Indian culture was most probably in vogue. Deganawida enlisted the help of a former Ononadaga chief, Hiawatha, to help carry his message in all its specifics to all the other nations.

The result was a detailed solution -- one that requires over a week to repeat by those who can still recite the Deganawida, but at its core is a solution with the simplicity of Occam's Razor: a forum will exist where all nations are represented, where "think-ing will replace violence" and "reason will prevail," with a cen-tral geographic location easily reached by all. In acts that further showed an underlying endosomatic wisdom, the Confederacy was divided into clans, irrespective of the participants' tribal ori-gin. The clan names were taken from animal species with whom the Indians share their ecosystem: Turtle, Bear, Wolf, Heron, Hawk, Snipe, Beaver, Deer, and Eel. Political power is not in-vested primarily in men. In a move that reflected the wisdom of culture that respects the equal importance that male and female play in a culture in equilibrium, the women of the clans meet under the leadership of a clan mother and select the men who assemble as chiefs in the Grand Council. To insure peace among the different Indian nations, "the Peacemaker proposed that the People of the Longhouse would be united in a brotherhood so strong that the people of the Turtle clan of the Senecas would view the people of the Turtle clan of the Mohawks as their own blood kin, and as such it would be unlawful for a person of one of these nations to marry a person of the other who was of the same clan, just as it would be wrong for a person to marry a sibling."

It is interesting that the Deganawida story describes an early opponent to the Plan for Unity that created the Federation. The oral tradition describes him an Onondaga war chief whose name was Tadodaho. He was said to be an "embodiment" of evil, one who had snakes woven into his hair to intimidate those around him. I believe this is Indian symbolism that, translated into the "language of the Axis," describes the "Darkness" that increases as one moves from left to right on the Exosomatic Axis. In continuing the symbolism, the tradition tells of the emergence of Jikohnsaseh, a woman chief of the Cat (or Neutral) Nation. "She suggested that (Tadodaho) could be won over by being offered the chairmanship of the Great League. When the nations assembled to make their offer, Tadodaho accepted. Jikohnsaseh, who came to be described as the Mother of Nations or the Peace Queen, seized the horns of authority and placed them on Tadodaho's head in a gesture symbolic of the power of women in Iroquois polity."

In comparing our own political and social order with that of the Iroquois Confederacy, several key features stand out -- and they show just how far we have allowed our worship of tools to remove us from the natural world. First, the strength of the "community" shines clearly among the Iroquois and nearly all indigenous tribes that one studies in North America. Their myths and symbolisms were rooted in the land and allowed them to have a deep and abiding relationship with the land. By contrast, our high entropy, highly exosomatic culture has invested itself largely in the individual. As Joseph Campbell notes, " . . . in the leading modern centers of cultural creativity -- people have begun to take the existence of their supporting social orders for granted, and instead of aiming to defend and maintain the integrity of the community have begun to place at the center of concern the development and protection of the individual -- the individual, moreover, not as an organ of the state but as an end and entity in himself. This marks an extremely important, unprecedented shift of ground . . ."[8]

Political economists who follow the theories of "social capital," understand the implications of these developments. For social capital is the glue that holds together both physical and human capital and makes them productive. "It refers to features of social organization, such as networks, norms, and trust, that facilitate coordination and cooperation for mutual benefit. Social capital enhances the benefits of investment in physical and human capital." The slow dying passage of American communi-

[8] Joseph Campbell, <u>Myths to Live By</u>, (New York: Penguin Group, 1972) 24.

354

ty is something social capital pioneer, Robert D. Putnam, makes clear in <u>Bowling Alone: The Collapse and Revival of American Community</u>.[9] Putnam is, however, a reformer without a sense of the tectonic shifts in politics that contribute to the collapse in the first place. You can't fix life on the surface when the underlying tectonic forces are programmed to make life above unstable. Investment in community, as Hume notes in his "farmer parable," is based on a confidence in reciprocity.[10] If the power structure has a center of gravity that is located at the top of the pyramid, where exosomaticity has created maximum centralization of authority, the very forces that create community vibrancy and potency have already been sucked out. Putnam does a superior job of identifying the problem -- not providing the solution.

I realized this while running my family's food company, Lumen Foods (soybean.com).[11] My employee number fluctuated anywhere between nine and forty-three employees over the years -- (I founded the company in Lake Charles, Louisiana in 1986). After a while, I noticed that my wife and I were the only ones who ever went to a voting booth to fulfill our civic duty on election day. I had extensive talks with employees, individually and in groups, to uncover why there was such a dearth of interest in the electoral process. If I had to sum up the sentiments of my workers, it would be: "What does it matter who gets elected? And even if my vote changed who got elected, what difference does that make to me or my life?"[12]

---

[9] Robert Putnam, <u>Bowling Alone: The Collapse and Revival of American Community</u>, (Simon & Schuster, 2001).

[10] R.D. Putnam, et al, <u>Making Democracy Work</u>, (Princeton, New Jersey: Princeton University Press, 1993), 163.

[11] See: www.soybean.com

[12] For those who think this reaction is isolated to those in lower socioeconomic strata, consider the experience of Dr. Daniel Goodenough of Harvard Medical School, who not long ago held three seminars on human health and global environment. The first seminar "was overflowing with energetic, aware, and concerned young medical students. Inexplicably, however, the second session was only half full. At the final seminar only half a dozen students showed up. When a perplexed Goodenough asked the students why attendance had fallen off so sharply, their responses were identical. The material was compelling, they said, but it engendered overwhelming personal reactions. The problems were so great, and the ability of the students to affect them so remote, that they could deal with their feelings of frustration and helplessness and depression only by staying away." Taken from Ross Gelbspan, <u>The Heat is On: The Climate Crisis, The Cover-Up, and The Prescription</u> (Cambridge, Massachusetts: Perseus Books, 1998), 172.

Centralized government and true democracy are contradictions in terms. The Iroquois understood this. That is why "tribal nationalism" was deliberately broken and destroyed with the institution of clans. The Indians understood that unless each and every citizen felt that his vote counted, that his opinion mattered -- or to borrow from Hume, that his effort in the field changed the fate of the crop,[13] that there could be no democracy, there could be no such a thing as representative government, there could be no peace, there could be none of the blessings that follow from endosomaticity.

The political culture that makes a *Meditopia* possible would have good government, with a political center of gravity that ascended no higher than a small city. Networking would be the order of the day. Such are the dictates of an endosomatically-leaning society.

---

[13] R.D. Putnam, ibid., 163.

Chapter 18

Brief Introduction to Chapter 19

Protecting lower entropy technologies is supported by the chapters leading up to this one. It ties previous concepts together in a way that describes the values that would be embodied by a vibrant, joyful, evolutionary society.

The original post was Chapter 14 of the original *Meditopia* draft, and it is still online.[1]

There are three remaining chapters that followed this one in the original *Meditopia* draft, all written in the days leading up to my re-imprisonment in 2004. However, they were never sufficiently developed to deserve further mention or inclusion in this volume.

---

[1] See: meditopia.org/old/chap14_2004.htm

Chapter: 19

Technological Development In A Meditopia: Protecting Lower Entropy Technologies

"Theuth, my paragon of inventors, the discoverer of an art is not the best judge of the good or harm which will accrue to those who practice it. So it is in this: you, who are the father of writing, have out of fondness for your offspring, attributed to it quite the opposite of its real function. Those who acquire it will cease to exercise their memory and become forgetful; they will rely on writing to bring things to their remembrance by external signs instead of by their own internal resources. What you have discovered is a receipt for recollection, not for memory. And as for wisdom, your pupils will have the reputation for it without the reality: they will receive a quantity of information without proper instruction, and in consequence be thought very knowledgeable when they are for the most part quite ignorant. And because they are filled with the conceit of wisdom instead of real wisdom they will be a burden to society."

Plato
Phaedrus

"Men have become tools of their tools . . ."

Henry David Thoreau

"Information . . . information . . . information . . . where's the transformation?"

Babaji
Famous saint and healer in southern India, upon being asked what he thought of the Internet

The word "technology" has become synonymous with "tool use," and in the battle between humanists and scientists the word is essentially a catch-all for all things exosomatic. The etymology of the word would suggest that even its use has moved right on the exosomatic axis over time -- for the word itself comes from the Greek "tekhnologia," roughly translating as "systematic treatment of an art or craft." Its two root words are "teknhe," or skill; and "logia," or study -- employing the art of reasoning.

The very transformation of the word tells us how our view of the world has been transformed over time. When you think of "Skill" normally refers to the innate abilities of a human, not of a machine; to the inner resources of the creator of the tool. And not those of the tool itself.

Today, the very word pays complete and unabashed homage to the glory of the tool. Gone are the humans who created it. Thoreau was right: we **have** become tools of our tools.

I begin this chapter on technology with a reassessment of what the word means, because for our purposes, we will need to think in more endosomatic terms. We will need to think of "technology" with the center of gravity returning to the inner man and not his tools. We will have to return to our roots and, once again, realize that the creator is more important than the created; the giver the true embodiment of skill, not his gift; and mind the true fountain of advancement and not the matter it creates.

The history of technological development over the last 200 years suggests that we have lost this wisdom to an extreme degree. We have allowed those in the power elite to suppress not just critically important health care technologies -- most of them surprisingly simple in nature. We have allowed those in charge to kill technologies that would have prevented the coming "high entropy" collapse from ever occurring. In concluding an overview of these suppressed technologies, Gerry Vassilatos was lead to pose the question, "What were the twisted intrigues which surrounded these deliberate convolutions of history? . . . Ours is a world living hundreds of years behind its intended stage of development. Complete knowledge of this loss is the key to recapturing this wonder technology."

A thorough study of Vassilatos's work demonstrates a common thread that runs throughout, one that parallels my experiences with suppressed medical knowledge that was central to

Alpha Omega Labs.[1] That common thread is the motivation behind the suppression: the desire to quash effective, low entropy, low profit, relatively non-proprietary, more ecologically benign, less exosomatic technology; so as to favor less effective, high entropy, high profit, more proprietary, ecologically damaging, more exosomatic technologies. The degree of police force has, over time, become more extreme and more outrageous, to the point where, as I showed in Chapter 3, traditional civil rights are being quickly eroded to support this continuing travesty that has brought, and will continue to bring a horrific blight to both humanity and the Earth.

The development and suppression of free energy, including Stubblefield's mastery of "Earth energy," Tesla's development of "broadcast technology," and Farnsworth's perfection of cold fusion, parallel the suppression of effective health care technologies,[2] as does the suppression of electrogravitic devices for transportation,[3] the suppression of Earth-based, wireless communications,[4] and the suppression of low entropy, all natural, lighting systems.[5]

As a people we could have obtained the promise of technology, held onto our endosomatic roots, and worked in harmony with the Earth. We chose instead to let the power elite force us into an extreme exosomatic culture, to poison the Earth, and to lead us down a path of destruction. And for what? So that a select few could make more money?

With the proper political and cultural infrastructure, technology could work for the common person, in harmony with Nature, sustainably and in accordance with good ecological practices, allowing and encouraging humanity's inner development.

Alas, that is not the case in the modern world.

---

[1] See: www.altcancer.com/

[2] Gerry Vassilatos, Lost Science, (Kempton, Illinois: Adventures Unlimited Press, 1999). See chapters 3 (Stubblefield), 4 (Tesla), 7 (Brown).

[3] Ibid., see chapter 7 on Thomas Townsend Brown.

[4] Ibid., see chapters 2 (Meucci) and 3 (Stubblefield).

[5] Ibid., see chapter 6 (Moray).

Living on the Precipice

Part III:

.

The Medical-Industrial
Complex,
Global Corruption
& The Corrosive
Influences of
Modernity

A Brief Commentary on Part III and Chapter 20

The criminal justice system in the U.S. is so unfathomably corrupt that it has become a caricature of itself, as I discuss in *Meditopia*, Chapter 3.[1]

I open Part III with this chapter because it provides the reader with my solid credentials as a first-hand witness before we enter this edifice of filth and corruption. True, the criminal justice system is but one arm of the medical-industrial complex, wherein the former is the brothel that services the vices of the latter. Nonetheless, it provides a worthy backdrop to first examine the endemic deficiencies of orthodox medicine and then expand this to paint an accurate picture of our current global civilization in the larger context. This chapter is abstracted from the original post, which is still online.[2]

---

[1] See: www.meditopia.org/chap3-1.htm

[2] See: www.altcancer.net/ashwin/ashw0908.htm -- (go to the first footnote).

Chapter 20:

Plea Agreement:
A Study in Torture & Coercion

*"Our healthy survival depends on us having nutritious
foods, clean water, healthy working environments and the ability
to take adequate exercise. On top of this we need to manage
stress and have good quality social interactions with the people
around us. These are the key requirements for good or optimal
health – not pharmaceutical drugs."*

Dr Robert Verkerk
*Executive & Scientific Director
Alliance for Natural Health*

On September 17, 2003, U.S. federal and local agents
raided our manufacturing facility, warehouses, and even
our home. They destroyed over 95% (roughly $500,000
worth) of our inventory, raw materials, and packaging; confiscated cash and library books from our home (only to later dra-
matically understate the total and claim that they "incinerated"
our property because they couldn't find us);[1] then worked with
not less than two competitors (that we know of) to assist in the
theft of our intellectual property.

After extracting a coerced plea, they threw me in prison
for what would end up being approximately 30 months, during
which they administered not one, but three, lie detector tests,
because a former associate and a competitor told them I had
millions of undeclared, untaxed dollars in Bahamian offshore
bank accounts.

Money they desperately wanted.

Money that never existed.

No one who has not witnessed federal agents behaving like
the mafia will quite grasp what all this means. Or, as author,

---

[1] See: www.altcancer.net/images/destroy_evidence.gif

365

Jordan Maxwell,[2] says, "You don't know what America is about until you get into trouble."

"United States of America vs. Gregory James Caton" contains so many instances of "government agents violating the law in the feigned effort to enforce the law" that it is the subject of Chapter 3 of *Meditopia*,[3] so I will not belabor the point here.[4] (For those who are having trouble seeing the FDA for the crime syndicate it has become, I recommend a free viewing of *We Become Silent: The Last Days of Health Freedom (2006)*, narrated by Dame Judi Dench, or Gary Null's *Prescription for Disaster (2006)*.)

Those who have followed our story know that our laboratory is now in Ecuador, a country that has freedoms in the area of health care that U.S. citizens can only dream of. We have reopened our online store and expanded our line with our old formulas, products that have been so successful in meeting consumer expectations that they are among the most trademark-violated in the short history of Internet commerce.

Plea Agreement: A Study in Torture & Coercion

Other notable figures have eloquently expressed in concrete terms how and why the modern "plea bargaining" process as perfected in the U.S. criminal justice system is an exercise in torture and coercion. Although the plea bargaining process has been depicted in U.S. media as an unending source of leniency for hardened criminals and all manner of no-do-gooders, the reality is that, more times than not, the plea agreement short-circuits justice, allows prosecutors to hide unspeakable crimes of their own, and provides the veneer that not only is criminal justice fair and efficient, but effective (after all, federal apologists

---

[2] See: www.coasttocoastam.com/shows/2005/04/19

[3] See: www.altcancer.net/docs/trademark_meditopia.pdf

[4] Yes, I won't belabor the point, but since those uninitiated in the true state of today's criminal injustice system should at least have some particulars, I provide the following. After all, to those who haven't been around, "coerced" is a strong word. What follows is an excerpt from *Meditopia*, Chapter 3.

like to brag that over 95% of all arrests end up in plea agreements). The truth is that it is difficult to conceive of a mechanism that would more perfectly act as a suppressor of truth and a determinant of real crime.

In federal prison, the saying goes: "There are two kinds of inmates. The ones who pled and the ones who wish they'd pled." I can say from personal experience that such a common penal saying sprouts from the shared experience of untold thousands of inmates. No one I spoke to in the entire time I was imprisoned would attempt to dispute the veracity of that adage: not those who committed real crimes, not those who are targeted for political reasons (a shockingly high percentage), and certainly not those who are railroaded by the U.S. Government's massive asset confiscation vacuum cleaner.

No words can begin to convey the experience of coming to court (in this case, with my wife and attorney), being presented with a nearly one-inch thick stack of papers, and being told that I had 30 minutes to read everything, sign it, and "plead" before a federal judge, especially when I had read a sufficient body of the text to know that the charges to which I was pleading were not only false, but were breathtakingly at variance with what I absolutely knew to be true. Now, a good criminal attorney would come to his client beforehand and discuss the documents in advance. Perhaps he might argue with the prosecutor that there might be advantages to crafting the plea documents so that they at least "sounded" truthful. Unfortunately, the $50,000.00 I paid to **Lewis Unglesby**, my defense counsel, was, by all appearances, insufficient to have included this in his services. In fact, I doubt that for all services rendered, Unglesby spent more than 25 hours on my case. I only met him five times, and all interactions were themselves exercises in legal minimalism and socially dysfunctional. His "bedside manner" was the worst of any professional whose services I have ever retained. As I told my wife, "Did we have to hire the Marquis de Sade to represent me?"

The untruthful foundations for the plea agreement weren't simply irritating for their inaccuracies, it was the knowledge that even the prosecutor knew they weren't truthful. (When one of our attorneys asked the lead prosecutor how he could present such a ridiculous document, he replied, "You do your job or you lose your job!") As the plea hearing got underway I realized I was travelling through a surrealistic legal version of "Alice in Wonderland."

> **Judge:** "Would you please explain to me in your own words what it is that you're here to do today."
> **Author:** "I'm here to enter pleas to protect my wife and my employees and others."[5]

That should do it, I thought. Perhaps the judge will see that this process is coercive and somehow the process will shift to something actually factual. Maybe.

> **Judge:** "Okay. But, now, you need to help me with this . . . Now I really need for you to help me with what you're actually saying . . ."[6]

Okay, well, up to this point, I had tried to be polite. That's important, right? I mean, I can't just stand here before the judge and say, "Listen, why can't we just be honest? You know this plea agreement is full of lies. I absolutely know it's full of lies. Is it that much trouble to come up with something that isn't fantasy?" And I had signed it at that point, skimming through it just to hit the high points, but I had not actually read it through thoroughly. There was no time for that. The courts don't think it's important for defendants to actually read the plea agreements that the DOJ comes up with. I know for a fact that Lewis Unglesby didn't care.).

> **Author:** "I understand, Your Honor. Well, there are accuracy issues in the pleas, but -- I'm sorry. Specifically, what do

---

[5] See: www.altcancer.net/docs/transcript_plea.pdf, p. 5, L. 22-25. For the rest of this chapter I will simply refer to this document as "Plea Transcript," rather than repeat the link.

[6] See "Plea Transcript," p. 6, L. 1-11.

you want to know, Your Honor?"[7]

This is about are far as a defendant in a U.S. criminal case can go to telling a judge in a plea hearing that he's being coerced with a plea agreement that is, to use vernacular well understood anywhere in America, full of bullshit. Did the judge take the hint? Did he think, "The Defendant has just told me that the plea agreement isn't accurate. Maybe I should ask why he thinks it's not accurate!"?

Of course not.

For the judge to be concerned about the accuracy of a plea agreement, facts have to matter. Truth must have meaning. In an out-of-control empire, like the U.S., the gravitational lines of power are warped around the desires of an executive branch that has completely subsumed the other two branches of government. All attempts at truthfulness are sucked into the prosecutor's black hole, something I still wasn't realizing.

> **Judge:** "Now, Mr. Caton, have you had ample opportunity to discuss your case with Mr. Unglesby?"
> **Author:** "Well, I just got the -- this paperwork -- just about an hour ago, so -- and I've signed it. So I would say I haven't had a lot of time, but I've had enough time to sign the documents." . . .
> **Judge:** " . . . do you feel like you need more time . . . "
> **Author:** "In all candor, Your Honor, I don't think it would affect the outcome."[8]

I'm not sure there is a way, in English, to more politely say to someone the truth doesn't matter. But I tried speaking more directly:

> **Author:** "If this document said I must serve five years in prison because I improperly emptied a kitty litter box, I would be forced to sign that. I don't really have a choice

---

[7] See "Plea Transcript," p. 6, L. 12-14; (emphasis added).
[8] See "Plea Transcript," p. 7, L. 24 to p. 8, L. 14.

in the matter . . . What this [plea agreement] says [is], it doesn't matter whether it's truth or not, I have to sign it."[9]

What ensued thereafter was a statement by the judge that he didn't think he could fairly accept my plea, followed by ramblings from my pseudo-defense lawyer, Lewis Unglesby, that was so at odds with my own knowledge of the facts and the underlying circumstances, that I had to butt in and interrupt my own attorney's conversation with the judge:

Author: "I don't necessarily agree with that."
Judge: "I'm sorry?"
Author: "I don't necessarily agree with that."
Judge: "Well, I tell you what I'm going to do, Mr. Unglesby . . . I'm going to go ahead and take my three o'clock matter. I'm going to give you and Mr. Caton until 3:30. We'll come back at 3:30 . . ."[10]

I could tell that Judge Melançon was trying to do the right thing, after all, he could have thrown the book at me for not being a good sport and just freely and willingly admitting to things that I knew were false. He was as polite as any judge could possibly be, but the hidden message of this latest instruction was the same: "Mr. Unglesby, you obviously haven't explained how this conviction mill works. You better grab a spare room in the back and explain to your client how things get done around here."

To this point, I made it clear to Judge Melançon that there was no deliberate intention to defraud anyone; that my wife, son, even my employees had been threatened, so thereby I was forced to go along with the plea. I had done everything I could think of to make it clear on the record that coercion was part and parcel of what was going on, without actually coming out and saying that the plea was a completely bogus document. I attempted to fall just short of the line. I was powerless to voice my objection to what was going on in any other fashion. (Again, all

[9] See "Plea Transcript," p. 9, L. 15-18 and p. 10, L. 5-6; (emphasis added).
[10] See "Plea Transcript," p. 12, L. 1-5.

of this can be read in the official plea transcript of that hearing.)

Apparently my objecting proved to be more than even Judge Melançon could tolerate. It was then that he interrupted the proceeding and had Unglesby take me and my wife, Cathryn, into a back area behind the courtroom and explain to me how the system "worked."

There was no recording equipment present, but from the recollection of my wife and me the meeting went something like this:

"Do you have any idea what you've just done!" Unglesby broke out steaming, just as soon as we had closed the door and sat down.

"How can you have me sign this?" I shot back. "Okay, so the prosecutor can lie all he wants to. But what about me? If I sign these documents, and you and I both know they contain false information, isn't that perjury on my part?"

"Who in the hell do you think you are?" Unglesby volleyed obliquely, ignoring my question, "There are Justice and FDA agents downstairs just hoping you screw this up so they can come back with more charges. They don't like this deal. They think you're coming out of this way too light. But hey, you want to fight the Federal Government, that's your business."

A short pause ensued. I said nothing. Neither did Cathryn.

"Governor Edwin Edwards[11] was a good friend of mine," Unglesby continued, almost musing. "He had access to millions of dollars and he thought he could take these guys on, too. You saw what happened to him, didn't you!"

Another pause ensued, at which point, sitting there in my orange prison garb, I was almost beyond words. I looked at Cathryn, knowing that one wrong move could mean her imprisonment and an uncertain future for my son. At issue, besides my disgust with the immorality of the entire process, was a series of yes-no questions that I, and all other federal inmates in my same position, must answer before a judge will accept a plea agreement.

"I tell you what, Lewis," I began bitterly, "I can't answer

[11] See: en.wikipedia.org/wiki/Edwin_Edwards

the questions without your input, because if I actually answer the questions that are on this piece of paper with what I know to be the truth, there is no way this judge will accept my plea. So here," and I symbolically handed Unglesby the pen that was on the table, "you take this pen and write 'Yes' and 'No' all the way down the plea agreement, so I don't have to think about what I'm doing and that's how we'll get through this thing."

I almost expected Unglesby to pause and question my approach. But, by now, dear reader, you should know that's pure fantasy. Without skipping a beat, Unglesby proceeded to take the pen and write my answers all the way down the plea agreement. It was then, and mind you, I can think of no more visceral words to convey how I felt in that moment, that I felt like I was no more than a fecal turd floating around in Unglesby's toilet; that he could not move fast enough to hit the flush handle; that he could not move fast enough to get rid of me and move onto the next case.

There is no question in my mind that if Lewis Unglesby were asked today if we ever had the above conversation, or if the details provided are accurate, he would deny it. He has to. He cannot admit to what happened. But this recounting is completely accurate to the best of my and my wife's recollection.

[Note: The following are excerpts from *Meditopia*, Chapters 1 and 3]:

Sue Gilliatt is a case study in just how outrageous civil litigation has gotten in the U.S. She purchased Cansema® from Alpha Omega Labs in September, 2002 and then claimed that it completely removed her nose. When I was served papers on the lawsuit, I immediately knew that the lawsuit was fraudulent. A close examination of the photographs she submitted with her lawsuit reveals images that can only be produced as a result of surgery. My extensive experience in working with escharotic preparations, an experience that led to my consulting with physicians all over the world, instantly told me that no escharotic preparation on Earth was capable of producing these perfect, symmetrical cut lines. Only a knife can do this. No herbal formula on Earth can. So how much were Sue Gilliatt and her attorneys rewarded for perpetrating a fraud on the State of Indiana and Federal courts? A cool $800,000 from my insurance company.

For filing claims concerning alleged injuries from our "H_3O" that could never have occurred, Sharon Lee and her attorney picked up the other $500,000. These parties will never be prosecuted for their crimes, simply because it is against Justice Department policy to admit that their own agents committed felonies in carrying out their duties. Far more likely is their participation in the cash windfall.

Incidentally, Sue Gilliatt's entire deposition can be viewed from this site. It is in DOC file format, nearly 1.2 megs in size, so please allow time for the download. [Case No. 1:03-CV-1183 LJM-WTL, Southern District of Indiana, Indianapolis Division; Sue Gilliatt (Plaintiff) vs. Gregory J. Caton, Lumen Foods Corporation d/b/a Alpha Omega Labs, Dan Raber, Appalachian Herbal Remedies, Pangea Remedies, The Deodorant Stone Co., and DSMC (Defendents).] Ms. Gilliatt sued even though she admitted under oath that her cancer was cured by Alpha Omega Labs' and/or Raber's products.[12]

[Note: The following is an excerpt from *Meditopia*, Chapter 1]:

The concept of "journalism as propaganda," like most things in life, is never grasped as vividly as when you are able to witness it close up. And so it came to pass that while I was in U.S. federal prison (2005), my wife, Cathryn, received a phone call from author, Dan Hurley, who indicated that he was calling to get information about my case. When the subject of FDA abuses came up from my wife, Dan Hurley was quick to interject, "Oh no. That's not what I'm writing about. I'm only out to write the truth."

Soon enough it became apparent that Hurley had already established his informational filters; if what he gathered was

---

[12] See: meditopia.org/docs/sue_depos.doc, read end of page 38 through middle of page 39 in the deposition.

largely supportive of orthodox medicine, it had a place in his forthcoming book; if it could discredit natural medicine, he was interested in doing so in the most sensational manner. A predetermined thesis had been created and the author wasn't about to veer from it.

In the end, my place in Hurley's book was not minor. It was upfront and center. In fact, the book begins with a nineteen page Prologue entitled, "Sue Gilliatt's Nose." The portrayal of this alleged victim is intimate, detailed, and sympathetic. He could have placed Sue Gilliatt's position juxtaposed to my own. He didn't. He could have listened to my or my wife's side of the events. He didn't. He could have received information showing that Sue Gilliatt and her attorney committed an enormous fraud upon the courts to pilfer $800,000 from my insurance company. None of those details made it into the book because the author made his goal plain and clear to my wife from their first conversation: his goal was to present **his** prepackaged truth, one designed to discredit an entire industry that competes with orthodox medicine.

Such is the goal, meaning and purpose of propaganda.

Associates who heard of the book told me to pay no mind. After all, the book (on my last investigation) never managed to ascend above #42,000 on Amazon.com's book sales list. (As one publisher told me jokingly, "That means your mother, two uncles, and a cousin bought` your book. It has no traction with a larger audience.") In fact, I have no doubt that my bringing it up on Meditopia will cause more copies to be sold via those who are merely curious than it has ever sold to date on its own.

But that misses the point entirely.

Endorsed, as it is by such orthodox medical figures as **Stephen Barrett** with Quackwatch ("a 'must' reading for all Americans ... ") and **Marcia Angell**, former editor-in-chief of the New England Journal of Medicine ("quite simply the best book I've seen on this important subject . . . authoritative"), I would have written *Meditopia* to counter the breathtaking collage of false and misleading statements if this book had sold no copies at all.

I would have written *Meditopia* if only because I know

that this book reflects how the established medical community thinks; that it is contemptuous of empirical reality; that it perversely opposes the application of a concept so basic and simple that you hear it at many sporting events: "May the best man win," which applied to medicine means "May the treatment that permanently cures the patient and is proven to do so safely, effectively, and inexpensively win"; that I had the power to expose the irreparable cracks in the foundation that is their paradigm, a system so astonishingly corrupt that it cannot be repaired.

Most books are written for far less noble reasons.

A Brief Commentary on Chapter 21

I've known Mike Adams since 1999, years before the stellar success of his website, *NaturalNews.com*.

This is a brief commentary on an article he wrote in late 2008. It is brief and to the point, the point being that corruption and bribery are the bedrock of orthodox medicine and the regulators who are purported to oversee its activities. This is part of a November 2008 post that is still online.[1]

---

[1] See: www.altcancer.net/ashwin/ashw1108.htm

Chapter 21:

When the Atrocities of Government Agents Exceed Those of Hardened Criminals

"Unless we put medical freedom into the Constitution, the time will come when medicine will organize itself into an under-cover dictatorship . . . "

Dr. Benjamin Rush *-- (1745-1813)*
Founding Father, United States of America
Co-Signer, Declaration of Independence[1]

"Stop throwing the Constitution in my face ! . . .
It's just a goddamned piece of paper !"

George W. Bush
U.S. President[2]

" . . . a new Bill of Rights shall be drafted and approved by . . . [oops!] . . . (that's) classified."

"Rep. John Haller"
Spoof video from Onion News Network
The Homeland Terrorism Prepareness Bill (HR 8791)
July, 2008[3]

S ome years ago I received an email containing a news article from an old friend, Mike Adams, the editor of Natu-
ral-News.com and now, former ex-pat.[4]

---

[1] McWilliams, Peter; Ain't Nobody's Business If You Do: The Absurdity of Consensual Crimes in a Free Society, (Los Angeles, California: Prelude Press, 1993), 561-570.

[2] With so many people hearing this comment at a White House meeting, you can see the quotation everywhere. We'll just quote Capitol Hill Blue.

[3] This biting satire comes from The Onion News Network. There is, of course, no Rep. Haller, but I include this piece of fiction simply because it frighteningly follows Shakespeare's observation, namely that "many a truth has been spoken in jest." It accurately depicts the level of contempt for which elected officials in the U.S. -- with the exception of a handful of remaining good souls, like Ron Paul -- have for those who elect them to office. See also on YouTube

[4] Mike Adams moved to Vilcabamba, Ecuador --- and was not shy about why he loved the place. Like another friend of ours who formerly lived there, Dr. Brian O'Leary, Mike decided to settle in the "Valley of Longevity." . . .
As an aside, when Mike Adams broke this story on the newest scam coming out of the FDA,

Mike Adams has uncovered a conspiracy within the FDA to shakedown natural product companies in order to extract

I called a friend in the U.S. who is still a natural products manufacturer there to get his take. I asked him because he regularly speaks with an FDA consultant who was a careerist (now semi-retired) with the FDA and assists members of the natural health community with questions about FDA policy and procedure. My conversion with my friend went something like this -- and I repeat it here only because it is quite instructive:

"Well, did you talk to your FDA consultant?," I asked.

"Sure did."

"Yeah? So what's the take-away?"

"He says Mike Adams is full of shit."

"How's that work?"

"Well, the report just isn't credible. FDA agents just don't do this kind of thing. There are procedures to be followed. Before the FDA ever targets someone, they get a 'Warning Letter' first. Plus, agents who take bribes have a way of getting caught."

"And you believe this?"

"Well, I guess. Why shouldn't I?"

"You know good-and-well that it doesn't comport with my own experience."

"I think your case is different."

"Meaning what? That I'm special? That the FDA just singled me out, decided to send Warning Letters to everybody else but me? That John Armand is the only bribe-taking FDA agent out there on the take? "

"Well, no, more like your case is not the norm."

"Oh really? What about the late James Kimball? He didn't get a Warning Letter, and, in fact, spent hundreds of thousands to get NDA approval with the FDA. He thought he was on good standing with the FDA the day he got arrested. And because of what they did to him in U.S. Federal prison he is now dead. Or Michael David Forrest? What about him? Did he get a Warning Letter when agents working with the FDA kidnapped him in Paraguay and brought him back to the U.S. under completely bogus 'child support' charges, when the guy doesn't even HAVE children, only to hit him with ever bigger, bullshittier FDA charges when they got him back in the U.S., charges so fictitious that they were too embarrassed to present them to corrupt, Paraguayan law enforcement agents? I could spend an entire day giving you cases that I know like these, the tip of the iceberg."

"OK, so what's your point?"

"I believe you were just given the 'common narrative' as it relates to FDA mythology."

"And what does that mean?"

"You got the 'Santa Claus' version of what goes on with these people. You got the version that is believable only by those who are still gullible enough to believe that the individual matters; that law and justice can be relied upon; that the purpose of law is to remove the caprice of powerful individuals; that truth matters, and someone will want to know it; that it makes sense to stand up and do the right thing"

"You're making this up, Greg."

"Well, actually, I'm sitting here, reading it from C. Fred Alford's book, Whistleblowers: Broken Lives & Organizational Power, but my point is that you were given a version that *would* be truthful if the FDA *did* follow the law, if the FDA had *not* descended into just another racketeering operation whose agents just carry these funny little metal badges"

"So this is your way of saying I have something to worry about?"

"Not necessarily, but what I am saying is that even though I have not spoken with any of Mike Adams' contacts, I find his report to not only be highly credible, but very consistent with everything I observed in how the FDA operates. And there are few people who have seen the FDA 'up close and personal' as I have. It is the face of an evil so vile that I cringe when I think about it, if only because I know that most Americans have no idea as to the degree to which their government has sold them out."

bribes. His allegations are very specific as to the process, and not so specific as to his news sources, since they are still in the U.S. and will only receive greater retribution if they were identified as those leaking the horrific details.[5] What makes this development newsworthy isn't the criminal extortion activity, per se, after all, both legislative houses of the U.S. Government flagrantly ripped off the American taxpayer for $700 billion, paying off irresponsible elitist bankers for years of breathtakingly bad business decisions.[6] Within the FDA itself, it has been known for years that "Big Pharma" has been funding the FDA with both overt and covert "user fees" (i.e. bribes).[7]

Some years ago in my online newsletter, the Ashwin,[8] I was specific about details of my own shakedown at the hands of the FDA. Moreover, I provided further details in a rebuttal to an extortion letter I received from Alpha Omega Labs' competitor and professional FDA snitch, Toby McAdams.

Far more important, however, is what these developments mean to ordinary Americans. The U.S. FDA is tasked with the responsibility of protecting the public in the areas of food, drugs, and cosmetics. In recent years, a veritable avalanche of dangerous drugs have flooded the market, harming, even killing, millions of consumers.[9]

Alpha Omega Labs came into existence with Cansema® in the early 1990s, but Cansema® itself is the descendent of a safe, effective, and inexpensive herbal formula that was announced to the world as a "cure for cancer" in 1858 from Middlesex

---

[5] See: www.naturalnews.com/024567_FDA_health_the.html, read Mike's article of October 21, 2008.

[6] By sheer coincidence, an article by former U.S. Assistant Secretary of the Treasury, Paul Craig Roberts, on this subject came out on the same day (10/21) as Mike Adam's news release. It is aptly entitled, "A Government of Thieves: When Greed is Rewarded."

[7] Laura Penny, Your Call is Important to Us: The Truth about Bullshit,(New York: The Crown Publishing Group (now part of the Penguin Random Group), 2005), 114. Read entire section on Big Pharma and FDA corruption, p. 113-139.

[8] See: www.altcancer.net/ashwin/ashw0908.htm

[9] The market is now awash with books that document the deceptive practices of the FDA. A handful that I recommend include: Stop the FDA by John Morgenthaler; Overdosed America: The Broken Promise of American Medicine by Dr. John Abrahamson; The Drug Lords: America's Pharmaceutical Cartel by Tonda R. Bian; What Doctors Don't Tell You: The Truth About the Dangers of Modern Medicine, by Lynne McTaggart; among many others. See: www.meditopia.org/chap2.htm

Hospital in London (then one of the world's most prestigious, orthodox medical institutions). In researching *Meditopia*, I discovered that the formulary knowledge goes back much farther, at least as far back as Paracelsus in the 1500s, a fact that forms the backbone of the second chapter of *Meditopia*.[10]

Can the public trust an institution that has been part of a massive cover-up to suppress a very simple method of curing cancer, for no less than 500 years? In exchange for bribe money?[11]

In this light, the latest criminal racket by FDA agents is but a small reflection of a larger, much more ominous phenomenon.

It is this larger deception of the public that should concern not just Americans, but consumers the world over.

---

[10] *Meditopia* is available online for free. The link above opens Chapter 2: Escharotics, 500 Years of Suppression. It is Chapter 5 in the current volume.

[11] I am well aware that the U.S. Food & Drug Administration, and the monstrous political creations that preceded it, have only been around since 1906. Nonetheless, that means that the FDA has scandalously partaken of the "great cancer cover-up" for at least a century of the 150 years since the directors of Middlesex Hospital announced to the world in 1858 that a predecessor to Cansema® was a proven, clinically tested cure for cancer. In all of recorded history I regard the FDA to be the single greatest suppressor of medical facts and discovery of any organization, anywhere. In the course of protecting its "pride, profits, and prejudices" it has killed more people than those consumed by all the the wars of modern times combined.

Chapter 21

A Brief Commentary on Chapter 22

It's one thing to defraud the public and put up every pretense to hide the details of nefarious activities. It is another thing to boldly proclaim pride in one's work. Such is the case of a disgusting website called QuackWatch, which has web pages devoted to denigrating the work of myself and about a half dozen of my friends in the medical research community, while proudly and arrogantly proclaiming in a sworn deposition to essentially be a paid shill of Big Pharma with the purpose "to discredit and cause damage and harm to health care practitioners, businesses that make alternative health therapies or products available, and advocates of non-allopathic therapies and health freedom."

Such a unique, twisted form of corruption merits including in this section of my book, taken from an April 2009 post which is still online.[1]

---

[1] See: www.altcancer.net/ashwin/ashw0409.htm

Chapter 22:

Quackwatch & Swine Flu: Confronting the MIC's Unending Cavalcade of Pathological Lies

"Dearest Cathryn,
It is my honor to order from your website. I took some time
to read a bit about your history. My family name is Bastida. Ro-
drigo Bastida,[1] the discoverer of Panama and the founder of the
first European colony in the Americas (Santa Marta,[2] Colombia)
was ambushed by his own men because he would not sell the
natives of Panama and Colombia. So, I am very much aware
of what happens when money is involved, how far some greedy
individuals will go for their sacred profits.
"Peace be with you, . . ."

Linda Bastida[3]
Personal email to Cathryn Caton, N.D. -- April 17, 2009

"The sole purpose of the activities of Barrett & Baratz are
to discredit and cause damage and harm to health care prac-
titioners, businesses that make alternative health therapies or
products available, and advocates of non-allopathic therapies
and health freedom."

Stephen Barrett, M.D.[4]
Creator / Operator / Disinformation
Specialist behind Quackwatch[5]
Author of "Don't Use Cancer Salves"[6]
[Statement made in a sworn deposition]

---

[1] See: en.wikipedia.org/wiki/Rodrigo_de_Bastidas

[2] See: en.wikipedia.org/wiki/Santa_Marta

[3] Those who want to debate the history may note that the "accepted" first European colony in the Americas is La Isabela or that Bastida was reported by his men to have been assassinated because of a refusal to share gold (incredibly unlikely, in my opinion). I make a major point in Chapter 4 of *Meditopia* of noting how and why conventional history is twisted to meet the objectives of whomever is in charge. (Or, as Henry Kissinger has noted, "History is the memory of States.") But, really, all of this misses the point of the letter, doesn't it?

[4] See Failed MD Stephen Barrett on the QuackPotWatch website. (www.quackpotwatch.org).

[5] See: www.quackwatch.org

[6] See: www.quackwatch.org/01QuackeryRelatedTopics/Cancer/eschar.html

"Greg . . .

"Public Relations" (PR) is a misnomer for the [black] art/ science of (1) spinning a story in such a way as to benefit (or trash) a given product, service, person, idea, political candidate, etc., and (2) "discretely" arranging for that suitably spun story to be published as 'objective news.' For the last 15-20 years, big business and big government have spent far more $$ on PR than on advertising as such. In fact, it is now estimated that 80%+ of all 'news' is the direct and/or indirect product of PR.

*"Just finished a quick read, 'The Whole Truth, '[7] a potboiler by David Baldacci. Central theme is 'perception management,' or PM for short--PR taken to the next level of **mind fuck**. As a character in the book says, 'Why waste time discovering the truth when you can so easily create it? PM's are not spin doctors because they don't spin facts; they create 'facts,' then sell them to the world as truth.'*

*"The DOD -- [U.S. Department of Defense][8] -- discusses PM in one of its in-house manuals: ' . . . **major untruths can be established so quickly and overwhelmingly across the world that no digging by any one after the fact can make a dent in public consciousness that they are actually not true at all . . . '** Example: journalists 'embedded' in the armed forces invading Iraq was highly touted as a way of 'getting the American public the real unvarnished story;' in fact, it was how the DOD took total control over the creation and 'legitimization' of its own stories created out of thin air.*

"Clearly, much of the 20% of the news that's not the product of PR is the product of PM. So much for the 'informed electorate' envisioned by Thomas Jefferson.

"Sound like anything that goes on with the FDA, Big Pharma, AMA, DOJ, FBI, etc., etc., ad nauseum?

Name Withheld
Private Letter to Greg Caton[9]
April 13, 2009

---

[7] See: www.amazon.com/gp/product/0446539686

[8] See: en.wikipedia.org/wiki/United_States_Department_of_Defense

[9] It is standard policy on our site not to reproduce the identity of any correspondent without their express permission.

S ome time ago I received a letter from a customer, asking why I had not yet written "a line by line refutation for the claims on Quackwatch's page about **escharotics**?"

There are really several reasons.

First of all, so many articles have been written before me, discrediting Mr. Quackwatch himself, **Dr. Stephen Barrett**, that I felt that beating the same pavement would be overkill. (Read Tim Bolen's excellent summation of Barrett's career.[10] In fact, Bolen has done such a good job of documenting the avalanche of lies generated by orthodox medicine as it pertains to alternative practices that you can get lost in hundreds of hours of reading on his website, QuackPotWatch,[11] with its numerous posts and links).

Secondly, I have already written a sidebar article on the quackery behind **Quackwatch** in Chapter 3 of *Meditopia*.[12] And lastly, there are so many pro-orthodox individuals, counterfeiters of our products, and paid FDA snitches, who have gleefully been singing, dancing, and feasting over "my corpse" during the years since the FDA's destruction of our lab in the States,[13] that I would have to morph into an obsessive polemicist to go after them all.

There are more important things in this world.

Nonetheless, since there are people out there who see the Quackwatch article on escharotics, which includes a diatribe on

[10] See: www.quackpotwatch.org/quackpots/quackpots/barrett.htm

[11] See: www.quackpotwatch.org

[12] See: www.meditopia.org/chap3-1.htm#quackwatch

[13] See: www.altcancer.net/ashwin/ashw0908.htm

Cansema® and yours truly, and wonder if any of it is true, I can see our customer's point.

A point-by-point decimation of Barrett's article, "Don't Use Cancer Salves," is linked below, appropriately entitled, "A Systematic Dismantling of Orthodox Medicine's Quack Attack on Escharotics."[14] If you won't take the time to read any of *Meditopia*, which clearly proves that escharotics have been used privately and successfully for hundreds of years, curing untold thousands of cancer patients, and have been constantly renounced by medical practitioners of each succeeding age for financial reasons, then at least read this piece.

This, of course, brings us to a much larger event in world news, the latest exercise in PM (Perception Management, see the third quote at the beginning of this chapter) to come out of the swine within the medical-industrial complex.

Swine flu.

Three days ago, I got a letter from a friend, himself a former resident of Mexico City, about the ever-dreaded swine flu, which read, in part:

> "Does anything about the super-hyped 'swine flu' strike anyone else as vaguely (or not so vaguely) fishy?
>
> "To wit: (1) 49 deaths so far in Mexico City from this 'horrific scourge???' Hell, there are almost that many homicides every 24 hrs in that benighted place, not to mention 4-5 times that many daily deaths from garden-variety flu/ague/bronchitis/asthma/pneumonia/emphysema/etc . . . (2) All of 20-40 instances of it so far in the entire United States??? Hell, on any given day there have to be that many people with the flu just in our small town [of 10,000]. (3) 'Anti-viral medications being rushed to the hinterlands???' Fact is, no such medications exist, or are at best only very marginally effective, and at that, with only a very small % of people. (4) 'A terrible public health threat???' Fact is, each year, approximately 350-500 million new cases of ma-

---

[14] See: www.altcancer.net/docs/quack/eschar.htm

laria kill between one and three million people, the majority of whom are young children--where the hell are the headlines and hyperventilating by talking heads about that?"

So . . . who's behind all the hype? What's the motive? Where does the money lead us?"

My private response, slightly rephrased for inclusion in this publication, ran along these lines:

During my imprisonment, it took me two or three readings of Machiavelli's, The Prince, before I finally realized that one of the principle functions of modern governance was jacking "the governed" around by the nose, scaring the shit out of them, and, in general, creating theatrical scenarios in the attempt to get people to believe that government, as it is known and practiced in the first world, was necessary. (It isn't, look at the Internet).

One of the points of Tainter's work (The Collapse of Complex Societies)[15] is that a government's highest necessity is the reinforcement of its own perceived justification for existence. As I point out in *Meditopia*:

'Hierarchy and complexity,' as Joseph Tainter has noted, 'are rare in human history, and where present require constant reinforcement. No societal leader is ever far from the need to validate position and policy, and no hierarchical society can be organized without explicit provision for this need.'

The Internet has opened people's eyes. The American people don't need their government. Their government needs them. Out of the sheer obviousness of this thermodynamic fact, comes bold observations, like that of the lead character in *V for Vendetta*, "People shouldn't fear their government, the government should fear its people."

---

[15] Joseph A. Tainter, The Collapse of Complex Societies, (Cambridge University Press, 1988), 59.

And because the host is getting tired of feeding this extremely ferocious parasite, the parasite is responding with something that will require people to ask for help. Swine flu is the parasite's way of trying to get the host to say, "You need us. You really, really need us."

My concern is that people are going to figure out how ludicrous this all is, just like you have, so the parasite will respond with something far worse, like maybe the World Trade Center Towers -- Act II, and then people will feel that they have no choice.

That's my greatest concern.

Ｎone of my political observations, or those of friends, should be interpreted as a denial of a real health threat. In fact, I personally side with Dr. Leonard Horowitz's rendition of events, which, reduced to its simplest terms goes something like this: (1) the H1N1-H5N1 flu outbreak has been engineered by an easy-to-identify pharmaceutical clique and their Anglo-American government toadies (more "mass killing of people for profit"), (2) the designer vaccines corresponding to the outbreak, rushed through the FDA approval process just in time for the crisis, which has already resulted in a huge run-up in stock price for those corporations involved, will be a major windfall for Big Pharma, and (3) the mechanics behind the outbreak mimic those of the conspiracy behind the 9/11 false flag attacks, a well-engineered, trillion dollar windfall for the "defense establishment." More simply restated, the swine flu outbreak is an attempt to recreate within the pharmaceutical industry, using the "Problem / Reaction / Solution" model made popular by David Icke, the same kind of profit vortex that was created by the military-industrial complex in its well-crafted execution of the 9/11 false flag attacks and their hysterical aftermath.

With reference to your own personal health, should you feel concerned? Mildly. (Read Julian Whitaker's medical advice[16] concerning the current outbreak.)

So there you have it.

[16] See: www.altcancer.net/docs/whitaker_swine_flu.htm

Swine flu.

It's good for Bigger Government, and its great for Bigger Pharma.

And as for the uninitiated plebs who die from these designer viruses? Oh, quit your sobbing, they'd end up dying from something else down the road anyway. And besides, can you think of a better way to introduce all these toxic, "ultra high profit margin" vaccines, so we can all do our part to help control world population? You lazy taxpayers need to stop your bitching, chatting on the Internet with all these deadbeat conspiracy theorists, especially that cancer fraud, Greg Caton, and get back to work!

Quack, quack, quack, quack, quack, quack, quack.

A Brief Commentary on Chapter 23

This brief essay on "mediated experience" plays off insights made by Jerry Mander in his groundbreaking book, <u>Four Arguments for the Elimination of Television</u>.[1] Interestingly, this was posted a little more than a month before my illegal kidnapping by U.S. government agents, which is the subject of Chapter 3, Section 3 of the online version of *Meditopia*.[2]

The original post is still online.[3]

---

[1] Jerry Mander, <u>Four Arguments for the Elimination of Television</u>. (New York: Quill Publishing, 1978). See also Bibliography.

[2] See: www.meditopia.org/chap3-3.htm

[3] See: www.altcancer.net/ashwin/ashw1009.htm

Chapter 23:

Mediated Experience & The End
of the Pharmaceutical Age

*"I began getting on to how degenerate things had really
become in 1955 when I worked for the movie industry on Park
Avenue in New York City. I met a man who began to show me
the power of propaganda, (as in "Federal" Reserve System).
Whoever penned the old saw about ... "the pen is mightier than
the sword . . ." really knew what he was talking about . . . I am
well aware of the stranglehold of the FDA as well as the AMA
(American Murderers Association). I appreciate very much the
sacrifices that you have made. If I wasn't so advanced in age
(83) I would leave the U.S. just as you have done. **The general
population here is so asleep you can hear them snoring out
beyond Jupiter.** Thanks ... again for what you are doing."*

[AO Customer -- name withheld][1]
Private Email to AO
October 27, 2009

"Most Americans spend their lives within environments
created by human beings. This is less the case if you live in Mon-
tana than if you live in Manhattan, but it is true to some extent
all over the country. Natural environments have largely given
way to human-created environments.

"What we see, hear, touch, taste, smell, feel and understand about the world has been processed for us. Our experiences of the world can no longer be called direct, or primary. *They
are secondary, mediated experiences.*

"When we are walking in the forest, we can see and feel
what the planet produces directly. Forests grow on their own
without human intervention. When we see a forest, or experience
it in other ways, we can count on the experience being directly
between us and the planet. It is not mediated, interpreted or
altered.

"On the other hand, when we live in cities, no experience
is directly between us and the planet. Virtually all experience is
mediated in some way. Concrete covers whatever would grow

---

[1] We have not yet obtained permission from the author of this email to use any other particulars.

from the ground. Buildings block the natural vistas. The water we drink comes from a faucet, not a stream or the sky. All foliage has been confined by human considerations and redesigned according to human tastes. There are no wild animals, there are no rocky terrains, there is no cycle of bloom and decline. There is not even night and day. No food grows anywhere.

"Most of us give little importance to this change in human experience of the world, if we notice it at all. We are so surrounded by a reconstructed world that it is difficult to grasp how astonishingly different it is from the world of only one hundred years ago, and that it bears virtually no resemblance to the world in which human beings lived for four million years before that. That this might affect the way we think, including our understanding of how our lives are connected to any nonhuman system, is rarely considered.

"In fact, most of us assume that human understanding is now more thorough than before, that we know more than we ever did. This is because we have (such) faith in our rational, intellectual processes and the institutions we have created that we fail to observe their limits."

Jerry Mander[2]

Years ago I was exposed to Jerry Mander's <u>Four Arguments for the Elimination of Television</u>[3]-- a penetrating set of polemics that outlines, from several vantage points, the dangers of television-watching and how the very medium itself is destructive and non-reformable.

Many unfamiliar with the work will laugh at the very notion, and I might well laugh, as well, were it not for the fact that in the 30+ years since

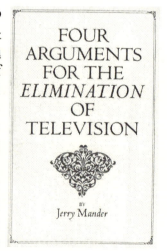

FOUR
ARGUMENTS
FOR THE
ELIMINATION
OF
TELEVISION

BY
Jerry Mander

---

[2] Jerry Mander, <u>Four Arguments for the Elimination of Television</u>, (New York: Quill Publishing, 1978).

[3] This article focuses on the first of the four arguments, "The Mediation Experience." The other three are: The Colonization of Experience, Effects of Television on the Human Being, and The Inherent Biases of Television.

Mander published his book, I have been able to observe the predictable outcome of avoiding the subject, which has become only more pronounced and horrifying.

I want to focus on just one of Mander's arguments, the first, in fact, as it would apply to medicine.[4]

As I detail extensively in *Meditopia*,[5] one of the unspoken, rarely considered assumptions of modern medicine is that progress is made through the march of technology. The idea that technology is the cure for our problems is ubiquitous in modern life. If my cellphone breaks, I take it to a phone technician. If my car breaks down, a mechanic. For my Mac, a computer tech. For my refrigerator, a "frig" guy. If I lose Internet service, I summon the cable guy. If I lose power, my provider sends an electrician.

And what do I do if I get sick?

Well, that's easy. I just go to a medical technician, a medical doctor or similar practitioner, depending on my problem, someone who has a technical solution, a scientific answer, someone in touch with the latest discoveries in that field. Makes sense, doesn't it?

Sure, it makes sense, but that's only because we live in a mediated environment that shields us from the obvious. We may live in world surrounding by technical man-made artifacts, but our bodies are not born of technology. They're born of nature. Only by living in a world that is so completely out of touch with nature could we be blinded to this self-evident fact.

The very foundation of modern pharmacology is based on a single principle that is as far removed from nature as one can imagine. It takes as gospel that the healing arts can only find perfection through the search for discrete, chemical, molecular entities, the vast majority of which cannot be found to exist within Nature herself. Moreover, these chemical entities must be unique and patentable, and they can only be discovered and sold by companies with sufficient capital (i.e., in the hundreds of mil-

[4] Ibid., 53-114.
[5] See: www.meditopia.org

lions of dollars per entity) to survive a vast bureaucratic maze, chock full of of regulatory bribe-takers, all working to prove that the chemical entity in question has at least **some** tangential effect on one or more disease conditions within the human body.

Only when all of these hurdles are negotiated can the substance, now called a medicine or a drug, receive the imprimatur of official medical science.

More perverse still, modern pharmacology gives little thought to the long-term, ill-effects of the drugs to which it gives its approval. At Alpha Omega Labs we deal with cancer patients the world over, and in the vast majority of cases the damage created by one or more therapies to which the patient has been subjected is greater than the original disease for which the patient sought help to begin with. This brings to mind the observation of the late Neil Postman, namely, that inventors and promoters of technology "are always given to telling the Public the wonderful things their invention will **DO** -- always neglecting to disclose what their invention will **UNDO**."[6]

T he first underlying principle behind the I Ching, the oldest and most revered work of ancient Chinese philosophy, is that "when things reach their extreme, they revert to their opposite." An American observer might use the pendulum to make the same observation.

The scientific community, specifically as it manifests itself in the drug industry, is insanely out of control, reaching levels of absurdity unimaginable in another time and another age. Mander himself used several examples in his book, even in the 1970s, such as a report from the *New England Journal of Medicine* that a team of doctors discovered that infant jaundice could be "cured by ordinary sunlight. This discovery led to a spurt of articles on the possibility that natural light might be healthy for humans. What a revelation!"[7]

---

[6] Neil Postman, Technopoly (1993). (New York: Vintage Books, 1993). The quote is paraphrased from the opening of the first chapter, discussed at greater length in Chapter 4, Section 3 of *Meditopia*. All of this material is contained within Chapter 6 of the current volume.
[7] Mander, 73

Or other "scientific findings" which Mander notes, which the New York Times reported in a "six-month period in 1973":

- A major research institute spending more than $50,000 to discover that the best bait for mice is cheese.
- Another study which found that mother's milk was better balanced nutritionally for infants than commercial formulas. (That study also proved that mother's milk was better for human infants than cow's milk or goat's milk.)
- A third study found that a walk is considerably healthier for the human respiratory and circulatory systems, in fact for overall health and vitality, than a ride in a car. Bicycling was also found to be beneficial!
- A fourth revealed that juice of fresh oranges has more nutritional value than either canned or frozen orange juice.
- A fifth discovered that infants who are touched a lot frequently grow into adults with greater self-confidence and have a more integrated relationship with the world than those who are not touched.[8]

What is amazing, as Mander notes, is that anyone should have found it necessary to conduct these studies in the first place. It confirms that "human beings no longer trust personal observation, even of the self-evident, until it is confirmed by scientific or technological institutions; human beings have lost insight into natural processes, how the world works, because natural processes are now exceedingly difficult to observe."

And it is in **this** environment that modern medicine has been allowed to evolve into pure, unadultered financial exploitation, for as Mander again notes, "Living within (these) artificial, reconstructed, arbitrary environments that are strictly the products of human conception, we have no way to be sure that we know what is true and what is not. We have lost context and

---

[8] Mander,. 53,54

perspective. What we know is what other humans tell us.[9]

And this is where the **I Ching** comes in.

All of my adult life I have been studying the many ways in which Western Civilization is "unsustainable." It is unsustainable because it has lost its natural mooring. It cannot stay alienated from Nature forever, just as the previous 26 major Earth civilizations that lived and breathed and died over the last 6,000 years. I cover this extensively in Chapter 5 of *Meditopia*.[10]

The pharmaceutical paradigm, which brought upon us this "Great Age of Iatrogenesis," will pass away, just as will the other components of our civilization to which it is tethered. And it is in that passing that members of humanity will then again be free to have a direct, primary experience of their world.

[9] Mander, 54

[10] See: www.meditopia.org/chap5.htm, This is Chapter 7 of the current volume.

Chapter 23

A Brief Commentary on Chapter 24

I wrote this chapter in September 2014,[1] three years after I returned to Ecuador following the 21 month ordeal that resulted from my illegal kidnapping in December 2009.[2]

What is reported here is surprisingly common: the mainstream news media, acting as a propaganda mouthpiece for Big Pharma interests, will take a spectacularly successful case within the Naturopathic community and twist it to make the success look like a failure. I saw the same thing happen in May 2017, when Dr. Oz did a hit piece of me in a remarkably audacious act of ambush tele-fake-journalism.[3]

There was no hearsay here: this involved one of our customers who removed a very difficult cancer using our Cansema in Australia, a case that had oversight from one of our in-house doctors.

In this instance I examine yet another, different sort of corruption that befouls the precincts of orthodox medicine.

---

[1] See: www.altcancer.net/ashwin/ashw0914.htm

[2] See: www.meditopia.org/chap3-3.htm

[3] See: www.altcancer.net/dr_oz_rebuttal.htm

Chapter 24:

Orthodoxy's Pathetic War Against Escharotics

From 'Missing Noses' to 'Holey Heads' The Scare Tactics of Modern Medicine's Apologists Shows No Bounds . . . or Capacity to Feel Embarrassment When Exposed

"The CIA owns everyone of any significance in the major media . . . We'll know our disinformation program is complete when everything the American public believes is false."

William Colby *(1981)[1]*
Former CIA Director

F irst of all, before I get started, I wanted to apologize for not "staying current." Some years ago a customer wrote to ask if we were still alive, since I hadn't updated my Ashwin[2] online blog in some time. In response I said: "Well, yes, we are alive and well, thank you for asking, and I apologize for not putting out more material. In defense, I should say that I haven't felt compelled to write a lot of articles in my Ashwin blog, unless something truly mind-blowing and uncovered elsewhere in the alternative media crosses my desk. Give me something original, head-spinning, which others cannot or will not discuss, and I'll pick up a pen."

---

[1] Please see: www.ldsfreedomforum.com/viewtopic.php?f=3&t=26909; lawrencerspencer. com/tag/william-colby/; www.conservativedailynews.com/2013/01/cia-admits-to-using-the-news-to-manipulate-the-usa-since-at-least-1975/; rense.com/general96/controll.html

[2] Ashwin: see Glossary.

That's what happened in this case.

Let me give a little background first.

Some years ago I got a series of emails from friends in Australia saying that a big media event had been set into motion there stating a 55-year old man had a huge hole in his head, resulting from the use of "Black Salve." I had no way of knowing whose salve they were  talking about, but this mainstream media event was obviously designed to go viral, and it did. The point of the event was to alert the public that this skin cancer treatment was "bogus," as stated in an article in the *Medical Journal of Australia*; articles carried warnings as to the graphic nature of the "images," and stated that the man in question narrowly escaped living the rest of his life with a hole in his head.

The sheer number of inaccurate statements made in both the mainstream media reports and in the Australian journal article did not surprise me. My online book, *Meditopia*,[3] is replete with one ridiculous "article of faith" produced by conventional medicine after another. You can't get very far in the study of medical orthodoxy before asking yourself, "Just how much more fraudulent can it get?" And the answer is, "It has no end." For as the William Colby quote at the beginning of this article illustrates, it is the very nature of "authority" to exercise its power to convince people of things that defy their own experience. You should expect nothing less, because that, in itself, is the true measure of power.

I learned this in 2003 during my ordeal with the FDA. The story of Sue Gilliatt[4] is a case-in-point. To this very day, you will hear physicians, nurses, and hospital personnel of every stripe talk about how using "black salve" causes people to lose body parts. "Look at the case of that poor woman, Sue Gilliatt." Apparently, it doesn't matter that in a July 2004 sworn deposition, Sue Gilliatt admitted under oath that she planned to sue us before she ever received any product, that she was cancer free after the

[3] See: www.meditopia.org

[4] See: www.meditopia.org/chap3-2.htm#trud

400

use of our salve, and, most astonishing of all, it was not our Cansema that caused her to lose her nose. In fact, she removed her own nose with embroidery scissors, a fact that caused one of our associates to remark in the aftermath, "I guess it really helps your product liability case if you're completely psychotic." (As a result of working with Federal prosecutors, Gillatt and her attorneys were able to nimbly extract $800,000 from my product liability policy in the States.) None of these facts,

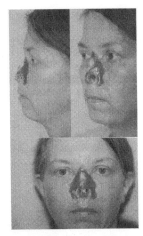

none of the astonishing revelations of this sworn deposition, made any difference to my U.S. Federal sentencing judge, Tucker Melançon, who threw me in prison for 33 months as a direct result of the Gilliatt matter. In fact, I later learned that it hurt my case that I pointed out how fraudulent the Gilliatt matter was, for, as the French philosopher, Voltaire, famously observed, "It is dangerous to be right when the government is wrong."

Fast forward to when, without any solicitation, we received a surprise email addressed to my wife, Cathryn, from the "55-year-old" man who was the subject of the "The Great Australian Black Salve Scare of 2014." (Note: he has asked for anonymity in anything we reproduce from this incident.) His letters below, like those in our Cansema Testimonial Section,[5] are unedited, except where indicated.

Hi Cathryn.

[snip: first five paragraphs]

. . . *some of my moles have been icebergs (one which got the titanic) here is the link from last year. Originally only a couple of mm across and it was 30mm across in the end.* ***I ended up at the doctors because of the pain and foolishly let the doctor***

---

[5] See: www.altcancer.net/cansema.htm#testimonials

***take a pic. Two journal articles later and it went viral in main-
stream media. It has completely healed with minor scarring.*** *[
Bold / underlined text added].*

    *www.australiandoctor.com.au/news/latest-news/black-
salve-leaves-man-with-hole-in-head*

[snip]

Thank you for your time

[Name Withheld]

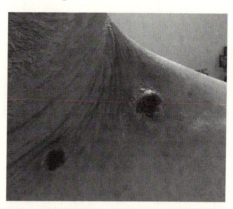

    The next day -- Sept. 2nd -- we received a follow-up email
providing proof-positive that this entire scare campaign was a
ruse. Please read the letter below carefully and then pay particular close attention to the last two images, which were never
reproduced in any follow-up story by the mainstream media, nor
will they ever be.

Hi Cathryn

    *I actually put some intrasite gel (soothing/hydrating gel a
little like vaseline) on the eschars last night, before receiving
your email. One eschar is now very active in wanting to pop this
morning. The others are showing positive signs as well.*
    *Please find the pics of the **"man with the hole in the head".**
As can be seen from the final pic, there is really only some skin*

discolouration, which is nothing in the big picture. *[Bold / underlined text added.]*

To explain why there is a hole in the eschar, the first application with bloodroot paste had the eschar pop within a couple of weeks, but it was not healing properly. A fresh application with amazon cream reveal the true extent of the mole. It took several weeks to finally come off, and the wound healed quickly.

I have taken well over a dozen moles off with bloodroot paste/[6] amazon cream[7] over the years. It is my luck that of late I have been finding some larger ones hiding under the skin.

Feel free to use these images as they are from my phone and I am the copyright owner. I wish to remain anonymous of course.

Many thanks & kind regards

[Name Withheld]

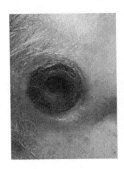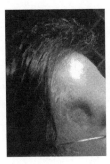

People who have read my previous articles on the official position of conventional medicine on a host of topics might get the impression that I regard orthodox clinicians as inveterate liars and fraudsters. For example, I've written a compelling paper as to WHY **modern medicine cannot and will not ever come up with a legitimate cure for cancer**[8] and I take the inarguable position that it was never possible for modern medicine **to heal**

---

[6] The customer is referring to: www.altcancer.net/bpaste.htm

[7] Amazon Cream is one of a variety of brands we use for our primarily formula, and its variations, which were originally branded as Cansema®. See: www.altcaner.net/cansema.htm

[8] See: www.altcancer.net/lysis5.htm, An abridged version of this piece is contained in Chapter 16 of the current volume.

more people that it has maimed, poisoned and killed.[9]

These claims are hardly original.

Ivan Illich created outrage in 1975 when he suggested that since *Homo sapiens* had no natural predators, the medical-industrial complex (MIC) has stepped in as a force of nature to fill the void.[10] Its job is to kill us and take our money with no less precision than meat-eating carnivores in the jungle hunt their prey, kill them, and eat their bodies.

I can think of no better, irrefutable example of orthodox medicine's disconnect from reality and unremitting perniciousness, even from modern medicine's most psychopathic apologists, than that of my own dealings with the U.S. FDA, which authoritatively sits at the very apex of the MIC.

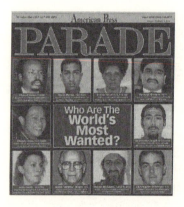

In 2008, the FDA had me placed as their "#1 Criminal" in an article they ran in *Parade Magazine*, entitled "Who Are the World's Most Wanted?" Realizing that when it comes to lying through your teeth, the sky's the limit if you're backed by the world's most powerful military and there are no punitive consequences, no matter what legal, ethical, or moral boundaries you cross, the FDA decided to elevate my case to a Twilight Zone episode. My picture, photoshopped to make me look bad, was placed in papers all over the U.S. with Osama bin Laden. I

[9] See: www.altcancer.net/ashwin/ashw0809.htm

[10] Ivan Illich, Limits to Medicine: Medical Nemesis, the Expropriation of Health (New York: Marion Boyars Publishers,
Ltd., 2002), 261.

was put on the Interpol Red List with a cascade of false claims, an event which the mainstream news media refused to touch, but which was subsequently covered by independent, Internet journalists, Mike Adams and Alex Jones.[11] Eventually I was kidnapped (Dec. 2, 2009) by the U.S. State Department in a scandalous event that violated so many laws that after I returned to Ecuador in 2011, a ministry of the Ecuadorean government held a special session that ruled that everything that had occurred to me was "without legal foundation." In other words, U.S. operatives had violated so many domestic and international laws in the course of my kidnapping, that my "deportation" would be expunged from government records in Ecuador. (Far more detail on this incident, along with supporting documentation, is provided in Chapter 3, Section 3[12] of *Meditopia*).

The same people who behave this way are the same people who will tell you that radiation or chemotherapy, with 2-3% survival rates,[13] are appropriate therapeutic approaches to treating cancer. And the same people who dispense your pharmaceuticals are the same people who measure their success, as Colby so elegantly puts it, by leading you to a point where "everything you believe is false."

Think about that the next time you read or hear of an article or news report about how someone's life was destroyed by using a natural product that has worked successfully (with little to no side effect) on ordinary people for centuries, if not millennia.

Get past the weather, sports, birth, marriage, and obituary sections of the daily newspaper and you quickly realize that the news doesn't exist to inform you.

It exists to test your stupidity and measure your gullibility.

---

[11] See: youtu.be/8q_mqlyNtGI

[12] See: www.meditopia.org/chap3-3.htm

[13] See also: www.burtongoldberg.com/home/burtongoldberg/contribution-of-chemotherapy-to-five-year-survival-rate-morgan.pdf; www.collective-evolution.com/2013/04/11/study-shows-chemotherapy-does-not-work-97-of-the-time/; www.whale.to/cancer/benjamin2.html#What_is_the_scientific_evidence_for_its_efficacy__; www.mercola.com/article/cancer/cancer_options.htm. See also: Ralph W. Moss, Questioning Chemotherapy: A Critique of the Use of Toxic Drugs (Brooklyn, New York: Equinox Press,1995).

A Brief Commentary on Chapter 25

Yes, "only idiots take herbal products." It must be true. The U.S. government wouldn't lie.

I first posted this in April 2015, shocked that I had just caught wind of something even more audacious than I had previously reported.

The original post is still online.[1]

---

[1] See: www.altcancer.net/ashwin/ashw0415.htm

Chapter 25:

Official U.S. Position:
"Only Idiots Take Herbal Products"

What the current herbal supplement scare in the U.S. looks like once you strip off the obnoxiously fictitious government / Medical Industrial Complex propaganda

Several years ago, I began to get emails from some of our customers asking for my take on the herbal supplement scare that was going on in New York. If you don't know what I'm talking about, allow me to give you some relevant background.

In late 2013, the mainsteam media began vigorously circulating a story that Canadian researchers tested "44 bottles of popular supplements sold by 12 companies"[1] and, using a form of genetic fingerprinting called "DNA barcoding," found that a large percentage were "bogus." Not only did many contain useless fillers, but some contained NONE of the herb that was purported to be in the bottle, or even WORSE, the bottle(s) contained herbal material that imparted medicinal effects quite contrary to those one would expect from the herb on the label. Lest anyone reading this should think that I would condone such obvious fraud, let me say before we begin in earnest that such corporate behavior is deplorable and should be punished.

Nonetheless, the story itself soon degraded into a twisted kind of resigned humor. As one associate told me in jest while making reference to this story, "Only major pharmaceutical companies with the financial clout to pay off all of our state and

---

[1] See: www.nytimes.com/2013/11/05/science/herbal-supplements-are-often-not-what-they-seem.html?_r=1

federal politicians should be allowed to rip off the public like that." Or as the late, political comedian, George Carlin[2] might have said, "They can't cheat the public like that! That's OUR f**kin' job!"[3] And, of course, the story did become fodder for Internet humorists, as well.[4]

Quite predictably, this discovery led to a coordinated, government manhunt, er, herb hunt, to go after the offending parties. Out of that effort came an announcement almost 14 months later by New York Attorney General, Eric Schneiderman, to four of the largest retail vendors of herbal products in the U.S., namely, GNC, Wal-Mart, Walgreens, and Target[5] telling them to drop entirely "herbs such as echinacea, ginseng, and St. John's wort." This AG's investigation found "supplements, including echinacea, ginseng, St. John's wort, garlic, ginkgo biloba and saw palmetto, were contaminated with substances including rice, beans, pine, citrus, asparagus, primrose, wheat, houseplant and wild carrot.[6] In many cases, unlisted contaminants were the only plant material found in the product samples."

Everybody covered this story: Yahoo,[7] ABC,[8] CBS,[9] New York Post,[10] Bloomberg,[11] Forbes, plus consumer protection organizations, like Food Safety News[12] and Consumerist,[13] to even

---

[2] See: youtu.be/acLW1vFO-2Q

[3] See: youtu.be/uwlVAkXcXOI

[4] See: youtu.be/pHJgmgflqRk

[5] See: www.bloomberg.com/news/articles/2015-02-03/gnc-wal-mart-found-by-new-york-to-sell-fake-herbal-supplements

[6] See: www.cbsnews.com/news/herbal-supplements-targeted-by-new-york-attorney-general/

[7] See: www.yahoo.com/lifestyle/investigation-of-supplements-at-target-walmart-109992906177.html

[8] See: abcnews.go.com/Health/bogus-herbal-supplements-fail-ingredient-test-investigation/story?id=28684472

[9] See: www.cbsnews.com/news/herbal-supplements-targeted-by-new-york-attorney-general/

[10] See: nypost.com/2015/02/04/most-herbal-supplements-arent-what-you-think-they-are/

[11] See: www.bloomberg.com/news/articles/2015-02-03/gnc-wal-mart-found-by-new-york-to-sell-fake-herbal-supplements

[12] See: www.foodsafetynews.com/2015/02/major-retailers-ordered-to-stop-selling-adulterated-and-mislabeled-supplements/#.WIUgbktG3ol

[13] See: consumerist.com/2015/02/03/ny-asks-stores-to-halt-herbal-supplements-after-tests-show-advertised-herbs-not-present/

prominent players in the alternative media, such as NewsMax.[14] To find a news story in New York that got more publicity than this, you just might have to go back to another well-orchestrated piece of government theater: 9/11.

Did the NY Attorney General seriously fine these offending merchants proportionate to the crime and then allow them to go about their business? No, no, no, of course not. That would defeat the purpose of why the exercise was engineered in the first place. Instead, New York's AG coordinated with 13 other U.S. state attorneys general to ask Congress to investigate the herbal supplements industry and consider giving the Food and Drug Administration "broadened ènforcement powers over the industry."[15] After all, who does a better job of protecting the American public against the nefarious activities of the medical-industrial complex than the FDA, right?

I've seen a lot in my 35 years in the alternative health care business. And, yes, somehow I have known that certain people didn't take this calling as seriously as I did, other herbalists included. I remember a meeting I had in Los Angeles in 1988 with one of the biggest players in the health food industry. Two years previously, I had founded a company called Lumen Foods, which made vegetarian jerky (later, the company was to be known as Soybean.com, which we sold in 2007). Among other things, we did vertical "form-fill-and-seal" work for other, larger companies on a subcontract basis. In any event, at this meeting, my counterpart was bragging that his multi-colored corn chips, which were a huge hit in health food stores throughout the country, would make "corn chip snacking" a healthy thing.

"Why do you say that?" I asked.

"Because they're lower in fat," came the knee-jerk response.

"How is that possible?" I responded without thinking,

---

[14] See: www.newsmax.com/TheWire/fake-herbal-supplements-walmart/2015/02/03/id/622342/
[15] See: www.nutraingredients-usa.com/Article/2015/04/02/Schneiderman-other-AGs-ask-Congress-to-investigate-herbal-supplements-industry

"Your product is fried, not baked. I can tell by the feel in my mouth and the organoleptics that your product is made just like Frito-Lay's corn chips. I don't have to test it. I can taste it." Realizing I was being too candid, I gave a big smile to try and spin my comments in a jovial, light-hearted way. But it was too late. My comments were interpreted as anything but light-hearted.

"You really don't understand this industry, do you?" was the response.

"I'm afraid I don't know what you mean," I replied, to which my counterpart made a very sad statement that I've never forgotten.

"People don't want to be saved of their sins. They want to be saved in their sins."

Extrapolated to the medicinal herbal business, that kind of thinking would translate into something like, "People don't need herbs that work. What people need are herbs that they THINK will work." That kind of exploitative thinking is why our planet is in the sorry condition it's in today; but the way that governments seize upon it and use it to their own manipulative advantage is the worst cut of all, for all of humanity. The following story out of New York is a good case in point. It leads to videos like the one below (put out by yet another "pharma shill") that despite thousands of years of successful ethnobotanical use, medicinal herbs have no value at all.[16]

Back in 2004, I wrote an article for inclusion in the first draft of *Meditopia*, entitled, "Gresham's Law: Its Treacherous Application."[17] In that piece, I explain how the FDA, the very same diabolical organization that former New York Attorney General, Eric Schneiderman, would have regulate all herbal supplements, secretly promoted adulterated, misbranded versions of our flagship product, Cansema®[18]

As a result of this experience, I came to understand that the FDA has no problems with deceptive consumer practices, as

[16] See: youtu.be/TrmvefreJwM
[17] See: www.meditopia.org/old/chap7_2004.htm, or see Chapter 11 in the current volume.
[18] See: www.altcancer.net/cansema.htm

long as it serves its political objectives. As I made clear in my online Ashwin blog,[19] neither truth nor the law itself have any meaning in the eyes of psychopathic rulers who feel they are beyond any legal constraints that are imposed on the rest of society with such gravity and fervor, to say nothing of the ethical and moral boundaries that are part and parcel of Natural Law.

It is for this reason that free markets (which do not currently exist in strictly regulated markets like the U.S.) are the only reliable way of weeding out "bad product" in the marketplace. No punishment is greater for bad producers than for consumers to strictly shun their products in favor of superior products that are made by their competitors. This is self-evident to everyone except the bureaucrats within organizations like the FDA who hide in the shadows while they cut secret deals with large industrial concerns who have no more ethics or morals than they do.

Give these people even more power?

I don't think so.

---

[19] See: www.altcancer.net/ashwin/ashw0914.htm

A Brief Commentary on Chapter 26

This is yet another entry that is quite personal. Bob Higgins is a personal friend and colleague in the alternative research community here in Cuenca, Ecuador. When a local "gringo publication" went after him for expressing his opinion about alternative treatments, the claws came out fully extended by a barrage of orthodox medical shills and apologists. Drives me nuts.

What resulted was a wide-ranging essay on the irreparable cracks in conventional medicine's well-crafted mythology. I think it is one of my better pieces.

The original post is still online.[1]

---

[1] See: www.altcancer.net/ashwin/ashw0615.htm

Chapter 26:

When Big Pharma Shills
Rule The Blogosphere

The Case of Bob Higgins,
Alternative Practitioner:
What Happens When Those of Us
Who Know Better Don't Speak Up?

"It is simply no longer possible to believe much of the clinical research that is published, or to rely on the judgment of trusted physicians or authoritative medical guidelines. I take no pleasure in this conclusion, which I reached slowly and reluctantly over my two decades as an editor of the New England Journal of Medicine."

Marcia Angel, M.D.
Longtime Editor-in-Chief
New England Medical Journal

"The case against science is straightforward: much of the scientific literature, perhaps half, may simply be untrue. Afflicted by studies with small sample sizes, tiny effects, invalid exploratory analyses, and flagrant conflicts of interest, together with an obsession for pursuing fashionable trends of dubious importance, science has taken a turn towards darkness."

Richard Horton, M.D.
Editor-in-Chief, ***Lancet***

L ife here in the high Andes -- (we live at close to 10,000 feet or 3,000 meters, take your pick) -- is pretty "tranquilo," as they say in Ecuador. There seems to be something in the water, the climate, the culture, or perhaps it's a combination, that resists the kind of contentiousness and never-ending conflict that grip so much of the rest of the world.

413

There is one notable exception, however: it is the mere mention of anything pertaining to health care that does not sing "hallelujah praises" to the great glory of the pharmaceutical industry. Yes, even in the remote part of the world in which I live, we're not immune to the drumbeat of pharmaceutical industry shills -- most of them on the payroll, some not -- standing guard over the comment sections of web pages where there is the slightest possibility these things can be discussed, fully "locked-and-loaded" and ready to pounce on anyone who commits the ultimate sin in their book: to express an independent line of thought that does not coincide with officially santioned **medical-industrial complex** doctrine and propaganda.

The truth of this hit home quite recently when a local alternative practitioner, Bob Higgins, wrote a series of articles for our local English-speaking online publication, Gringo Tree,[1] expressing his very personal journey in the world of cancer treatment. [Readers can contact Bob at: cuencaholisticguide@gmail.com].

He first published an article, entitled "Cancer and Institutionalized Medicine: Who's the Real Enemy?" Then he followed that up with "Cancer vs. Institutionalized Medicine," for which the comment section has to contain some of the most foul flaming I've ever seen in my 20+ years on the Internet. And then just a few days ago, Gringo Post Forum, an unrelated local forum, had an entire page of posts in which Higgins was included, even though he had never participated in the discussion. (It concerned an MMS Conference that was to take place in Vilcabamba, about 5 hours south of Cuenca. Neither Bob nor I were attending.) Fact is, Bob knew nothing about the MMS conference. Nonetheless, the MMS matter was used as a opportunity by shills to seriously flame[2] Higgins. He was sandbagged for an issue in which he took no part.

Since over 99% of my clients are outside of South America, it might appear that my presentation here is starting to appear provincial. However, I have seen this same treatment of alter-

---

[1] See: www.gringotree.com

[2] See: gringopost-forum.blogspot.com/2015/07/mms-is-it-safe.html

native practitioners for years on other blog sites, and yet I have chosen to say nothing. Should I have? Or should I have said something?

After meeting with Bob to discuss what had happened him, I composed the following response, which I sent to the editors of Gringo Tree. It contains compelling arguments that anyone can use against shills for the medical-industrial complex.

Addressing Robert Higgins' "Alternative Cancer" Articles
by Greg Caton -- Herbalist

I watched with interest as the responses to Robert Higgins' recent articles on alternative cancer therapies poured in, and I was somewhat surprised by the level of vitriol by some of our more spirited defenders of the medical-industrial complex: Charlie, Victor, Mark Zuckerburglar, William Baker, Kenneth Merena, some names real, some fake, it doesn't matter. You guys know who you are. You are the dominant bacterial organisms who have made the blogosphere your primary intestinal habitat, if only because ordinary people have more important things to do.

Since the possibility exists that some misinformed individuals could read this mindless drivel and take it seriously, I thought it might be refreshing to let some of this propagandistic fog clear and deal with established facts. I will also attempt to transcend personal attacks on Bob's character, cheesy, though predictable, because when the therapies you're defending produce such disastrous therapeutic results, what other fig leaf are you going to reach for besides deflection? Let's bring the focus back to where it belongs.

I'll make this easy with a simple numbering system and footnotes for those who want documentary support. I provide hundreds more references in *Meditopia*.

(1) **There is no convincing evidence anywhere that supports conventional cancer therapy.**

As I detail extensively in Chapter 4 of *Meditopia*,[3] there is absolutely no credible evidence, anywhere, in any language, in any country, in any time period, in any of the existing literature, on this planet and quite likely any other, that supports the notion that most conventional therapies for serious degenerative disease, but most particularly any conventional cancer therapy, actually work. There is, however, plenty of credible evidence that supports the fact that few things are as effective in KILLING people as conventional cancer treatment. It was not without sound foundation that the late two-time Nobel Prize winner, Dr. Linus Pauling, could say, **"Everyone should know that most cancer research is largely a fraud, and that the major cancer research organizations are derelict in their duties to the people who support them."**[4] (Try to keep in mind that when it comes to Nobel Prizes, Linus Pauling, unlike Barack Obama, actually EARNED his.) If you knew what I knew, you would, as do I, regard Pauling as being excessively diplomatic when he said this, if not downright obsequious, given his standing in the orthodox scientific community. This only makes it a more astonishing admission.

This is why you have medical renegades who have introduced the revolutionary concept of "evidence-based medicine." And, believe me, it is truly revolutionary. Why? Because it defies the conventional medicine position that it is perfectly acceptable to foist incredibly expensive, dangerous medical products, procedures, and modalities upon the public using fake data (as "Isabella" pointed out in her post) all the while pointing a finger at those "outside" the system as quacks and snake oil salesmen and whatever other pejoratives you can construct using the 26 known letters of the English alphabet. As Dr. Barbara Starfield[5] so aptly pointed out, where there is increased expenditure within the modern medical model, there is more death and disease. Ours is the Age of Iatrogenesis: death from doctoring.

[3] See: www.meditopia.org/chap4.htm, this is Chapter 6 in the current volume.

[4] See: On the mortality of conventional cancer treatment, see: www.naturalnews.com/033847_chemotherapy_cancer_treatments.html; Dr. Linus Pauling, with reference, is taken from Chapter 1 of *Meditopia*.

[5] See: www.drug-education.info/documents/iatrogenic.pdf

Over the years I have constructed several models to assist those who are cerebrally challenged to get their heads around the simple, historical observation that the cancer industry has nothing to do with coming up with a cancer cure and everything to do with suppressing those who do. I have created corollaries of Parkinson's Law,[6] put together a short treatise tying together the time-honored principle of planned obsolescence in business administration with the NEED FOR iatrogenesis,[7] shot holes the size of beach balls through orthodox media campaigns designed to deceive the public,[8] and the first four chapters of *Meditopia* itself, a free read at meditopia.org, stand as an indictment of this incredibly corrupt system, replete in its filth, devoid of any moral or ethical fiber.[9]

(2) There is nothing "scientific" about "medical science." And this is because orthodox science has nothing to do with the impartial quest for knowledge, but rather the quest for consensus within a privileged, professional, authoritative elite.

One of the things I do in Chapter 4 of *Meditopia*[10] is dissect Thomas Kuhn's famous landmark work, "The Structure of Scientific Revolutions" to show that science is a control system. It isn't about the quest for impartial knowledge.

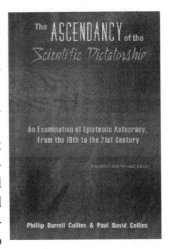

But apart from that, throughout my entire career, I have seen one ridiculous article of faith that carried all the weight of gravity and feigned sincerity by established medicine after another, obliterated by people who

---

[6] See: www.altcancer.net/lysis5.htm

[7] See: www.altcancer.net/ashwin/ashw0809.htm

[8] See: www.altcancer.net/ashwin/ashw0914.htm; also: www.altcancer.net/ashwin/ashw0415.htm

[9] See: www.meditopia.org

[10] See: www.meditopia.org/chap4-3.htm, or see Chapter 6 in the current volume.

were smarter, more brilliant, more creative, more resourceful, only to see their lives destroyed for attempting to inject a little verifiable truth into what author, Thomas Sheridan, calls our global "psychopathic control grid."[11] I could come up with a hundred examples, but for brevity's sake I'll just take two salient, poignant, and very personal examples.

EXHIBIT A: In 2000 I was exposed to a researcher who claimed that he created a formula to rapidly accelerate the healing of broken bones. Upon investigation, I quickly realized that one of the hidden assumptions of his formula is that the body utilizes silicon to create calcium compounds.[12] This angered me at first, because as anybody who was paying any attention during their high school chemistry classes knows, elemental transmutation is impossible, right? I mean, the entire scientific establishment wouldn't lie about something that fundamental, now would they? Subsequent to this, the researcher in question led me to thoroughly examine the work of Professor C.L. Kervran,

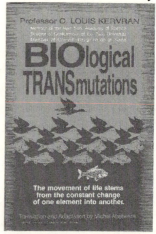

whose thoughts are summarized in his seminal work, "Biological Transmutations." I was willing to make this effort, because I really wanted to know how this "bone builder" formula worked, and I couldn't come up with an alternative explanation as to why it was so effective to save my life.

Just like with the apologists for the medical-industrial complex, the simple observable facts of daily life become obscure when you have people in authority telling you what to believe and to trust THEM rather than your own experience.

Like what comes out of a chicken's rear end. Well, yes,

---

[11] Thomas Sheridan, Puzzling People: The Labyrinth of the Psychopath (Velluminous Press, 2011).

[12] Out of this experience, we used to carry a product called Bone Builder: www.altcancer.net/bb.htm

I'm talking about eggs. But did you know that the egg shell is made of calcium carbonate, and that if you deliberately deprive a chicken of calcium its entire life, the eggs it produces will still be covered in shell that is made of calcium carbonate? Where does the calcium come from if the chicken isn't producing it internally from other elements? Kervran provides countless other examples that science cannot and will not explain. Not now. Not ever. Why should they? Science is not about knowledge, and its proponents take delight in suppressing observations that clearly defy their cherished theories.

EXHIBIT B: I make a product called H_3O (Calcium Sulfate Hydronium Solution).[13] In October 2001, I was in Washington D.C., giving a demonstration of this material along with its companion product, HRx.[14] What is the difference? H_3O (the chemical shorthand for hydronium) has a pH of close to 0.0, yet is non-caustic and non-corrosive to animal tissue; while HRx has a pH of close to 14.0 and is similarly non-caustic and non-corrosive to animal tissue. I produced a website devoted to the hundreds of truly scientific tests that we conducted to show the properties of these products.[15]

Okay, so back to the Expo East show. About halfway through my demonstration, I did a live example showing that when H_3O and HRx are combined, that is to say, an extreme acid with an extreme alkaline, they produce no exothermic reaction and the resulting solution has a pH that is close to 7.0.

If you know anything about inorganic chemistry, you know that all the chemistry books will tell you that this isn't possible. Is this registering with you yet, dear reader? I had just done a live demonstration showing that one of the bedrock principles of inorganic chemistry has at least one provable exception.

A professor from Georgetown University approached me, business card in hand. I looked at it and saw that he had a Ph.D.

[13] See: www.altcancer.net/h3o.htm. It should be pointed out that the demonstration had to do with chemical properties. No mention was made of medical properties. I was, after all, in Washington, D.C. . . .

[14] See: www.altcancer.net/hydrox.htm

[15] See: www.gregcaton.com/natura/

in chemistry

"How did you do that?" he asked.

"What do you mean?" I replied.

"What's the trick? Are the pH strips you're using artificially marked?"

"No," I replied. "There's no trick. I use ColorpHast strips from EM Science, imported from Germany, and we make these solutions here in the States. These products really do have the properties I've indicated."

Suddenly, the man's face grimaced and as he turned to walk away, he muttered, "What a con artist!"

The truth is that this professor was more committed to believing a mythology that was central to his position, authority, standing, and world view than he was in trusting his own eyes. This is what historian Gary North is referring to when he says, "Always beware respectable people, because they are beholden to the institutions that are the source of that respectability!" And this is what those in authority count on: that you're dumb enough, gullible enough, foolish enough to believe whatever they come up with, even when it defies what your own senses tell you. People will believe a medical doctor, who frequently has financial motives that conflict with the interests of the patient, over their own body, which has NO INTEREST apart from that of the patient. A doctor will lie to you. Your own body will not. I learned this from Jerry Mander,[16] though a more convincing look at how divorced "modern science" is from reality and how it has been transformed into a twisted religious cult, can be found in Phillip Collins' work.[17]

---

[16] Mander wrote a book in 1976 called "Four Arguments for the Elimination of Television," which deals extensively with the use of television as a programming tool, and how deftly it gets people to do things that are against their own best interest. The title is deceiving, in as much as the book stretches the mind well beyond what you expect of the initial subject to be covered.

[17] Phillip Darrell Collins, et al., The Ascendency of Scientific Dictatorship: An Examination of Epistemic Autocracy, From the 19th to the 21st Century, (USA: BookSurge Publishing)

(3) A world without conventional cancer therapy, or pharmaceutical drugs, for that matter, produces no deficiencies.

Everyone knows that the body needs a variety of macronutrients, vitamins, minerals, and enzymes in order to function properly. What happens when your body doesn't get any one of the many nutrients that it needs? It gets diseased, right? Insufficient vitamin C leads to scurvy; insufficient vitamin B3 leads to pellagra; insufficient iodine leads to goiter, etc.

In fact, there is not one thing that the body needs which is essential (that is to say the body cannot manufacture it) whose deficiency will not result in a diseased condition. And why is that? Because the body requires it. It's essential to good health.

My world, the world of phytopharmacology, is filled with thousands of various natural chemicals which belong to different classes of organic compounds whose deficiency results in harm to the body. This is because naturopaths, like myself, will only deal in things that the body *needs*. We're not in the business of creating Frankensteinian molecular structures that can be found nowhere in this entire universe, filing a patent for it, claiming ownership, and then attempting to sell the public on the idea that our completely artificial molecule is somehow necessary for a restored, natural function of the body.

If I told you that I have a special kind of mud on my property which, if put into your gas tank, will improve your car's performance, would you be dumb enough to believe me?

No? Well, anybody who agrees to go in for chemotherapy or radiation therapy buys that logic, so why won't you? After all, **THERE IS NO SUCH THING AS BEING CHEMOTHERAPY OR RADIATION THERAPY DEFICIENT!** Such a physical state does not exist.

The word "pharmacology" comes from the ancient Greek root, meaning "poison."[18] This is not an accident. The fathers of modern medicine knew what they were doing, and this is conveyed in the word they chose to describe their art: using materials that are foreign to the body, unnecessary for its optimal function, the absence of which cannot possibly produce a deficiency, all while extolling its vital curative properties. The very etymology of the word provides us with a clue as to what cancer therapy itself is about: poisoning the patient so that further treatment will be required. This fits perfectly with the "problem, reaction, solution" Hegelian model that rests at the very foundation of modern government, and make no mistake about it, modern medicine is a form of governance.[19]

(4) The majority of medical doctors who administer chemotherapy would not undergo it themselves.

The figure from a 2014 study was 88%.[20] However, I have seen higher. But surveys aside, I can personally attest that Cathryn and I have talked to scores of medical doctors over our 25 years of working together who have told us privately that they would *not* undergo chemotherapy or radiation therapy themselves and the only reason they prescribe these approaches is because they risk losing their licenses if they don't.

How many cancer patients who get sold a bill of goods on the "chemo / radiation good-time choo-choo train" understand that there is a greater than 50% chance (and that's an extremely conservative figure) that the medical doctor who sold them on that therapy would not undergo it themselves because they know it's too dangerous. That they know it doesn't work. That they know there are better alternatives. That they know that chemotherapy "kills cancer patients faster than no treatment at all."[21]

Probably not many.

---

[18] See: en.wikipedia.org/wiki/Pharmacology

[19] See: www.infowars.com/the-hegelian-dialectic-and-its-use-in-controlling-modern-society/

[20] See: www.dailymail.co.uk/health/article-2643751/Most-doctors-terminally-ill-AVOID-aggressive-treatments-chemotherapy-despite-recommending-patients.html

[21] See: www.naturalnews.com/048827_chemotherapy_cancer_treatment_patient_survival.html

(5) Anecdotal trumps JAMA any day.

I get sick and tired of hearing about how something is valid only if has been confirmed by a triple blind study. Do you have any sense of how ridiculous this is? If I'm walking down the street and I see a woman violently raped to the point of hospitalization, do you understand that my testimony is of no value to the police if I applied these people's logic? It is only what I saw or heard, so how could my testimony have any valid meaning? Only a qualified controlled study could confirm that this woman was raped and who did it!

As I discuss in Chapter 4 of *Meditopia*, the first American Medical Pharmacopeia consisted almost exclusively of "cures" that were stolen from native American Indians. It was all anecdotal. And what does anecdotal mean? It means knowledge that has not yet received the imprimatur of people in authority who view you as little more than cattle, something to be milked until you're ready for the clinical cancer slaughterhouse.

In fact, the working knowledge of indigenous people all over the world is based on anecdotal observations. Bob Higgins' naysayers would argue that none of these natural medicines have any value, after all, they haven't been "triple blind studied" and had their results published in the *Journal of the American Medical Association* by a pharmaceutical company.

I beg to differ.

It might be different if these studies were "legit," but the FDA routinely helps Big Pharma pull off studies that are hugely fraudulent.[22] To put it bluntly "most medical research is false."[23] And what happens to those who blow this whistle on this kind of fraud? They get punished for being honest.[24]

Is this really the kind of medical system that we should honor, respect, support, and follow?

Strangely, the posters who were unjustifiably gunning for Robert Higgins' article and his personal character certainly

[22] See: retractionwatch.com/2015/02/09/fda-repeatedly-hidden-evidence-scientific-fraud-says-author-new-study/

[23] See: www.naturalnews.com/039416_medical_research_scientific_fraud_false_data.html

[24] Example: healthimpactnews.com/2014/the-vaccine-autism-cover-up-how-one-doctors-career-was-destroyed-for-telling-the-truth/

think so.

(6) You wouldn't trust a local "mafia don" with your health care needs. So why would you trust an oncologist without question?

I remember having a phone conversation in the mid-1990s with Canadian physician, Dr. Guylaine Lanctôt, M.D. She was in the process of releasing her book, The Medical Mafia.[25] This was an important checkpoint in my ongoing education as to just how criminal the medical establishment is. There is no room in the conventional medical establishment for objectivity. It is a world, like that of George W. Bush's, ". . . where you're either with us, or you're a terrorist."

In 2010, in the aftermath of my celebrated kidnapping,[26] while imprisoned in Beaumont, Texas, I spent a good deal of time with James T. Hill, M.D. He was a physician who, like Guylaine, had come to the conclusion that few of the practices and principles of the medical-industrial complex were sound. Unlike most physicians he worked with his patients on improving their diets. He frequently recommended nutraceuticals, medicinal herbs, vitamin and mineral supplements, and he prescribed a fraction of the pharmaceutical drugs that most physicians prescribe. The local licensing board found out and wasn't pleased. In the end, federal charges were brought against Dr. Hill involving a single prescription and he was sentenced to more than ten years.

But imprisoning practitioners using fake charges and fictitious allegations isn't good enough anymore. Those who follow the long list of "unconventional" scientists who have died in recent years of strange, mysterious, unusually violent deaths[27] are now having to add medical practitioners to their lists.[28] I personally know of practitioners myself who are petrified of the wave of murders that is taking place to physicians who don't "toe the party line."

[25] Guylaine Lanctôt, M.D , The Medical Mafia. (Here's the Key, Inc., Morgan, VT, 1995). See: www.altcancer.net/lysis.htm#book16
[26] See: www.meditopia.org/chap3-3.htm
[27] See: www.stevequayle.com/index.php?s=146
[28] See: www.infowars.com/alternative-health-practitioners-death-is-third-in-past-two-weeks/

And how is this relevant to the current discussion?

Simple: if you represented a system of health care, especially as it relates to conventional cancer treatment, that had any validity to it, if your therapeutic approaches were better, safer, more effective, and superior to those offered by the naturopathic community, would it really be necessary to falsely imprison contrarians or pay assassins to violently murder those who did not agree with your system?

Now, you might say, "But wait, my doctor (or my oncologist, or my pharmacist, or my pathologist, or my registered dietitian, etc.) doesn't have anything to do with this!"

They don't have to.

They are the foot soldiers in a system that has other operatives who *do*. And just like "The Matrix," as long as they are plugged into this system, this vast abyss of endless corruption, well-meaning though they might be, they are participants who profit from it. They belong to a club that rewards adherents for conformity, and swiftly punishes those who express independent thought or give credence to empirical evidence. [Forget "1984." Welcome to the Borg!]

Therefore, you have a right to question their recommendations.

Ask yourself: is a system that behaves this way a system that you can trust with life-and-death decisions? I believe this is something that deserves serious attention before giving any heed to critics of alternative practitioners like Bob Higgins, who is merely suggesting that there may be a better way.

(7) And finally if these fundamental principles still elude you, I devote the better part of two hours on one of my interviews explaining them![29]

---

[29] See: youtu.be/p14sSMQtGII In even providing this link, I wish to note that since interviews are "extemporaneous," mistakes are made. Early in this interview, for example, I use the word "months" instead of "years" at one important juncture. A little later on I slip and mention that my wife received her bachelor's and master's from Texas A&M (true), and then a Doctorate in Naturopathy at Clayton "School of Business," when it should have been Clayton College of Natural Health -- an institution that prior to its closing in 2010 was, predictably, under constant attack from conventional medical interests.

A Brief Commentary on Chapter 27

This is a brief post I made in February 2017.[1] It is important, because despite its brevity, it sets the stage for two upcoming posts that extend the argument that "Fake News" is a subset of a much larger phenomenon: a global culture where there almost isn't anything that *isn't* fake.

---

[1] See: www.altcancer.net/ashwin/ashw0217.htm

Chapter 27:

Forget Fake News . . .

"The greatest challenges of our time are Fake Science, Fake Medicine, and Fake Education confronting a horrifically suppressive, global system designed to keep us misinformed, chronically ill, and just plain stupid."

"We must either defy the corporate state
Or accept our extinction as a species.
We have been stripped of the power
To express dissent or effect change.
Rebellion is the only way to remain fully human."

Chris Hedges

Since Cathryn and I moved to Ecuador in 2007, I have repeatedly told friends that the place of my birth, The United States of America, has morphed into something I scarcely recognize. It has become truer with each passing year, with a critical component of that assessment being the degree to which so much of what constitutes ordinary life is riddled with the fake and the fabricated. The entire FDA case against me, which stole eight years of my life[1] (2003-2011), was riddled with preposterous claims, culminating in Hillary Clinton (then U.S. Secretary of State) signing an order to have me illegally kidnapped in 2009,[2] an act that was later condemned by the Ecuadorian government. If I seem somewhat bold in my description of our "life in the Matrix," it is only because I have seen it "up close and personal" in a way that few citizens ever do.

Occupying much of the current social and political discourse today is this pejorative meme, **Fake News**, an expression that the mainstream media conjured up to excoriate their blossoming competition in the "Alternative Media," only to see the effort result in egg on their face, as they themselves became identified with the very 'fakeness' they so assiduously attempted to ascribe to others.

Those who have read any part of my free online book, *Meditopia*, know that for many years I have been sounding the alarm about the perniciousness of the ubiquitous fakery that is neither isolated in geography to the U.S., nor in content to current affairs. It is a virus that affects every aspect of our lives worldwide.

I was reminded of the incorrigible character of this virulent malignancy when *Scholar Open Access*, a website designed to help expose the exploding tsunami of fake scientific journal articles, was unceremoniously shut down[3] in January. No one who works inside the closed world of scientific journals is unaware of this scandalous development, which is probably why a few at the top have thrown in the towel and gone public.[4] (A professor of molecular oncology in Australia has recently started up her own "truth journal" to expose "fake science."[5] We'll see how far she gets before she is closed down. And the same goes

---

[1] See: www.meditopia.org/chap3-1.htm

[2] See: youtu.be/8q_mqlyNtGI

[3] See: www.iflscience.com/editors-blog/website-that-tracked-fake-science-journals-has-suddenly-vanished/

[4] See: www.altcancer.net/ashwin/ashw0615.htm

[5] See: www.naturalnews.com/2017-01-31-cancer-researcher-now-crusading-against-fake-science-journals-after-finding-published-fake-papers.html

for *NaturalNews's* new offering, *FakeScience.news*, which has more fake science reports at its disposal than it can ever expect to cover. This may have contributed to the actions of Google, another gem of a 5-star brothel whose clients include large corporate and government vested interests, which recently targeted *NaturalNews.*)[6]

Nonetheless, these developments appear to have done little to reeducate the general public, who still rely on the exudate of the establishment's information sewer system to make life-and-death decisions, particularly as it pertains to health care. How do I know this? Because, to cite just one example among many, we talk daily to people who have been duped by their physicians into chemotherapy, not knowing that this conventional cancer therapy has a 97% failure rate.[7] And few things in this world are so vigorously supported by fake facts and fake science as conventional cancer therapies.

The exploitative underpinnings of our surreal global culture have their roots in poor education. You can't very well be expected to control the minds of a citizenry that is well-educated and informed. I realized this some years ago while reading Alexander Fraser Tytler's <u>Elements of General History, Ancient and Modern</u>, a history book for children written in the early 1800s. (I keep a copy of it in my library.) Twelve year olds routinely read this work as part of a basic education, and today you'd be hard-pressed to find college graduates who could thoroughly comprehend it. So rich is the language, grammar, syntax, the extensive vocabulary, complex sentence structures, etc. Tytler's work is an ancient American relic from a time and place where the purpose of education was to educate and not indoctrinate.

Which brings me to the purpose of this essay: that you cannot, as Chris Hedges would say, retain your humanity unless you exert the effort to resist a system intent on dehumanizing you, using you, exploiting you, and then discarding you. This begins

---

[6] See: www.naturalnews.com/2017-02-28-google-censorship-of-natural-news-statement-from-the-health-ranger.html

[7] See: www.altcancer.net/with_chemo.htm

with a firm commitment to your own self-education, your own quest to uncover truths that your overlords are intent on suppressing. You cannot expect to rise above the fakery unless you become your own authority.

Chapter 27

A Brief Commentary on Chapter 28

I wrote this chapter in May 2017, four months after the pre-vious chapter.[1] Here's a question: if you have an entire industry, health care, built on a cultural foundation of fraud and corrup-tion, should you have any reason to believe that the inner sanc-tum of medical science's "double-blind" studies and "peer-re-viewed" articles would not be similarly affected?

Of course not.

This article gets into the specifics.

Chapter 28:

The Unmasking of Conventional Medicine As Fake Health Care, Medical Authorities as Shock Jocks

"Fake clinical studies, fake journal reports, and Dr. Oz . . . Just when you thought it couldn't get any more surreal . . ."

"One of the most salient features of our culture is that there is so much bullshit."

Harry G. Frankfurt
On Bullshit
Princeton University Press

" The truth is so fragile, it needs a bodyguard of lies to protect it."

Winston Churchill

In April 2017, I received an email from *GreenMedInfo*,[1] highlighting an article by Jefferey Jaxen,[2] entitled, "Retractions and Errors Driving Loss of Faith in the Peer Review Process."[3] The lead-off sets the tone: "Establishment medical professionals are quick to hold up peer-reviewed studies as the gold standard, argument-ending proof in an attempt to shut down valid discussions around 'alternative' health and healing. Major medical and science journals have long-been considered the sacred cows from which information gets disseminated down

---

[1] See: www.greenmedinfo.com
[2] See: www.jeffereyjaxen.com/about.html
[3] See: www.greenmedinfo.com/blog/retractions-errors-driving-loss-faith-peer-review-process

through the roots of mainstream medicine with unquestioning adherence mirroring religious dogma. **What if this peer-reviewed research was flawed? What if major medical journals acted as gatekeepers long-crafting a health paradigm that favored only limited and dangerous pharmaceutical interventions?"** [emphasis added]

The article then goes on to discuss the recent retraction of 107 research papers by *Tumor Biology*, which released a statement that read: *"The current retractions are not a new case of integrity breach but are the result of a deeper manual investigation which became necessary after our previous retractions from Tumor Biology in 2016. The extent of the current retractions was not obvious from the earlier investigations in 2015. We are retracting these published papers because the peer review process required for publication in our journals had been deliberately compromised by fabricated peer reviewer reports. "* None of this is news to established, practicing naturopaths, who have to battle disinformation every day of their career. I began an article in my *Ashwin* blog in June 2015 with quotes from Marcia Angel, M.D., former Editor-in-Chief of *The New England Journal of Medicine* and Richard Horton, M.D., former Editor-in-Chief of *Lancet*, who both have decried the increasingly fraudulent character of the peer-review process and the unreliability of most published clinical studies, in general.[4] (Moreover, both of them figure prominently in the *GreenMedInfo* article cited above.) Going farther back, I've written a series of articles about the untruthful, dishonest character of "official information." I've written about the unjustified war against herbal products[5] (April 2015); the disinformation campaign against escharotics[6] (September 2014); orthodoxy's campaign against reputable alternative companies and their websites

---

[4] See: www.altcancer.net/ashw0515.htm or Chapter 26 in the current volume.

[5] See: www.altcancer.net/ashwin/ashw0415.htm, or Chapter 25 in the current volume.

[6] See: www.altcancer.net/ashwin/ashw0914.htm, or Chapter 24 in the current volume.

using WOT[7] (August 2012); convention's art of disinformation using mediated experience[8] (October 2009); and the deliberate lies that spew forth from that beacon of official medical lies that's known as *Quackwatch* ("Confronting the MIC's Unending Cavalcade of Pathological Lies")[9] (April 2009). And none of this addresses the unending lies that the FDA's minions of darkness used in connection with their attacks on me since 2003 (see Chapter 3 of *Meditopia*.)[10]

Do the lies that emanate from anything that's remotely connected with conventional medicine never end?

Apparently not.

On May 10, 2017, the Dr. Oz Show aired a segment on "Black Salve," based on a private interview I gave to Dr. Oz himself on April 17, 2017. I have to hand it to Dr. Oz's staff: they did an incredible job in the editing room of twisting everything I said and crafting a hit piece on my person, such that anyone who didn't know me or my work would be quite convinced that I deserved a place among the world's most notorious criminals, somewhere between Osama bin Laden, Al Capone, and Jack the Ripper.

Even worse, Dr. Oz made so many provably false statements about Black Salve, that I had to respond with a lengthy, comprehensive rebuttal of my own.[11]

The interesting thing about Harry Frankfurt's work, with whose quote I began this chapter, is that he has found the extreme lack of truthfulness so prominent in our culture that it has lead to him to produce a Unified Theory of Bullshit. Prominent within Frankfurt's theory is the idea that the "value" of spoken communication is its ability to persuade, with no mind as to whether or not it's truthful. "The liar cares about the truth and attempts to hide it; the bullshitter doesn't care if what they say is true or false, but rather only cares whether or not their listener

---

[7] See: www.altcancer.net/ashwin/ashw0812.htm.

[8] See: www.altcancer.net/ashwin/ashw1009.htm, or Chapter 23 in the current volume.

[9] See: www.altcancer.net/ashwin/ashw0409.htm, or Chapter 22in the current volume.

[10] See: www.meditopia.org/chap3-1.htm.

[11] See: www.altcancer.net/dr_oz_rebuttal.htm.

is persuaded." With that standard in mind, it has become all too obvious that the medical-industrial complex has filled its ranks with wall-to-wall bullshitters.

On inconsequential matters, it's easy to ignore this feature of our culture. But when the **Theory of Bullshit** is applied to organized medicine, it leads to disastrous decisions by ordinary people on matters that, all too often, turn out to be a matter of life and death.

And all of this returns us to our raison d'être at Alpha Omega Labs: supplying raw, verifiable information that consumers can use to make their own health care decisions, void of the tendency of those in the orthodox medical community to tell anyone who will listen to them whatever they want, no matter how provably false it is, as long as it makes more money for the medical-industrial complex.

More than ever, it's important for consumers to think for themselves, knowing that those in authority do not live to provide the public with what's in their best interest. Never before has it been more important to think independently and do one's own research.

Chapter 28

A Brief Commentary on Chapter 29

This article segues from the previous two chapters, continuing with the theme of the supremacy of "fake." It was posted in June 2017, the month after the previous chapter.[1] The difference here is that I initially focus on one particular medical journal article that attempts to speak with authority on the subject of Black Salve (escharotics), making a host of statements, favorable to the orthodox medical view, that I know to be empirically untrue. For 28 years I have been observing medical phenomena that directly contradict the content of this article.

The thought here, and this appears to have become ubiquitous in the world of scientific reporting, is that if you lie often enough, convincingly enough, with passion and an air of authority, some kind of journalistic alchemy will kick in and your lies will be transformed into the truth.

It is a deceitful virus has infected our culture to the core, touching everyone and everything.

And it is now threatening, as I point out in Part I, the very sustenance of life on this planet. Those who want to see stronger causal connections can find them in my previous book.[2]

---

[1] See: www.altcancer.net/ashwin/ashw0617.htm

[2] See: Caton, The Joys of Psychopathocracy, (Miami, USA: Herbologics, Ltd., 2017)

Chapter 29:

"First We Ban Black Salve . . .
Then We Ban Water."

*"A global culture that cultivates all things fake:
fake news, fake education, fake medicine,
fake science, as long as it serves a financial
or political agenda, is the hallmark of a system that
can ban anything useful to humanity, or even things
vital to the sustenance of life on this planet."*

I n May 2017 I posted an article to my Ashwin,[1] online blog that covered just now fake and fraudulent the world of orthodox medicine, in general, and peer reviewed medical studies, in particular, had become.[2] If you haven't read the article, you should, because it segues into what I'm going to talk about in the following pages.

Hindawi Publishing Corporation
Evidence-Based Complementary and Alternative Medicine
Volume 2017, Article ID 9184034, 11 pages
http://dx.doi.org/10.1155/2017/9184034

Review Article
A Review of Black Salve: Cancer Specificity, Cure, and Cosmesis

Andrew Croaker,[1,2] Graham J. King,[1] John H. Pyne,[3] Shailendra Anoopkumar-Dukie,[4] and Lei Liu[1]

[1] Southern Cross Plant Science, Southern Cross University, Lismore, NSW 2480, Australia
[2] Wesley Medical Research Institute, Wesley Hospital, Auchenflower, QLD 4066, Australia
[3] School of Medicine, University of Queensland, St Lucia, QLD 4072, Australia
[4] School of Pharmacy, Griffith University, Gold Coast Campus, Gold Coast, QLD 4222, Australia

Because so many people know that I work as both an herbalist and a medical researcher, I routinely get email from people who want my opinion about this study or that, the majority of which are, like the studies mentioned in my Ashwin blog, peer-reviewed and/or made available through publication in a prominent medical journal. A couple months ago, I was sent

---

[1] Ashwin: see Glossary

[2] That Ashwin article is Chapter 28 in the current volume.

a PDF of a review article from Australia entitled, "A Review of Black Salve: Cancer Specificity, Cure, and Cosmesis."[3] The person who sent me the reference said I really ought to read it, because several of the citations were taken from my own work, though overall not in a complimentary light. (Do these people know Dr. Oz?) Before I get started, I want to make it clear that I'm not here to trash the entire endeavor. (The authors make clear in their introduction that "herbal medicines should not be dismissed without consideration," which is somewhat encouraging.) In fact, the article made some points that I myself have emphasized, but the "review," authored by five contributors straight from the bowels of orthodoxy, is not without a self-serving slant, which is, in the points I enumerate below, at odds with the experiences of naturopaths worldwide who are well versed in the practice of using escharotics. (Note that in my discussion below, I leave out, as much as possible, any reduplication of the studies / footnotes cited, as this is unnecessarily repetitive. Since I proceed through the review article's main points in the same order they appear in the document, readers can easily follow without undue redundancy.)

Let's go through my points of contention:

1. Recent Origins of Black Salve.

This may seem unimportant, but early in this document, the authors lay the origin of "Black Salve" at the feet of American surgeon, Dr. Jesse Fell, circa 1858. I am not unfamiliar with Fell's work, as I wrote about this in *Meditopia* thirteen years ago.[4] But if we broaden our search for "Cancer Salves" with caustic properties, we could confirm its origins at least to Hildegard of Bingen in the 12th Century.[5]

But even if we restrict ourselves to Black Salves with zinc chloride as an ingredient, our search would take us back thousands of years to ancient Egypt. As I make clear in my page on

---

[3] See: www.altcancer.net/docs/review%20of%20black%20salve%2001%202017.pdf

[4] Chapter 2 in the original *Meditopia* draft, Chapter 5 in the current volume.

[5] Naiman, Ingrid, Cancer Salves, (Suquamish, Washington: Seventh Ray Press, 1999), 3.

zinc chloride,[6] Christopher Dunn has unearthed evidence that zinc chloride was clearly being manufactured inside the Great Pyramid of Giza. Although its varied uses in antiquity are unclear and our evidence circumstantial, are we to believe that the ancient Egyptians manufactured zinc chloride thousands of years ago, and were somehow ignorant of its ability to be mixed with a wide range of botanical material and work in the treatment of malignancies? Remember, we're talking about an advanced civilization which produced feats of engineering that we cannot duplicate to this very day.

Yeah. Sure.

My problem with this insignificant piece of poor research is that it's based on an attempt to delegitimize Black Salves by insinuating that they're of recent development, a good 100 years into the industrial age. This runs parallel to their argument that Black Salves are untested and unproven (which I'll examine more closely shortly). After all, in the over 150 years that Black Salves have been more aggressively used around the world, studied and tested, with numerous books written about them, we couldn't possibly have accumulated enough evidence to know what they are, what they do, and the most effective formulary combinations, now could we?

2. "Black Salve isn't natural."

Here's their logic: (1) Zinc Chloride & DMSO are "synthetic chemicals." (2) Both chemicals are frequently used to make Black Salve (particularly the former). (3) Therefore, Black Salve can't be a natural product.

It isn't just that these two compounds are frequently used. The authors say that "black salve contains significant quantities of synthetic chemicals." (Plural.) And since we all learned new math in school, we all know what a huge number two is.

First of all, the truth is that DMSO is rarely used to make Black Salve. At Alpha Omega Labs we only use it to make a variation called "Deep Tissue," and the only reason we use DMSO is because it enhances transdermal penetration. However, it is

---

[6] See: www.altcancer.net/zinc.htm

hardly a "requirement" to make an effective topical escharotic. Of all the U.S. patents that are cited in Chapter 1 of *Meditopia*, none that I know of lists DMSO as an ingredient.[7]

Furthermore, the authors work even more vigorously to test the stupidity of their readers by openly admitting that DMSO is found in "cereals, fruits, and vegetables," which presumably even the authors might admit are natural in origin, but since commercially sold DMSO is made from lignins, the suggestion that it's natural is somehow made illegitimate. The authors are insinuating that a molecule of DMSO, dimethyl sulfoxide, or (CH3)2SO from nature is different than a molecule of DMSO made synthetically. This is reminiscent of the work of Durk Pearson and Sandy Shaw, who in their international bestseller, Life Extension (1982), devote an entire chapter making light of those who would suggest that natural molecular structures and the very same compounds made synthetically were somehow different.[8] What bothers me is that the language used by the authors is intended to make it "sound" more artificial: "DMSO's chemical synthesis utilizes lignins free methyl radicals; these are coupled to sulphur and then oxidized." This is true, but so what?

What if we tell consumers instead that DMSO is a powerful scavenger of hydroxyl free radicals, "which are responsible for much of the damage which occurs following a crushing injury and which have also been implicated in arthritis."[9] Or that its use in Black Salve is aided by the fact that "DMSO penetrates the skin, acting as a powerful inhibitor of free radical activity . . . (that it) reduces the free radical damage and thereby allows faster healing."[10] What would such a revelation do to the ridiculous statement made in the authors' closing paragraph on this subject: "This knowledge may alter the treatment choices of CAM patients, a population often wanting to reduce their exposure to

---

[7] See Chapter 4 in the current volume.

[8] Durk Pearson and Sandy Shaw, Life Extension: A Practical Scientific Approach (New York: Warner Books, 1982), 52-55.

[9] Ibid., 347

[10] Ibid., 347-348.

unnatural compounds."[11]

Now let's go back to the one remaining "unnatural" compound mentioned in the paper: zinc chloride. Although the authors admit that zinc chloride occurs naturally in the rare mineral, simonkolleite, they use the same ridiculous logic as they do with DMSO to suggest that because it is commercially "manufactured," it must somehow be artificial. Yes, zinc chloride is made from zinc metal and hydrochloric acid, both of which are found in huge supply throughout nature. What we have here is a simple inorganic chemical reaction. How else would the authors propose that you make it? Is one molecule of $ZnCl_2$ derived from simonkolleite any different than one molecule of $ZnCl_2$ made by combined zinc and hydrochloric acid? Does the fact that zinc chloride is "manufactured" make it any less natural?

What bothers me about this entire polemic, and I see it all the time in my work, is that given who is delivering the message, what we're dealing with here is what psychologists call reverse projection. The entire pharmaceutical industry is awash with molecular entities that exist nowhere in the natural world. Not on this planet. Not on any other planet. Not in our galaxy, and quite possibly in no other galaxy. This is true by definition and is a fundamental principle of patent medicine. If you want a proprietary "drug," you need to create a molecular entity that has not, hitherto, existed and been in commerce. Moreover, you need to construct fraudulent clinical studies that give lip service to the precautionary principle. How else are you going to prove that your new pharmaceutical drug, an unnatural molecular entity that can be found nowhere else in the known universe, is "completely safe"?

Zinc chloride and DMSO may not be found in abundant amounts throughout nature, but at least they exist. In addition, their judicious use does not bring a laundry list of side effects that are now part and parcel of most pharmaceutical drugs.

The authors of this paper are not going to tell you any of this, so I will.

3. Black Salve indiscriminately attacks both healthy

[11] Croaker, et al. 2.

and malignant cells.

The authors then spend the next two and half pages with a section entitled, "Black Salve Cancer Specificity and Normal Tissue Toxicity."[12] They begin with a footnote on the subject, taken from *Altcancer.com FAQ*,[13] where I indicate that a well made escharotic (i.e., "Black Salve") attacks cancerous and not healthy tissue. I stand by this statement because it comports with my experience in working with escharotics since 1989, and communicating with thousands of end users, falling into three categories: people who have used a Black Salve I made, people who have used a Black Salve made by another company, and people who have made Black Salve for themselves. The exception is certain systemic conditions to which I devote a separate page.[14]

Before we delve into the minutia of this section, let me say at the outset that this is yet another area of misinformation that I have to deal with routinely. If what the authors say in this section were true, I wouldn't get so many people calling me, asking why a Black Salve they have applied to a benign growth that they "thought" might be a malignancy, induces no reaction. This would not be possible if the authors or the authorities they cite in their footnotes knew what they were talking about. Additionally, if you simply peruse our pictorial and testimonial section, you can visually examine the high degree of differentiation exerted by the action of Cansema®,[15] a property shared with any well-prepared "Black Salve."

The authors make their position clear in the closing paragraph of this section with the simple statement, "black salve can also cause normal tissue necrosis." It goes without saying that misuse of any product, natural or otherwise, has the potential to bring unintended results. But to get Black Salve, at least the variations we make, to actually kill healthy cells requires you

---

[12] Croaker, et al., 2-5.

[13] See FAQ. In Croaker et al., it appears as Footnote #57.

[14] See: www.altcancer.net/insitu.htm

[15] See: www.altcancer.net/cansema.htm

to ignore the instructions,[16] usually by way of using the Salve excessively or with longer "residence times." Many natural products will do this. Recently, I did an experiment on myself that resulted in a significant burn on my head. Like a lot of men my age, I have alopecia (male pattern baldness), so I was experimenting with a combination of an Andean hot pepper oil from "Rocoto"[17] (*Capsicum pubescens*) and mutamba (*Gauzuma ulmifolia*). I made a paste from this, applied it to my head, and then went to bed. I woke up about four hours later with an intense burning sensation, at which point I went to the bathroom and saw that I had actually burned myself. Quite simply, I had used too much cayenne oil. I removed the paste, applied H_3O, and the burn was healed within an hour. I realize now that most any *Capsicum* would have induced this reaction. Had I applied Tabasco® sauce to my head under the same conditions, I would have gotten the same reaction if I'd left it on long enough. Considering the ways one can misuse hot peppers, maybe we should get them regulated as a potentially dangerous natural plant. Do you see how absurd this can get?

Going back to the review paper at hand, what follows is a breakdown of individual phytopharmacological constituents of common Black Salve botanicals in a series of convoluted arguments (supported by numerous citations from orthodox sources) so absurd that it brings to mind Winston Churchill's famous quip concerning the grave danger to the English language of ending a sentence with a preposition: "This is errant pedantry up with which I shall not put!"

First the paper focuses on the alkaloids of bloodroot (*Sanguinaria canadensis*), in particular, sanguinaria. The examples that follow are flawed at the onset by one simple proposition: "As a therapeutic product containing multiple bioactive compounds, the discriminating ability of black salve can be gauged by the cytotoxic potential of its individual constituents against malignant and normal cells."[18] In other words, if you tear Black

---

[16] See: www.altcancer.net/can5.htm

[17] See: en.wikipedia.org/wiki/Capsicum_pubescens

[18] See: Croaker, et al., 2.

Salve down to its individual phytochemicals, the entire composition can be judged based on the isolated property exerted by one particular component.

No, it can't.

Let me give you an example:

My first mentor in the use of escharotics was Dr. Russell Jordan, whose work and influence on my own career was substantial.[19] Dr. Jordan was a co-founder of not one, but two, successful, conventional pharmaceutical companies. Towards the end of his career, he began to realize how grossly flawed the fundamental principles guiding the pharmaceutical industry were, and he openly expressed this to me. (I created a theoretical framework to explain it in *Meditopia*.[20])

His first pharmaceutical company was Vipont Pharmaceutical, which made a very effective dentifrice that contained both zinc chloride and bloodroot, which makes this example particularly relevant. After his company was sold to Colgate-Palmolive[21] for $88 million, the geniuses at Colgate thought they'd improve on Vipont's toothpaset formula by getting rid of the bloodroot, and use extractions of bloodroot to try and improve the formula. Apparently, it made no difference that Jordan and Vipont Pharmaceutical had 15 U.S. patents on bloodroot in connection with its use as a dentifrice, and were really quite knowledgeable on the subject of bloodroot and its properties. Certainly, the technical team at Vipont was infinitely more knowledgeable than the authors of this review paper we've been discussing and the researchers and studies they use to populate their footnote section.

The result? A dismal failure.

Jordan told me that Colgate's resulting formulations actually made the product less efficacious. And why was that? Well, as any experienced herbalist will tell you, the broken down constituents of an herbal preparation rarely exert the same properties as the unfragmented botanical preparation. A true herbal

---

[19] See: www.meditopia.org/chap1.htm, or Chapter 4 in the current volume.

[20] See: www.meditopia.org/chap5.htm, or Chapter 7 in the current volume. Go down to: "Premise #4: Cleaving Wholeness for Fragmentationalism was the first step in the development of modern medicine."

[21] See: www.referenceforbusiness.com/history2/2/Colgate-Palmolive-Company.html

preparation is a living, biochemical symphony. Sure you can segregate out the components of an orchestra into its violinists, violists, clarinetists, etc., but you can't change the fact that there is a whole that is greater than the sum of the parts. The very foundation of modern pharmacology is an attempt to negate this Natural Law. No orthodox clinician can appreciate this fact and stay true to their work. Russell Jordan, my mentor, (who has since passed on), spent an entire lifetime working in the trenches of the medical-industrial complex before coming to grips with this reality.

Going back to the review article, the text goes from one fragmentational study to another, one on the effects of sanguinarine on A431 epidermoid carcinoma; another showing that cell death is induced, one in the case of squamous cell carcinoma by apoptosis, in the case of keratinocytes, by necrosis; etc. The isolated effects of different herbal preparations used with escharotics, some of which we ourselves originated as the online pioneers of Black Salve beginning in 1995,[22] are then covered.

Next, the viability of Black Salve is questioned because of variances in the bio-active principles in various botanical substances. One study in particular is mentioned stating that "bloodroot rhizomes have been shown to have an up to fifteenfold variation in sanguinarine concentration."[23] No mention is made of the fact that herbal manufacturers can create their own systems of quality control to ensure that their end products exhibit consistent results. [As an aside, when I was learning the techniques used by various herbalists and shamans in the Amazon, I found it interesting that they use organoleptics (primarily appearance, taste, and smell) to decide what plants they were going to use. Orthodox clinicians will scoff at this, and yet, many of these same indigenous practitioners are hounded by foreigners who seek them out because they so frequently deliver better results than even the best conventional practitioners. You get a sense of

---

[22] See: www.altcancer.net/ashwin/ashw0712.htm

[23] Croaker et al., 2. Study is footnote #81. B.C. Bennett et al., "Geographic variation in alkaloid concent of *Sanguinaria canadensis*," 1990.

this if you see Nick Polizzi's documentary, *The Sacred Science*[24] (2011) or spend time on their website.[25] Watch Nick's documentary.[26]

Taking into account these various framentation exercises posing as officialdom's divinely-inspired decree, the authors issue their edict: "With a number of black salve constituents possessing in vitro normal cell cytotoxicity at low concentrations, health claims regarding black salve tumour specificity appear false." This is followed by a section entitled, "In vivo evidence of nonselectivity: histology," which findings are self-evident on the basis of the section's title. This, despite the fact that this runs counter to the empirical findings of thousands of naturopaths and alternative practitioners who are skilled in the escharotic art. This, despite the fact that I know of numerous practitioners in third world countries who use Black Salve as a diagnostic tool, something that would be impossible and make no sense whatsoever if Black Salves possessed no tumor cell specificity. This, despite the fact that it is evident on its face that Black Salve would never have achieved the popularity that it has if Black Salve possessed no specificity in its action,[27] which simply means that we're seeing more "reverse projection," because, by stark contrast with Black Salves which do not kill cells indiscriminately, chemotherapy really is an indiscriminate killer of cells.[28]

The review article then moves on to: "In vivo evidence of non-selectivity: Mohs Paste." I knew this was coming because, as I point out in Chapter 1 of *Meditopia*,[29] the add-on of a surgical process is essential to making escharotic use more profitable for Big Medicine. They need to bring in the apologists to explain this away. The truth is that if orthodox clinicians were ever, even for a moment, to admit that Black Salve was selective in its action, then they would automatically be admitting that Mohs sur-

---

[24] See: www.thesacredscience.com/screening.html

[25] See: www.thesacredscience.com/

[26] See: youtu.be/h-R2E5JiNVg

[27] Croaker, et al., 4.

[28] See: www.altcancer.net/with_chemo.htm

[29] See: www.meditopia.chap1.htm, or Chapter 4 in the current volume.

gery is a fraud. They cannot do that. Not now. Not ever.

They go on to say: "Using the fixed tissue method, Mohs 5-year cure rate, despite a complicated case load where 20% of patients had recurrent disease was 99.3% for BCC based on 7,257 cases and 94.4% for SCC based on 2,551 cases."[30] I'm not impressed. If you're a naturopath using a well-prepared escharotic and you cannot achieve percentages at least this good, then you're incompetent. The authors cite these figures so that people will think that the high success rate is attributable to the surgery. It's not. It's attributable to the escharotic. Attributing these success rates to the Mohs surgical component is just misdirection.

4. Is Black Salve effective at curing cancer?

The authors start out by stating that there are a mere "14 journal articles and abstracts that report the use of black salves derived from S. canadensis in 19 pathology confirmed skin cancers from 15 individuals." They continue, stating, "a number of Internet sites suggest that black salve can be used to treat melanoma effectively. The scientific literature does not support this claim."[31] Of course, it's not going to "support this claim."

I suppose that I should write the untold number of people who have used Black Salve that I have communicated with over the years and inform them that the melanoma they got rid of years ago is a myth. They're wrong. Their doctors are wrong. The pathologists who confirmed their cancer-free state are wrong. And why are they wrong? Because their cures fall outside the propagandistic boundaries of conventional, extant, scientific literature.

The authors continue by noting instances where patients are told that their use of Black Salve was unsuccessful, so conventional intervention was required. This is both predictable and, in my experience, routine. In one case, the patient dies of "metastatic BCC despite radical neck lymphadenectomy and adjuvant radiotherapy." The implication here is that the patient might be

[30] Croaker, et al., 4, citing footnote #88.
[31] Croaker, et al., 5.

alive today had they not used Black Salve. Is it possible that the patient could have died from the surgery and radiotherapy, both highly invasive? No, of course not. Let's not give that a second thought.

From there, the report boasts high rates of success for surgical intervention, something that contradicts what I see in my world. A huge percentage of our customers over the years have come to us as a result of metastasis following surgery. And why not? Physicians have known for 2,400 years that surgical intervention in treating cancer is inherently metastatic.[32]

The authors then emphasize that "without an understanding of skin cancer biology and behavior, unsuitable lesions can be selected by patients for black salve topical treatment, placing them at increased risk of recurrence and metastatic disease."[33] Just what is that risk? 2%? 5%? I'm only asking because when Black Salve is used properly, recurrence should be rare, and metastasis should be almost nonexistent. Seeing the results that I have seen over the past 28 years, you would think that I live in a completely different universe from that of the authors.

5. Does Black Salve cause less scarring than surgery?

The authors note that the filling in of the decavitation, which is a natural part of the escharotic process, takes place through "secondary intention" healing. Automatically, the assumption is made that this is inferior to post-surgical wound healing after the wound edges are placed in apposition.

This sounds logical, but, again, it does not comport with our experiences. I myself have treated 12 to 15 different malignant growths since 1989, depending on how you count them: under my eye, at the edge of my lips, right clavicle, left cheek, armpit, and back, in some places where there were multiple growths. In every case, there was minimal scarring and in most of those locations, you cannot even tell that the area was ever treated. I even posted pictures of my self-treatment at various locations

---

[32] See: www.altcancer.net/cutting.htm

[33] Croaker, et al., 6.

at the bottom of QuackWatch rebuttal page,[34] which I posted in 2009.

Because a large percentage of the people I work with have also had cancer growths surgically removed, they have a basis to make a comparison. What am I told? That in the vast majority of cases, the end result is less scarring and a more aesthetic appearance.

Does any of this make any difference in the orthodox world? Of course not. It hasn't received the imprimatur of medical authorities, nor has it gotten funding from a pharmaceutical company so that the results could be published in medical journal.

So, it couldn't possibly be true.

It's "anecdotal," a curse word to orthodox clinicians, principally because they can't control people's perceptions with fake information the way they can in stuffing medical journals with fake, self-serving, highly misleading, clinical data.

The authors also cite two cases where "the most extensive destruction however occurred with two female patients having the majority of their nose destroyed by black salve." There are two citations: #54 and #55. The latter involves a woman I know quite well named Sue Gilliatt, who admitted in a sworn deposition in July 2004, that she used a variety of different products to treat her nose, so she doesn't even know which one was responsible for damage. She also admits under oath that, in frustration, she removed her own nose with embroidery scissors, something I have to believe that most physicians would not recommend.

I go into considerable detail in Chapter 3 of *Meditopia*[35] as to just how fraudulent the Sue Gilliatt case is, wherein she and her doctors skillfully used the criminal justice system to get $800,000 in reparations out of my insurance company.

What the authors leave out of their paper is the fact that in a highly litigious environment, "patients" will work with the plaintiff lawyers to make their case look as troubling as possible. They are highly incentivized to do this because the finan-

---

[34] See: www.altcancer.net/docs/quack/eschar.htm
[35] See: www.meditopia.org/chap3-1.htm

cial stakes are high and the elements necessary to secure the sympathies of a jury are well established. Product liability cases involve far more histrionics than they do factual representation. Any defense attorney specializing in product liability cases will tell you that.

That said, let me tell what I know about escharotically derived decavitations that do not fill in completely, having worked with thousands of cases in 28 years -- either using one of my products, or somebody else's. First of all, they are quite rare. I can recall no more than eight cases. Most occur in one of the following locations: nose, cars, or breasts. I know of one case involving an ear (a customer we had in Canada), three cases involving the nose (and, for the sake of argument, I am including the case of Sue Gilliatt),and four cases involving the breast. In every one of these cases, the extent of the cancer growth was quite extensive, in terms of mass and area. In almost all of these cases, the doctor or doctors who were behind the original diagnosis recommended radical surgery to remove the affected part(s).

For those practicing the escharotic art, let me tell you what we recommend: if you're dealing with a large cancer over an extensive area, know that the growth should always be removed in stages. Never attempt to take the growth all out at one time -- unless the growth is life-threatening, and physicians have advised that the patient has a limited amount of time to live. By attacking a growth "in stages," there is sufficient cell memory to fill in the resulting decavitation completely. Instead of one significant "escharotic cycle," you have divided up the treatment to a series of "removal stages." One complete cycle is "shown" on our escharotic cycle page.[36]

I am personally aware of two extreme cases, and in both cases the physicians who did the diagnosis recommended surgical removal from the outset, requiring cosmetic surgery in the aftermath, where cosmetic surgery was required. In both cases, it involved the nose, and in both cases, the patient was satisfied with both the end result of the use of Black Salve, and the work

[36] See: www.altcancer.net/can2.htm

done by their respective cosmetic surgeons.

The authors then close with this damning indictment: "While portrayed as a cosmetically superior treatment to surgery, black salve's mechanism of action and suspected indiscriminate toxicity suggest this is not the case. Black salve has not spared a number of patients from requiring surgery to correct cosmetic damage or treat persisting malignancy." There are two issues here: cosmetic damage and persisting malignancy. As to "cosmetic damage," in my personal experience, this is very rare. A handful out of thousands of cases. As to "persisting malignancy," this is even more rare. I *am* aware of the following unfortunate case. A man had a persistent SCC[37] that covered a very large area of his right arm. The doctors recommended the amputation of the arm. We worked with this individual for several months, and although progress was made, the cancer grew faster than Black Salve could remove the cancer. In the end, the arm was amputated, as per the recommendation of the original physicians. It is the only such case that I have encountered in my many years of working with escharotics.

6. Discussion:

The authors start off by attacking the Internet as an unregulated space where "there is the potential for inaccurate or misleading claims to result in choices leading to harmful health outcomes." This might be one of the few areas in which I agree with the authors' assessment. As I have previously written in my Ashwin blog,[38] there are "bullshitters" in both the field of conventional and alternative medicine. However, only in conventional medicine has unending "bullshit" (I'm using Harry Frankfurt's definition for the term) been so thoroughly institutionalized, standardized, and made acceptable. When I hear conventional doctors talk about unreliable information on the Internet, I do not disagree with them. But I cannot help but take note of the "reverse projection."

I maintain that if you took out the fake, fraudulent, and

[37] Squamous cell carcinoma.

[38] See: www.altcancer.net/ashwin/ashw0517.htm

rigged peer-reviewed studies, there would be very little to publish. Most medical journals would have to go out of business. As far back as November 2010, *The Atlantic* put out an article, entitled "Lies, Damned Lies, and Medical Science,"[39] which opens with Greek hospitals duping immigrants by diagnosing them with appendicitis that they don't have, and moves on to other areas of official jaw-dropping fraud. The article's highlighted biostatistician, George Salanti, found after years of subsequent investigation that "as much as 90 percent of the published medical information that doctors rely on is flawed."

Hmmm, 90% -- that's kind of high, isn't it?

Is that why 90% of the information provided in this article review doesn't comport with my professional experience? Is there a correlation there?

Fake studies in the medical field are now so prolific that according to a Guardian article published in August 2015, retractions in academic journals have gone up more than 10 times,[40] and keep in mind that medical journals have no built-in financial incentive to annoy their contributors by retracting their submissions or implying that they're flawed. All of this has lead to a deep mistrust in official medical research and the articles that come out of them. It even lead Curt Rice to write an article in February 2013, entitled, "Why you can't trust research: 3 problems with the quality of science,"[41] in which he concludes, "We have a system for communicating results in which the need for retraction is exploding, the replicability of research is diminishing, and the most standard measure of journal quality is becoming a farce." Although the article states that "ranking journals" are the problem, and that the system is so broken that "it should be abandoned," I suspect that something deeper is afoot.

Truth just doesn't matter anymore.

Like telling people that Black Salve isn't a natural product,

[39] See: www.theatlantic.com/magazine/archive/2010/11/lies-damned-lies-and-medical-science/308269/

[40] See: www.theguardian.com/science/2015/aug/22/can-we-trust-science-academic-journal-peer-review-retraction-

[41] See: curt-rice.com/2013/02/06/why-you-cant-trust-research-3-problems-with-the-quality-of-science/

when it is.

Like telling people that Black Salve is indiscriminate in its action, when anyone who has experience with well-crafted escharotics knows this is patently false.

Like telling people or suggesting that Black Salve produces more scarring than surgery, etc., when it is the overwhelming collective experience of those who have experienced both that this is patently untrue.

The authors continue with a celebration of the success of the highly profitable Mohs procedure, followed by a statement that is so breathtakingly inane that I had to read it twice to confirm what I'd read: "Substituting **highly effective conventional therapies** with an unproven alternative such as black salve should not occur outside the framework of a clinical trial." [emphasis added][42] Can we make that clinical trial fraudulent, too, just so we're consistent?

Earlier in their review article, the authors acknowledged that people were flocking to alternative medicine and the Internet in record numbers (presumably in connection with cancer, the subject of the review article.)

Is there anybody with an IQ above mid-double-digits who would believe that people would do this if conventional therapies, most of which are paid for by the government and insurance companies, rather than the patient, were highly effective?

From this point, the authors segue into lamenting the availability of black salve, going so far as to cry over individuals making their own. (How dare people ever have the right to prepare their own health product for their personal use.) The unquestionable "takeaway" from this one section is that Black Salve should be banned at all cost.

When you read between the lines, there is no other way to interpret what the authors are recommending.

Conclusion: More studies are needed. Yes. Always more studies. They're very profitable, you know! If you don't believe

---

[42] Croaker, et al., 7.

that Black Salve has been studied to death, go ahead and read Chapter 2 of *Meditopia*.[43] Sixteen years ago, I wrote an essay entitled, "Impossible Dream: Why the Cancer Industry is Committed to Not Finding a Cure, and If They Do Run Across One, Suppressing It!"[44] If you think that there is anything about this article that is "fair and balanced," read that essay.

7. Competing Interests.

This entire section, resting just above the Reference section, is just one sentence long: "The authors declare that they have no conflicts of interest."

And with that little jewel, I rest my case as it relates to their "review article."

I might close on that note, except that I am unnerved by the tone and obvious recommendation of the article, as much or more so as Dr. Oz's recommendation to have all Black Salve banned.

The problem in our time is that the general public has become so oblivious to the machinations of authority and so immersed in the prevailing "hive mentality," that with enough effort, authorities can ban almost anything.

With enough effort, you can get anything banned. You can get ordinary plants banned (i.e. marijuana). You can get Black Salve banned. Hell, you can get people to agree to ban or highly regulate *water*.

Back in 2006, Penn & Teller did a social experiment where they got everyday citizens to sign a petition, banning water. Yes, banning water.[45] Now, granted, they used the term "dihydrogen monoxide" (H_2O), but even if you flunked high school chemistry, would you be gullible enough to sign a petition to ban water? Before signing such a petition, might it seem reasonable to ask just what "dihydrogen monoxide" is?

If you think this is an anomaly, Alex Jones did the same

---

[43] See: www.meditopia.org/chap2.htm, or Chapter 5 in the current volume.

[44] See: www.altcancer.net/lysis5.htm, relates to Chapter 16 in the current volume.

[45] See: youtu.be/yi3erdgVVTw

social experiment ten years later and got the very same result.[46]

Question: If you can find people who are stupid enough to sign a petition to ban water, how much easier would it be to get people to sign a petition banning Black Salve?

It scares me to contemplate the answer to my own question.

That is why it is more important than ever for people to stand up for their own sovereignty and speak the truth. Because if you don't, you get people who will read review articles by those advancing the tyranny of medical authorities. But even worse, you'll get people who just might be gullible enough to believe them.

---

[46] See: youtu.be/zfTUklMF9Wg

Part IV:

All Things Return
to Source

Chapter 30:

To Know the Place
For the First Time

"We now live in a global community where
Doctors destroy health,
Lawyers destroy justice,
Universities destroy knowledge,
Governments destroy freedom,
The press destroys information,
Religion destroys morals,
And our banks destroy the economy."

Chris Hedges[1]
Paraphrased

"We shall not cease in our explorations
And at the end of all our exploring
Will be to arrive where we started
And to know the place for the first time."

T.S. Eliot
Four Quartets (Little Gidding)[2]

It is a weighty thing to come to the conclusion that there is no element of your culture – in this case, our Western global culture – that isn't infected with mean-spirited exploitation, intractable corruption, all-pervasive "bullshit," and the celebratory elevation in status of all things fake, fabricated, tawdry, and irrelevant. If we could cordon off the limits of this infection, its effects might not be so disconcerting, but we cannot.

[1] See: https://www.goodreads.com/quotes/825055-we-now-live-in-a-nation-where-doctors destroy-health. I say "paraphrased" because the original quote has "nation" instead of "global community." The severity of the problems and inherent contradictions in this quote may vary from nation to nation, but they are still pervasive on a global scale.
[2] T.S. Eliot, The Complete Poems and Plays, (New York: Harcourt, Brace & World, Inc., 1952),145

Incapable of confining itself to the boundaries of its own autolysis, Western Civilization seeks to extend its decomposition to "all four corners" and ensure the disintegration of the rest of the planet's ecosystems.

Ours is a world comparable to an apple in which there is no place one can take a bite without getting a mouthful of worm. Without a dramatic course correction, these preconditions carry with them equally weighty consequences, nearly all of them dire.

We live on a planet managed by apex predators – collectively, "that's us" – who have, either proactively or through indifference, acted as if they're on a kamikaze mission to make their planet sanitized and completely lifeless in order to terraform it for another purpose.

I did not come to these conclusions with haste, but rather over many years of study and reflection. In fact, these same themes appear prominently in my previous two books.[3]

In a world teeming with evidence of intelligent design, so ubiquitous that I wonder why the public would ever contemplate the converse from lesser intellects, the current state of our world begs us to assign a purpose. Why would any Creator allow any corner of His universe and the supposed object of his affection to fall into such morbid disrepair? It would be easy enough to fall back on the despair of Marcion and assume that "the god who created our cosmos couldn't possibly be good."[4] But I see a deeper significance to our present decrescence.[5]

If I've learned anything at all from the many hundreds of entheogenic journeys I've taken, it is that the search for the divine, for the highest knowledge that men are capable of acquir-

---

[3] Greg Caton, The Joys of Psychopathocracy (Miami: Herbologics, Ltd., 2017) and The Gospel of 2012 According to Ayahuasca (Miami: Herbologics, Ltd., 2012)

[4] We covered the thoughts of Marcion in the book review section of Chapter 7 above in discussing The Lucifer Principle.

[5] Similar thoughts, perhaps not as well-developed, are covered in Greg Caton, The Gospel of 2012 According to Ayahuasca (2012).

ing, is an arduous, painstaking one. If a soul is to attain to a divine consciousness, it must first travel the ends of the universe to fully attain to a conscious awareness of all that is ***not*** divine.

To fully appreciate the light, you must comprehend the darkness, and the myriad combinations of shadows that their interplay produces. The farther back the archer draws the bowstring, the farther the arrow is projected in the opposite direction. In this the mettle of the soul is tested and its character forged.

Any athlete knows that greater performance lies in discipline and a willingness to put the body through greater challenges. As painful as it is, particularly if you're a "sensitive" to begin with, to live in a world that is seemingly bereft of divine goodness, therein lies our redemption. We have collectively circumnavigated the multiverse, going from union with the divine to the far depths of hell, and now we have the opportunity to see our way home. And truly, this world, now, in this moment, at this juncture of its history, really is hell.

But dramatic course corrections, even when the state of the world is as seemingly hopeless as it is now, are possible. In fact, they appear to be "baked" into the design of things.

In late October 2016, I had a San Pedro journey,[6] which lasted for about 12 hours. During this vision quest, I saw our current global civilization and its inhabitants on a train, headed for unspeakable calamity. Suddenly, at the last moment, the tracks were switched taking the train in a much more positive direction. I pondered the significance of this for quite some time, and might have disregarded the vision were it not for the fact that many of the things revealed actually occurred within the weeks and months that followed.[7]

---

[6] Next to ayahuasca and psilocybin mushrooms, San Pedro cactus (L. Echinopsis pachanoi) is probably the next most popular entheogenic for divination purposes here in Ecuador.

[7] As it turns out, the U.S. Presidential election occurred just 10 days later. So, by way of example, I was "told" that although the results and its aftermath would be contentious, Donald Trump, for all his obvious faults and narcissistic tendencies, would win. Conversely, on a parallel universe, I saw a "timeline" with Hillary as President, with the U.S. convulsing in the throws of World War III by no later than early 2018. Strangely, I saw Trump, completely ignorant of "higher influences" going on around him, being shepherded into office as a result of "outside influences." It just so happens that none of these significant influences has anything to

It would seem that Natural Law, itself, dictates that something truly climactic is afoot. It is not by accident that our greatest euphoria in the arts comes from stories where darkness prevails and all seems hopeless, then suddenly, as if by magic, the forces of good prevail and negativity is subdued. This is not how the story begins. It is how it ends. And then a new cycle begins.

I won't go into all the astonishing correlations I've found in those who have shared their subconscious revelations about "a coming Event," a true climactic ending to our current tale, because I do so exhaustively in previous works.[8] However, by all accounts, this coming Event involves a dramatic shift in consciousness. It truly means an end to all our exploring, the arrival to the point in Creation where we started, and a knowing of "the place for the first time."

Through the portal of all that is not divine, we will come to know and appreciate the divine. The true love, bliss, and fulfillment which is the sum and substance that gave birth to creation to begin with – an "article of faith" on the part of every experienced psychonaut through his or her own direct experience and cognition.

In this all things will be made clear, and in retrospect, we will see why everything unfolded exactly as it had to.

We will understand that it could not have unfolded in any other way.

In this we will know our true divine heritage.

Life as we know it was meant to be lived.

Life as we know we were meant to live it.

---

do with Russia, or any other terrestrial state government. Additionally, I was shown that misdeeds of the Elite at the pinnacle of power would begin to filter out to the public, adding to a growing awareness about the true nature of those in authority. With ongoing revelations about Pizzagate, pedophilia rings in high places, and the Satanic, ritual sacrifices of small children, this vision has already been made manifest.

[8] Greg Caton, The Joys of Psychopathocracy, (Miami: Herbologics, Ltd., 2017), Chapters 8 and 9; see also Greg Caton, The Gospel of 2012 According to Ayahuasca, (Miami: Herbologics, Ltd., 2012)

Chapter 29

Glossary

The vast majority of the terms used in this book are commonly understood, defined in the text or via external link, usually the former. The terms below, however, have unique applications or nuances for which this Glossary has been prepared.

Alpha Omega Labs: One of the "DBA's" for Herbologics, Ltd., an herbal company established by the author in 1992 in Louisiana that has been in continuous operation since. The company operates multiple websites.[1]

antiscorbutic: Literally, efficacious against scurvy, as the term was created long before the discovery of Vitamin C. The term now most often refers to foods or natural sources for ascorbic acid.

Ashwin, The: An online "blog" created in October, 2001, by the author. It has had postings at irregular intervals since that time, excepting two periods of incarceration at the hands of the U.S. FDA.[2] His FDA issues are covered in exhaustive detail in Chapter 3 of the original Meditopia draft.[3]

Barlow's disease: May refer to mitral valve prolapse, as the term references two distinct medical conditions. For the purposes of this volume, it refers strictly to infantile scurvy, which was later shown to be the same condition as adult scurvy.

Bruner/Postman experiments: Also known as the "red playing card" experiments, conducted in 1949.[4] These experiments resulted in a paper which is a classic in the field of psychology, "On the perception of incongruity: a paradigm." They deal with the nature of selective perception. Details are provided in Chapter 6.

black salve: See "Cansema."

Cansema®: A U.S. registered trademark of Herbologics, Ltd., which the author founded in 1992. The word has become synonymous with "Black Salve," or topical escharotic preparations with a long history of safe, effective use in the removal of basal and squamous cell carcinomas, melanoma, and related malignancies in the skin (i.e. skin cancers). This is covered in Chapters 4 and 5 of the current volume.

---

[1] See: www.altcancer.net/order_instruct.htm

[2] See: www.altcancer.net/ashwin/

[3] This matter is covered exhaustively online, beginning at: www.meditopia.org/chap3-1.htm

[4] See: psychclassics.yorku.ca/Bruner/Cards/

endosomatic: A thing or resource found within the body of an organism or accessible within same. The antonym is "exosomatic," which is a thing or resource found outside the body of an organism. These terms play prominently in Chapter 10 of the current volume.

exosomatic: See "endosomatic."

Godel's Incompleteness Theorem: There are actually a set of principles incorporated into Godel's Incomplete Theorem, now a basic concept in mathematical logic. The theorem is mentioned in passing in Chapter 6. Fundamentally, the theorem states that if a mathematical formula is logically valid, then there is a finite deduction of the formula.[5]

Gresham's Law: Stated in its simplest terms, "bad money drives out good." It's a basic observation in finance and economics with applications to other disciplines.[6]

Hegelian model: (problem / reaction / solution) – this is a limited application of Hegel's dialectic and is a term used to describe the method by which a governed people or cohort can be led to agree to actions that are against their own interests.[7]

Holocene extinction: Also referred to as the "sixth extinction" or "Anthropocene extinction." This is a reference to the current, ongoing extinction event occurring in the present Holocene epoch.[8]

hypoascorbemia: Vitamin C (ascorbic acid) deficiency insufficient to cause scurvy, but sufficient to support other subclinical medical conditions. The observation, first articulated by Dr. Irwin Stone, is discussed extensively in Chapter 6 of the current volume.

I Ching: Also known as the "Book of Changes," the I Ching is the oldest of the known, ancient, Chinese philosophical texts.[9]

iatrogenesis: (from the Greek, meaning "brought forth from the healer"). The term traditionally means the effects brought about a health care professional that oppose the objective(s) of the patient, or person being treated. This is increasingly seen as a euphemistic, such that the word in everyday usage increasingly refers to doctor screw-ups or even death brought about by

---

[5] See: plato.stanford.edu/entries/goedel-incompleteness/
[6] See: www.britannica.com/topic/Greshams-law
[7] See: www.bibliotecapleyades.net/biggestsecret/esp_icke22.htm
[8] See: en.wikipedia.org/wiki/Holocene_extinction
[9] See: en.wikipedia.org/wiki/I_Ching

medical incompetency.

Interpol: "International Criminal Police Organization" is an international organization with worldwide affiliates which coordinates international police cooperation. Interpol plays prominently in the false prosecution of the author.[10]which is detailed at: http://www.meditopia.org/chap3-3.htm

Meditopia®: An online book that the author began in June, 2004, using the domain, meditopia.org. For yearly 14 years additions and changes were made to this book, which is still online. Numerous corrections have been made to the book, which, prior to the publication of Living on the Precipice, had no parts of it ever put into print. The best parts of this work have been incorporated into the current work.

Peak Oil: The theory, first expounded by M. King Hubbert, that a point would be reached when the maximum rate of petroleum could be extracted, after which there would be a terminal decline.[11]

Quackpot Watch: an effort by alternative practitioner, Tim Bolen, to expose the political and economic agenda of the Quackwatch organization. [12] See Quackwatch entry.

Quackwatch: a disreputable network of affiliates and websites (21 as of this writing), founded by a Dr. Stephen Barrett in 1996 and funded by pharmaceutical interests. (Its principal English-speaking website is quackwatch. org.) Although its ostensible purpose and mission statement is to "combat health-related frauds, myths, fads, fallacies, and misconduct," it actually serves to mislead the public as to healing practices, products, and practitioners in the alternative community, particularly those which are efficacious, while glorifying orthodox treatments through omission. The site, therefore, works to redefine what constitutes quackery as that which does not provide allegiance to the medical-industrial complex or revenue to any of its stakeholders.

---

[10] Detailed at: www.meditopia.org/chap3-3.htm
[11] See: en.wikipedia.org/wiki/Peak_oil
[12] See: www.quackpotwatch.org/

Living on the Precipice

Bibliography

The bibliography below contains the complete list of published books referenced in this work. Since the newer book cataloging software programs often make searching easier using ISBN numbers, either the 10 or 13 ISBN number is provided, where available.

Abramson, John, M.D. Overdosed America: The Broken Promise of American Medicine. New York: HarperCollins Publishers, Inc., 2005. ISBN: 0060568534.

Ackerknecht, Erwin H., M.D. A Short History of Medicine. Baltimore: The John Hopkins University Press, 1982. ISBN: 0801827264.

Adams, Richard Newbold. Energy and Structure: a Theory of Social Power. Austin: University of Texas Press, 1975. ISBN: 0292720122.

Alford, C. Fred. Whistleblowers: Broken Lives and Organizational Power. Ithaca, New York: Cornell University Press, 2001. ISBN: 0801487803.

Allan, D.S., J.B. Delair. Cataclysm! Compelling Evidence of a Cosmic Catastrophe in 9500 B.C. Rochester, Vermont: Bear & Company, 1997. ISBN: 1879181428.

Ausubel, Kenny. When Healing Becomes a Crime: The Amazing Story of the Hoxsey Cancer Clinics and the Return of Alternative Therapies. Rochester, Vermont: Healing Arts Press, 2000. Most recent ISBN: 0892819251.

Axelrod, Robert. The Complexity of Cooperation. Princeton University Press, Princeton, NJ, 1997. ISBN: 0691015678.

Axelrod, Robert. The Evolution of Cooperation. Perseus Publishing New York, 2006. ISBN: 0465005640.

Backster, Cleve. Primary Perception: Biocommunication with Plants, Living Foods, and Human Cells. Anza, California: White Rose Millenium Press, 2003. ISBN: 0966435435.

Barzun, Jacques. From Dawn to Decadence (1500 to the Present): 500 Years of Western Cultural Life. New York: HarperCollins Publishers, 2000. ISBN: 0060175869.

Bauman, Zygmunt; Modernity and the Holocaust. Ithaca, New York: Cornell University Press, 1989. ISBN: 0745606857.

Becker, Robert O., M.D., and Gary Selden. The Body Electric, New York: William Morrow and Company, 1985. ISBN: 0688069711.

Becker, Robert O., M.D. Cross Currents: The Perils of Electropollution, The Promise of Electromedicine. Los Angeles: Jeremy P. Tarcher, Inc., 1990. ISBN: 0874775361.

Berman, Morris. The Twilight of American Culture. New York: W.W. Norton, 2000. ISBN: 039332169X.

Berman, Morris. Dark Ages America. New York: W.W. Norton, 2006. ISBN: 0393058662.

Bernays, Edward. Propaganda. New York: Ig Publishing, 2005. ISBN:

2004016015.

Bian, Tonda R.. The Drug Lords: America's Pharmaceutical Cartel. Kalamazoo, Michigan: No Barriers Publishing, 1997. ISBN: 0965456803.

The Bible, Authorized King James Version. containing the Old and New Testaments translated out of the original tongues: and with the former translations diligently compared and revised, by His Majesty's special command, Zondervan Bible Publishers, Grand Rapids, MI; hardbound: 918 pages; 1983.

Blake, T.T. Cancers Cured Without the Use of the Knife. New York: J. J. Reed, 1858.

Bloom, Howard. The Lucifer Principle: A Scientific Expedition into the Forces of History. New York: The Atlantic Monthly Press, 1995. ISBN: 0871135329.

Blum, William. Rogue State: A Guide to the World's Only Superpower Monroe, Maine: Common Courage Press, 2000. (ISBN for newest (3rd Edition, 2005) version: 1567513743.)

Borjesson, Kristina, ed. Into the Buzzsaw: Leading Journalists Expose the Myth of a Free Press. New York: Prometheus Books, 2004. ISBN: 1591022304.

Bown, Stephen R. Scurvy: How a Surgeon, a Mariner, and a Gentleman Solved the Greatest Medical Mystery of the Age of Sail. New York: Thomas Dunne Books / St. Martin's Press, 2003. ISBN: 0312313918.

Braden, Gregg. Secrets of the Lost Mode of Prayer: The Hidden Power of Beauty, Blessings, Wisdom, and Hurt. Carlsbad, California: Hay House, 2005. ISBN: 1401906834.

Brown, Courney. Cosmic Explorers. New York: New American Library, 1999. Most recent ISBN: 0451201051.

Browne, Harry. Why Government Doesn't Work. New York: St. Martin's Press, 1995. ISBN: 0965603601.

Buck, Albert H. The Growth of Medicine from the Earliest Times to About 1800. Kessinger Publishing (re-print of original published by Yale University Press, 1917). ISBN: 0766196054.

Bucke, Richard Maurice, M.D, Cosmic Consciousness: A Study in theEvolution of the Human Mind. Philadelphia, Pennsylvania: Innes & Sons, 1901. ISBN: 0525472452.

Byden, S.V., ed. The Impact of Civilization on the Biology of Man. Canberra, Australia: National University Press, 1970. ISBN: 0802017282.

Cameron, Ewan and Linus Pauling. Cancer and Vitamin C. New York: W.W. Norton and Co., 1979. ISBN: 0393500004

Campbell, C.J. The Coming Oil Crisis. Brentwood, Essex, England: Multi-Science Publishing Company & Petroconsultants, S.A., 1997, updated 2004 edition: 0906522110).

Campbell, Joseph. Myths to Live By. New York: Penguin Group, 1972. (ISBN: 0140194614; Peguin classic edition).

Carpenter, Kenneth J. The History of Scurvy & Vitamin C. Cambridge

University Press, Cambridge; 1986. ISBN: 0521347734.

Carr, Anthony. Cheiro: Prophet of the End Times. Toronto, Canada: Carrino Publishing, 2002. (ISBN: 0973222204).

Carter, James P., M.D., Dr. P.H. Racketeering in Medicine. Norfolk, Virginia: Hampton Roads Publishing Company, 1992. ISBN: 187890132X.

Carter, Mary Ellen. Hugh Lynn Cayce. ed. Edgar Cayce on Prophecy. taken from Edgar Cayce, Modern Prophet, Four Complete Books. New York: Gramercy Books, 1990. ISBN: 0446351962.

Caton, G.J. Lumen: Food For A New Age. Lake Charles, Louisiana: Calcasieu Graphics & Pressworks, 1986. ISBN: 0939955008.

Caton, Greg. MLM Fraud: A Practical Handbook for the Network Marketing Professional. Self-published, 1990. ISBN: 0939955032. Ordered removed from the market by court order, plus gag order -- plus to an astonishing $133,000,000.00 judgement against the author (defendant), under the pretense that the author's (defendant's) deposition responses were incomplete (1996).

Caton, Greg. The Gospel of 2012 According to Ayahuasca: The End of Faith and the Beginning of Knowingness. Miami, Florida: Herbologics, Ltd., 2012. ISBN: 978-0939955091.

Caton, Greg. The Joys of Psychopathocracy: Why Criminality Is Essential To Effective Modern Government, Our Rebirth In The Wake of Their Destruction of Our World. Miami, Florida: Herbologics, Ltd., 2017. ISBN: 0939955016.

Caton, Hiram. The Politics of Progress: The Origins and Development of the Commercial Republic, 1600-1835. Gainesville, Florida: University of Florida Press, 1988. ISBN: 0813008476.

Catton, Jr., William R. Overshoot: The Ecological Basis of Revolutionary Change. Champaign, Illinois: University of Illinois Press, 1980. (ISBN: 0252009886).

Cheraskin, Dr. Emanuel, M.D., D.M.D. The Vitamin Controversy: Questions & Answers. Wichita, Kansas: Bio-Communications Press, 1988. ISBN: 0942333012.

Cheraskin, Dr. Emanuel, W.M, Ringsdorf and Emily L. Sisley. The Vitamin C Connection: Getting well and staying well with Vitamin C. New York: Harper & Row, 1983. ISBN: 0060380241.

Chomsky, Noam. Rogue States: The Rule of Force in World Affairs. Boston, Massachusetts: South End Press, 2000. ISBN: 0896086119.

Chomsky, Noam. 9-11. New York: Seven Stories Press, 2001. ISBN: 1583224890.

Chomsky, Noam. Manufacturing Consent: The Political Economy of the Mass Media. New York: Pantheon Books, 2002. ISBN: 0375714499.

Chomsky, Noam. Media Control: The Spectacular Achievements of Propaganda. New York: Seven Stories Press, 2002. Originally published in 1997, the material in the book became more relevant after '9/11' -- though

Chomsky refuses to go so far as to admit what most savvy observers and masters of common sense have already figured out: that "9/11" was an inside job. ISBN: 1583225361.

Chomsky, Noam. Hegemony or Survival. New York: Metropolitan Books/ Henry Holt, 2003. ISBN: 0805076883.

Cichoke, Anthony J., D.C., Ph.D. Secrets of Native American Herbal Remedies, A Comprehensive Guide to the Native American Tradition of Using Herbs and the Mind/Body/Spirit Connection for Improving Health and Well-Being, New York: Avery/Penguin Putnam, Inc., 2001. ISBN: 158333100X.

Cipolla, Carlo M.. The Economic History of World Population, 6th ed. Baltimore, Maryland; Penguin Books, Inc., 1974. (ISBN: 0064911381).

Cockburn, William. Sea diseases: or, a treatise of their nature, causes, and cure. Also an essay on bleeding in fevers; 3rd ed. Farmington Hills, Michigan: Gale Ecco, 2010. ISBN: 1140886061.

Collins, Phillip Darrell and Paul David Collins. The Ascendancy of the Scientific Dictatorship: An Examination of Epistemic Autocracy, From the19th to the 21st Century. Charleston, South Carolina: BookSurge Publishing, 2006. ASIN: B01N9LKDZQ.

Constantine, Alex. Psychic Dictatorship in the U.S.A. Port Townsend, Washington: Feral House, 1995. ISBN: 0922915288.

Constantine, Alex. Virtual Government: CIA Mind Control Operations in America. Port Townsend Washington: Feral House, 1997.

Constantine, Alex. The Covert War Against Rock. Port Townsend, Washington: Feral House, 2000. ISBN: 092291561X.

Cooper, William. Behold a Pale Horse. Sedona, Arizona: Light Technology Publishing, 1991. ISBN: 0929385225.

Cremo, Michael A., Richard L. Thompson. Forbidden Archeology. Nadia, West Bengal: Torchlight Publishing, 1998. ISBN: 0892132949.

Cremo, Michael A., Richard L. Thompson. The Hidden History of the Human Race. Nadia, West Bengal: Torchlight Publishing, 1999. (ISBN: 0892133252).

Crick, Francis. Life Itself: Its Origin and Nature. New York: Simon & Schuster, 1981. ISBN: 0671255630.

Crile, George, Jr., M.D. Cancer and Common Sense, New York: Viking Press, 1955.

Dawkins, Richard. The Selfish Gene. 30th anniversary ed. Oxford, England: Oxford University Press, 2006. ISBN: 0199291152.

Deffeyes, Kenneth S. Hubbert's Peak: The Impending World Oil Shortage. Princeton, New Jersey: Princeton University Press, 2001. ISBN: 0691116253.

DeMeo, James, Ph.D. The Orgone Accumulator Handbook. Ashland, Oregon: Natural Energy Works, 1999. ISBN: 0962185507.

Denevan, William M. The Native Population of the Americas in 1492. Madison, Wisconsin: The University of Wisconsin Press, 1976. ISBN:

0299134342.

Dermer, Gerald B. The Immortal Cell. Garden City Park, New York; Avery Publishing Group, Inc., 1994. ISBN: 0895295822.

Desalvo, John A. The Complete Pyramid Sourcebook. Great Pyramid of Giza Research Association, 2003. ISBN: 1410780422.

Desborough, Brian. They Cast No Shadows: A Collection of Essays on the Illuminati, Revisionist History, and Suppressed Technologies, San Jose, California:Writers Club Press, 2002. ISBN: 0595219578.

Diamond, Stanley. In Search of the Primitive: A Critique of Civilization. New Brusnwick, New Jersey: Transaction Publishers, 1981. ISBN: 087855582X.

Donnelly, Ignatius. Ragnarok: The Age of Fire and Gravel. Fairford, United Kingdom: Echo Library, 2007. ISBN: 1406840246. (originally published in 1894).

Dossey, Larry. Healing Words: The Power of Prayer and the Practice of Medicine. New York: Harper Collins Publishers, 1997. ISBN: 0061043834.

Dreyfus, Jack. A Remarkable Medicine Has Been Overlooked. New York: Continuum Publishing, 1997. ISBN: 0826410693.

Drosnin, Michael. Bible Code II: The Countdown. New York: Penguin Books, 2003. ISBN: 0142003506.

Dubos, René J. Man Adapting. New Haven: Connecticut: Yale University Press, 1965. ISBN: 0300004370.

Dubos, René J. A God Within. New York: Charles Scribner's Sons, 1972. ASIN: B000E1EO8Y.

Dubos, René J. Louis Pasteur: Free Lance of Science. New York: Da Capo Press, Inc., 1986. ISBN: 0306802627.

Dubos, René J. Mirage of Health: Utopias, Progress, and Biological Change. New Brunswick, New Jersey: Rutgers University Press, 1996. First published in 1959 by Harper & Brothers, New York. ISBN: 0813512603.

Dyer, Joel. The Perpetual Prisoner Machine: How America Profits from Crime. Boulder, Colorado: Westview Press, 2000. ISBN: 0813335078.

Easton, David. A Framework for Political Analysis. Englewood Cliffs, New Jersey: Prentice-Hall, 1965. ISBN: 0226180158.

Eco, Robert. The Name of the Rose. Boston, Massachusetts: Mariner Books, 2014. ISBN: 0544176561.

Eisen, Jonathan. Supressed Inventions & Other Discoveries. New York: Berkley Publishing Group, 1999. ISBN: 0399527354.

Eliade, Mircea. Shamanism: Archaic Techniques of Ecstasy. Princeton, New Jersey: Princeton University Press, 1972. ISBN: 0691017794

Eliot, T.S. The Complete Poems and Plays. New York: Harcourt, Brace & World, 1952. ISBN: LCC Number: 52-11346

Encyclopaedia Brittanica, s.v. "The Great Books of the Western World." Volume 39 (of 54). An Inquiry into the Nature and Causes of the Wealth of Nations, Adam Smith. Chicago, Illinois, Encyclopaedia Britannica, Inc.,

1952. ISBN: 0852295316

Epperson, Ralph. The Unseen Hand: An Introduction to the Conspiratorial View of History. Tucson, Arizona: Publius Press, 1985. ISBN: 0961413506.

Epperson, Ralph. New World Order. Tucson, Arizona: Publius Press, 1990. ISBN: 0961413514.

Epstein, Samuel. The Politics of Cancer - Revisited. Fremont Center, New York: East Ridge Press, 1998. ISBN: 0914896474.

Farrow, Ruth T. Odyssey of an American cancer specialist of a hundred years ago. Baltimore, Maryland: Johns Hopkins University Press, 1949. ASIN: B0007HF4T8.

Farly, Fred. Royal R. Rife: Humanitarian, Betrayed and Persecuted. Spring Valley, California: R.T. Plasma Publishing, 2001. ISBN: 0965961311.

Fell, J.Weldon. A Treatise on Cancer. London: John Churchill, 1857. ASIN: B0006AF5GI.

Feuer, Elaine. Innocent Casualties: The FDA's War Against Humanity. Pittsburgh, Pennsylvania: Dorrance Publishing Co., 1996. ISBN: 0805938192.

Fiennes, Ranulph. Captain Scott. London: Coronet Books, 2004. ISBN: 0340826991.

Firestone, Richard, Allen West and Simon Warwick-Smith. The Cycle of Cosmic Catastrophes: Flood, Fire, and Famine in the History of Civilization, Rochester, Vermont: Bear & Company, 2006. ISBN: 1591430615.

Fishbein, Morris. Fishbein's Illustrated Medical and Health Encyclopedia. Westport, Connecticut: H.S. Stuttman, Inc., 1981. ISBN: 0874752000.

Friedman, Milton and Rose D. Friedman. Free to Choose, New York: Harcourt Brace and Company, 1979. ASIN: B000N55A48.

Forte, Robert ed. Entheogens and the Future of Religion. San Francisco, California: Pine Forge Press, 2000. ISBN: 1889725048.

Frankfurt, Harry G. On Bullshit. Princeton, New Jersey: Princeton University Press, 2005. ISBN: 0691122946.

Frankl, Victor. Man's Search for Meaning: An Introduction to Logotheraphy, New York: Pocket Books, 1971. ISBN: 0671781383.

Fraser, Sheila Snow and Carroll Allen. Essiac, Buffalo, New York: New Action Products. (No publication date provided).

Frazier, Claude A., M.D. Faith Healing: Finger of God? or Scientific Curiosity?. New York: Thomas Nelson, Inc., 1973. ASIN: B0006C94AY.

Gallert, Mark L. New Light on Therapeutic Energies. London: James Clarke & Co., Ltd., 1966. ISBN: 0718890086.

Garrett, Laurie. The Coming Plague: Newly Emerging Disease in a World Out of Balance. New York: Farrar, Straus and Giroux, 1994. (Reprint edition, ISBN: 0140250913).

Garrett, Laurie. Betrayal of Trust: The Collapse of Global Public Health. New York: Hyperion, 2000. ISBN: 0786884401.

Garrison, Fielding H., A.B., M.D. An Introduction to the History of Medicine. Philadelphia, Pennsylvania: W.B. Saunders Company, 1929. (Amazon notes earlier 1914 edition). ASIN: B0008901BC.

Gelbspan, Ross. The Heat is On: The Climate Crisis, The Cover-Up, and The Prescription. Cambridge, Massachusetts: Perseus Books, 1998. ISBN: 0738200255.

Ghadiali, Dinshah. Spectro-Chrome-Metry Encyclopedia. 4th ed. Malaga, New Jersey: Dinshah Health Society, 1997. ISBN: 0933917163.

Gifford, Eli and R. Michael Cook. How Can One Sell The Air?. Summertown, Tennessee: Natives Voices, 2005. ISBN: 1570671737.

Gleick, James. Chaos: Making A New Science. New York: Penguin Books, 1988. ISBN: 0140092501.

Goodman, Sandra, Ph.D. Vitamin C: The Master Nutrient. New Canaan, Connecticut: Keats Publishing, 1991. ISBN: 0879835710.

Goodrick-Clarke, Nicholas. Paracelsus: Essential Readings, Berkeley, California: North Atlantic Books, 1999. ISBN: 1556433166.

Greider, William. Who Will Tell The People? : The Betrayal Of American Democracy. New York: Simon & Schuster, 1993. ISBN: 0671867407.

Haley, Daniel. Politics in Healing: The Suppression and Manipulation of American Medicine. Washington, DC: Potomac Valley Press, 2000. ISBN: 0970115008. More information can be found on this well-written introduction to medical suppression at the Politics in Healing web page.

Hall, Manly P. Paracelsus: His Mystical & Medical Philosophy. Los Angles, California:Philosophical Research Society, 1997. ISBN: 0893148083.

Hallinan, Joseph T. Going Up the River: Travels in a Prison Nation. New York: Random House, 2003. ISBN: 0812968441.

Hapgood, Charles. Path of the Pole. Kempton, Illinois: Adventures Unlimited Press, 1999 (originally published in 1952). ISBN: 0932813712.

Hartmann, Franz, M.D. Paracelsus: Life and Prophecies. Blauvelt, NY: Rudolph Steiner Publications, 1973. ASIN: B000EBI5IE.

Hartmann, Thom. The Last Hours of Ancient Sunlight. New York: Harmony Books, 1998. (Updated, ISBN: 1400051576).

Hartwell, Jonathan. Plants Used Against Cancer: A Survey. Lawrence, Massachusetts: Quarterman Publications, 1984. ISBN: 0880001305.

Harvie, David I. Limeys: The True Story of One Man's War Against Ignorance, the Establishment and the Deadly Scurvy. Phoenix Mill, United Kingdom: Sutton Publishing, 2002. ISBN: 0750927720.

Heinberg, Richard. The Party's Over: Oil, War and the Fate of Industrial Societies. Gabriola Island, British Columbia, Canada: New Society Publishers, 2003 ISBN: 0865715297.

Heinberg, Richard. Memories and Visions of Paradise: Exploring the Universal Myth of a Lost Golden Age. Wheaton, Illinois: Quest Books, 1989 ISBN: 083560716X.

Hickey, Steve and Hilary Roberts. Ascorbate: The Science of Vitamin C. Morrisville, North Carolina: Lulu, 2004. ISBN: 1411607244.

Hill, Napolean. Think & Grow Rich. New York: Fawcett Crest, 1960. Issue shown on Amazon (among many) for this best-selling classic is reissue by Tarcher (2005). ISBN: 1585424331.

Hitchens, Christopher. Thomas Jefferson: Author of America. New York: HarperCollins, 2005. ISBN: 0060598964.

Horn, Arthur David with Lynette Anne Mallory-Horn. Humanity's Extraterrestial Origins: ET Influences on Humankind's Biological and Cultural Evolution. Lake Montezuma, Arizona: A & L Horn, 1996. Original ISBN: 3931652319.

Horowitz, Dr. Leonard G. Healing Celebrations: Miraculous Recoveries Through Ancient Scriptures, Natural Medicine & Modern Science. Sandpoint, Idaho: Tetrahedron Publishing Group, 2000. ISBN: 0923550089.

Hoxsey, Harry M., N.D. You Don't Have To Die. New York: Milstone Books, Inc., 1956. ASIN: B0007E65V2. *(Author's Note: The link on Hoxsey's name above brings you to the Wikipedia article on "Hoxsey Treatment," since, despite his notoriety, it would appear that he doesn't merit his own biographical entry. It is a decidedly biased presentation, catering to the orthodox community; nonetheless, we provide it for its instructive value in proving our point about suppression, if not its entertainment value.)*

Huntford, Roland and Paul Theroux. Scott and Amundsen: Their Race to the South Pole (The Last Place on Earth). London: Abacus, 2000. ISBN: 0349113955. Carpenter sites the original 1985 edition, entitled simply "Scott and Amundsen" by Roland Huntford (singular).

Hutchens, Alma R. Indian Herbology of North America. Boston, Massachusetts, Shambhala Publications, Inc., 1973. ISBN: 0877736391.

Huxley, Elspeth. Scott of the Antartic. New York: Atheneum, 1978. ASIN: B000J3JQH6.

Icke, David. I am Me, I Am Free - The Robot's Guide to Freedom, San Diego, California: Truth Seeker, 1996. ISBN: 0952614758.

Icke, David. The Biggest Secret: The Book That Will Change the World. Scottsdale, Arizona: Bridge of Love Publications, 1999. ISBN: 0952614766.

Icke, David. Children of the Matrix. Wildwood, Missouri: Bridge of Love Publications, 2001. ISBN: 095388101.

Icke, David. Tales from the Time Loop: The most comprehensive exposé of the global conspiracy ever written and all you need to know to be truly free, Wildwood, Missouri: Bridge of Love Publications, 2003. ISBN: 0953881040.

Icke, David. And the Truth Shall Set You Free. Wildwood, Missouri: Bridge of Love Publications, 2004. ISBN: 0953881059.

Icke, David. Lifting the Veil. San Diego, California: Truth Seeker, 1998. ISBN: 0939040050.

Illich, Ivan. Limits to Medicine, Medical Nemesis:The Expropriationi of Health, London: Marion Boyars Publishers, Ltd., 2001, ISBN:1842300075.

Jackson, Frederick George. A Thousand Days in the Arctic. New York:

Harper & Brothers, 1899, ASIN: B0008693BS.

Jaynes, Julian. The Origin of Consciousness in the Breakdown of the Bicameral Mind. Boston, Massachusetts: Houghton Mifflin Company, 1976. ISBN: 0395207290.

Jenkins, John Major. Maya Cosmogenesis 2012: The True Meaning of the Maya Calendar End-Date. Rochester, Vermont: Bear & Company, 1998. ISBN: 187918148.

Jensen, Derrick. The Culture of Make Believe, White River Junction, Vermont: Chelsea Green Publishing Company, 2004. ISBN: 1931498571.

Johnson, Chalmers. Blowback: The Costs and Consequences of American Empire. New York: Metropolitan / Owl Book, 2000. ISBN: 0805075593.

Johnson, Chalmers. The Sorrows of Empire: Militarism, Secrecy, and the End of the Republic. New York: Owl Books, 2003. (New 2004 reprint, ISBN: 0805077979).

Kaku, Michio. Hyperspace: A Scientific Odyssey Through Parallel Universes, Time Warps, and the 10th Dimension. New York: Doubleday, 1994. ISBN: 0385477058.

Kaku, Michio. Visions: How Science Will Revolutionize the 21st Century, New York: Doubleday, 1997. ISBN: 0385484992.

Kaku, Michio. Parallel Worlds: A Journey Through Creation, Higher Dimensions, and the Future of the Cosmos. New York: Doubleday, 2005. ISBN: 0385509863.

Kaminski, John. America's Autopsy Report: The Internet Essays of John Kaminski. Tempe, Arizona: Dandelion Books, 2003. ISBN: 1893302423.

Keith, Jim. Mind Control, World Control. Kempton, Illinois: Adventures Unlimited Press, 1998. ISBN: 0932813453.

Keith, Jim. The Octopus: Secret Government and the Death of Danny Casolaro. Los Angeles: Feral House, 2003. ISBN: 0922915911.

Kenyon, J. Douglas, ed. Forbidden History: Prehistoric Technologies, Extraterrestrial Intervention, and the Suppressed Origins of Civilization. Rochester, Vermont: Bear & Company, 2005. ISBN: 1591430453.

Kervran, C. Louis. Biological Transmutations (The movement of life stems from the constant change of one element into another). Translation and adaptation by Michel Abehsera, Jacques de Langre, Ph.D., ed. Magalia, California: Happiness Press, 1988 (2nd printing). ISBN: 0846401959.

Klare, Michael T. Resource Wars: The New Landscape of Global Conflict. New York: Henry Holt & Company, 2001. ISBN: 0805055762.

Klaw, Spencer. The New Brahmins: Scientific Life in America. New York: William Morrow & Company, 1968. ASIN: B000FMPV02.

Knishinsky, Ran. The Clay Cure: Natural Healing from the Earth. Rochester, Vermont: Healing Arts Press, 1998. ISBN: 089281775.

Koch, William Frederick, M.D. The Survival Factor in Neoplastic and Viral Diseases: A Study of the Phenomena of the Free Radical, the Double Bond, and its Alpha Placed Hydrogen Atom in the Pathogenesis and Correction of Neoplastic, Viral and Bacterial Diseases, with Supplement. Self-published by William Koch, 1 January 1958. ASIN: B0007KAJE0.

Kuhn, Thomas S. The Structure of Scientific Revolutions. Chicago: University of Chicago Press, 1962. ISBN: 0226458083. This book is hugely important and the internalization of its major concepts should be considered elemental to being an educated person in the 21st century. Known for having coined the expression "paradigm shift," the book is a highly damaging critique of scientism. Even one of its fiercest critics, Steven Weinberg, has remarked, "Structure has had a wider influence than any other book on the history of science." It is not enough to know that Truth is not a criterion of scientific theory. It is more important to know why.

Kuhn, Thomas S. The Copernican Revolution: Planetary Astronomy in the Development of Western Thought. Cambridge, Massachusetts: Harvard University Press, 1992. ISBN: 0674171039.

La Boétie, Étienne de. Politics of Obedience: the discourse of voluntary servitude. Trans. Harry Kurz. Montréal: Black Rose Books, 1997. (Different version available from Amazon, ISBN: 1419178091).

Lanctôt, Guylaine. The Medical Mafia. Morgan, Vermont: Here's the Key, Inc., 1995. ISBN: 0964412608.

Laszlo, Ervin. The Chaos Point: The World at the Crossroads (Seven Years to Avoid Global Collapse and Promote Worldwide Renewal). Charlottesville, Virginia: Hampton Roads Publishing, 2006. ISBN: 1571744851.

Leakey, Richard and Roger Lewin. The Sixth Extinction. New York, Doubleday, 1995 ISBN: 0385424973.

Liebig, Justus von. Animal Chemistry, or Organic Chemistry in Its Applications to Physiology and Pathology. London: Forgotten Books, 2018. ISBN: 0265752094.

Lovelock, James. The Revenge of Gaia, New York: Allen Lane / Penguin Books, 2006. ISBN: 0713999144.

Lynes, Barry. The Cancer Cure That Worked!. Queensville, Ontario: Marcus Books, 1987. Also published by CompCare Publishers (1987). ISBN: 0919951309.

Lynes, Barry. The Healing of Cancer: The Cures -- the Cover-Ups and the Solution Now!. Queensville, Ontario: Marcus Books; 1989. ISBN: 0919951449.

Machiavelli, Niccolo. The Prince. Translated by Daniel J. Donno. New York: Bantam Books, 1981. ISBN: 0553212788.

Magner, Lois N. A History of Medicine. New York: Marcel Dekker, Inc., 1992. ISBN: 0824786734.

Mander, Jerry. Four Arguments for the Elimination of Television. William Morrow & Company, Inc., 1978. ISBN: 0688082742.

Mander, Jerry. In the Absence of the Sacred: The Failure of Technology & the Survival of the Indian Nations. New York: Sierra Club Books, 1992. ISBN: 0871565099.

Mann, Charles C. 1491: New Revelations of the Americas Before Columbus. New York: Alfred A. Knopf, 2005. ISBN: 2004061547, is the hardbound edition from which I quote. Amazon shows the paperback as 1400032059.

Marrs, James. PSI Spies. Phoenix, Arizona: AlienZoo Publishing, 2000. ISBN: 1588790231.

Marrs, Jim. Crossfire: The Plot That Killed Kennedy. New York: Carroll & Graf Publishers, 1990. ISBN: 0881846481.

Marrs, Jim. Alien Agenda. New York: HarperTorch, 1998. ISBN: 0061096865.

Marrs, Jim. Rule by Secrecy: The Hidden History That Connects the Trilateral Commission, the Freemasons, and the Great Pyramids. New York: Harper-Collins Publishers, 2000. ISBN: 0060931841.

Marrs, Jim. Inside Job: The Shocking Case for a 9/11 Conspiracy. San Rafael, California: Origin Press, 2005. ISBN: 1579830188.

May, James A. The Miracle of Stevia: Discover the Healing Power of Nature's Herbal Sweetener. New York: Kensington Publishing Corp., 2003. ISBN: 0758202202.

McDougall, John A., M.D. and Mary A. McDougall. The McDougall Plan, Piscataway, New Jersey: New Century Publishers, Inc., 1983. (ISBN: 0832903922).

McKenna, Terence. The Invisible Landscape: Mind, Hallucinogens, and the I Ching. New York: HarperCollins Publishers, 1975. ISBN: 0062506358.

McKenna, Terence. Food of the Gods: The Search for the Original Tree of Knowledge, A Radical History of Plants, Drugs, and Human Evolution. New York: Bantam Books, 1992. ISBN: 0553371304.

McKeown, Thomas. The Role of Medicine: Dream, Mirage or Nemesis, Princeton, New Jersey: Princeton University Press, 1979. ISBN: 0691082359. A most interesting work, showing just how powerful Illich's Medical Nemesis has been. The Preface to the Second Edition (cited above) immediately opens by attempting to distance himself from Illich, lest his work, too, be interpreted as "an attack on clinical medicine." McKeown, highly regarded in his field, proves in his defensiveness that -- once again -- we should follow Paracelsus' advice and we wary of respectable people. "For respectable people are loath to question the system which is itself the source of their respectability." Nonetheless, McKeown's own arguments paradoxically DO damage orthodox medicine's credit-taking for a host of positive nutritional, environemental, and behavioral changes. In this respect, he is an unwitting aid to Illich. In either event, me thinketh he doth protesteth too much. His work is, nonetheless, powerful, compelling, well-documented and quite relevant to the current volume.

McKeown, Thomas. The Origins of Human Disease. Oxford, England: Basil Blackwell, 1988. ISBN: 0631179380.

McMoneagle, Joseph. Mind Trek: Exploring Consciousness, Time, and Space Through Remote Viewing. Charlottesville, Virginia: Hampton Roads,

1993. (ISBN for newer 1997 edition: 1878901729).

McTaggart, Lynne. The Cancer Handbook. Bloomingdale, Illinois: Vital Health Publishing. 1997. ISBN: 1890612189.

McTaggart, Lynne. What Doctors Don't Tell You: The Truth About the Dangers of Modern Medicine. New York: Avon Books, 1998. ISBN: 0380807610.

McWilliams, Peter. Ain't Nobody's Business If You Do: The Absurdity of Consensual Crimes in a Free Society. Los Angeles, California: Prelude Press, 1993. ISBN: 0931580536.

Mettrie, Julien Offrey De La. Man a Machine. La Salle, Illinois: Open Court, 1991. Title Notes: French-English, including Frederick the Great's "Eulogy" on La Mettrie and Extracts from La Mettrie's "The Natural History of the Soul" -- Philosophical and Historical Notes by Gertrude Carman Bussey, M.A., Wellesley College, Open Court, La Salle, Illinois. The portion I quote from is tranlated from the original 1748 tract, "Man a Machine," which begins on page 83. There is no ISBN or ASIN number assigned to this version. I do not have it in my personal library, but instead pulled it from www.questia.com, where I have a membership. Amazon shows several recent republications, including one by Cambridge University Press and another by Hackett Publishing.

Miller, Neil Z. Vaccines: Are They Really Safe & Effective?. Santa Fe, New Mexico: New Atlantean Press, 2002. ISBN: 1881217302.

Miller, Jr., Tyler. Energetics, Kinetics and Life. Belmont, California: Wadsworth Publishing Co., 1971. ISBN: 053400136X.

Mohs, Frederic E., M.D. Chemosurgery: Microscopically Controlled Surgery for Skin Cancer. Springfield, Illinois: Charles C. Thomas Publisher, 1978. ISBN: 0398037256.

Moolenburgh, Hans C. As Chance Would Have It: A Study in Coincidences, Essex, United Kingdom: Saffron Walden, The C.W. Daniel Company Limited, 1998. ISBN: 0852073178.

Morehouse, David. Psychic Warrior. New York: St. Martin's Press, 1996. ISBN: 031296413.

Morgenthaler, John. Stop the FDA. Menlo Park, California: Health Freedom Publications, 1992. ISBN: 0962741884.

Morris, Nat. The Cancer Blackout. 5th ed. Los Angeles, California: Regent House, 1977. Amazon edition cited was a reprint put out by the author in 1976. The original was published in 1958.

Moss, Ralph W. Free Radical, Albert Szent-Gyorgyi and the Battle over Vitamin C. New York: Paragon House Publishers, 1988. ISBN: 0913729787. Listed in Amazon under: ASIN: B000FH86BI.

Moss, Ralph W. Questioning Chemotherapy. Sheffield, United Kingdom: Equinox Press, 1995. ISBN: 188102525X.

Moss, Ralph W. Herbs Against Cancer: History and Controversy. Sheffield, United Kingdom: Equinox Press, 1998. ISBN: 1881025403.

Naiman, Ingrid. Cancer Salves and Suppositories. Cundiyo, New Mexico: Seventh Ray Press, 1994. ISBN: 1882834151.

Narby, Jeremy. The Cosmic Serpent: DNA & the Origins of Knowledge. New York: Jeremy P. Tarcher/Putnam, 1999. ISBN: 0874779642.

Newbold, H.L., M.D. Vitamin C Against Cancer. New York: Stein & Day, 1981. ISBN: 0812881672.

Noah, Joseph. Future Prospects of The World According to the Bible Code. Boca Raton, Florida:New Paradigm Books, 2002. ISBN: 1892138077.

Novak, David. Downtime: A Guide to Federal Incarceration. David Novak Consulting, Inc., 2003. Recent (2005) edition's ISBN: 0971030626.

Olsen, Cynthia. Essiac: A Native Herbal Cancer Remedy. Pagosa Springs, Colorado: Kali Press, 1996. ISBN: 0962888257.

Orme-Johnson, David W., Ph.D. and John T. Farrow, Ph.D., eds. Scientific Research on the Transcendental Meditation Program. Vlodrop, Holland: Maharishi European Research University Press, 1977. ISBN: 3883330019.

Pancoast, S. Blue and Red Light: Or, Light and Its Rays as Medicine; Showing That Light Is the Original and Sole Source of Life, as It Is the Source of All the Physical and Vital Forces in Nature; and That Light is Nature's Own and Only Remedy for Disease. Marrickville, New South Wales, Australia: Wentworth Press, 2016. ISBN: 1360645160.

Paoletti, Rodolfo. Vitamin C: the state of the art in disease prevention sixty years after the Nobel Prize, New York: Springer-Verlag, 1998. ISBN: 8847000270.

Parenti, Christian. Lockdown America: Police and Prisons in the Age of Crisis. New York: Verso, 2000. ISBN: 1859843034.

Parkinson, C. Northcote. Parkinson's Law And Other Studies in Administration. New York: Houghton Mifflin Co., 1957. (1962 update, ISBN: 0395083737).

Pattison, John. Cancer: Its nature and successful and comparatively painless treatment without the usual operation with the knife. London: H. Turner & Co., 1866.

Pauling, Linus. Vitamin C and the Common Cold. San Francisco, California: W. H. Freeman & Company, 1972. ISBN: 0716701596.

Pauling, Linus. Vitamin C, the Common Cold, and the Flu. San Francisco, California, W. H. Freeman & Company, 1976. ISBN: 0716703610.

Penny, Laura. Your Call is Important to Us: The Truth about Bullshit. New York: The Crown Publishing Group, 2005. ISBN: 1400081033.

Perkins, John. The World is as You Dream It. Rochester, Vermont: Destiny Books, 1994. ISBN: 0892814594.

Perkins, John. Confessions of an Economic Hit Man. San Francisco, California: Berrett-Koehler Publishers, Inc., 2004. ISBN: 1576753018.

Pert, Candace B., Ph.D. Molecules of Emotion. New York: Scribner, 1997. ISBN: 0684846349.

Pinchbeck, Daniel. Breaking Open the Head: A Psychedelic Journey into the Heart of Contemporary Shamanism. New York: Broadway Books, 2003. ISBN: 0767907434.

Planck, Max. Scientific Autobiography and Other Papers. Santa Barbara, California: Greenwood Publishing, 1968. ISBN: 0837101948

Postman, Neil. Technopoly: The Surrender of Culture to Technology. New York: First Vintage Books, 1993. ISBN: 0679745408.

Poundstone, Williams. Prisoner's Dilemma. New York: Doubleday Books, 1992. ISBN: 038541580X.

Price, Weston A., D.D.S. Nutrition and Physical Degeneration. 14th printing. La Mesa, California: The Price-Pottenger Nutrition Foundation, Inc., 2000. ISBN: 0879838167.

Putnam, Robert. Bowling Alone : The Collapse and Revival of American Community. New York: Simon & Schuster, 2001. ISBN: 0743203046.

Putnam, Robert, and Lewis M. Feldstein, with Don Cohen. Better Together: Restoring the American Community. New York: Simon & Schuster, 2004. ISBN: 0743235460.

Putnam, Robert D., Robert Leonardi and Rafaella Y. Nanetti. Making Democracy Work: Civic Traditions in Modern Italy. Princeton, New Jersey: Princeton University Press, 1993. ASIN: B00087IC4YM.

Quigley, Carroll. The Evolution of Civilizations: An Introduction to Historical Analysis. Indianapolis, Indiana: Liberty Fund, 1961. ISBN: 0913966576.

Quigley, Carroll. Tragedy & Hope: A History of the World in Our Time. New York: The Macmillan Company, 1966. ISBN: 094500110X.

Rappoport, Jon. Oklahoma City Bombing: The Suppressed Truth. Escondido, California: Book Tree, 1997. ISBN: 1885395221.

Rappoport, Jon. The Secret Behind Secret Societies: Liberation of the Planet in the 21st Century. San Diego, California: Truth Seeker, 1998. ISBN: 0939040085.

Rappoport, Jon. The Ownership of All Life. San Diego, California: Truth Seeker, 1999. ISBN: 0939040360.

Rappoport, Jon. AIDS, Inc.: Scandal of the Century. Escondido, California: Namaste Publishing, 2003. ISBN: 0954659015.

Rath, Matthias. Ten Years That Changed Medicine Forever. Santa Clara, California: MR Publishing, Inc., 2001. ISBN: 0967954630.

Rath, Matthias. Wny Animals Don't Get Heart Attacks . . . But People Do!. Fremont, California: MR Publishing, Inc., 2003. ISBN: 0967954681.

Rees, Martin. Our Final Century: Will Civilization Survive the Twenty-First Century?. London: Arrow Books, 2003. ISBN: 0099436868.

Rees, Martin. Our Final Hour (A Scentist's Warning: How terror, error, and environmental diaster threaten humankind's future in this century -- on earth and beyond). New York: Basic Books, 2003. ISBN: 0465068626.

Rescher, Nicholas. Scientific Progress: a Philosophical Essay on the Economics of Research in Natural Science. Pittsburgh, Pennsylvania: University of Pittsburgh Press, 1978. (Basil Blackwell edition, ISBN: 0631179801).

Rifkin, Jeremy with Ted Howard. Entropy: A New World View. New York: Bantam Books, 1980. (Updated 1981 version, ISBN; 0553202154; see Wiki article on this book).

Roberts, Paul Craig; and Lawrence M. Stratton. The Tyranny of Good Intentions: How Prosecutors and Bureaucrats Are Trampling the Constitution in the Name of Justice, Rocklin, California: Prima Lifestyles, 2000. ISBN: 076152553X.

Rossiter, Clinton, editor. The Federalist Papers. First Mentor printing. New York: New American Library, 1999. (ISBN for Signet edition, 2003: 0451528816).

Rost, Peter, M.D. The Whistleblower: Confessions of a Healthcare Hitman, Brooklyn, New York: Soft Skull Press, 2006. ISBN: 193336839X.

Russell, Walter. Atomic Suicide: What Radioactivity Is, Why and How It Kills, What To Do About It. Swannanoa, VA: University of Science & Philosophy, 1981. Originally published in 1957. ISBN: 1879605112.

Sahlins, Marshall D. and Elman R. Service, eds. Evolution and Culture. Ann Arbor, Michigan: University of Michigan Press, 1960. ISBN: 0472087762.

Sauder, Richard. Underground Bases & Tunnels: What is the Government Trying to Hide?, Adventures Unlimited Press, 2014. ISBN: 1939149266.

Sauder, Richard. Underwater and Underground Bases, Surprising Facts the Government Does Not Want You to Know. Kempton, Illinois: Adventures Unlimited Press, 2014. ISBN: 1939149282.

Schultes, Richard Evans and Robert Francis Raffauf. Vine of the Soul: Medicine Men, Their Plants and Rituals in the Colombian Amazonia, Santa Fe, New Mexico: Synergetic Press, 1992. ISBN: 090779131X.

Service, Elman R. The Law of Evolutionary Potential. Indianapolis, Indiana: Bobbs-Merrill, 1960. (ASIN B0007FXMZI).

Seton, Ernest Thompson. The Gospel of the Red Man. New York: Doubleday, 1936. (ASIN B00088XIT4).

Sheffrey, Stephen. Vitamin C Under Attack: Unfair trials bombard high-dose benefits: separating fact from fiction to ensure proper dose. Ann Arbor, Michigan: published by author, 2000. ISBN: 0962937215.

Sheldrake, Rupert. A New Science of Life: The Hypothesis of Formative Causation. Los Angeles, California: Jeremy P. Tarcher, Inc., 1981. (Updated edition: A New Science of Life: The Hypothesis of Morphic Resonance, Park Street Press, 1995, ISBN: 0892815353).

Shope, Robert E. and Joshua Lederberg, Stanley C. Oaks, Institute of Medicine Committee on Emerging Microbial Threats to Health. Emerging Infections: Microbial Threats to Health in the United States. Washington, DC: National Academy Press, 1993.

Shorter, Edward. The Health Century. New York: Doubleday, 1987. ISBN: 0385242360.

Siegel, Bernie. Love, Medicine & Miracles: Lessons Learned About Self-Healing From a Surgeon's Experience With Exceptional Patients. New

York: Harper Perennial, 1990. ISBN: 0060919833.

Sitchin, Zacharia. The 12th Planet. New York: HarperCollins, 1999. ISBN: 038039362X.

Sitchin, Zacharia. The End of Days: Armageddon and Prophecies of the Return. New York: HarperCollins Publishers, 2007. ISBN: 0061238236.

Smith, Adam. An Inquiry Into the Nature and Causes of the Wealth of Nations. New York: Bantam Classics, 2003. ISBN 0553585975.

Smith, Huston. Cleansing the Doors of Perception. Boulder, Colorado: Sentient Publications, 2003. ISBN: 1591810086.

Solomon, Susan. The Coldest March: Scott's Fatal Antarctic Expedition. New Haven, Connecticut: Yale University Press, 2002. ISBN: 0300099215.

Spengler, Oswald. The Decline of the West. New York: Vintage Books, 2006. I recommend this abridgement of the original, classic work by Spengler (1880-1936), first published in German in the early 1920's. ISBN: 1400097002.

Steiger, Brad. The Philadelphia Experiment & Other UFO Conspiracies. New Brunswick, New Jersey: Inner Light Publications, 1990. ISBN: 0948395970.

Stich, Rodney. The Real Unfriendly Skies: Saga of Corruption. Alamo, California: Diablo Western Press, Inc., 1991. ISBN: 0932438024. The original book title was "Unfriendly Skies." Because of the tactic to dilute the effect of the book on the public, influencial government agents had Doubleday publish an unsubstantial book by the same exact name. This is detailed in Defrauding America, p. 513-516. ISBN: 0932438024.

Stich, Rodney. Defrauding America: A Pattern of Related Scandals. Alamo, California: Diablo Western Press, Inc., 1994. ISBN: 0932438075.

Stone, Irwin, M.D. The Healing Factor: "Vitamin C" Against Disease. New York: Putnam Publishing Group, 1974. ISBN: 0448116936.

Sumner, Judith. The Natural History of Medicinal Plants. Portland, Oregon: Timber Press, Inc., 2000. ISBN: 0881924830.

Tainter, Joseph. The Collapse of Complex Societies. Cambridge: Cambridge University Press, 1988. ISBN: 052138673X.

Targ, Russell. Limitless Mind: A Guide to Remote Viewing and Transformation of Consciousness. Novato, California: New World Library, 2004. ISBN: 1577314131.

Taylor, Steve. The Fall: The evidence for a Golden Age, 6,000 years of insanity, and the dawning of a New Era. Hants, United Kingdom: The Bothy, John Hunt Publishing, Ltd., 2005. ISBN: 1905047207.

Tocqueville, Alexis de. Democracy in America and Two Essays on America. Translated by Gerald E. Bevan. New York: Penguin Classics, 2003. ISBN: 0140447601.

Tompkins, Peter with Christopher Bird. The Secret Life of Plants: a fascinating account of the physical, emotional, and spiritual relations between plants and man. New York: Harper & Row, 1973. ISBN: 0060143266.

Tonry, Michael. Thinking About Crime: Sense and Sensibility in American Penal Culture. New York: Oxford University Press, 2004. ISBN: 0195141016.

Toynbee, Arnold J. and D.C. Somervell. A Study of History: Abridgment of Volumes I-VI. New York: Oxford University Press, 1987. ISBN: 0195050800. I make no apologizes in using the Somervell abridgements over the original texts. Toynbee himself lavished praise on the authenticity of these volumes, and it is said that except for having to truncate the abundance of examples provided in the original, the Somervell abridgements are quite faithful to Toynbee's work -- so says Toynbee himself in the Preface.

Toynbee, Arnold J. and D.C. Somervell. A Study of History: Abridgment of Volumes VII-X. New York: Oxford University Press, 1987. ISBN: 0195050819.

Thompson, David. Scott's Men. London: Allen Lane, 1977. ISBN: 0713910348.

Trudeau, Kevin. Natural Cures They Don't Want You To Know About. London: Alliance Publishing, 2004. ISBN: 097559950X / 3413410296.

Trull, Louise. The Cancell Controversy, Norfolk Virginia: Hampton Roads Publishing Co., 1993. ISBN: 1878901761.

Tsu, Lao. Tao Te Ching. New York: Vintage Books, 1972. ISBN: 039471833X.

Twain, Mark. The Mysterious Stranger and Other Stories. New York: New American Library, 1980. ISBN 0451520696.

Vacca, Roberto. The Coming Dark Age. New York: Doubleday & Company, 973. ISBN: 0385063407. Translated from the Italian, "Medioevo Prossimo Venturo" by Robert Vacca; Arnoldo Mondadori Editore, 1971.

Vassilatos, Gerry. Lost Science. Kempton, Illinois: Adventures Unlimited Press, 1999. (Originally published in 1997 by Borderland Sciences Research). ISBN: 0945685254.

Velikovsky, Immanuel. Worlds in Collision. New York: Simon & Schuster, Inc., 1977. First published in 1950, my copy is the cheap mass paperback. ISBN: 067181091X.

Velikovsky, Immanuel. Earth in Upheaval. New York: Simon & Schuster, Inc., 1977. First published in 1955. ISBN: 0671823396.

Velikovsky, Immanuel. Mankind in Amnesia. New York: Doubleday & Company, Inc., 1982. ISBN: 0385033931.

Vogel, Virgil J. American Indian Medicine. Norman, Oklahoma: University of Oklahoma Press, 1990. ISBN: 0806122935.

Vonnegut, Kurt. A Man Without a Country. New York: Random House, 2007 (hardback edition, 2005). ISBN: 081297736X.

Vidal, Gore; Perpetual War For Perpetual Peace : How We Got To Be So Hated. New York: Nation Books, 2002. ISBN: 156025405X.

Waite, Arthur Edward. ed. The hermetic and alchemical writings of Paracelsus the Great. Edmonds, Washington: The Alchemical Press, 1992. (Originallly published in 1984).

Walker, Morton. How Not to Have a Heart Attack. New York: New Viewpoints/Vision Books, 1980. ISBN: 0531099199.

Warburg, Otto. The Prime Cause and Prevention of Cancer. Wurzburg, Germany: Konrad Triltsch, 1967.

Wasserman, Gerhard D. From Occam's Razor to the Roots of Consciousness: 20 Essays on Philosophy, Philosophy of Science and Philosophy of Mind, Hants, England: Avebury, Ashgate Publishing Limited, 1997. ISBN: 1859722857.

Waters, Frank. Book of the Hopi. New York: Penguin Books, 1977. ISBN: 0140045279.

Weaver, Richard M. Ideas Have Consequences. Chicago. Illinois: The University of Chicago Press, 1948. (Reprint, 1984; ISBN: 0226876802).

Weaver, Richard M. The Ethics of Rhetoric. Chicago, Illinois: The University of Chicago Press, 1953. (Reprint, Lawrence Erlbaum Associates, 1985; ISBN: 0961180021).

Weaver, Richard M. Visions of Order: The Cultural Crisis of Our Times, Baton Rouge, Louisiana: Louisiana State University Press, 1964. (Reprint, Intercollegiate Studies Institute, 1995; ISBN: 1882926072).

Weil, Andrew, M.D. Ask Dr. Weil: Vitamins & Minerals. New York: Ivy Books, 1997. ISBN: 0804116725.

Wesley, John Benjamin. Primitive Physick Or An Easy And Natural Method Of Curing Most Diseases. Andesite Press, 2017. ISBN: 1376140594.

White, John. Pole Shift. Virginia Beach, Virginia: A.R.E. Press, 1991. ISBN: 08786041624).

Wittgenstein, Ludwig. Tractatus Logico-Philosophicus. Translated by D.F.Pears and B.F. McGuinness. London;: Outledge Classics, 1921. ISBN: 0415254086.

Whitman, Walt. Leaves of Grass. 2nd edition. New York: Modern Library, 1891. ISBN: 0679600760.

Wilkins, Harold. Mysteries of Ancient South America. Kempton, Illinois: Adventures Unlimited Press, 2000. ISBN: 0932813267.

Williams, Walters. A History of Northwest Missouri Vol. III. Chicago/New York: The Lewis Publishing Company, 1915. p. 1463-1464. See pages one and two of the relevant article within the book.

Wohl, Stanley, M.D. The Medical Industrial Complex. New York: Harmony Books, 1984. Original Random House edition ISBN: 0517553511.

Wolfram, Stephen. A New Kind of Science. Champaign, Illinois: Wolfram Media, Inc., 2002. ISBN: 1579550088.

Woodall, John. The Surgeon's Mate. Bath, England: Kingsmead Press, 1978. ISBN: 0906230152.

Wright, Jonathan V., M.D. Dr Wright's Guide to Healing with Nutrition. Emmaus, Pennsylvania: Rodale Press, 1984. ISBN: 0878574859.

Zerzan, John. Against Civilization: Readings and Reflections. Los Angeles, California: Feral House 1999. ISBN: 0922915989. John Zerzan is one of the few authors by whom **I won't** have to worry about getting sued. His publisher's page reads, "Selections by the following authors, **anti-copyright @ 2005, 1999 may be freely pirated and quoted:** Anti-Authoritarians Anonymous . . . " etc. Love him or not, John stands by what he believes.

Zerzan, John. Running on Emptiness: The Pathology of Civilization. Los Angeles, California: Feral House, 2002. ISBN: 092291575X.

Zinn, Howard. A Peoples's History of the Unites States: 1492-Present. New York: HarperCollins Publishers, 2005. ISBN: 0060838655.

Index

Note on Indexing: I choose to index this work by hand. As an avid reader myself I find most indices today to be cluttered by words, often common nouns not important to the author's message, that no one would ever reference. The introduction of indexing software, with or without subsequent thorough editing, has only added to the clutter. This is predictable because no indexing software can discriminate with a sense of reference value as can the work's creator.

I also don't reference words of high frequency, except for words with important introductions, definitions, or varied uses attached to them. Additionally, I left in all bibliographed authors (the primary authors), but not their book titles. That's what the bibliography is for. I did, however, allow for a handful of notable exceptions.

Attention was placed on words and phrases that were most likely to be referenced by the book's readers. Page numbers set in **bold** have added importance. Other words and phrases are in bold, italics, underlined, presented parenthetically ( ), or otherwise altered as to help visually navigate through the Index. Where you see "bb" following a page number, this indicates reference to a published work that appears in the Bibliography. G.C.

467.
apricot seeds, 89, 90.
Arawak, 217.
Aristotle, 300.
arrest (FDA), 32, 45
arsenic sulfide, 57.
Arteriosclerosis, (medical journal),
149, 152, 153, 155, 324.
ascorbic acid – (see Vitamin C), 111,
112, 142, 143, 144, 146, 147.
467, 468.
Auschwitz (concentration camp),
107.
Australia, 49, 141, 142, 168, 398,
400, 428, 440, 472, 483.
aveloz (Euphorbia tirucalli), 113.
avitaminosis (deficiency disease),
145
ayahuasca, 25, 26, 99, 129, 273,
274, 462, 463, 464, 473.
Axelrod, Robert, 229, 252, 471.

B

Babaji, 359.
Bachstrom, John Friedrich, 132.
Backster, Cleve, 250, 471.
Bacon, Francis, 264 ,
Banks, Mr. R.L., 87.
Baños (Tungurahua Province, Ecua-
dor), 20.
Barlow's disease, 140, 142, 467.
Barrett, Stephen (M.D., Quack
watch creator/spokesman and
self-professed apologist and
fraudster for Big Pharma and the
medical-in dustrial complex),
374, 383, 385, 469.
Bartolo, Don, 23.
Barzun, Jacques, 110, 212, 471.
basal cell carcinoma (BCC), 115.
Bauman, Zygmunt, 81, 471.
Bear, Rex, 3.
Beaumont (prison; FCI Beaumont,

Texas), 11, 98, 167, 260, 424.
Beck, Robert C., 93.
Becker, Robert O., 93, 471.
Benton County, Iowa, 69.
Berman, Morris, 27, 95, 471, 472.
Bible (The Holy), 22, 218, 248, 472,
475, 482.
Biological Transmutations, 324,
418, 479.
black salve, 32, 400, 401, 433, 438,
439, 440, 441, 442, 443, 444,
445, 447, 448, 449, 450, 452,
453, 454, 455, 456, 457, 467.
Blake, T.T., 53, 68, 472.
Blanchot, Maurice, 102.
Blane, Gilbert (Adm.), 178.
Blanton, Zane, 37, 38.
blogosphere, 413.
bloodroot (Sanguinaria canadensis),
38, 39, 40, 43, 44, 47, 60, 63,64,
74, 113, 308, 403, 445, 446, 447.
Bloom, Harold, 230, 231, 232, 246,
392, 472.
Bloomberg News, 408.
Bolen, Tim, 385, 467.
Bone Builder, 199, 418.
Bown, Stephen R., 114, 115,116,
117, 118, 119, 120, 121, 126,
127, 132, 178, 472.
Bowser, Andrew (M.D.), 72.
Brazil, 15, 142.
British Medical Association, 138.
Brown, Thomas Townsend, 39, 119,
361, 472.
Browne, Harry, 317, 318, 472.
Bruner/Postman experiments, 189,
191, 467.
Bucke, Richard Maurice, 13, 14,
239, 327, 472.
Burzynski, Stanislaw, 96, 97, 151.
Bush, George W., 104, 377.

C

Copernican Revolution, The, 192, 480
Cosmic Consciousness, 13, 239, 242, 327, 472
Cosmic Serpent, The: DNA and the Origins of Consciousness (book review), 482.
Cremo, Michael A., 211, 352.
Crick, Francis, 215, 216, 238.
crustal displacement, 243.
Cuenca (Azuay Province, Ecuador), II, 3, 11, 412, 414.
Cultural Operating System – (see: Global Cultural Operating System), 33, 79, 82, 109, 123, 204, 205, 206, 211, 225, 226, 229, 241, 258.
Cycle of Cosmic Catastrophe, The (book review), 476.

D

Dawkins, Richard, 227, 251.
Darwin, Charles, 264, 323.
De La Boétie, Étienne, 313, 315, 480.
Declaration of Independence, U.S., 160, 341.
deficiencies (nutritional), 140, 150, 152, 325, 364, 423.
Deganawida, 352, 353.
Dermatology Times, 72.
Dermer, Gerald B., 186, 187, 188, 206, 231, 475.
Desborough, Brian, 319, 475.
Descartes, 195, 212, 230, 264.
Devereux, George, 268.
Dirac, Paul, 203.
Domagaia, 115.
Diamond, Jared, 253.
Diamond, Stanley, 54.
DMSO, 441, 442, 443.
"Dr. Oz Show," The (see Oz, Mehmet). 398, 433, 435, 440.

Dunn, Christopher, 43, 441.
Dyer, Gary A. (M.D.), 72, 475.

E

eBay, 72.
Ecuador, II, 3, 11, 12, 15, 18, 20, 22, 23, 25, 27, 129, 261, 273, 366, 377, 398, 405, 412, 413, 427, 463.
Ecuador Passion Fruit, 25.
Eddy, David (M.D.), 162, 163, 164.
Edgar Cayce, 12, 473.
Edwards, (Former Louisiana Governor) Edwin, 80, 371.
"ego explosion," 233, 238, 239.
Egypt, 440.
Einstein, Albert, 243.
ELE (extinction level event), 11, 12.
endosomatic, 285, 287, 288, 289, 298, 303, 304, 325, 326, 330, 331, 332, 343, 344, 345, 346, 350, 352, 353, 360, 361, 468
Enigma Files, 5.
entitlements, 350.
entropy, 204, 205, 212, 264, 276, 278, 280, 282, 285, 286, 287, 306, 329, 330, 331, 335, 341, 345, 354, 359, 360, 361, 484.
Epperson, Ralph, 239, 319, 475.
escharotics, 32, 38, 39, 40, 41, 42, 43, 45, 46, 48, 49, 50, 52, 53, 55, 57, 59, 60, 67, 68, 72, 75, 81, 85, 86, 87, 184, 275, 302, 337, 380, 385, 386, 399, 438, 440, 444, 446, 447, 453, 455.
Essiac: A Native Herbal Cancer Remedy (book review), 88, 89, 97, 165, 275, 476, 483.
ethnobotany, 44, 59, 264.
Evolution and Culture, 264, 276, 329, 485.
exosomatic, 282, 285, 287, 289, 289, 298, 302, 304, 322, 325,

transcendental meditation (TM), 483.
Trull, Louise B., 96, 487.
Tumor Biology, 434.
"Turtle Island," 22.
Tuttle, Ed, 25.
Twain, Mark (Samuel Clements), 247, 487.
Tytler, Fraser, 429.

U

Unglesby, Lewis, 367 - 372.
"Unified Theory of Bullshit,", 435.
University of Michigan, 45, 264, 276, 329, 485.
University of New York, 61.
U.S. Central Intelligence Agency, 268.
U.S. Congress, 183.

V

Vale, Jason, 90, 105, 166.
Vassilatos, Gerry, 55, 91, 92, 360, 361, 487.
Velikovsky, Immanuel, 215, 219, 232, 234, 238, 239, 244, 245, 487.
Verkerk, Dr. Robert, 365.
Vilcabamba (Loja Province, Ecuador), 377, 414.
Vipont Pharmaceutical, 41-43, 446.
Virchow, Dr. Rudolf, 53.
violet (viola odorata), 113.
Vipont Pharmaceutical, 41, 42, 43, 446.
Vitamin B3, 421.
Vitamin C, 33, 111, 112, 115, 116, 123, 126, 130 – 134, 139, 142, 144 -151, 153 -155, 157, 158, 182, 421, 467, 468, 472, 473, 482, 483, 485, 486.

Vogel, Virgil J., 79, 115, 160 – 162, 270, 487.
Voltaire, 70, 401.
Vonnegut, Kurt, 246, 247, 487.

W

Warburg, Otto, 33.
Waters, Frank, 22.
Watson, James (M.D.), 80.
Weaver, Richard M., 260, 263, 265, 266, 270, 271, 274, 275, 487, 488.
Weil, Andrew (M.D.), 147, 231, 488.
Wesley, John, 79.
Whale.to, 72, 405.
whistleblowers, 80, 98, 99, 100 – 102, 105, 108, 110, 169 – 171, 173, 378, 471.
Whistleblowers: Broken Lives and Organizational Power (book review), 98, 100, 169, 378, 487.
Whistleblower, The: Confessions of a Healthcare Hitman (book review), 170.
Whitaker, Julian, 388.
Who will tell the People (book review), 175, 349, 477.
Wigington, Dane, 4, 7, 13.
Wilkins, Harold, 218, 237, 488.
William of Occam, 282, 289, 298, 299, 300 – 304, 329, 335, 353, 487.
"wisdom gathering," 21-22.
Witort, Mike, 105.
Wittgenstein, Ludwig, 237, 488.
Wohl, Stanley, 33, 36, 488.
Wolfram, Stephen, 220, 221, 222, 223, 224, 235, 239, 240, 248, 249, 252, 259, 298, 300, 301, 488.
World Is As You Dream It, 261, 273, 483.

World Without Cancer (book review), 90.
Worlds in Collision (book review), 215, 232, 244, 487.
Wright, Jonathan (M.D.), 112, 115, 151, 488.

X-Y-Z

About the Author

Greg Caton is an American herbalist, inventor and manufacturer. He is the co-founder of Alpha Omega Labs (altcancer. com) and lives outside the city of Cuenca, Ecuador, with his wife, Cathryn.

More complete information on his work can be found at: **gregcaton.com**

Made in the USA
Columbia, SC
08 March 2019